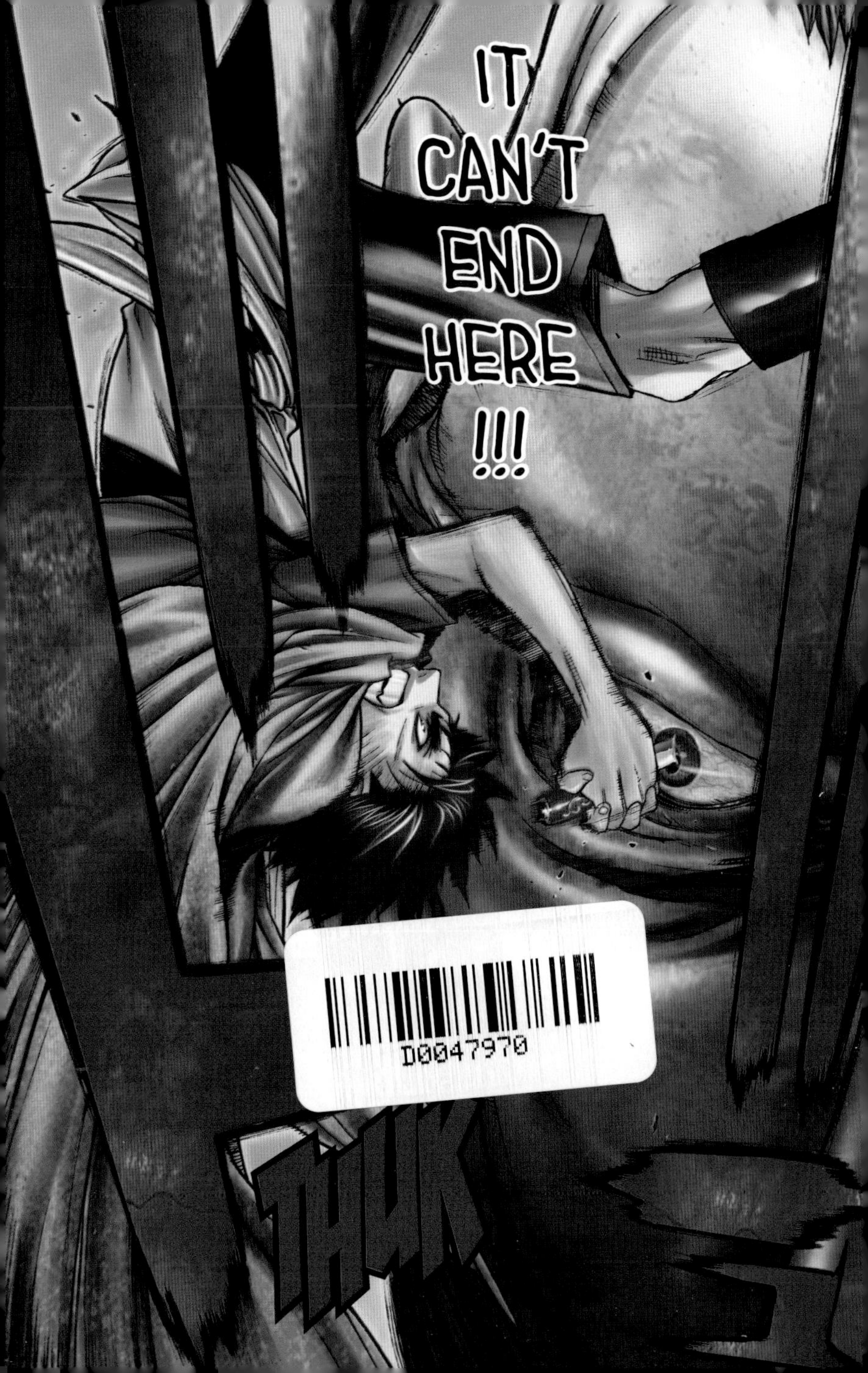
IT CAN'T END HERE!!!
THUK

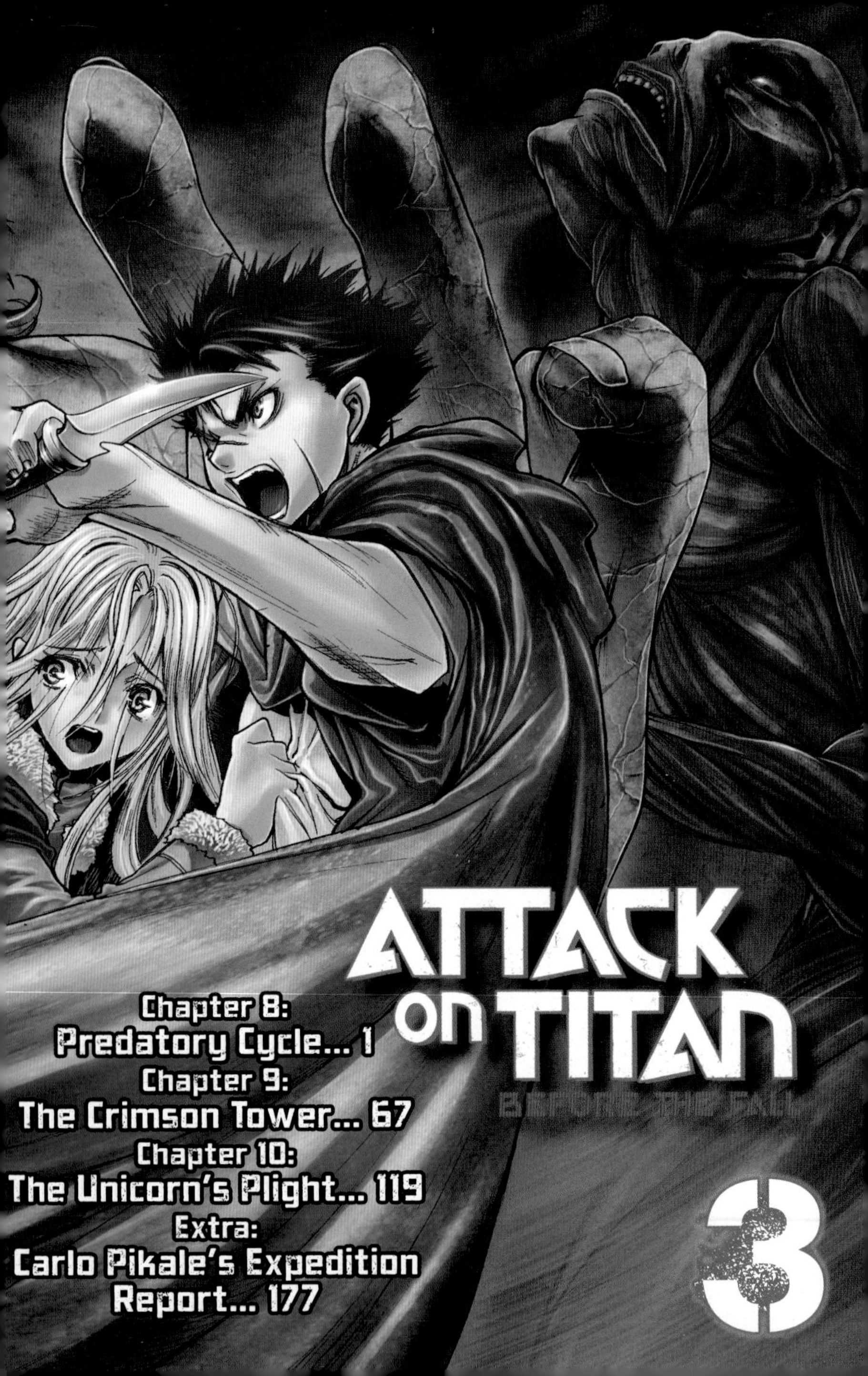

ATTACK ON TITAN
BEFORE THE FALL

3

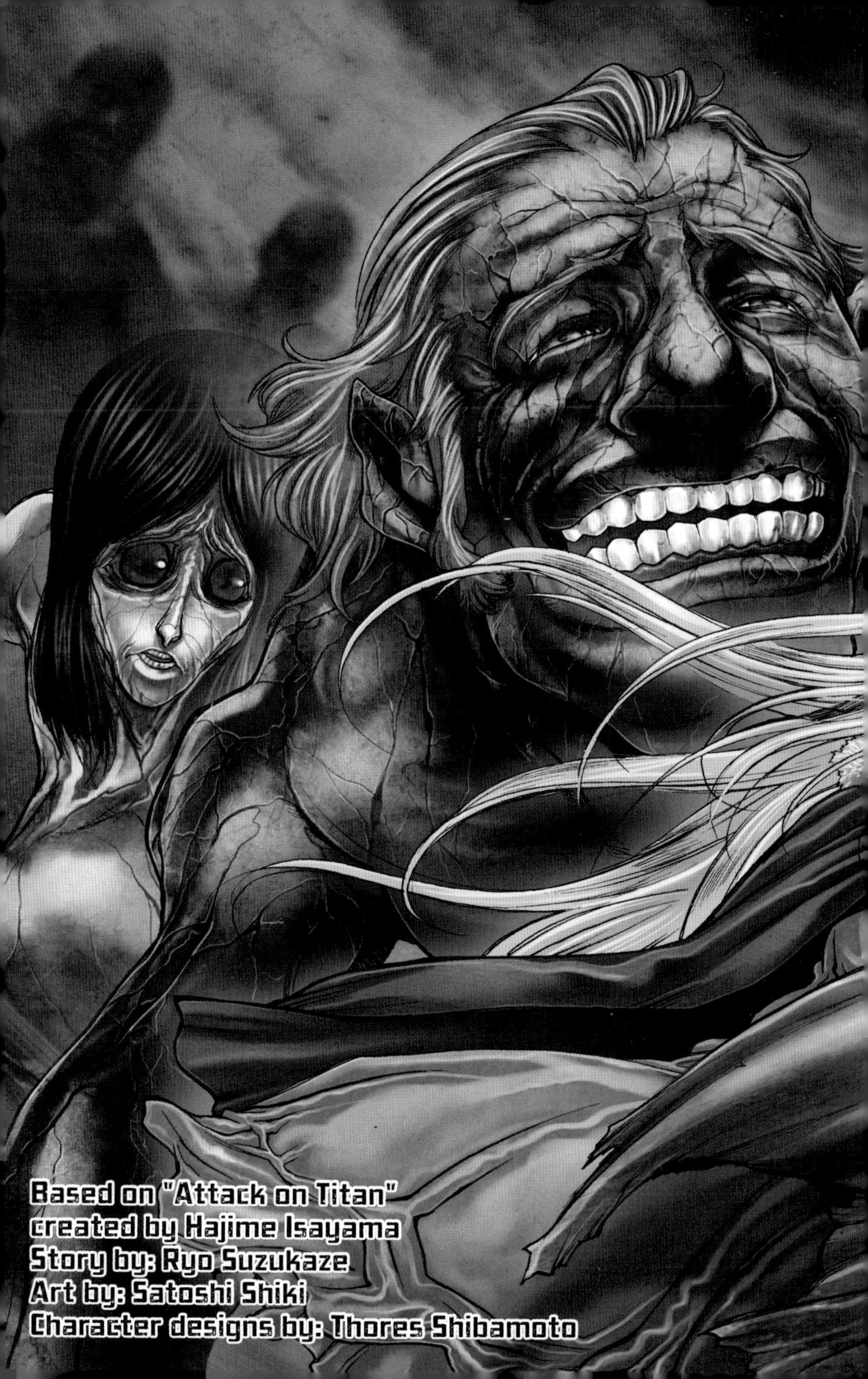

Based on "Attack on Titan"
created by Hajime Isayama
Story by: Ryo Suzukaze
Art by: Satoshi Shiki
Character designs by: Thores Shibamoto

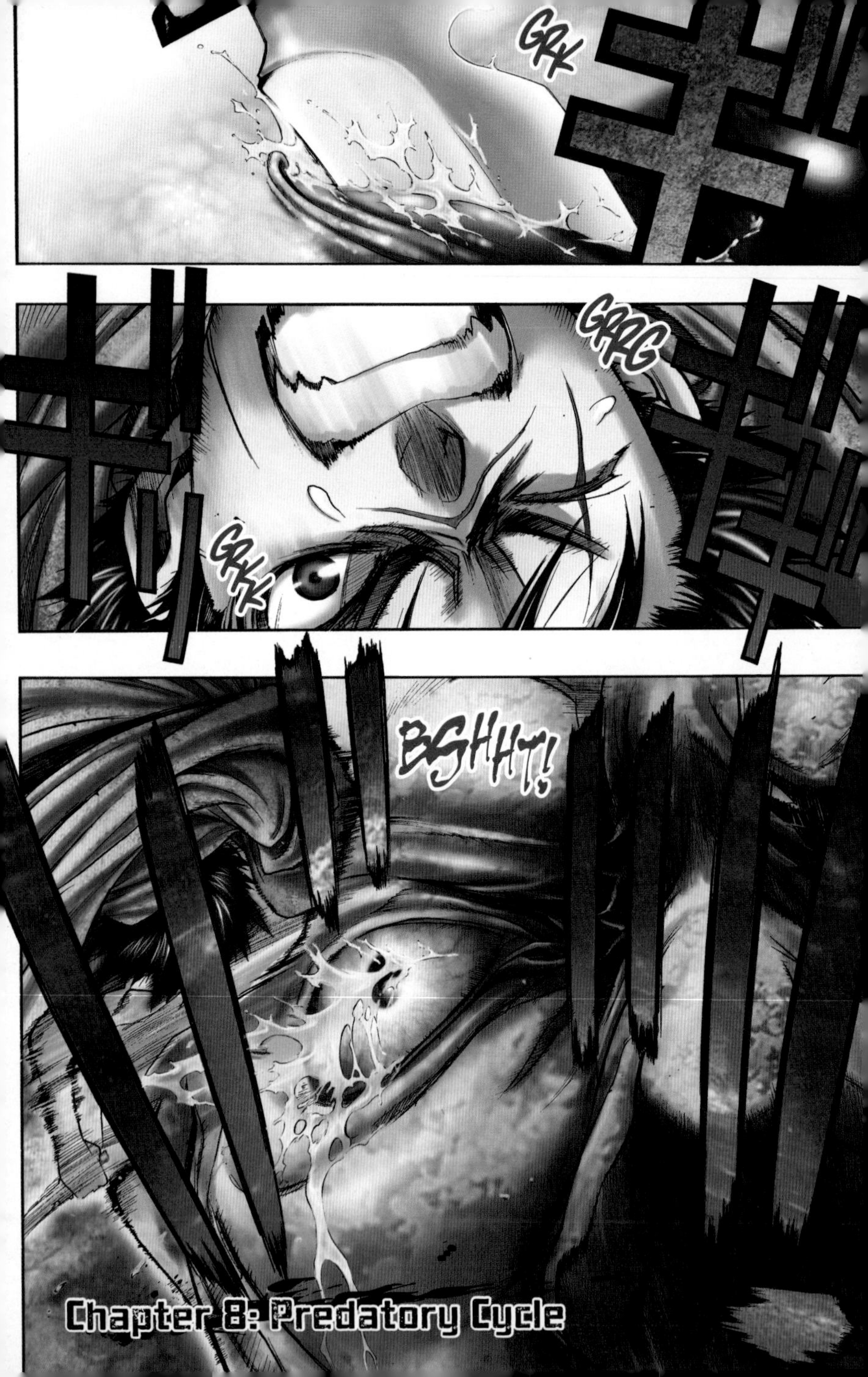
GRK
GRRG
GRK
BGHHT!

Chapter 8: Predatory Cycle

Character Profiles

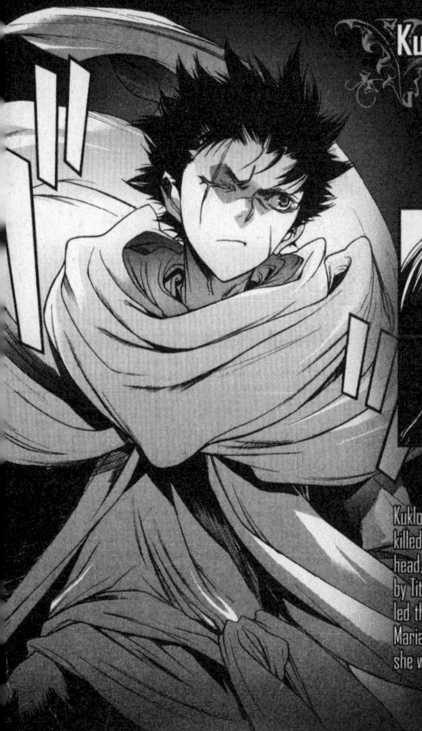

Kuklo

Kuklo was born from a dead body packed into the vomit of a Titan, which earned him the moniker, "Titan's son." The wealthy Inocencio family bought him from a sideshow hut. His father was Heath Mansel, squad leader in the Survey Corps, and his mother was Elena, who helped bring a Titan inside the walls. He escaped the Inocencio mansion when it was attacked by Titan-worshipers. He is now 15 years old.

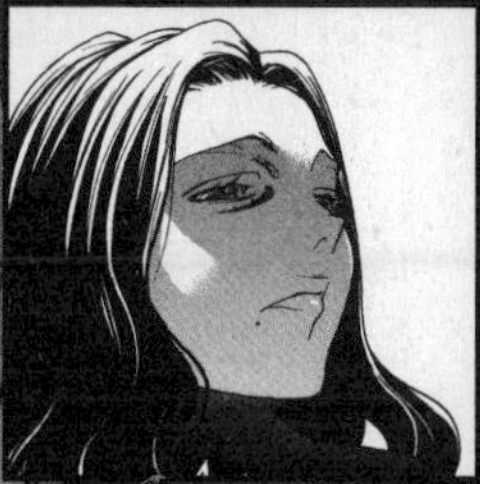

Elena

Kuklo's mother. Her husband Heath was killed by a Titan. When she saw his severed head, she went mad, and was manipulated by Titan-worshipers. Heavy with child, she led the campaign to open the gate in Wall Maria. When a Titan made its way inside, she was the first eaten.

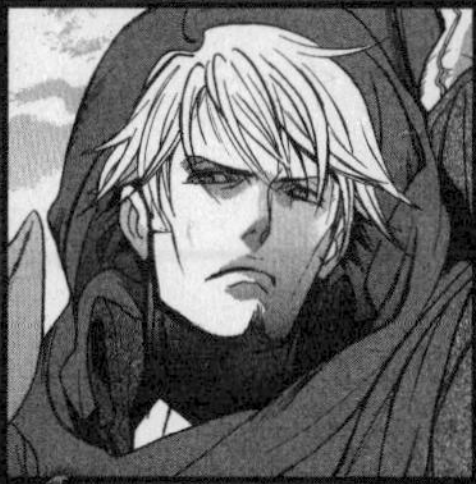

Carlo Pikale

Survey Corps captain. He was age 18 in the first chapter, having joined at the same time as Heath, Kuklo's father. He discovered Elena's remains in the Titan's vomit, and witnessed Kuklo's birth. Now the captain of the newly-reformed Survey Corps, he is 33 years old.

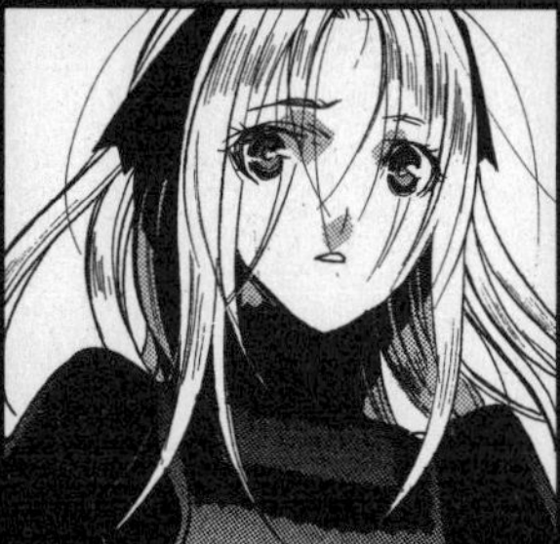

Sharle Inocencio

First daughter of the Inocencio family. She attempted to kill Kuklo after he was brought to the mansion, but became his only friend when she realized that he was human, not a monster. When Titan-worshipers invaded her home, she left with Kuklo, saying goodbye to her brother Xavi. She is now 15 years old.

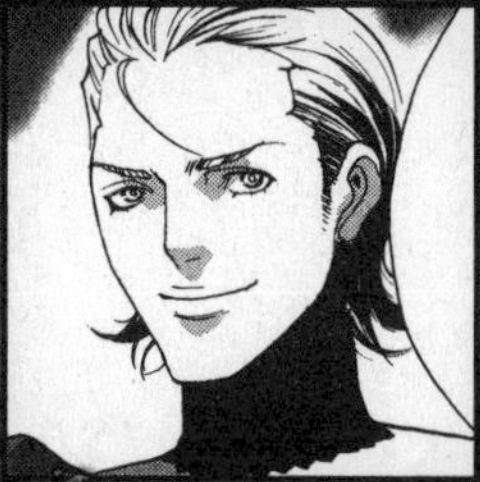

Xavi Inocencio

Sharle's brother, firstborn of the Inocencio children. His father Dario raised him to lead the military. He beat Kuklo nearly every day for two years, claiming to have "conquered the Son of a Titan." This gave him an arrogant leader's air. He believes that Kuklo let the Titan-worshipers into his home.

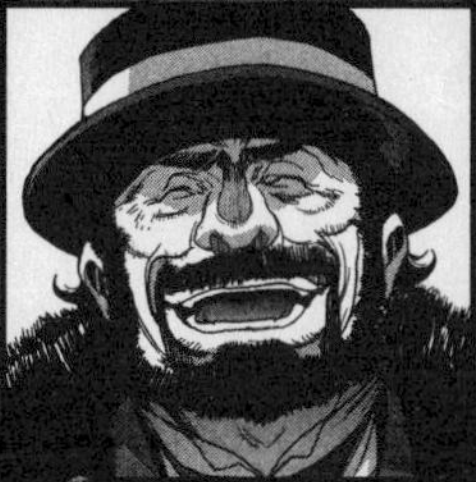

Dario Inocencio

One of the top merchants behind Wall Sheena, innermost of the walls. He has close ties to politicians, and hoped to arrange a marriage between Sharle and the son of Bruno Baumeister, a prominent conservative leader. He was slain at the hands of Titan-worshipers who intended to free Kuklo.

The Story So Far

Fifteen years ago, a Titan terrorized Shiganshina District and left behind a pile of vomit. In that pile was a pregnant corpse, rom which a baby boy was miraculously born. This boy vas named Kuklo, the "Titan's son," and treated as a ideshow freak. Thirteen years later, the wealthy nerchant Dario Inocencio bought Kuklo to serve as a ounching bag for his son, Xavi. Meanwhile, Xavi's sister harle, who was terrified of the Titans, felt a secret duty o purge their house of the so-called monster. But when he approached the chained Kuklo with murderous intent, he realized that he was a human being like any other, and decided to teach him what it meant to be human nstead.

Kuklo put together an escape plan over two ong years, but on the day of the escape, tragedy struck he Inocencio mansion. A group of Titan-worshipers nvaded, seeking to take back the Titan's son. They nurdered Dario and many of the mansion servants. uklo narrowly managed to save Sharle and Xavi from arm, but Xavi accused him of being in league with the ttackers, and put out his right eye. Kuklo took Sharle and escaped from Wall Sheena into Shiganshina.

DMM
DMM
DMM
DMM
DMM
DMM

In Shiganshina District, the Survey Corps was back in action, preparing for its first expedition outside of the wall in 15 years. Kuklo wanted to see a Titan to confirm that he was indeed a human being. He left Sharle behind and snuck into the expedition's cargo wagon. As he hoped, the Survey Corps ran across a Titan, but it was ar worse of a monster that he expected. The group urned around to retreat to Wall Maria, but the Titan crushed the wagon at the rear. Kuklo and the coach driver were caught in the creature's terrible clutches.

WUH!
AA
AAAA
AH!

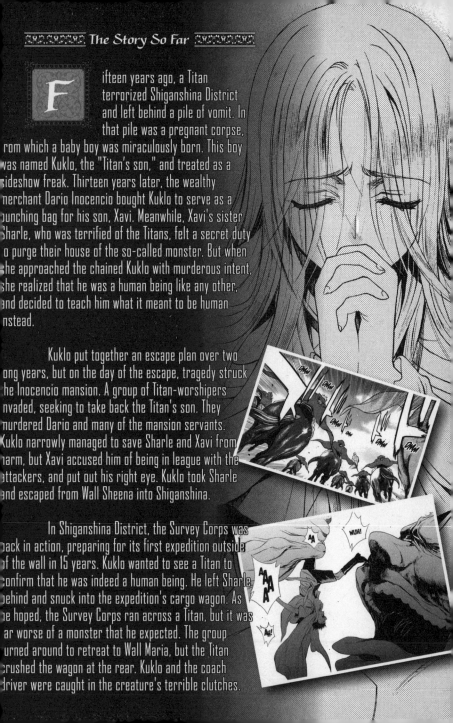

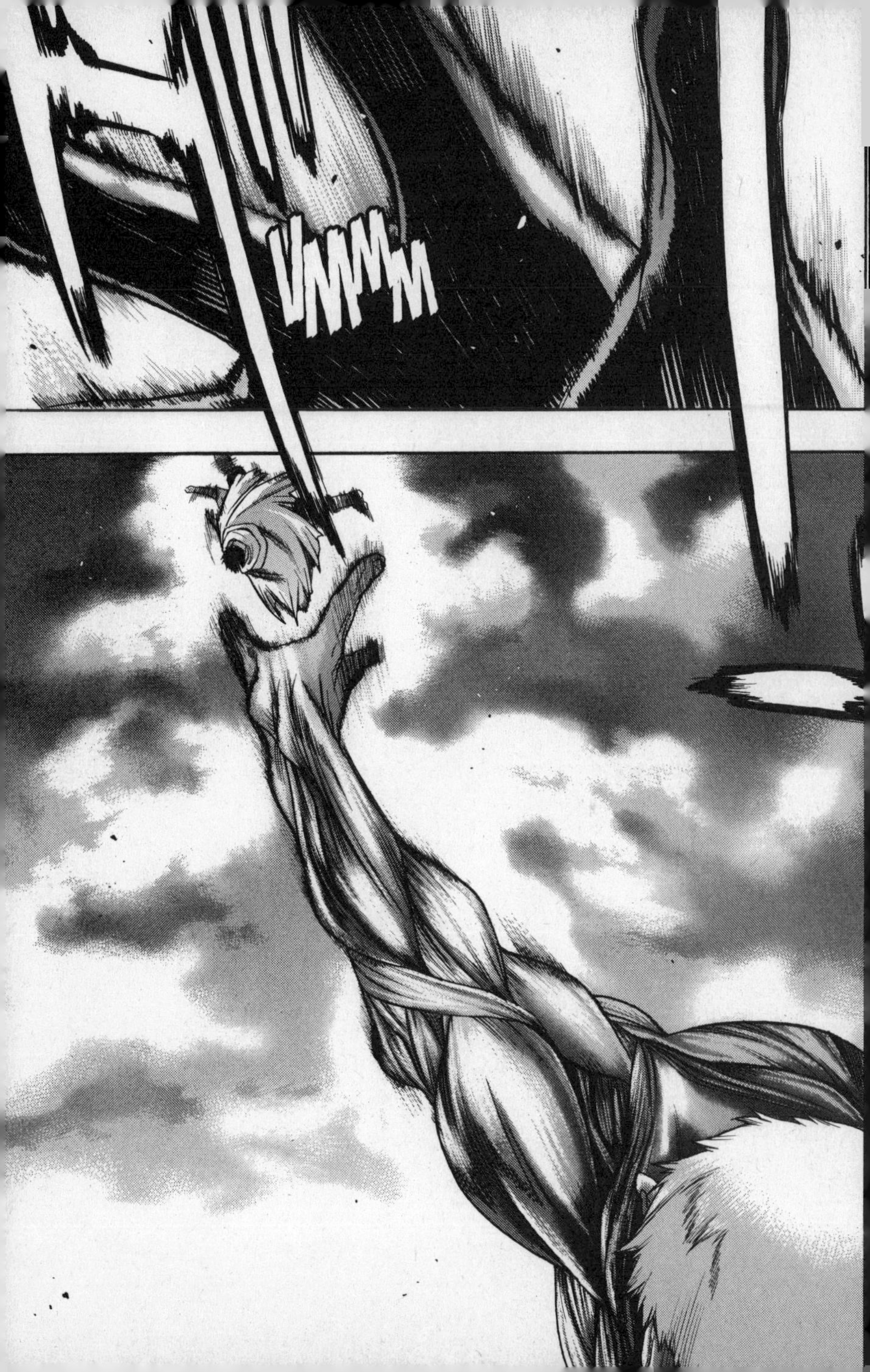
VMMM

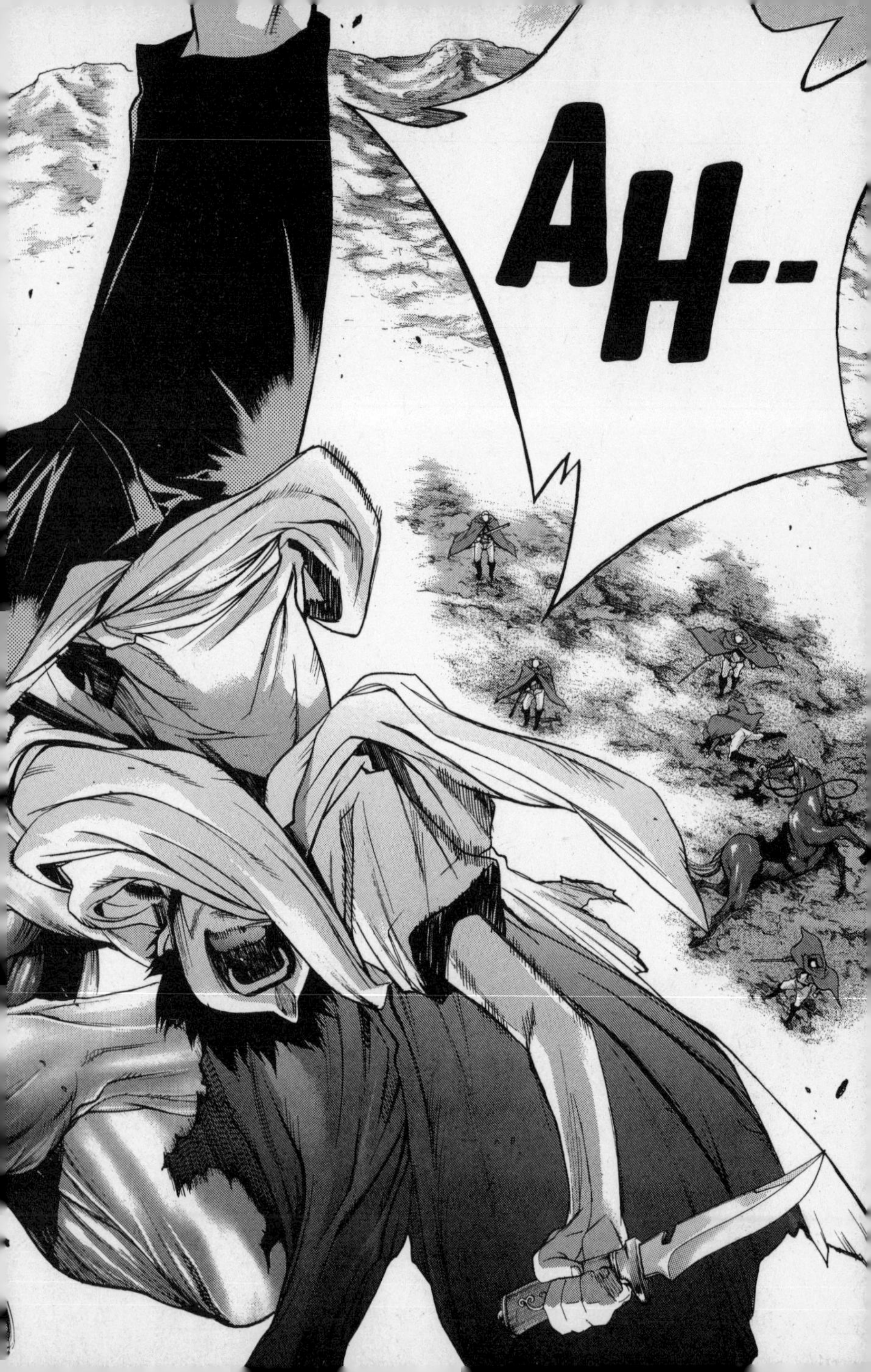
AH--

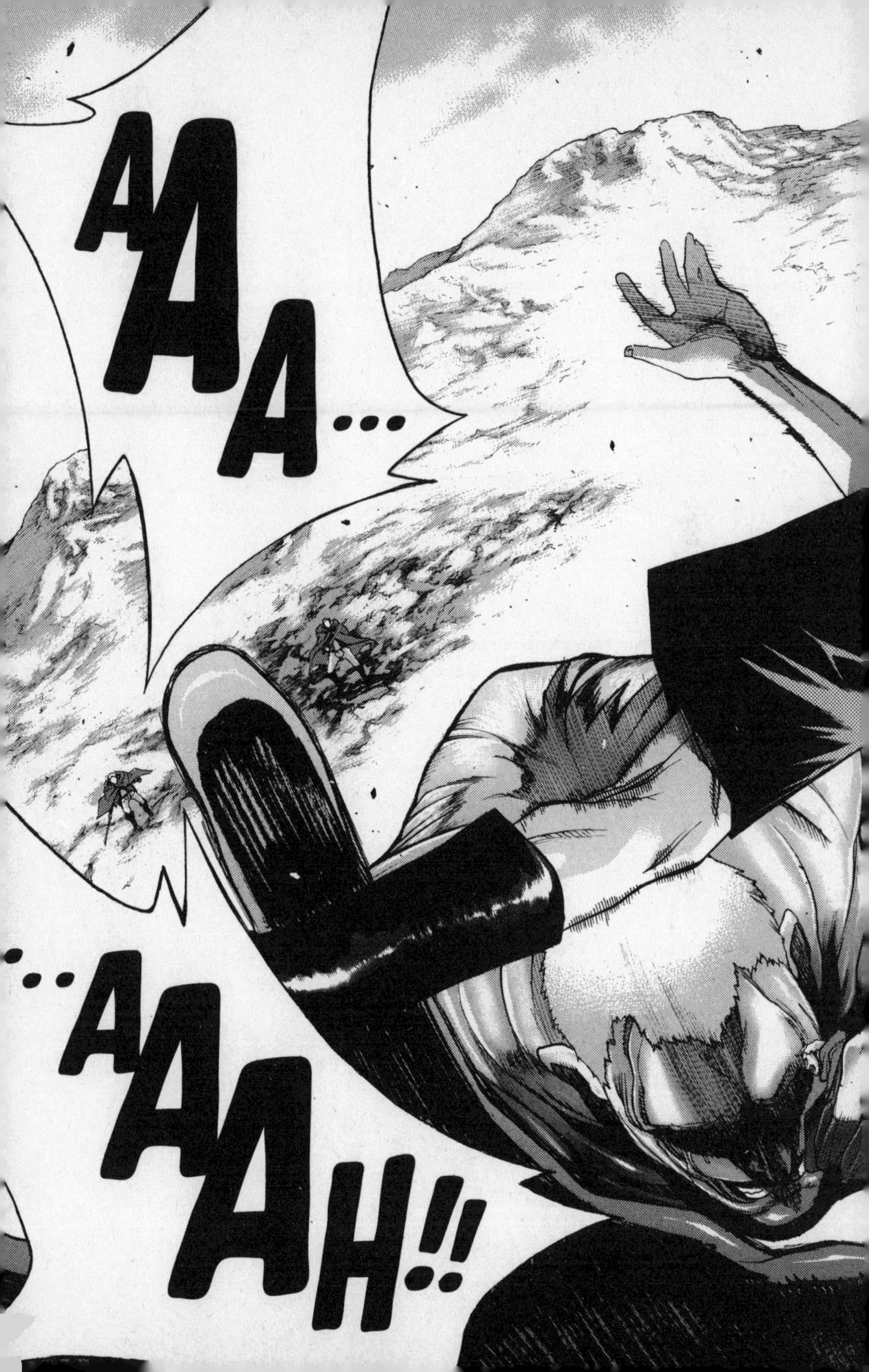
AAAA...
...AAAAH!!

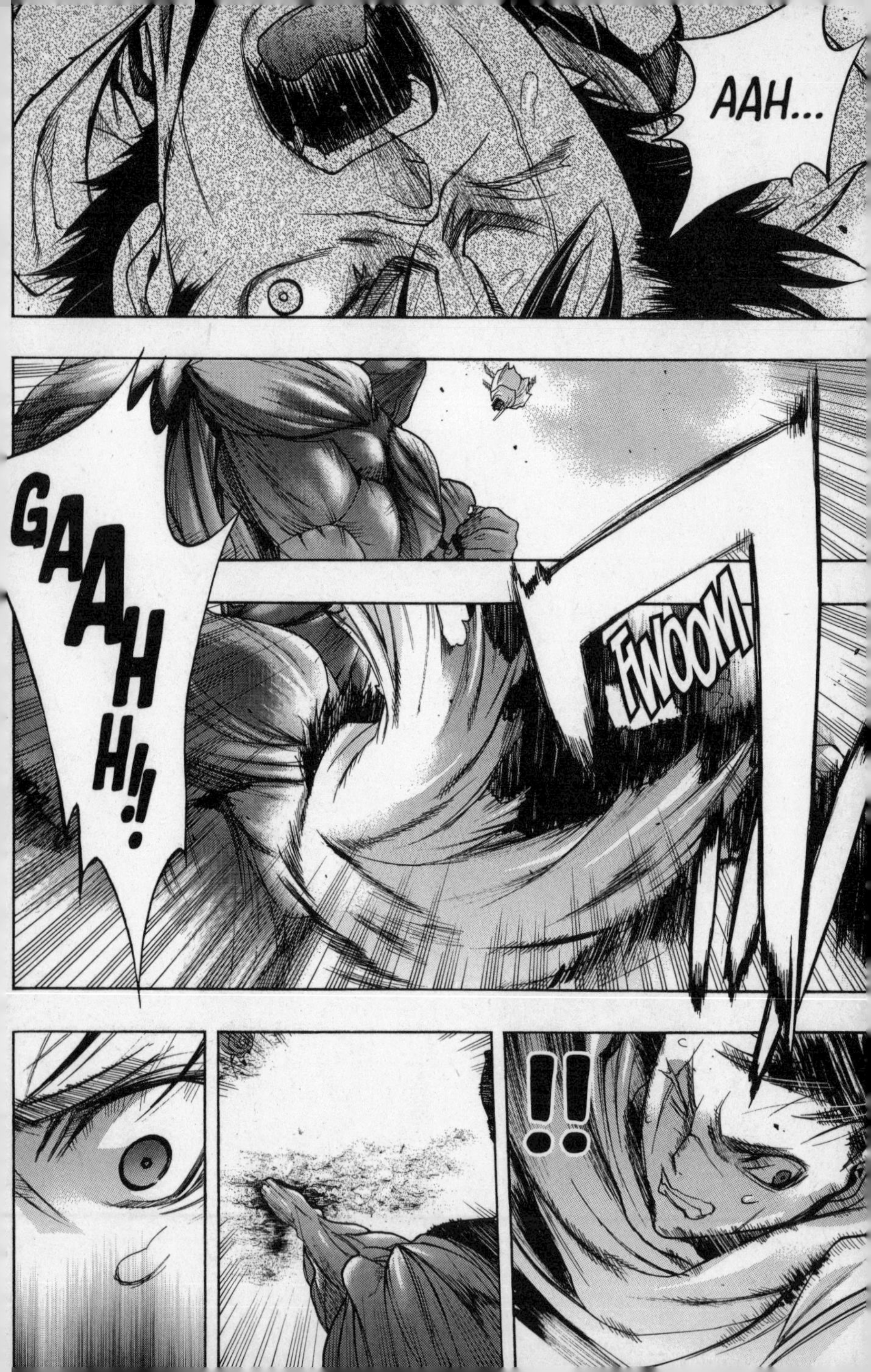
AAH...
FWOOM
GAAHH!!
!!

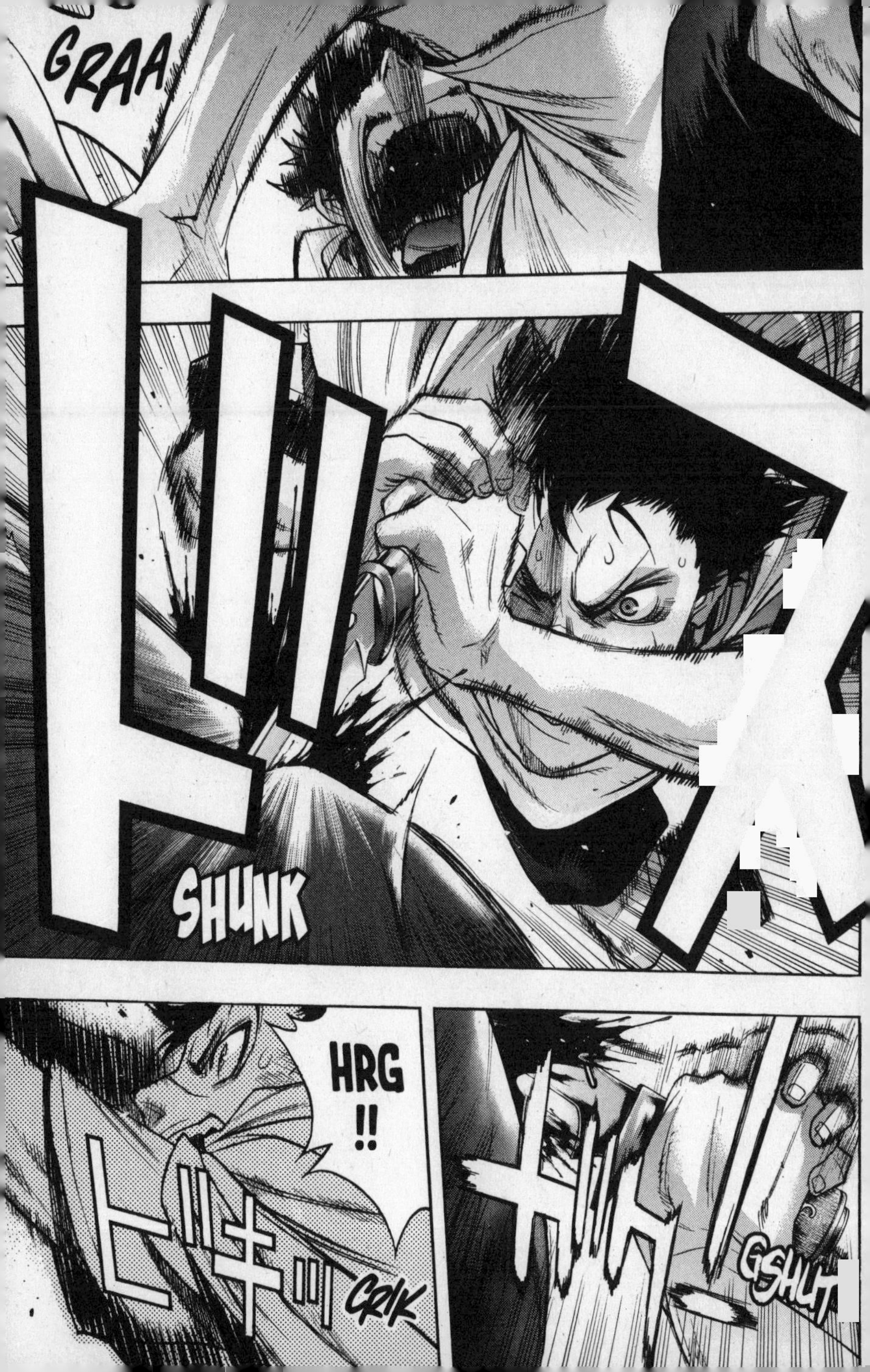
GRAA
SHUNK
GSHUT
HRG !!
CRIK

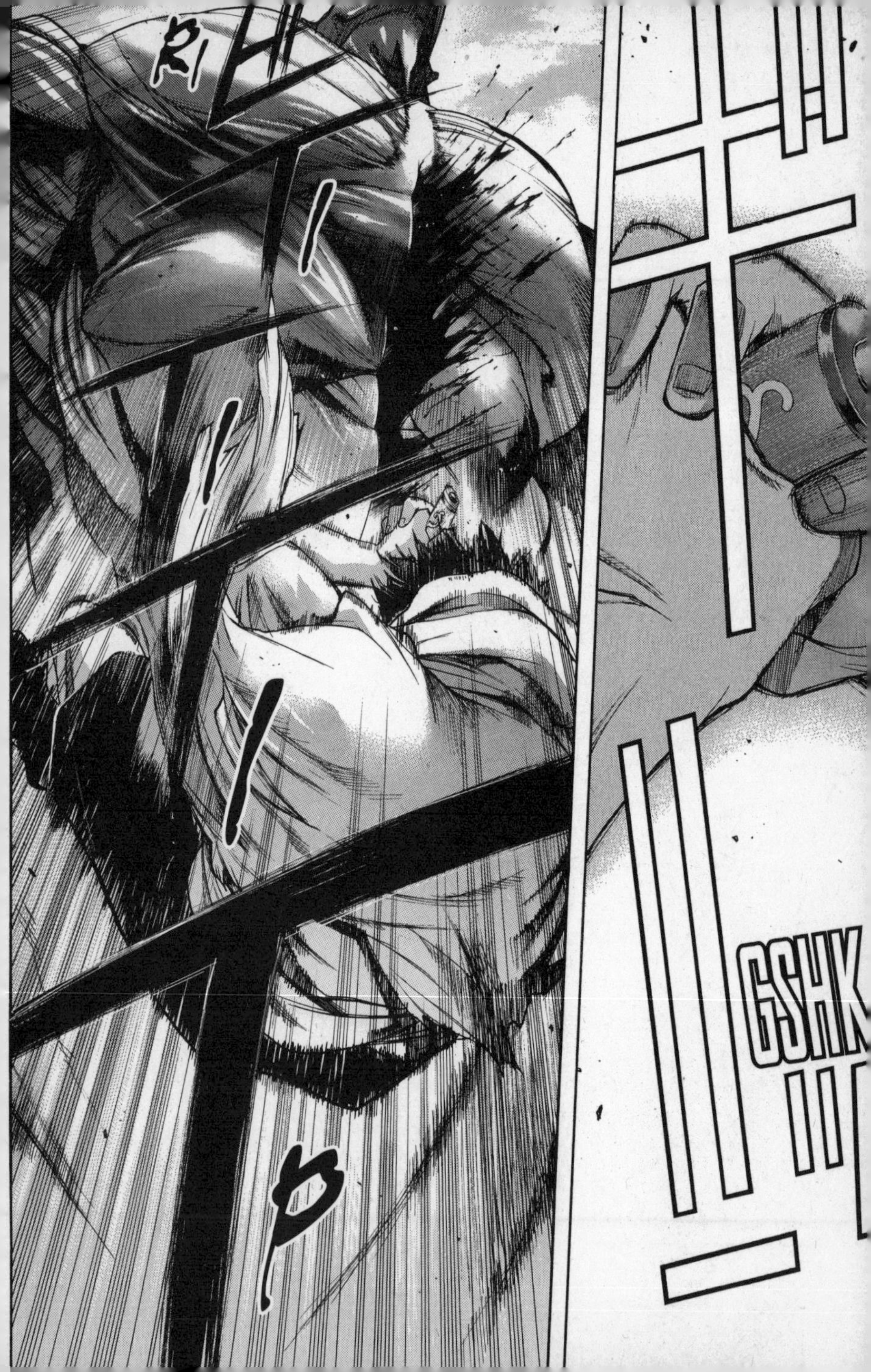
GSHK
RIIIIP

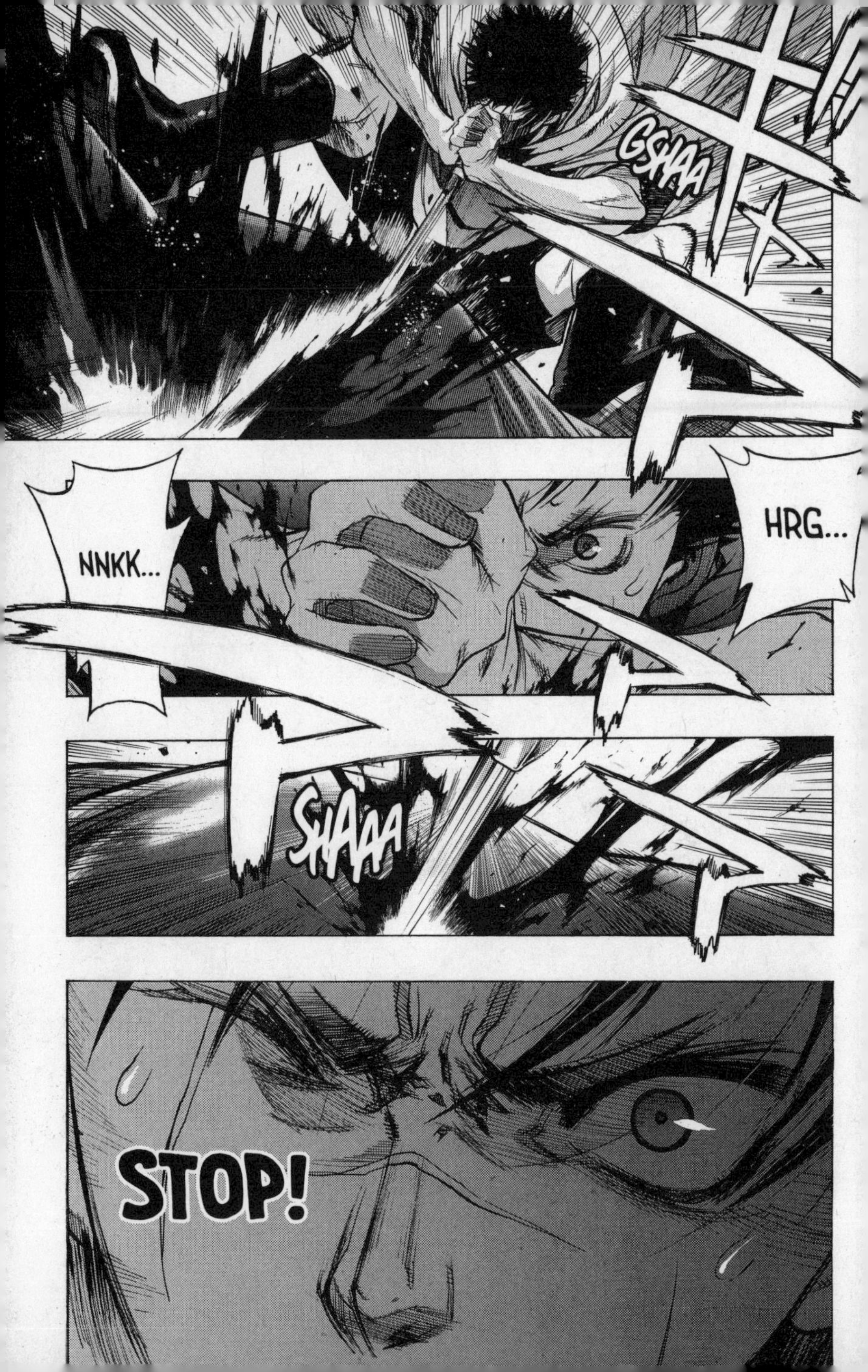
GSHAA
HRG...
NNKK...
SHAAA
STOP!

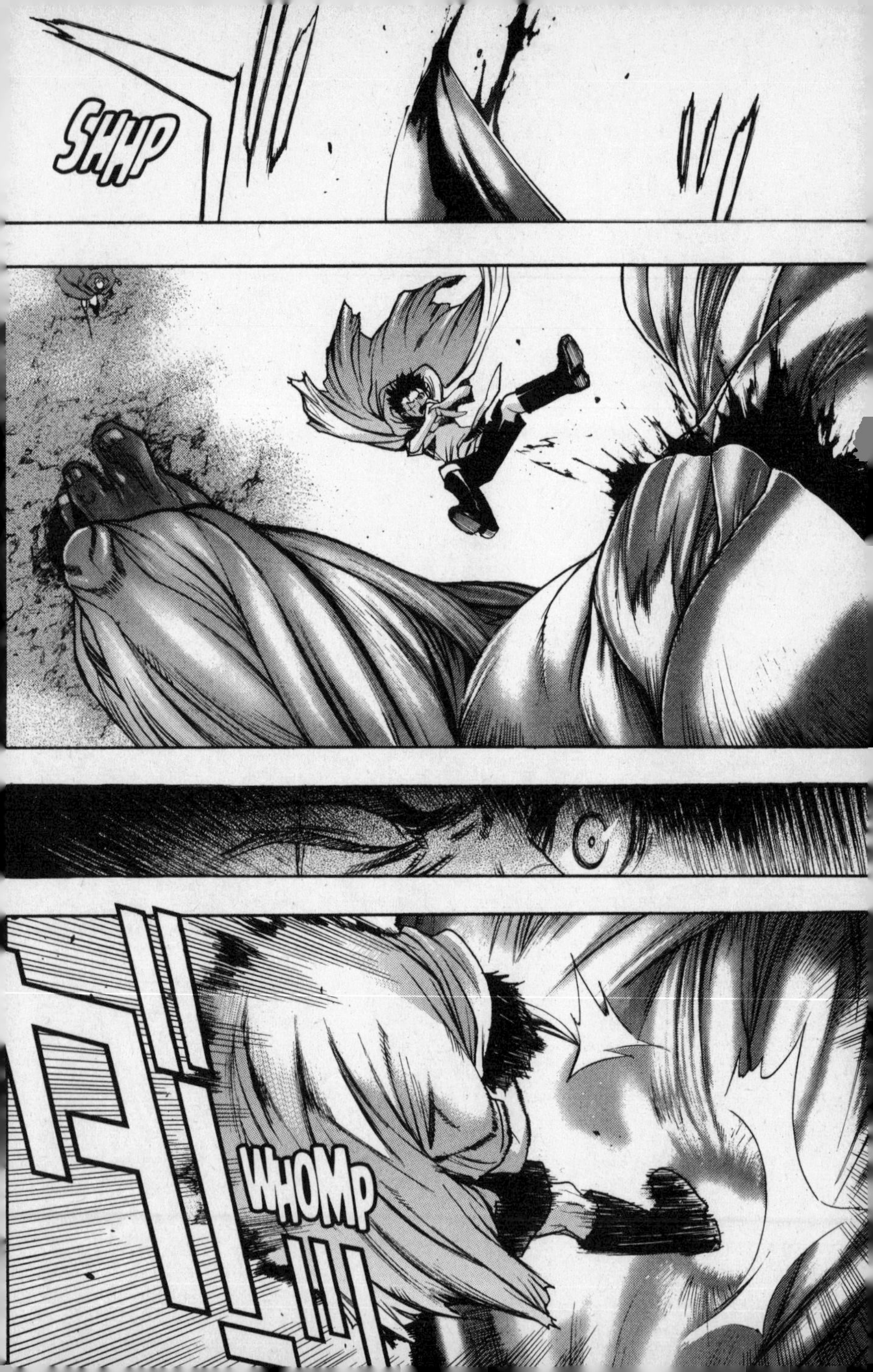
SHHP
WHOMP

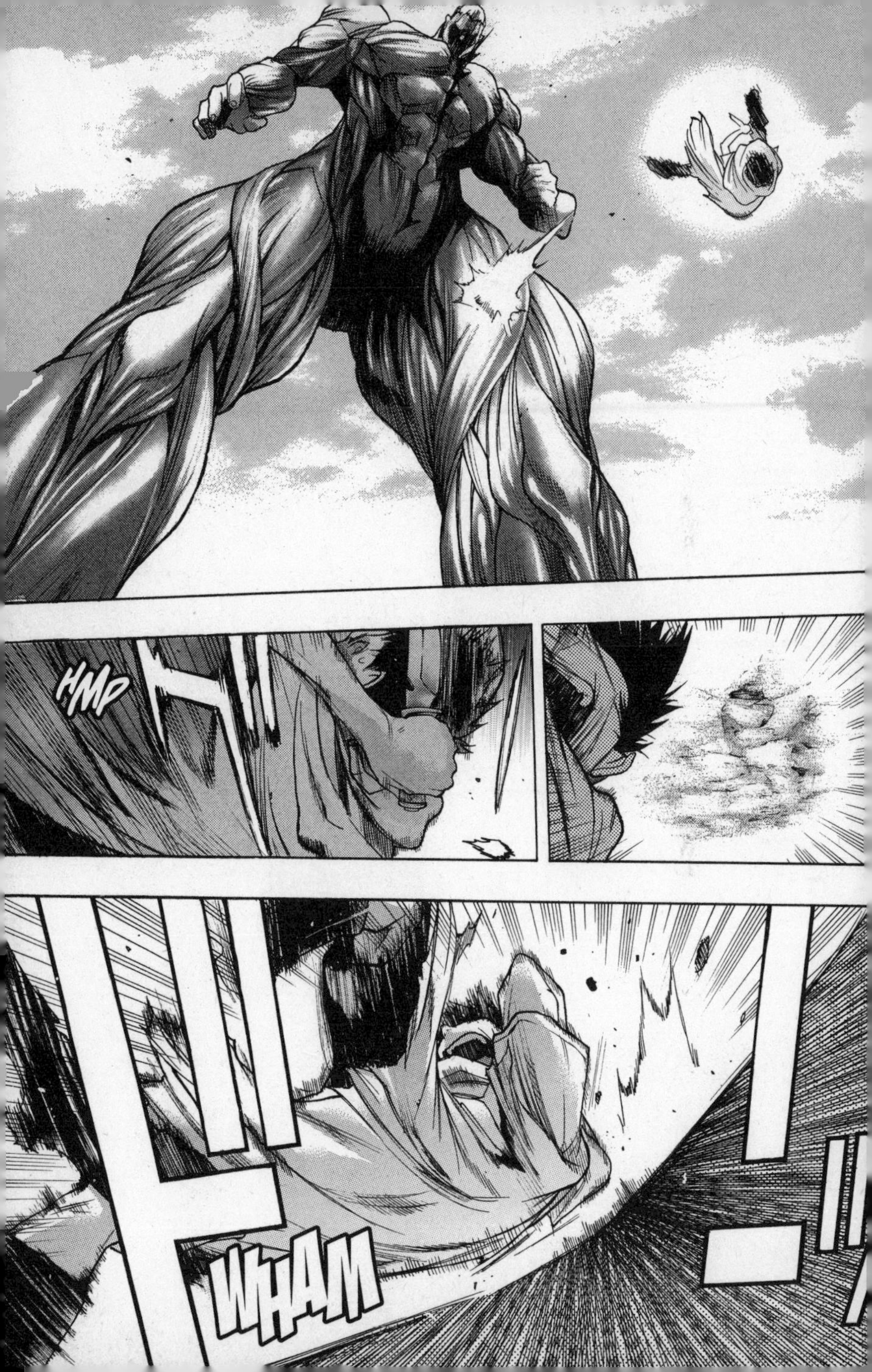
HMP
WHAM

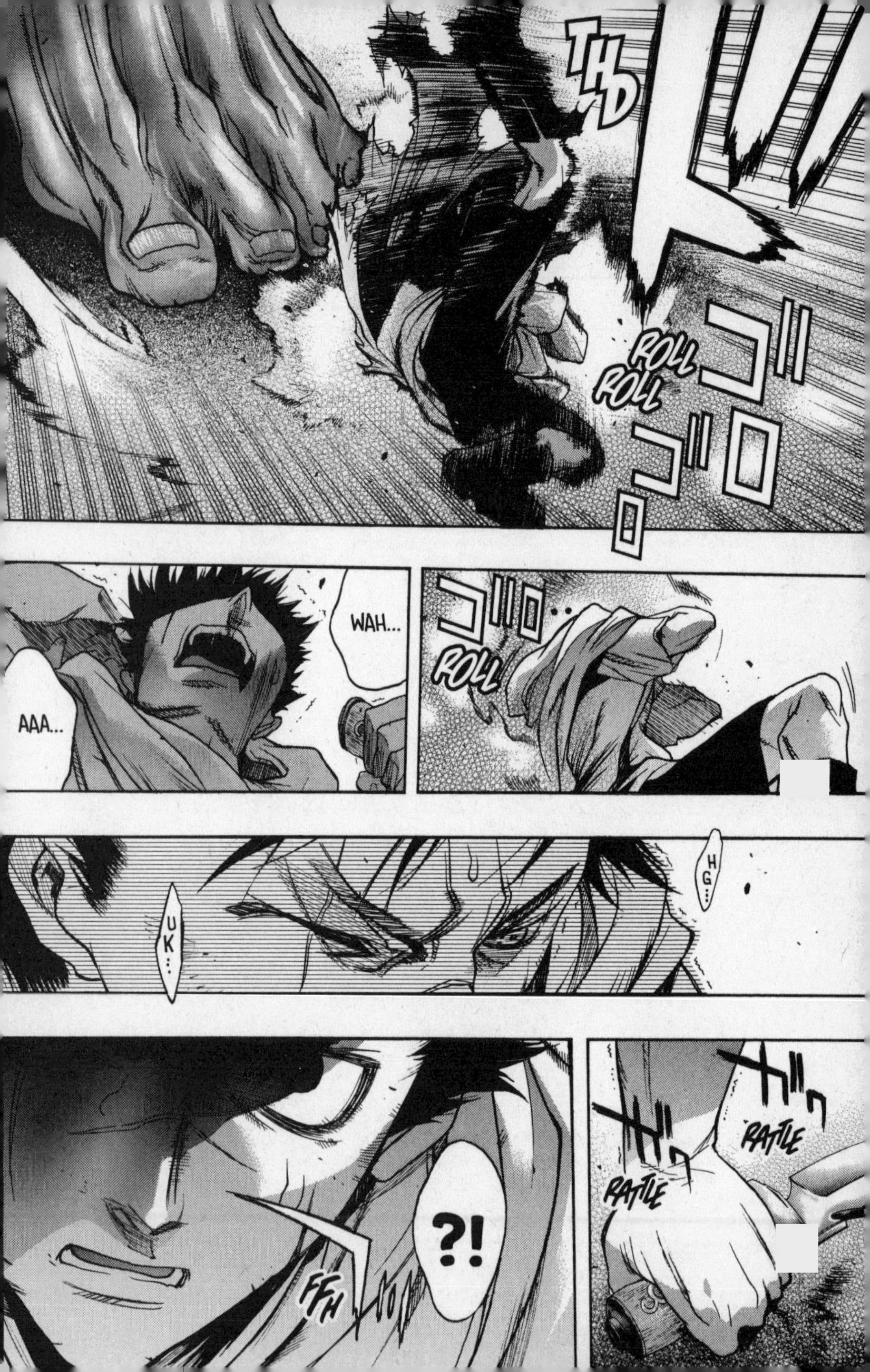
THD
ROLL
ROLL
ROLL
WAH...
AAA...
HG...
UK...
RATTLE
RATTLE
?!
FFH

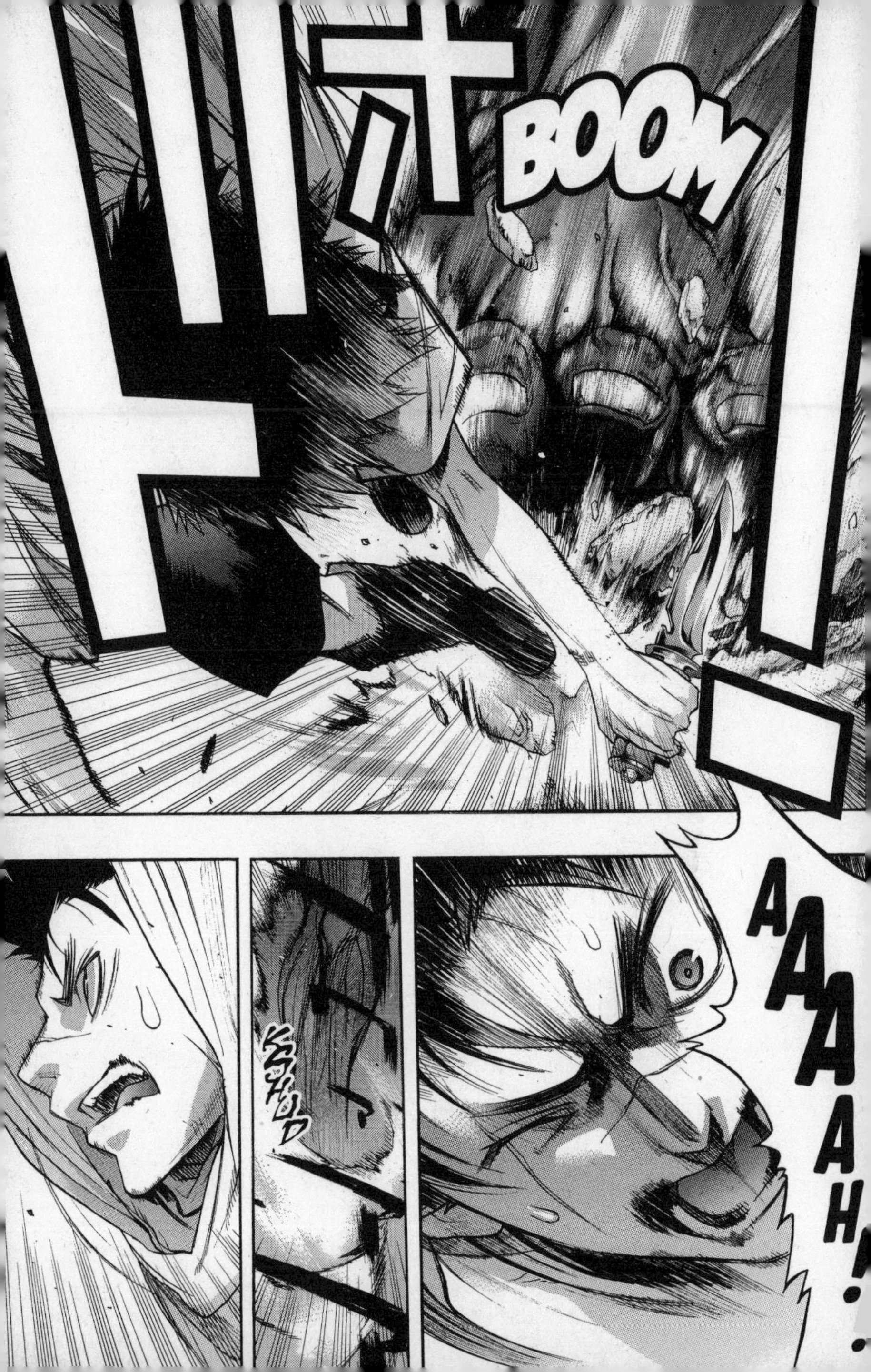
ドォ
BOOM
AAAAAH!!
KSHOD

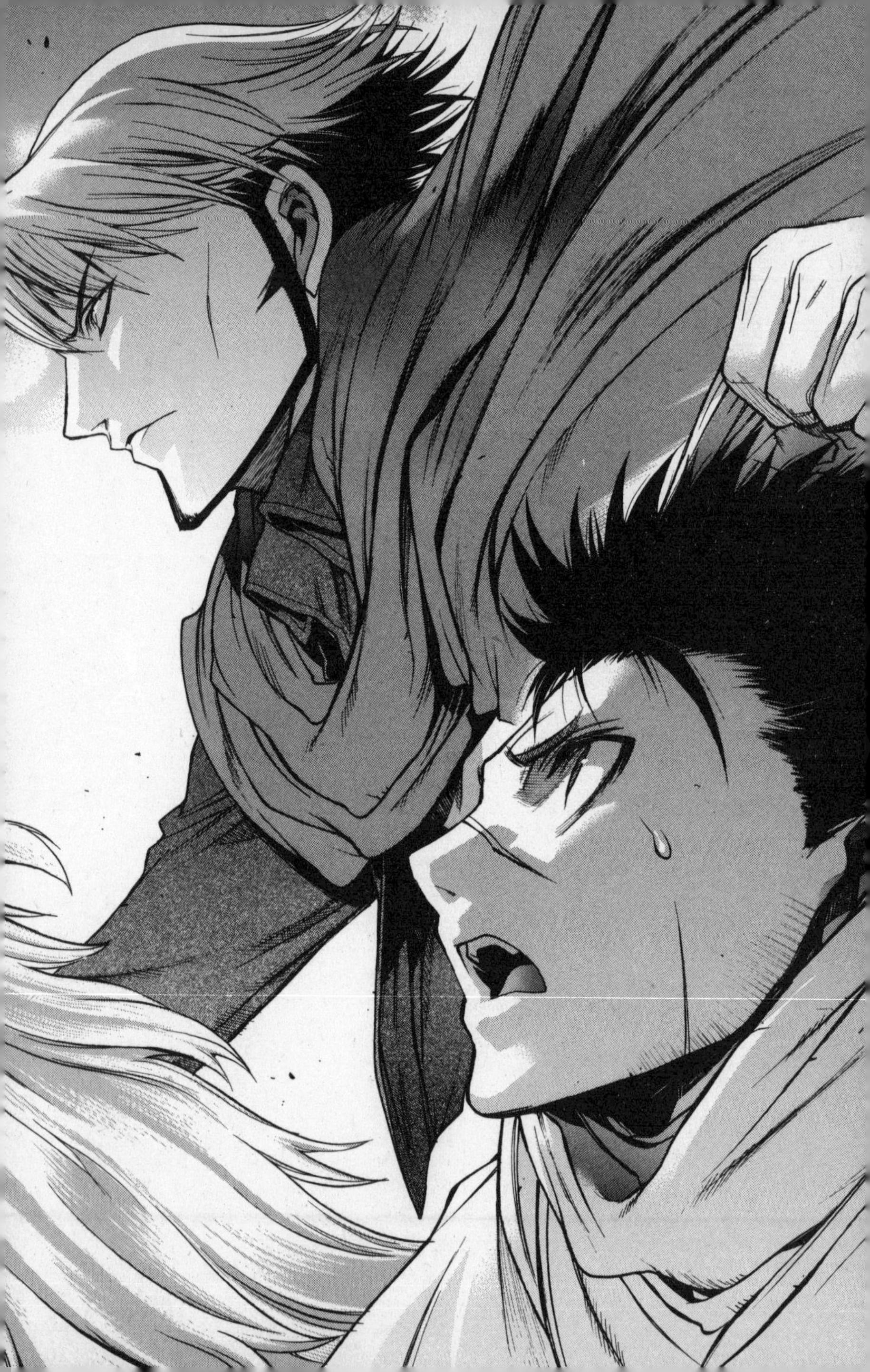

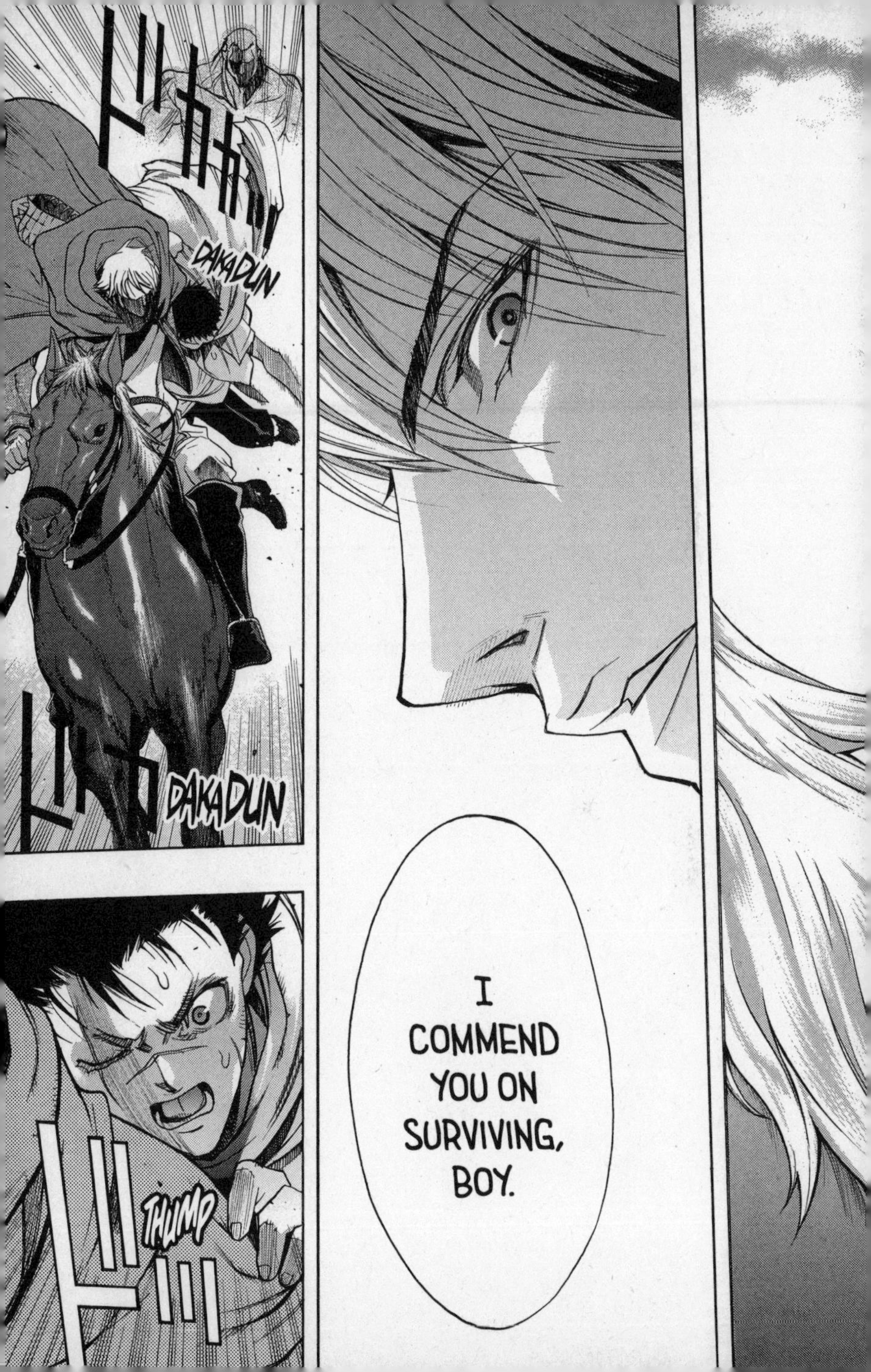
I COMMEND YOU ON SURVIVING, BOY.
DAKADUN
DAKADUN
THUMP

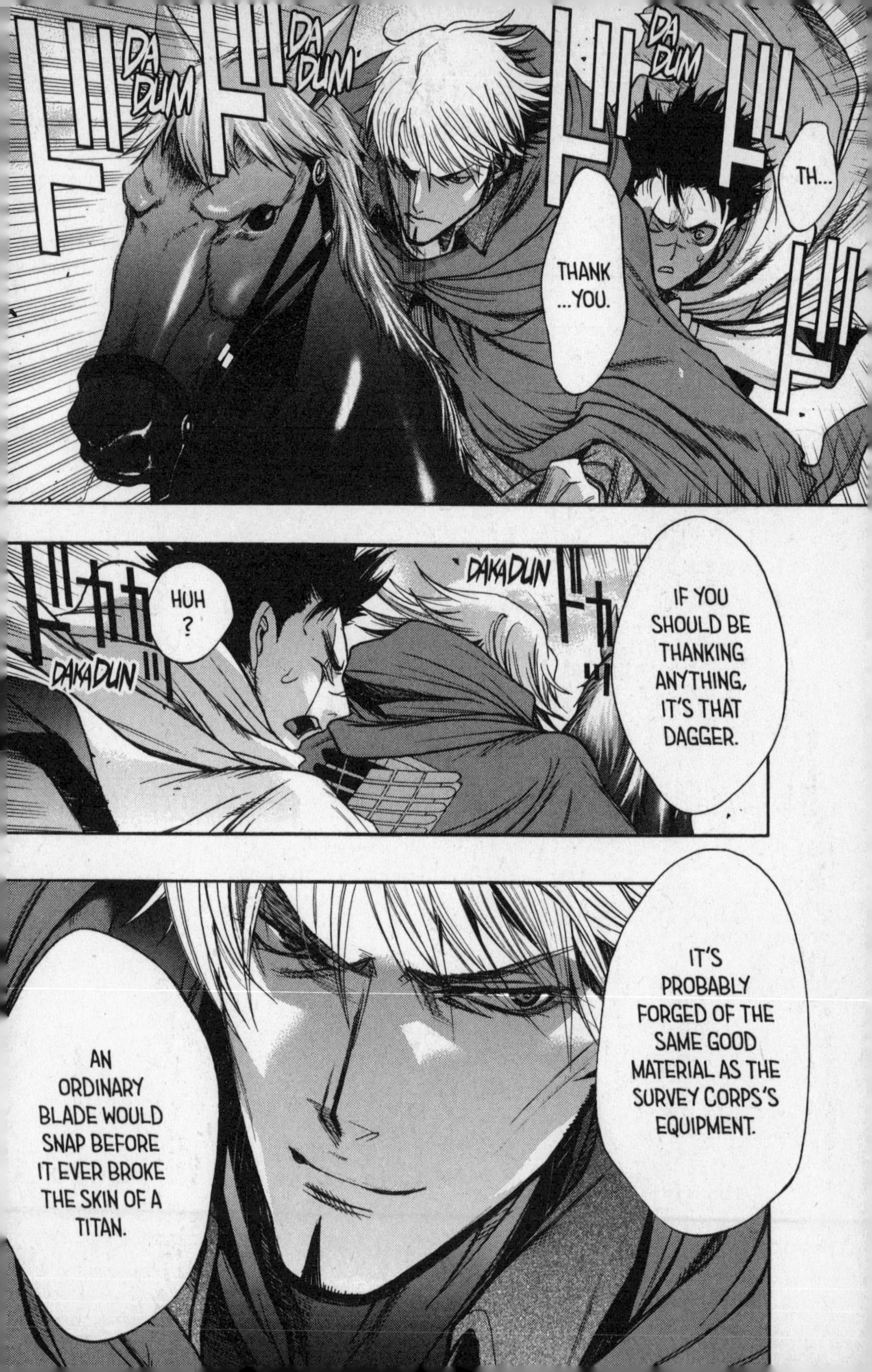
DA DUM
TH...
THANK ...YOU.
DA DUM
DA DUM
IF YOU SHOULD BE THANKING ANYTHING, IT'S THAT DAGGER.
DAKADUN
HUH ?
DAKADUN
IT'S PROBABLY FORGED OF THE SAME GOOD MATERIAL AS THE SURVEY CORPS'S EQUIPMENT.
AN ORDINARY BLADE WOULD SNAP BEFORE IT EVER BROKE THE SKIN OF A TITAN.

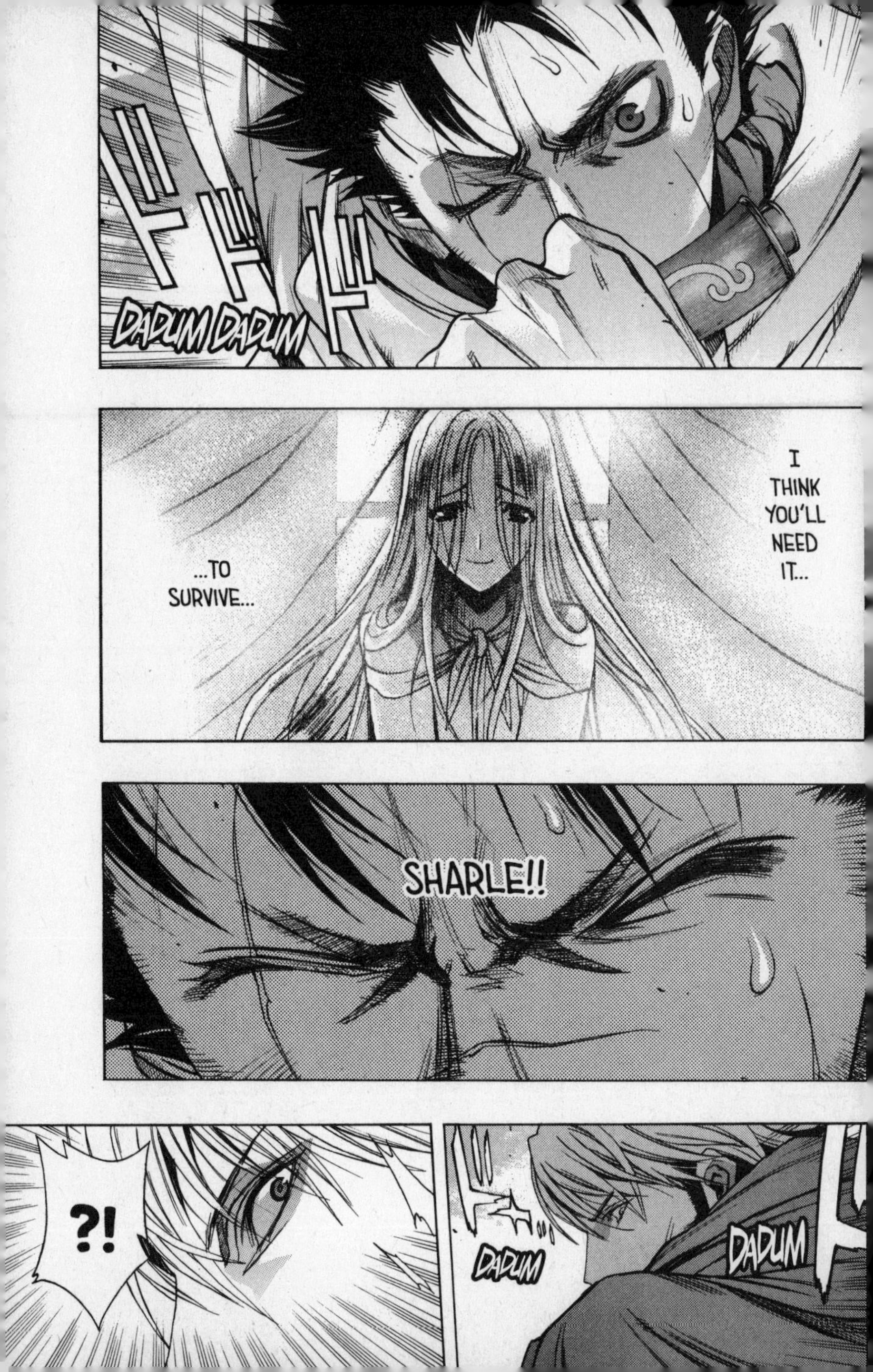
DADUM DADUM
I THINK YOU'LL NEED IT...
...TO SURVIVE...
SHARLE!!
DADUM
DADUM
?!

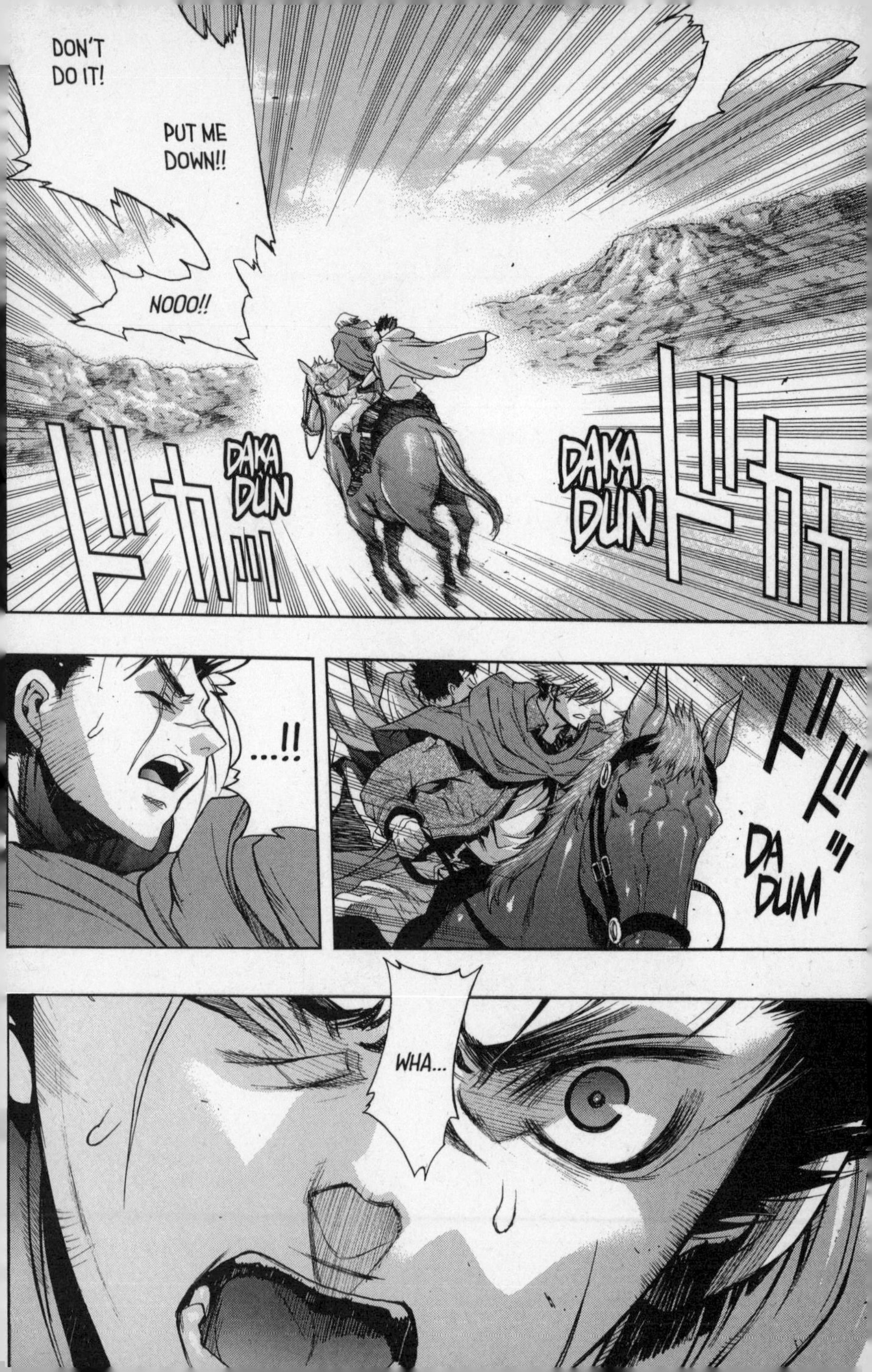
DON'T DO IT!
PUT ME DOWN!!
NOOO!!
DAKA DUN
DAKA DUN
DA DUM
...!!
WHA...

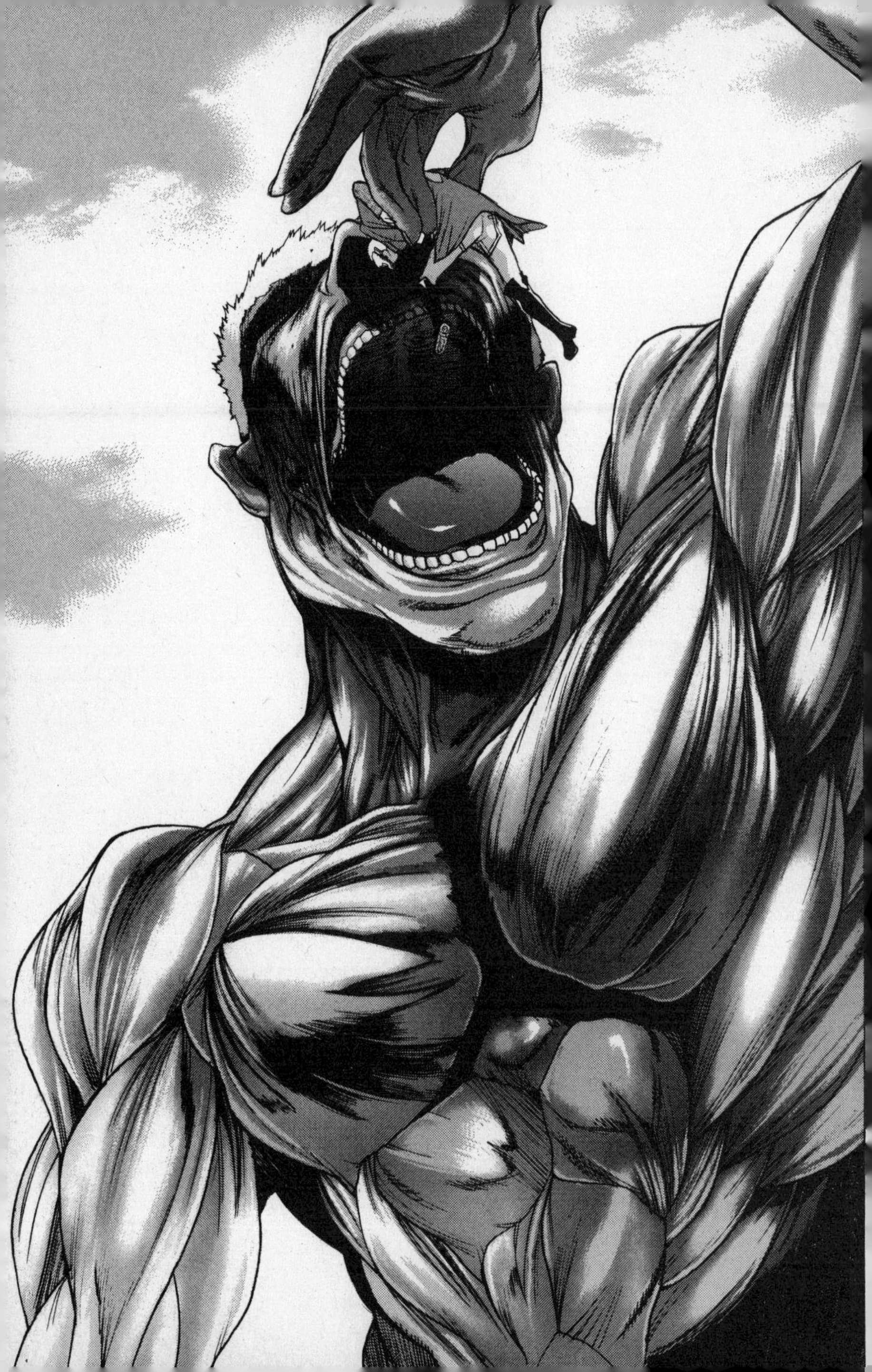

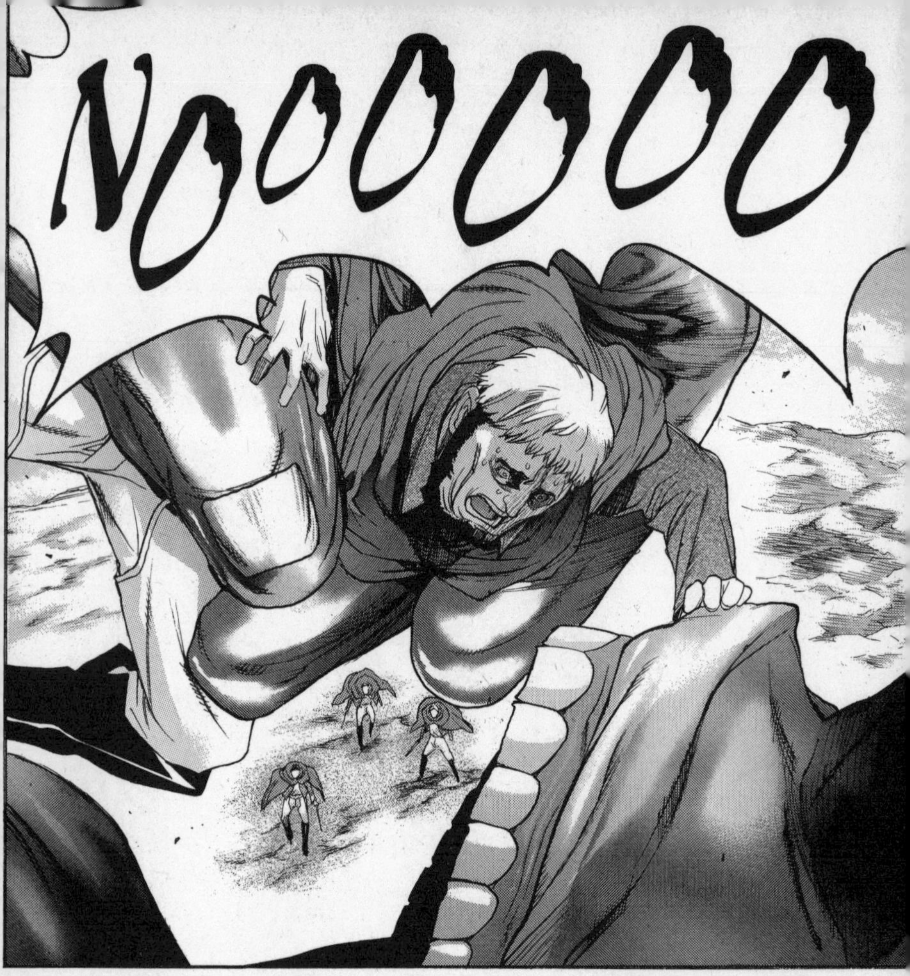
NOOOOOO
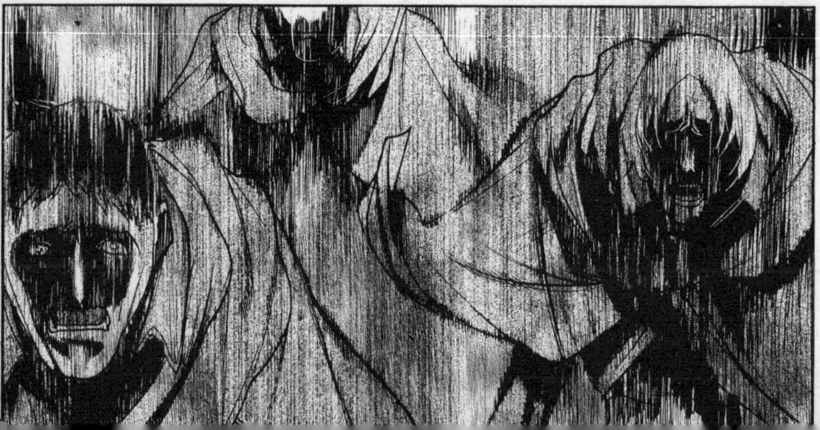

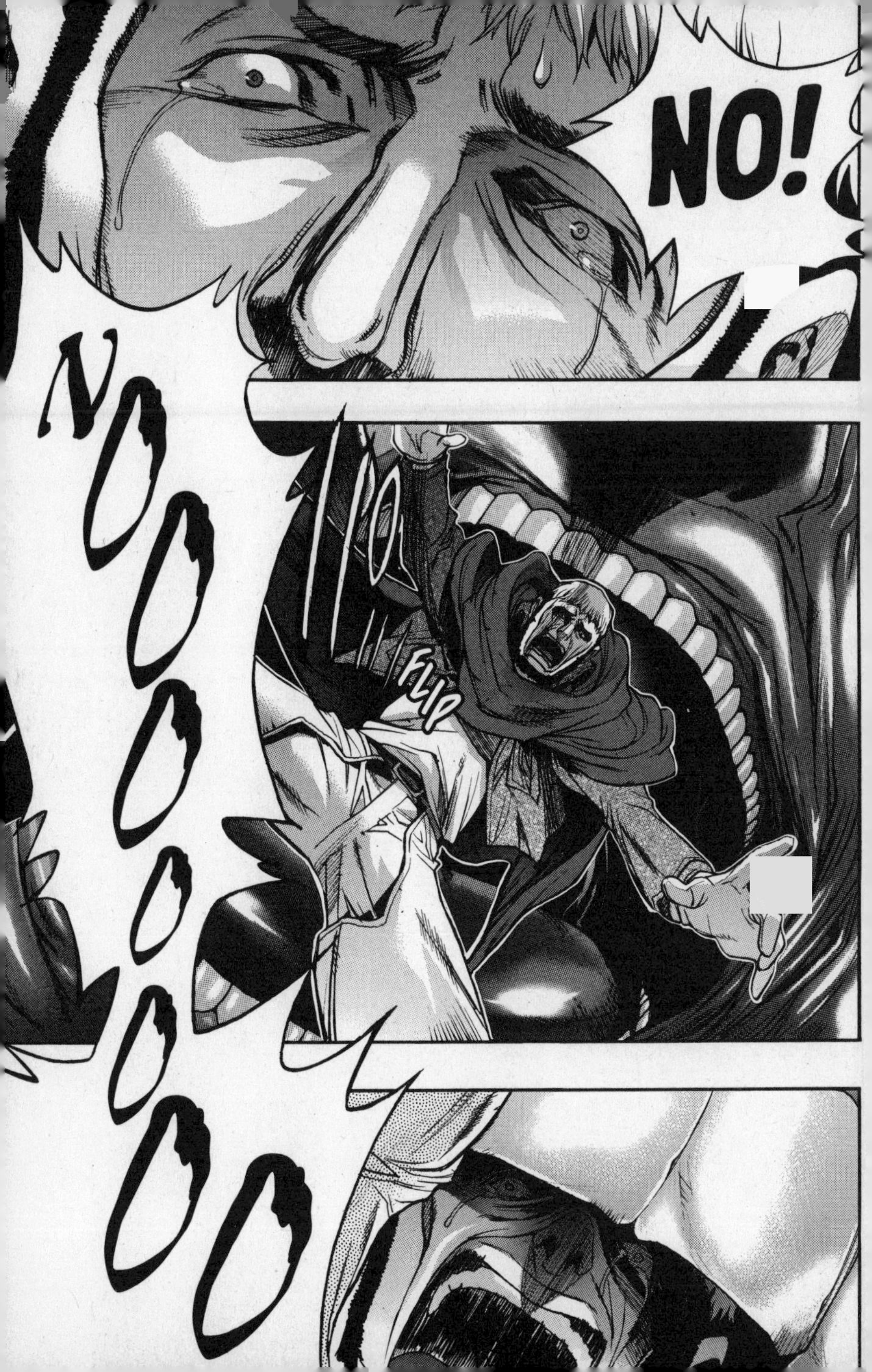
NO!
FLIP
NOOOOOOO

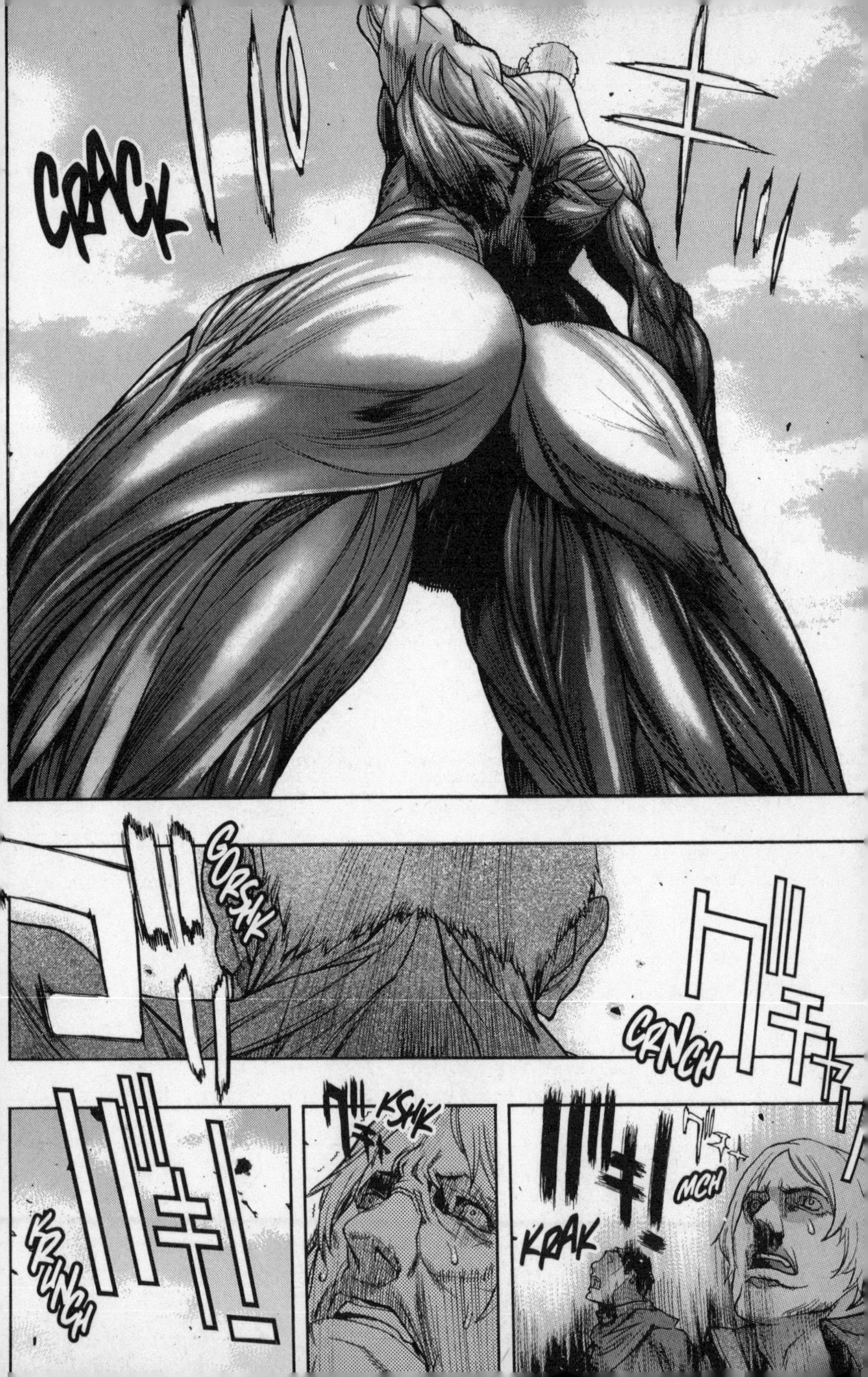
CRACK
CRNCH
GORSHK
MCH
KRAK
KSHK
KRUNCH

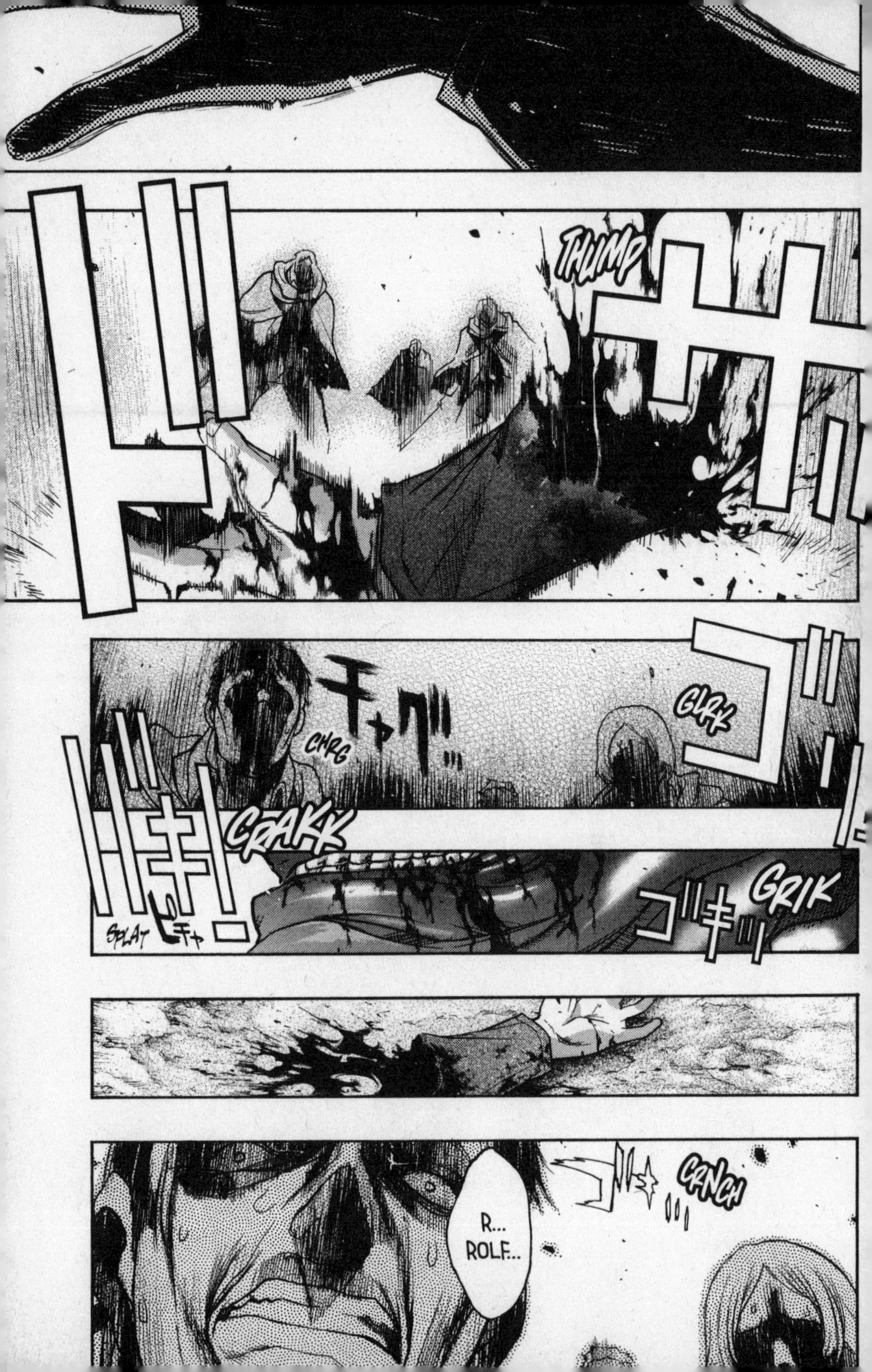
THUMP
GLRK
CHRG
GRIK
CRAKK
SPLAT
CRNCH
R... ROLF...

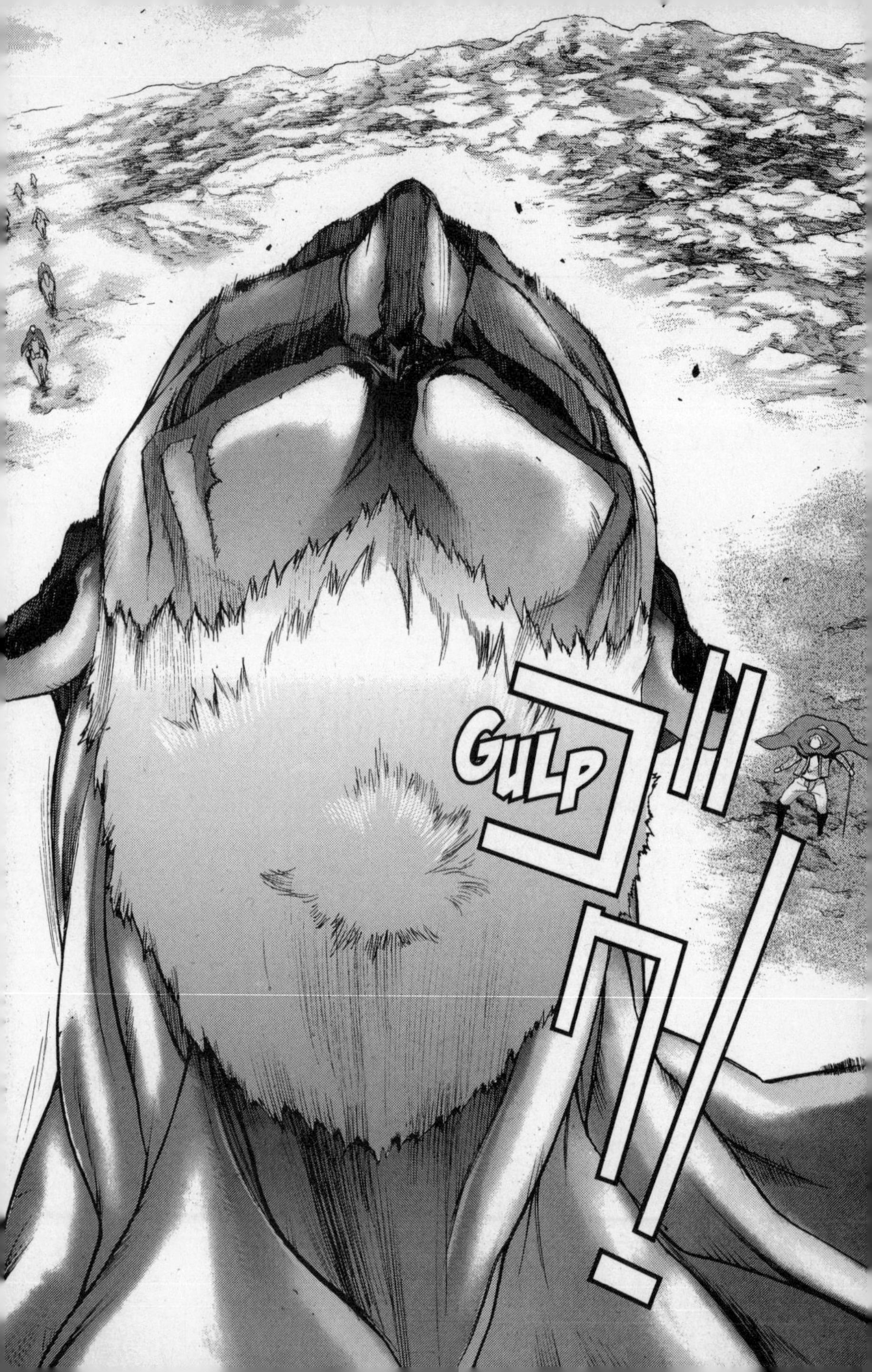
GULP

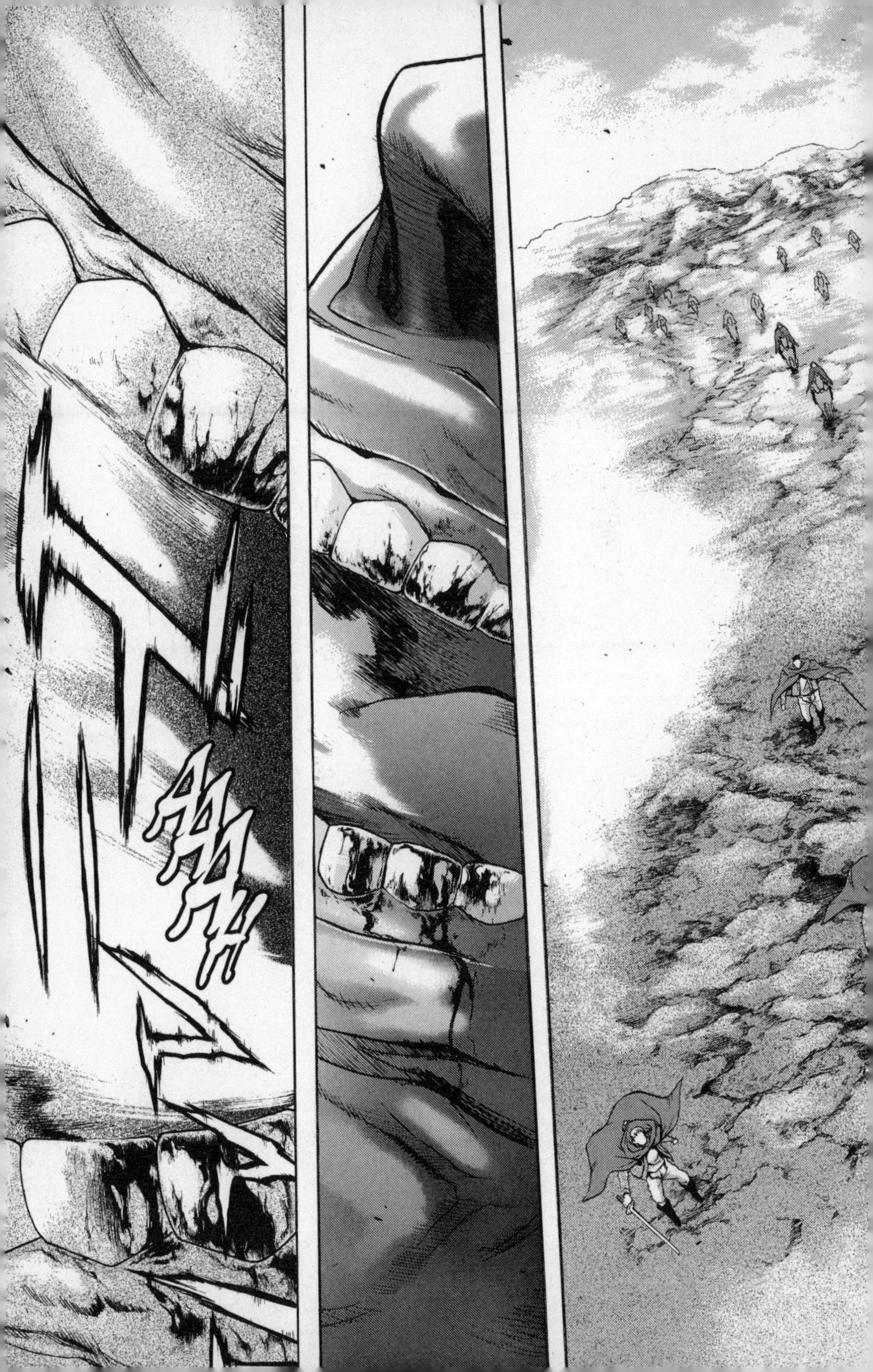
AAAAH

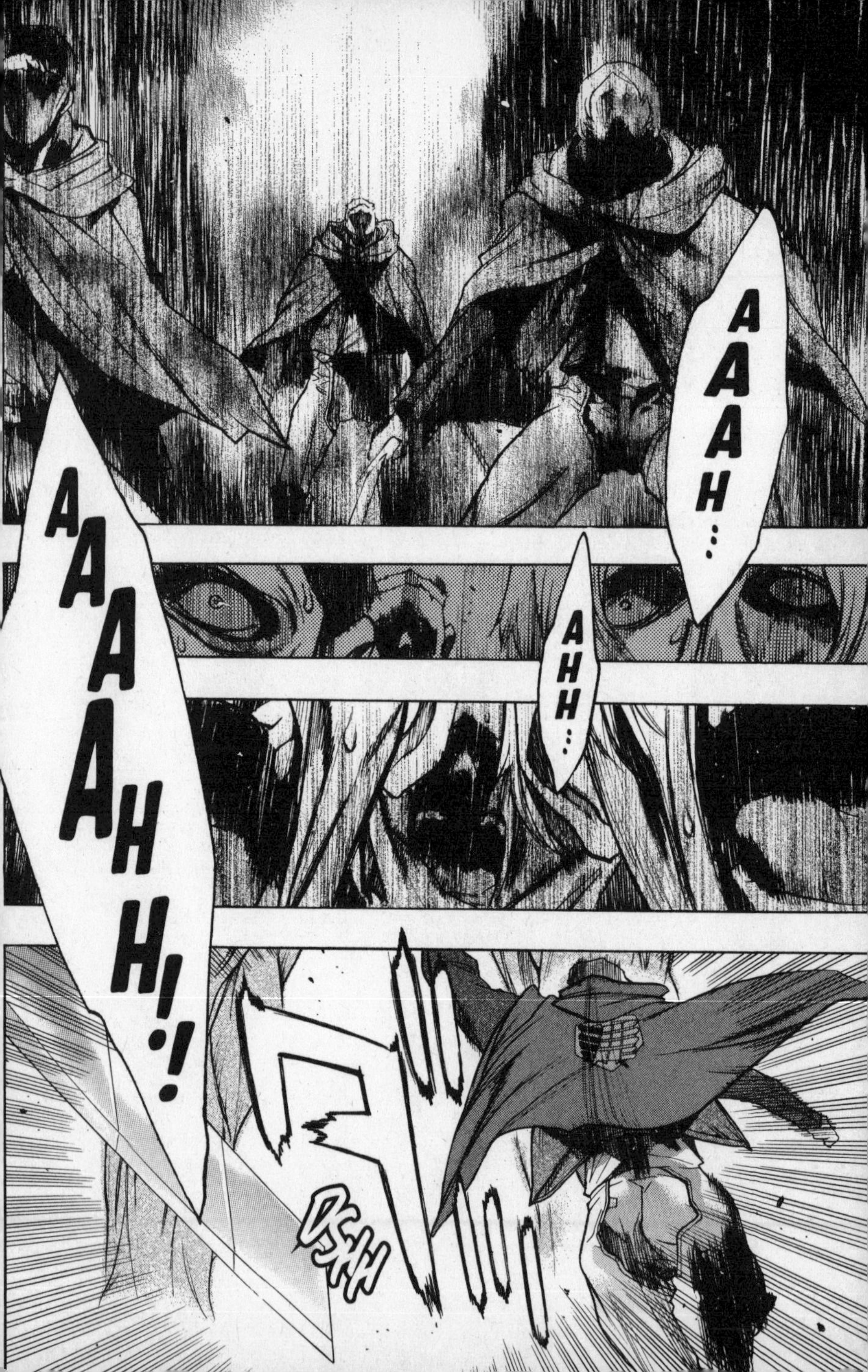
AAAH...
AHH...
AAAAAHH!!
DSHH

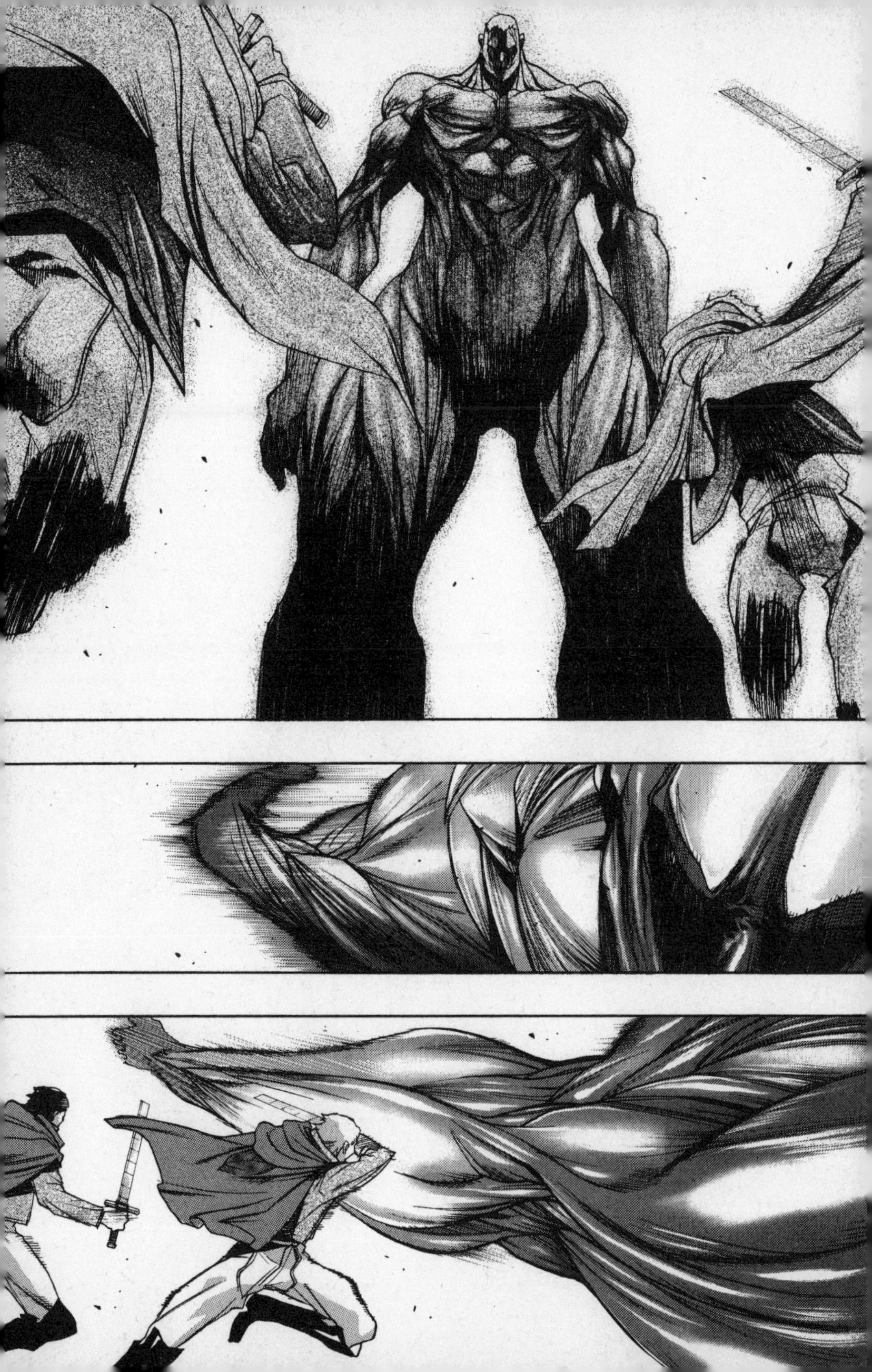

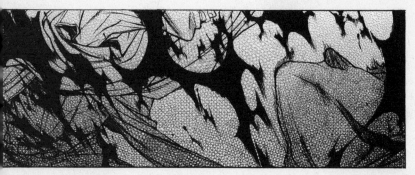

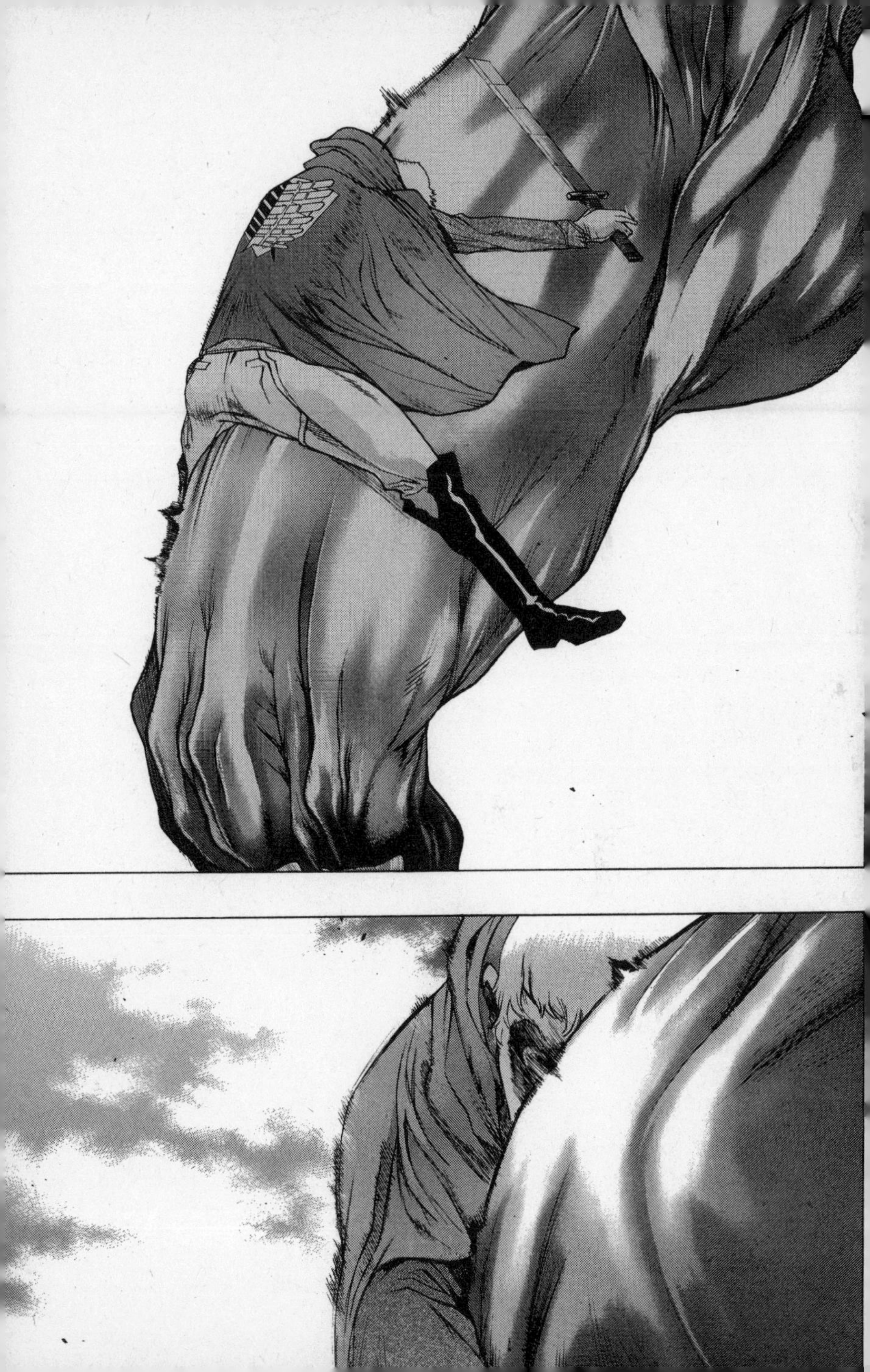

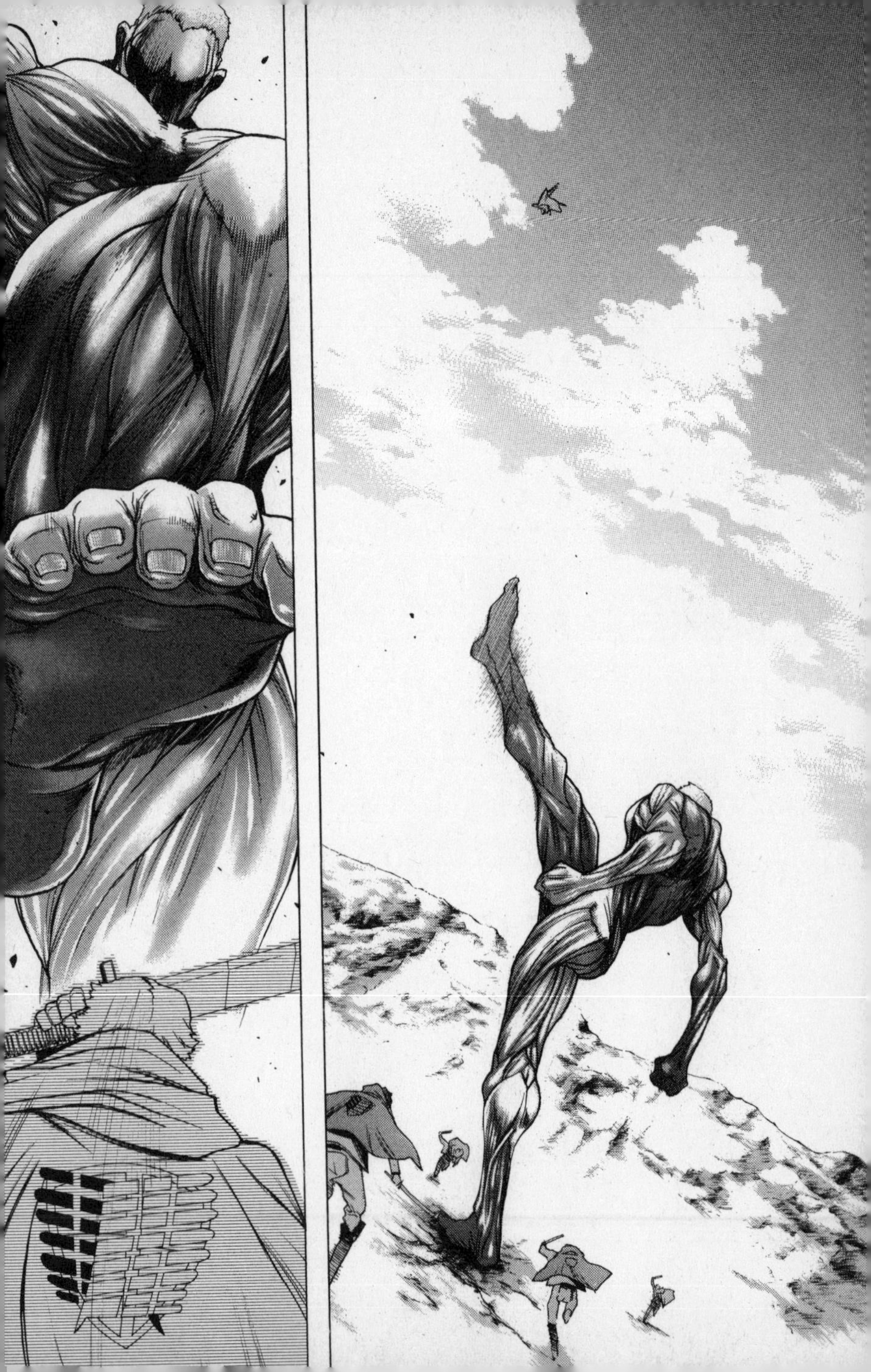

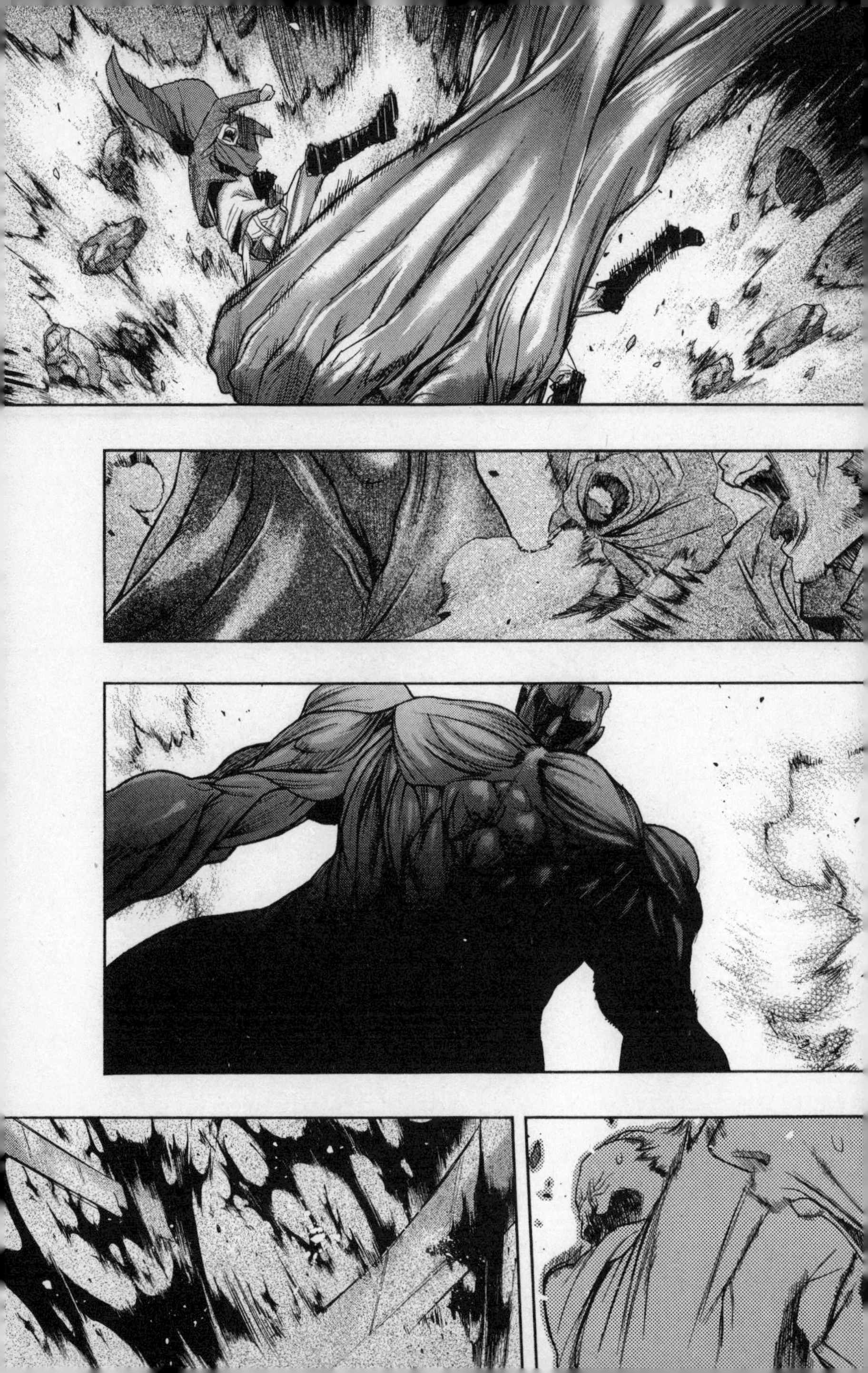

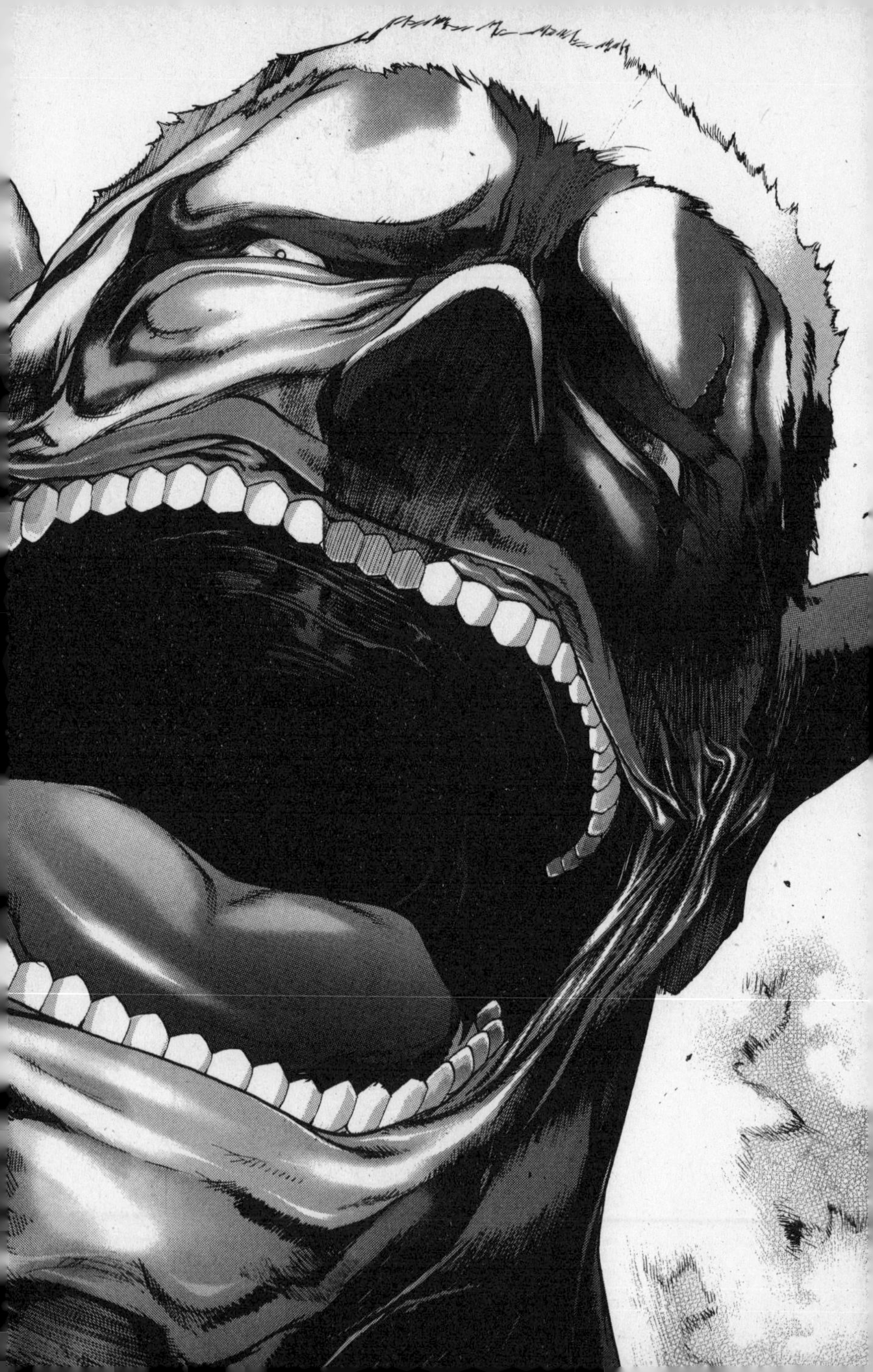

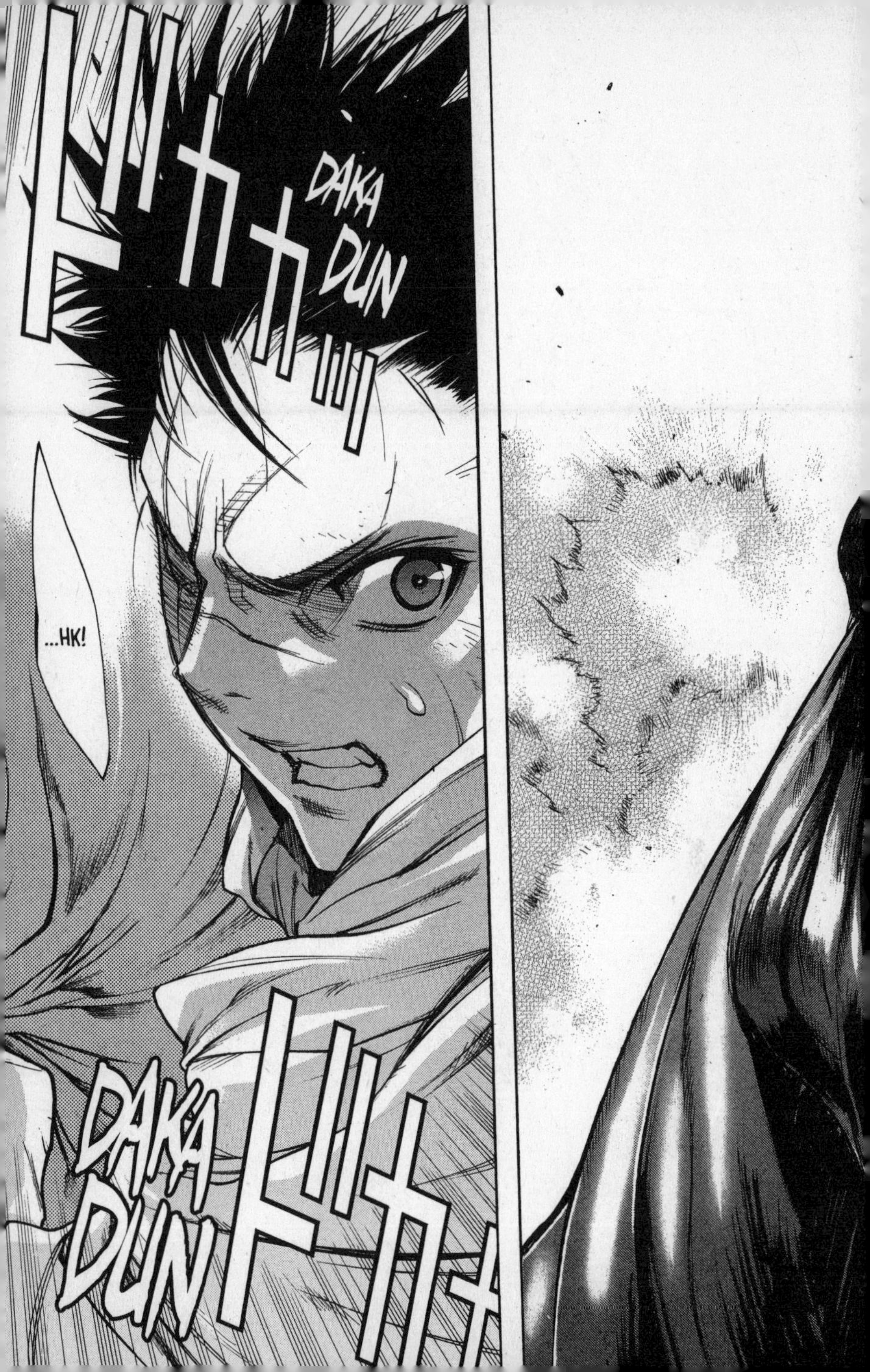
DAKA DUN
...HK!
DAKA DUN

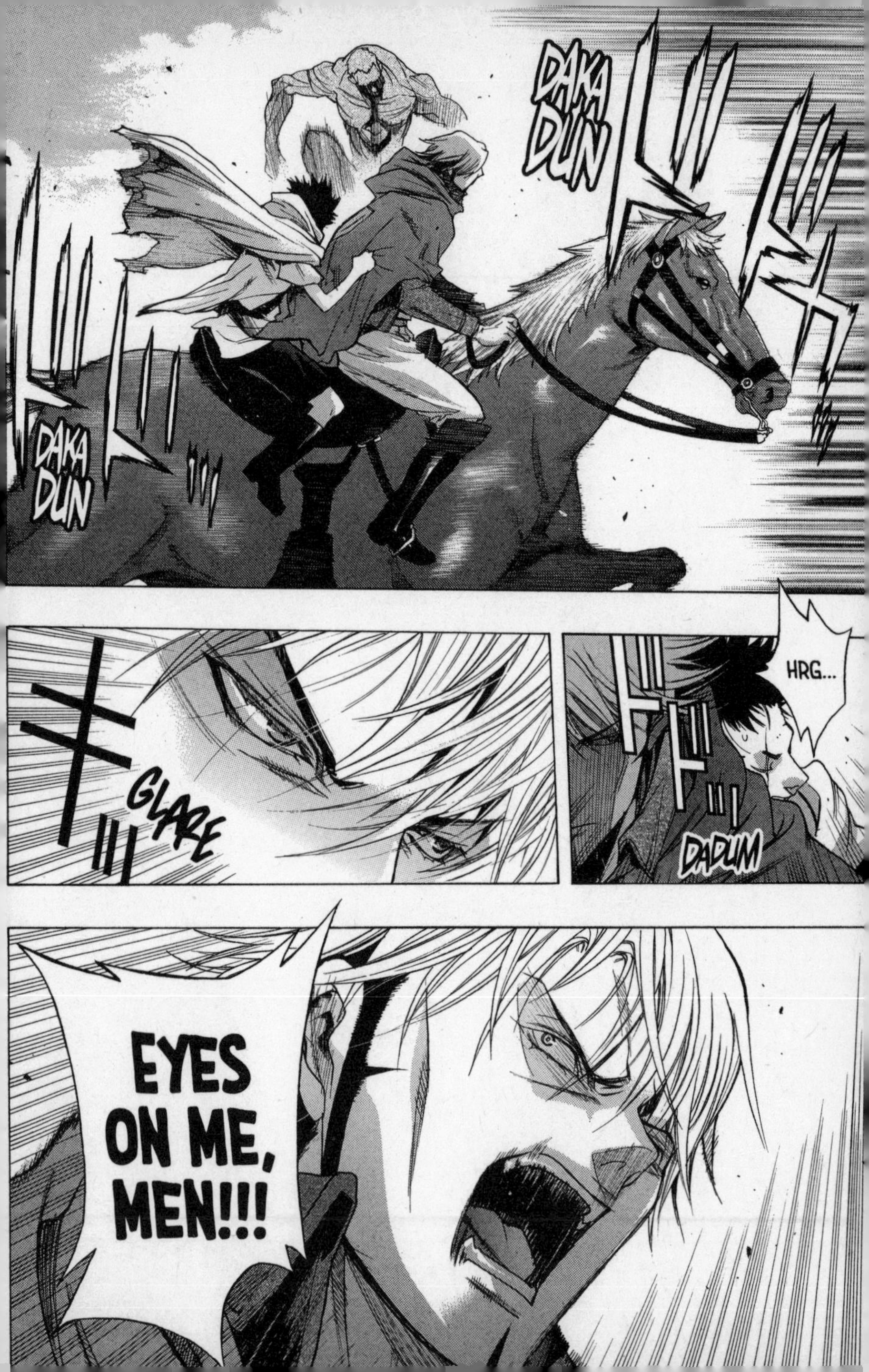
DAKA DUN
DAKA DUN
HRG...
DADUM
GLARE
EYES ON ME, MEN!!!

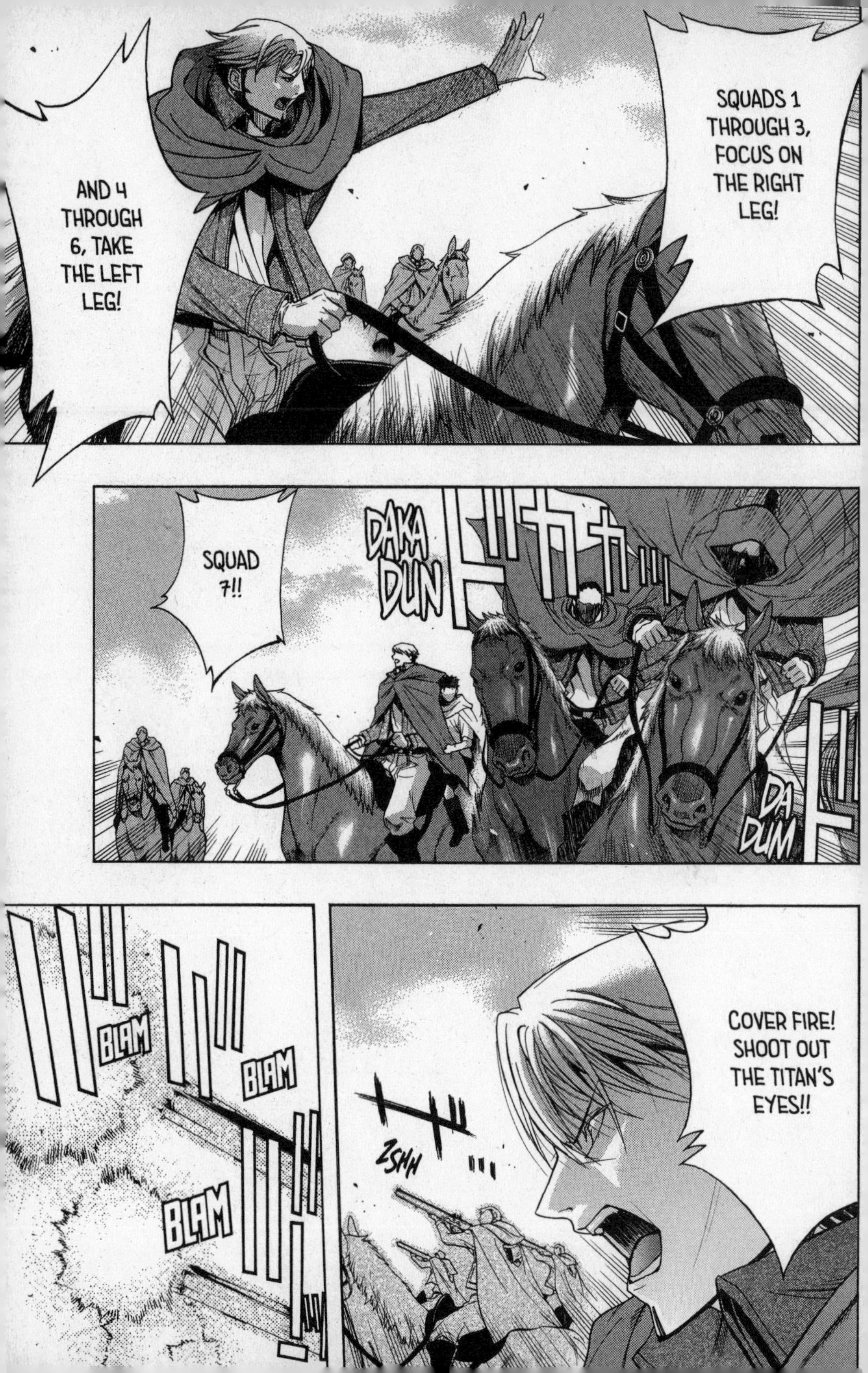
SQUADS 1 THROUGH 3, FOCUS ON THE RIGHT LEG!
AND 4 THROUGH 6, TAKE THE LEFT LEG!
DAKA DUN
SQUAD 7!!
DA DUM
COVER FIRE! SHOOT OUT THE TITAN'S EYES!!
ZSHH
BLAM
BLAM
BLAM

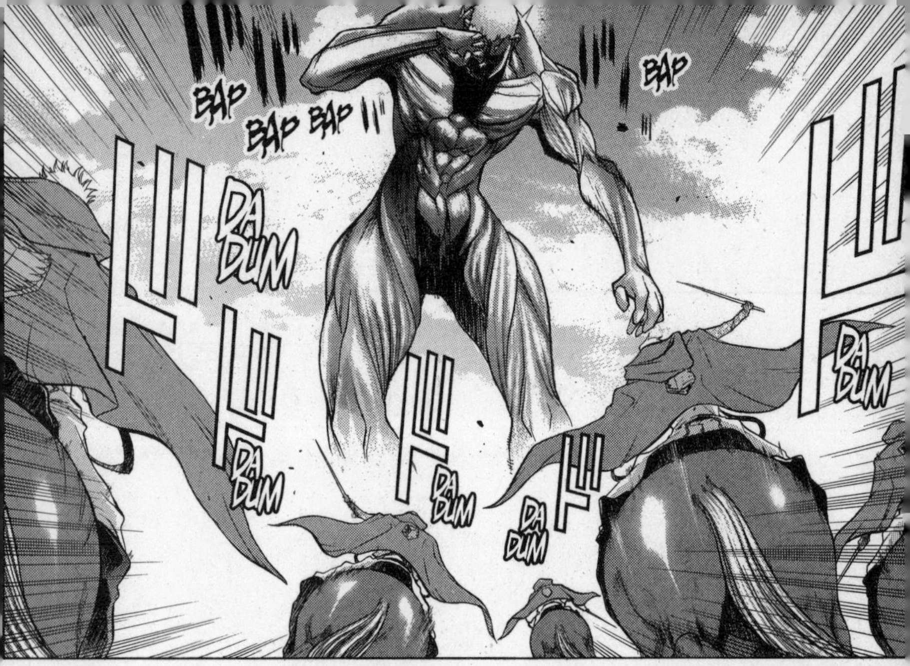
BAP
BAP
BAP BAP
DA DUM
DA DUM
DA DUM
DA DUM
DA DUM
DA DUM
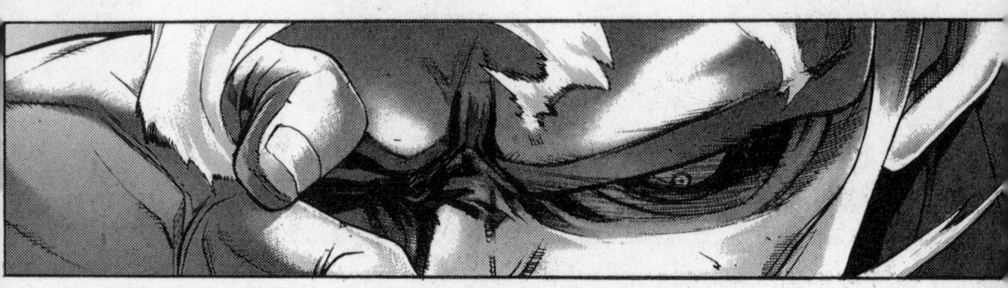
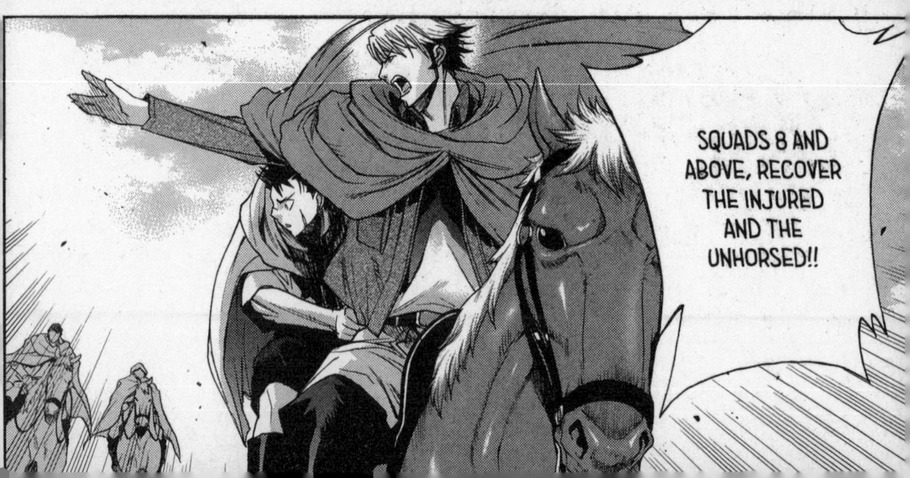
SQUADS 8 AND ABOVE, RECOVER THE INJURED AND THE UNHORSED!!

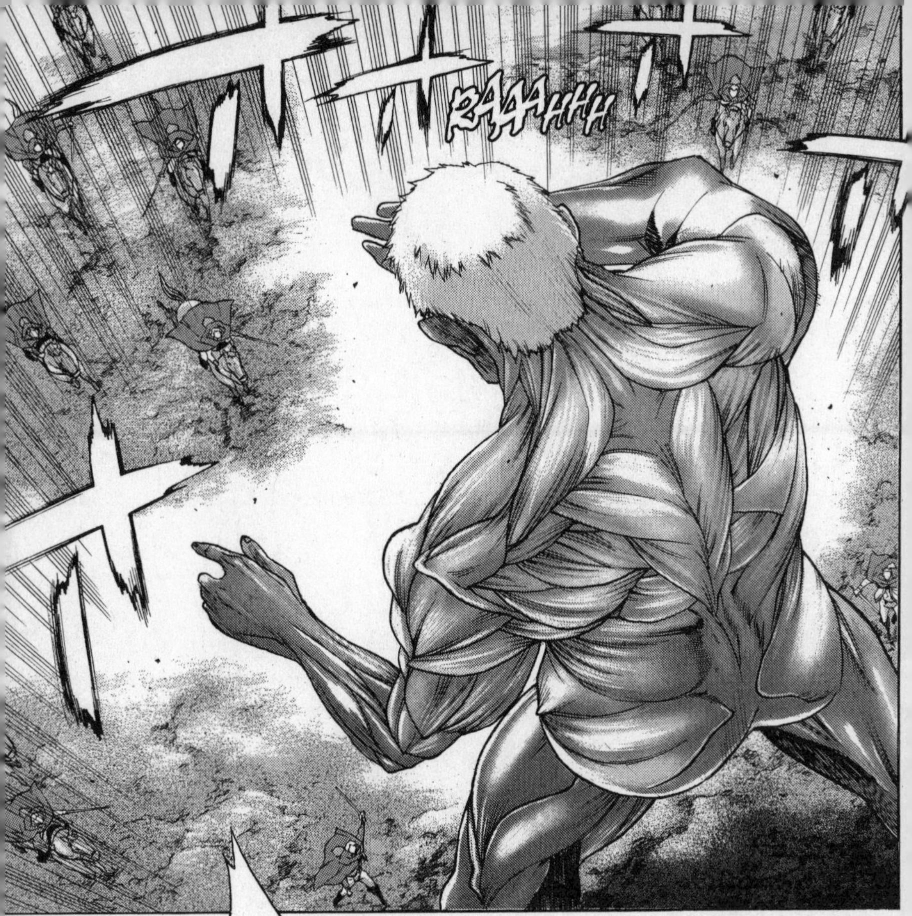
RAAAHHH

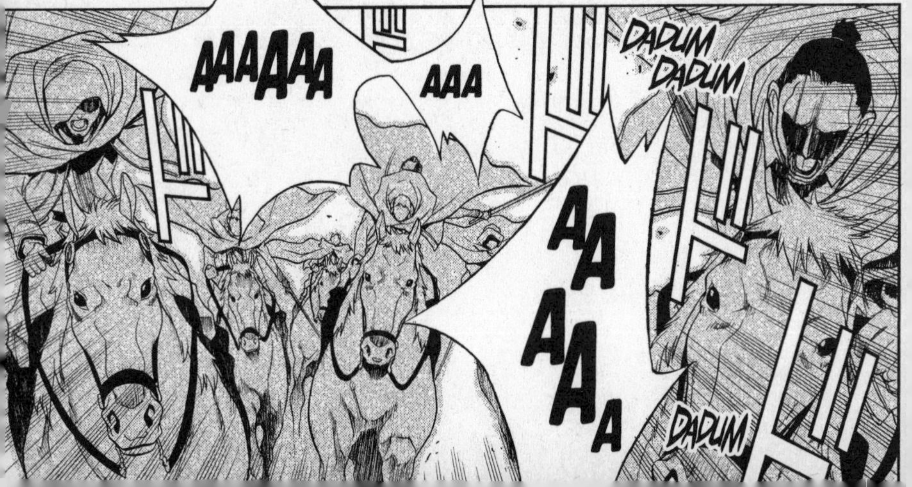
DADUM
DADUM
AAAAAAA
DADUM
AAAAAA
AAA

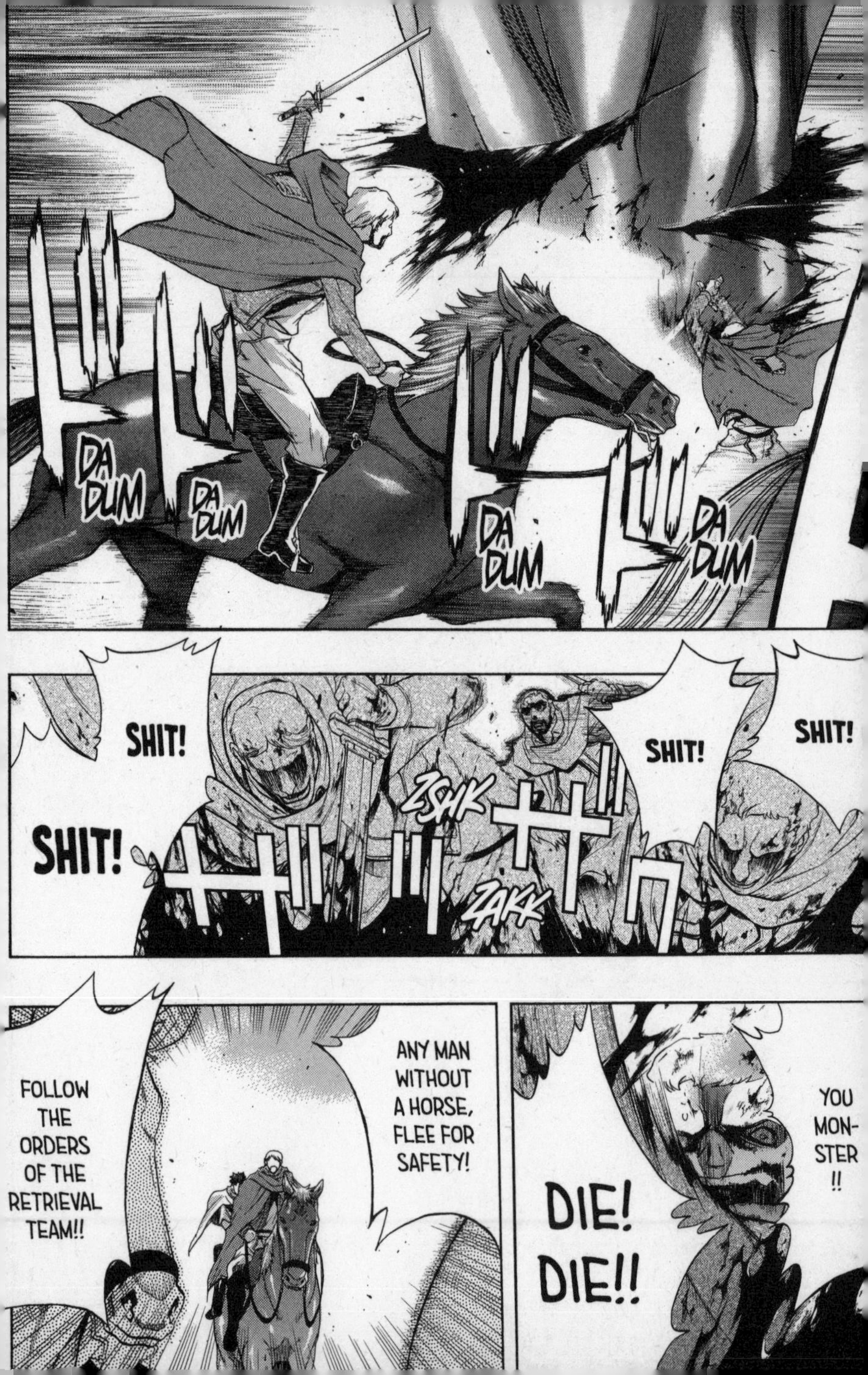
DA DUM
DA DUM
DA DUM
DA DUM
SHIT!
SHIT!
SHIT!
SHIT!
ZSHK
ZAKK
ANY MAN WITHOUT A HORSE, FLEE FOR SAFETY!
FOLLOW THE ORDERS OF THE RETRIEVAL TEAM!!
YOU MON-STER !!
DIE! DIE!!

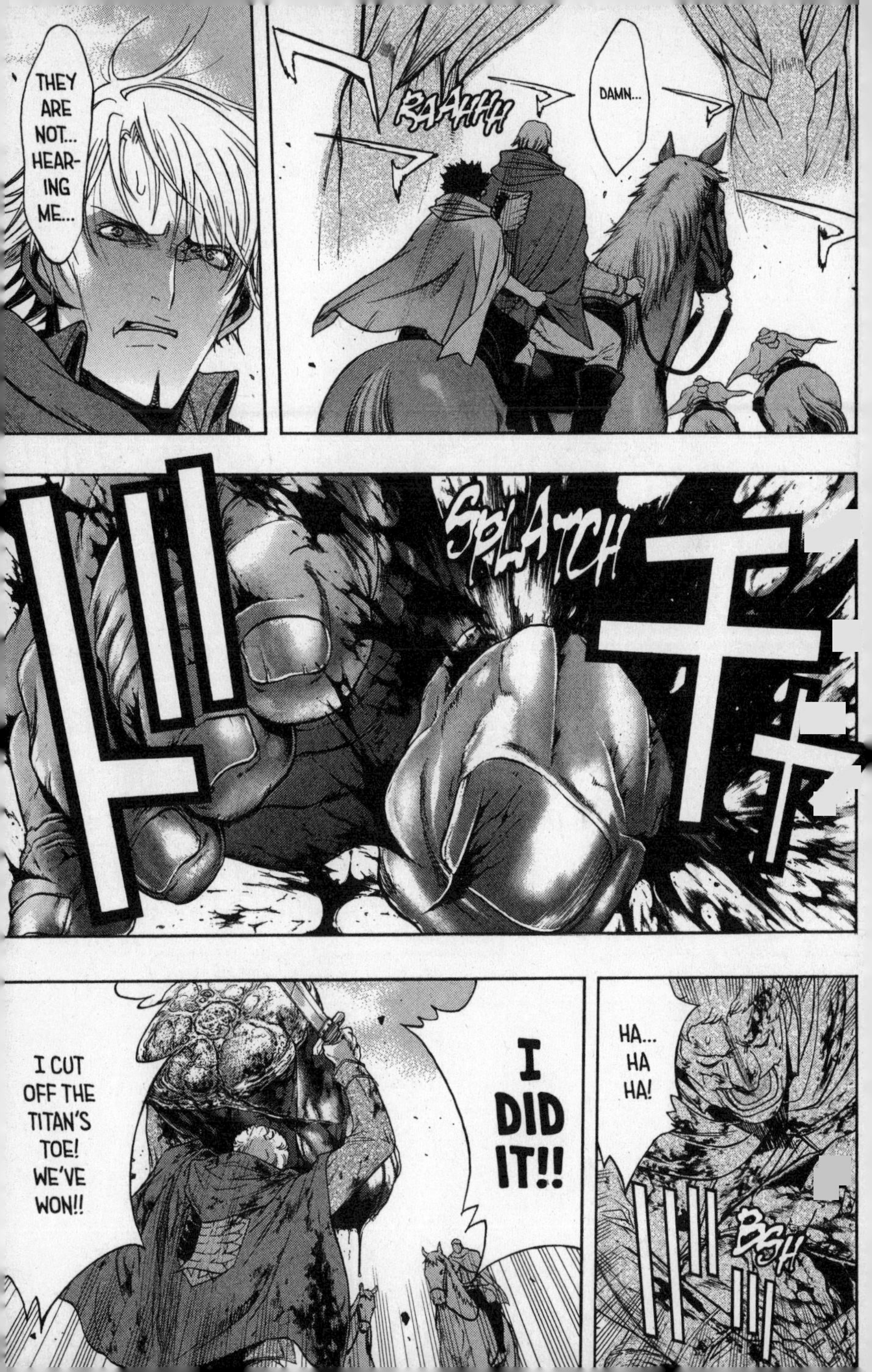
DAMN...
RAAHH!!
THEY ARE NOT... HEAR-ING ME...
SPLATCH
HA... HA HA!
BSH
I DID IT!!
I CUT OFF THE TITAN'S TOE! WE'VE WON!!

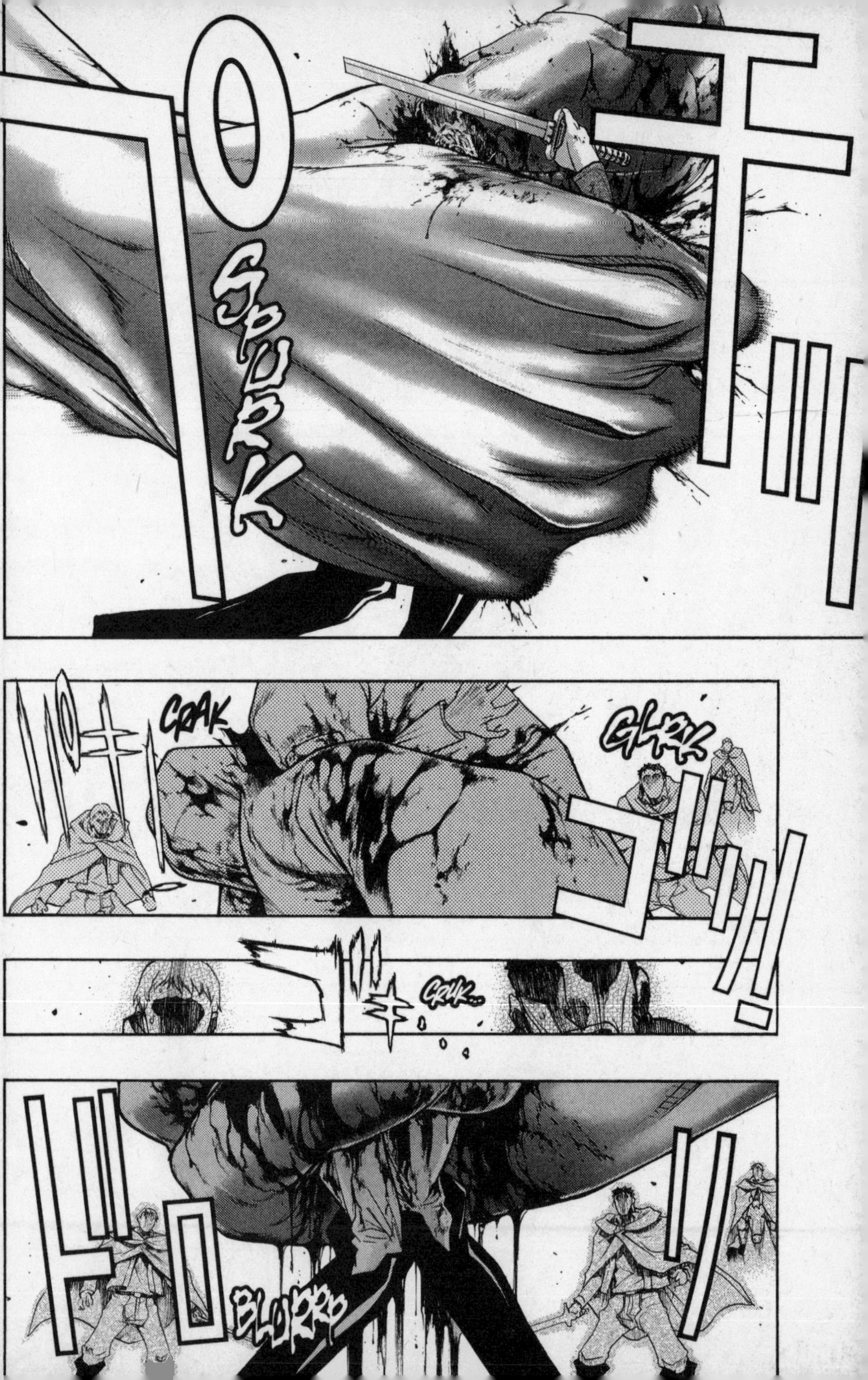
SPURK
GLRK
CRAK
CRUK...
BLORRP

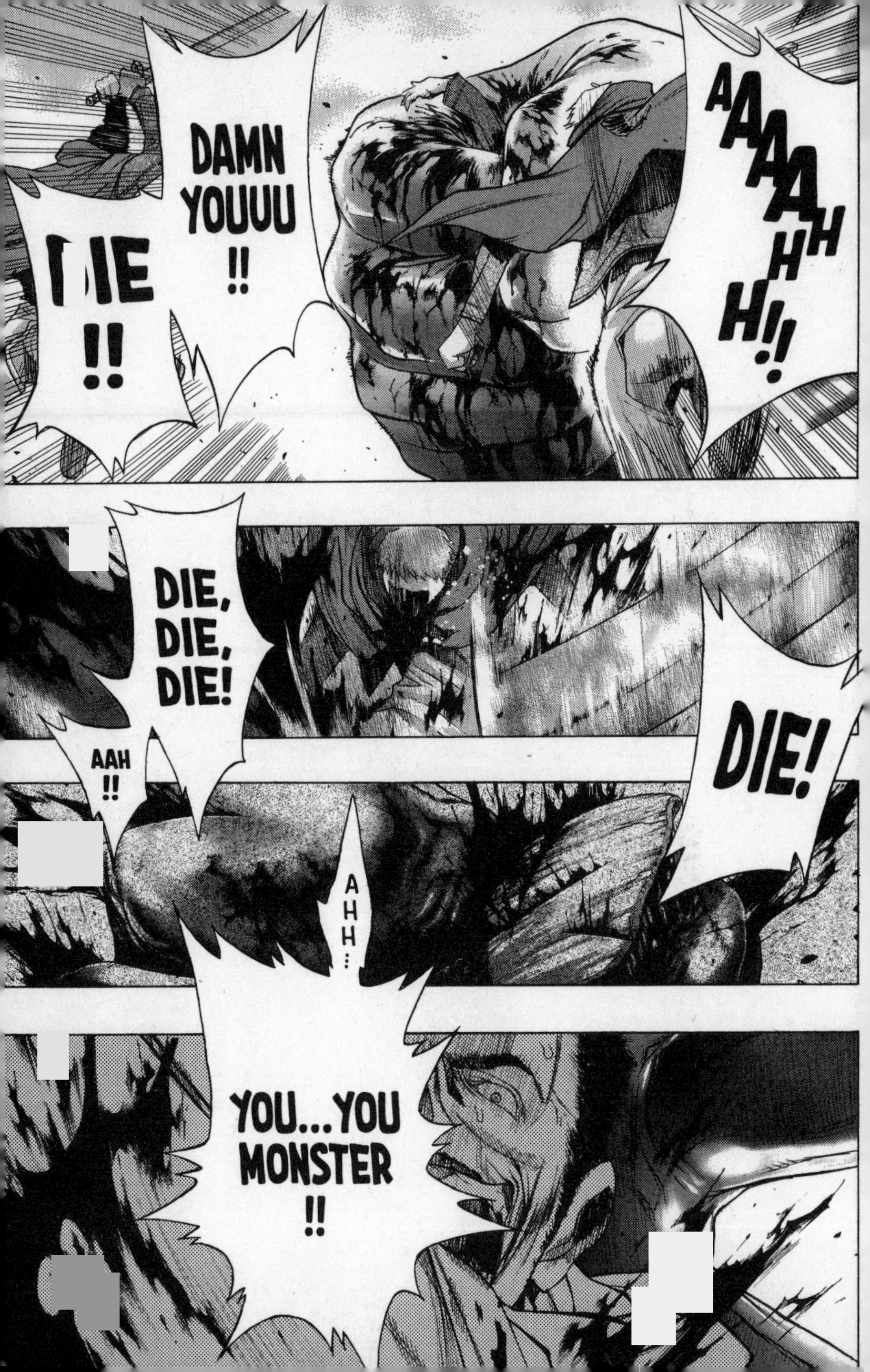
AAAAAHHH!!
DAMN YOUUU!!
DIE!!
DIE!
DIE, DIE, DIE!
AAH!!
AHH...
YOU...YOU MONSTER!!

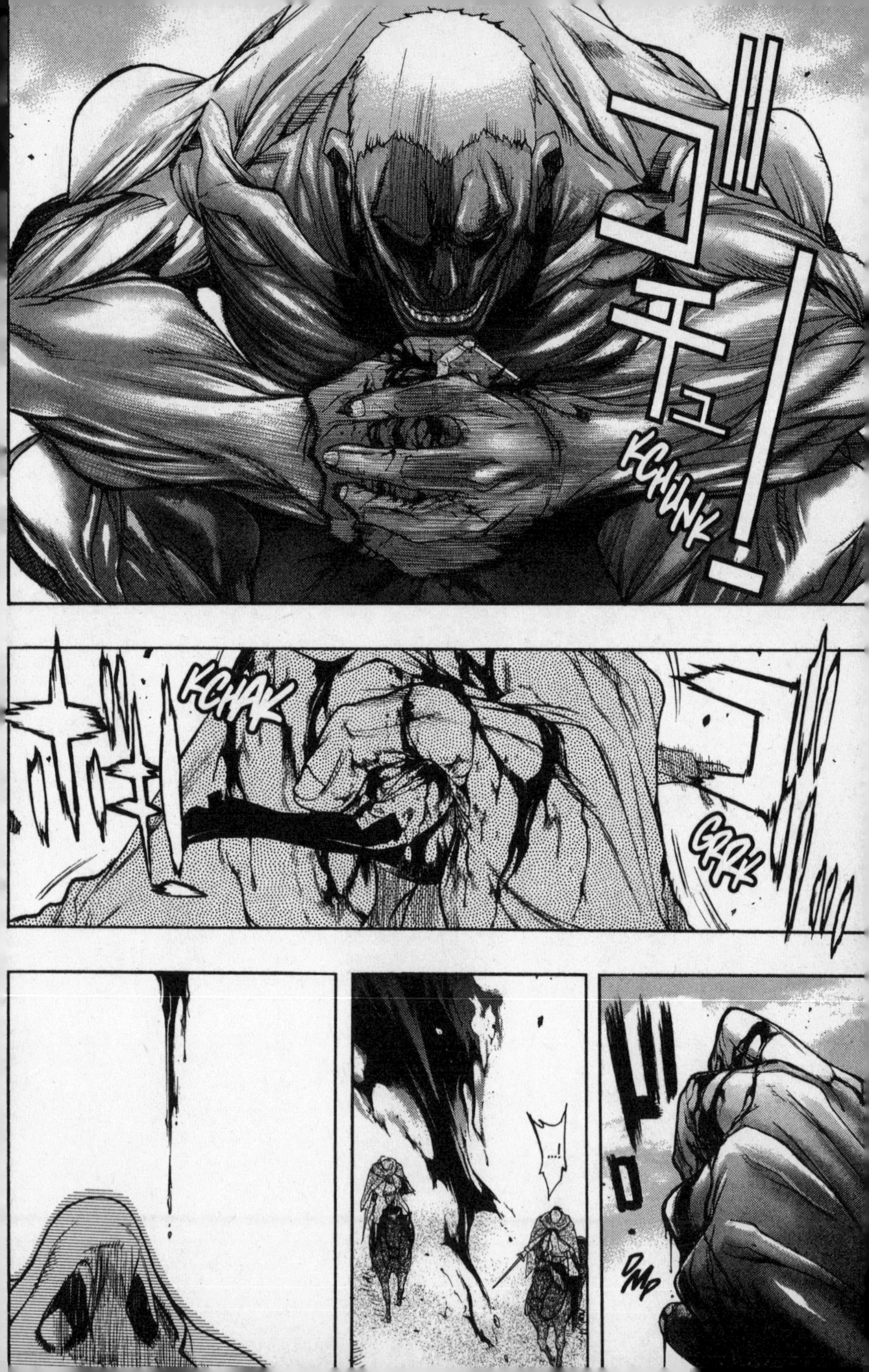
ゴキュ
KCHUNK
GRRK
KCHAK
DMP
...!

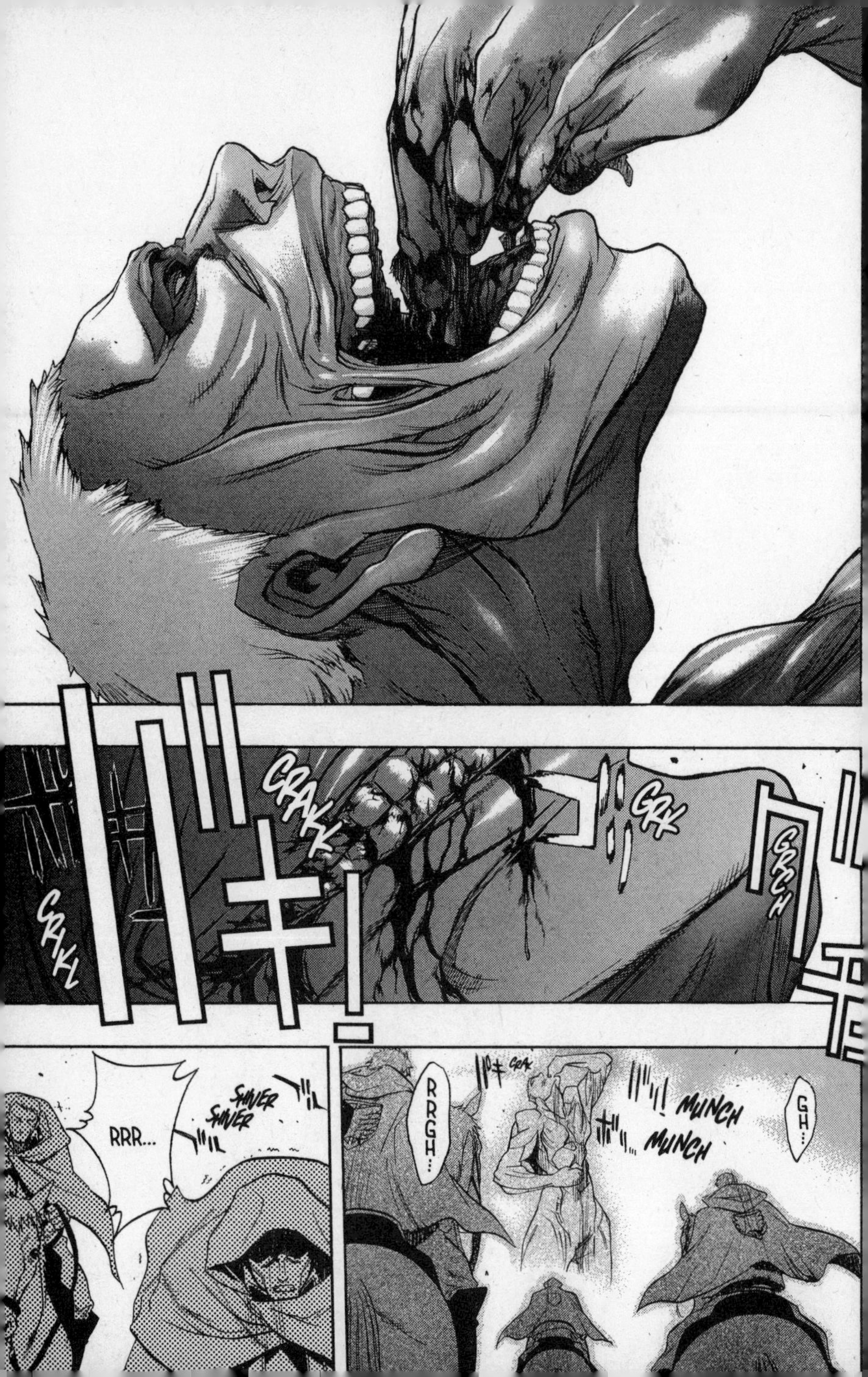
GRCH
GRK
CRAKK
CRAKL
GH...
MUNCH
MUNCH
GRAK
RRGH...
SHIVER SHIVER
RRR...

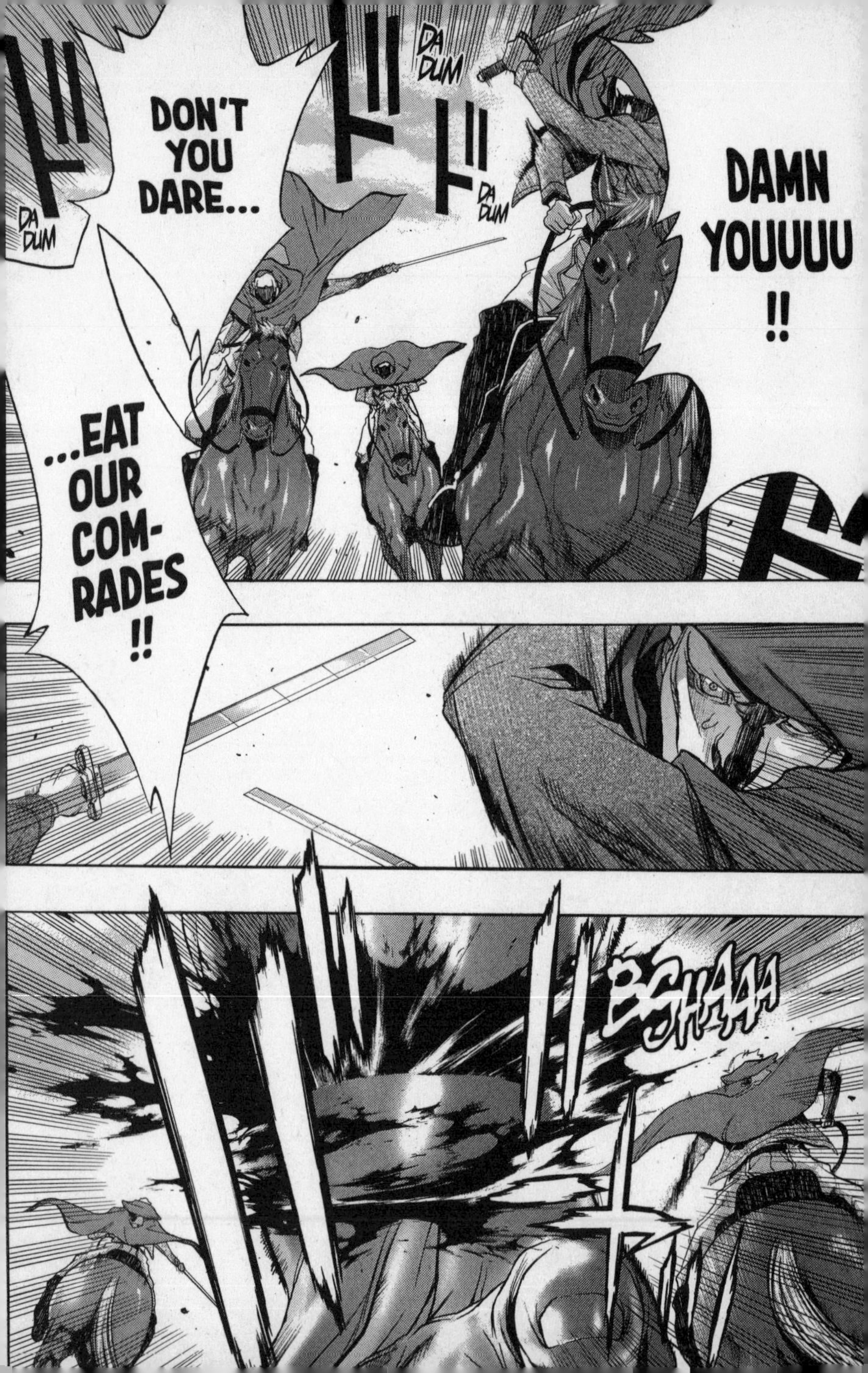
DAMN YOUUUU !!
DA DUM
DA DUM
DON'T YOU DARE...
DA DUM
...EAT OUR COM-RADES !!
BSHAAA

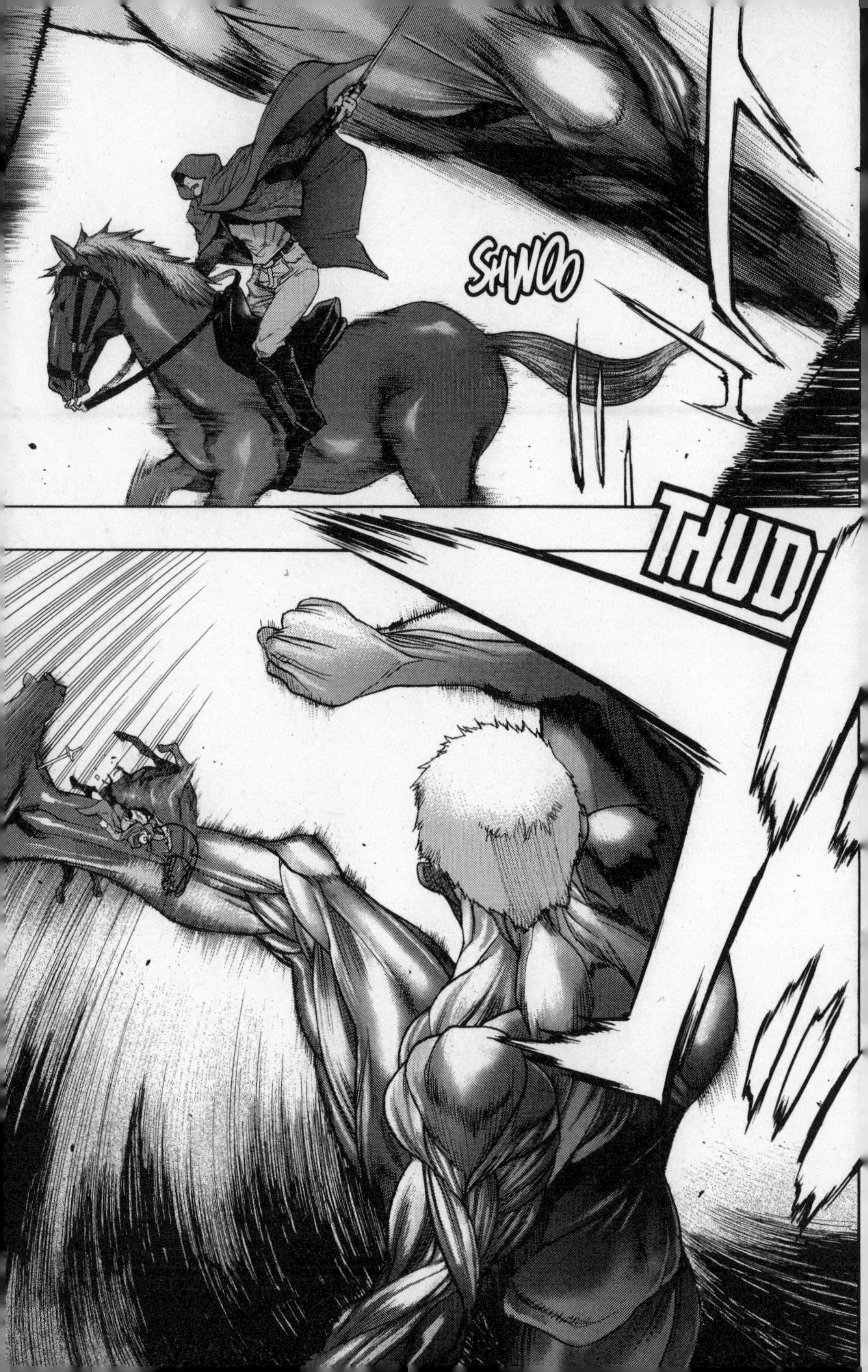
SHWOO
THUD

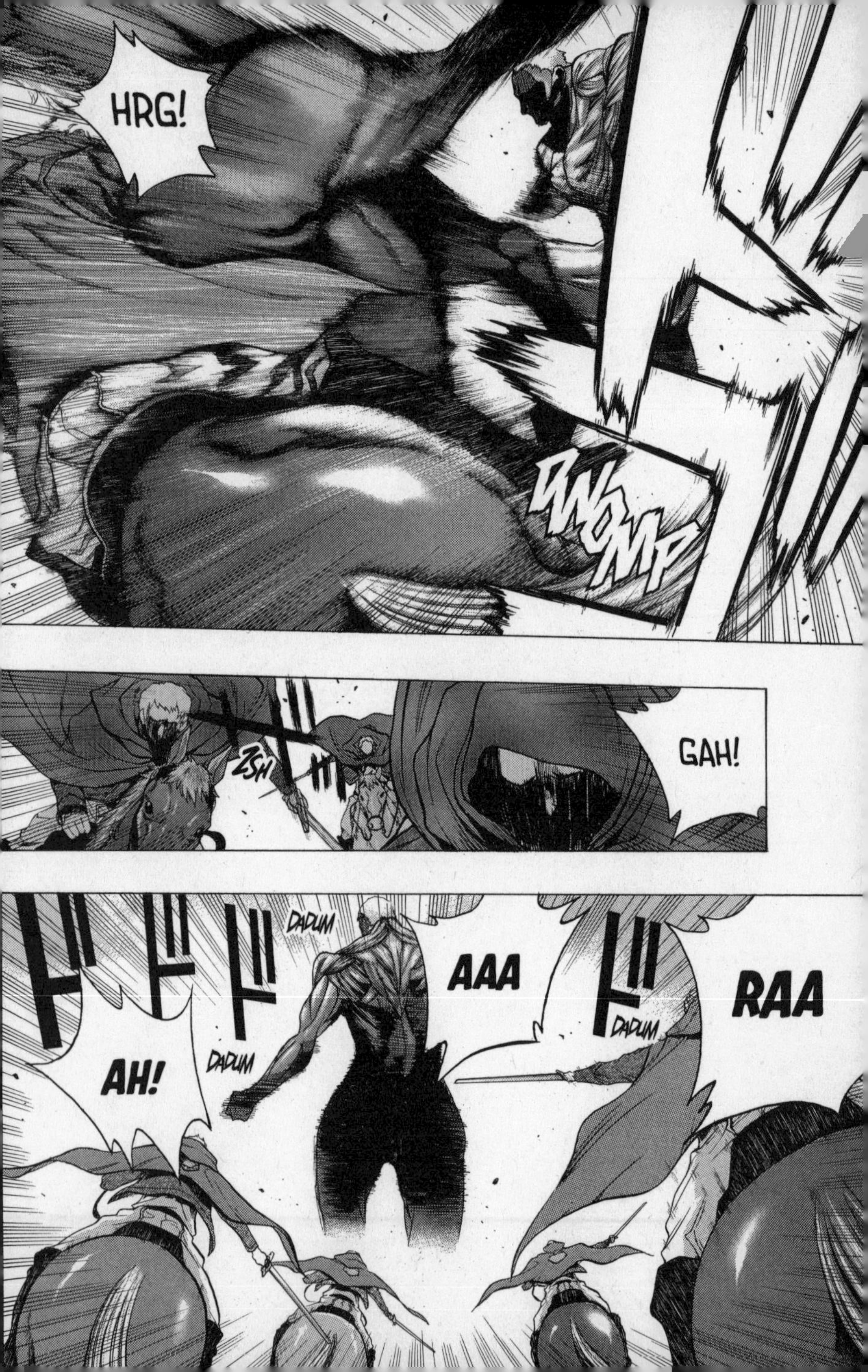

HRG!
DWOMP
GAH!
ZSH
DADUM
RAA
DADUM
AAA
DADUM
AH!

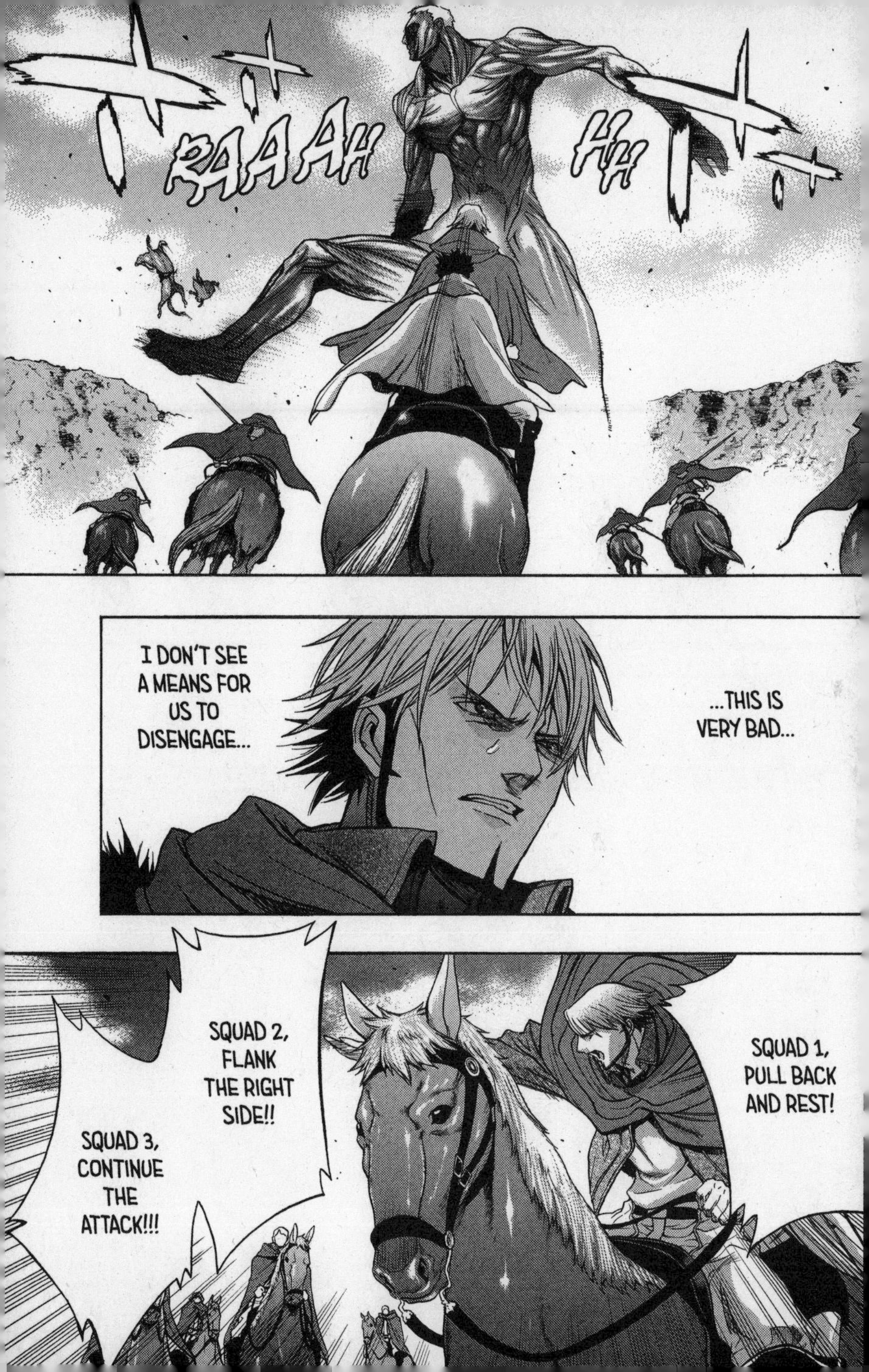
RAAAH HH
...THIS IS VERY BAD...
I DON'T SEE A MEANS FOR US TO DISENGAGE...
SQUAD 1, PULL BACK AND REST!
SQUAD 2, FLANK THE RIGHT SIDE!!
SQUAD 3, CONTINUE THE ATTACK!!!

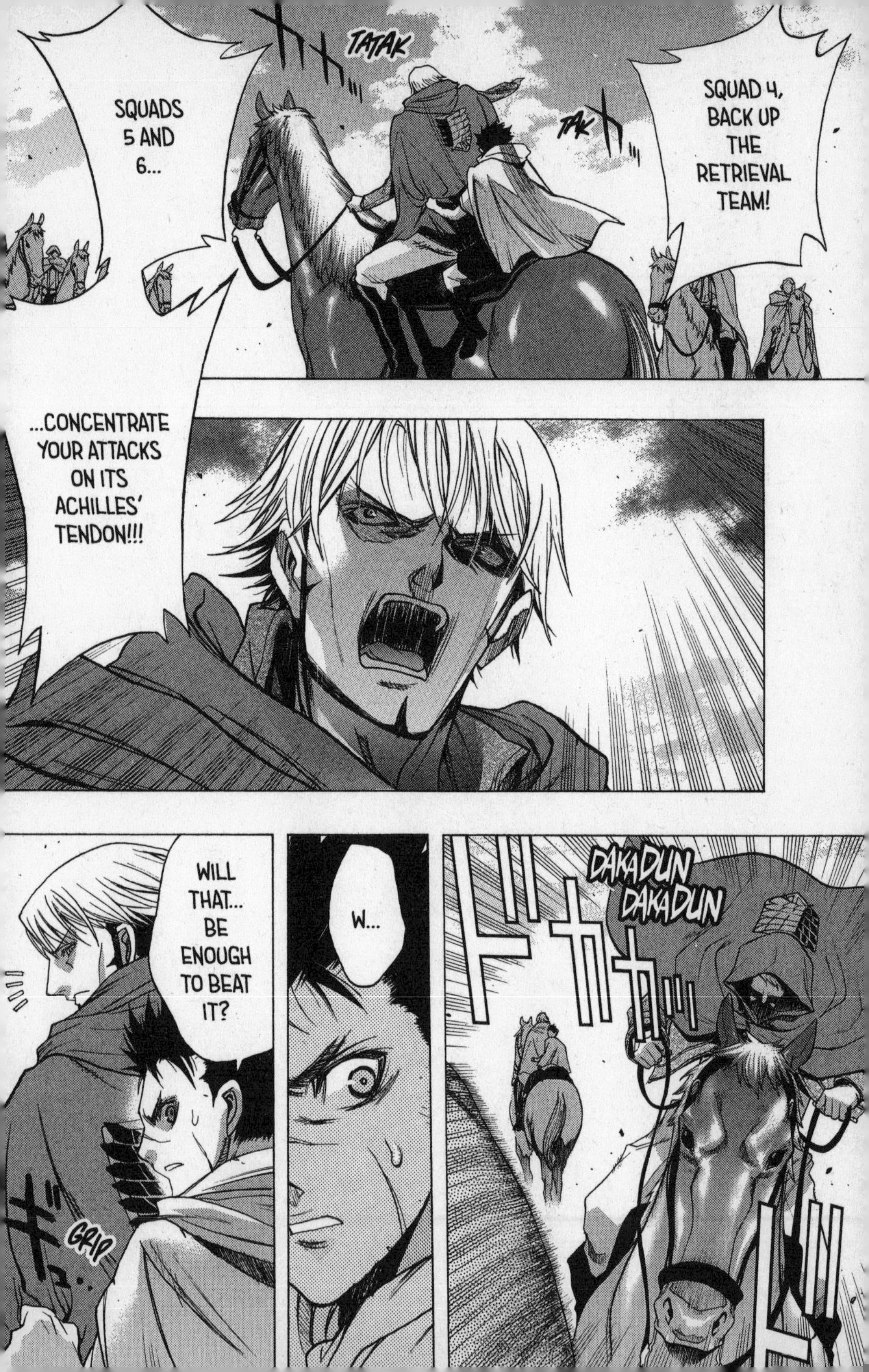
SQUAD 4, BACK UP THE RETRIEVAL TEAM!
TATAK
TAK
SQUADS 5 AND 6...
...CONCENTRATE YOUR ATTACKS ON ITS ACHILLES' TENDON!!!
DAKADUN DAKADUN
W...
WILL THAT... BE ENOUGH TO BEAT IT?
GRIP

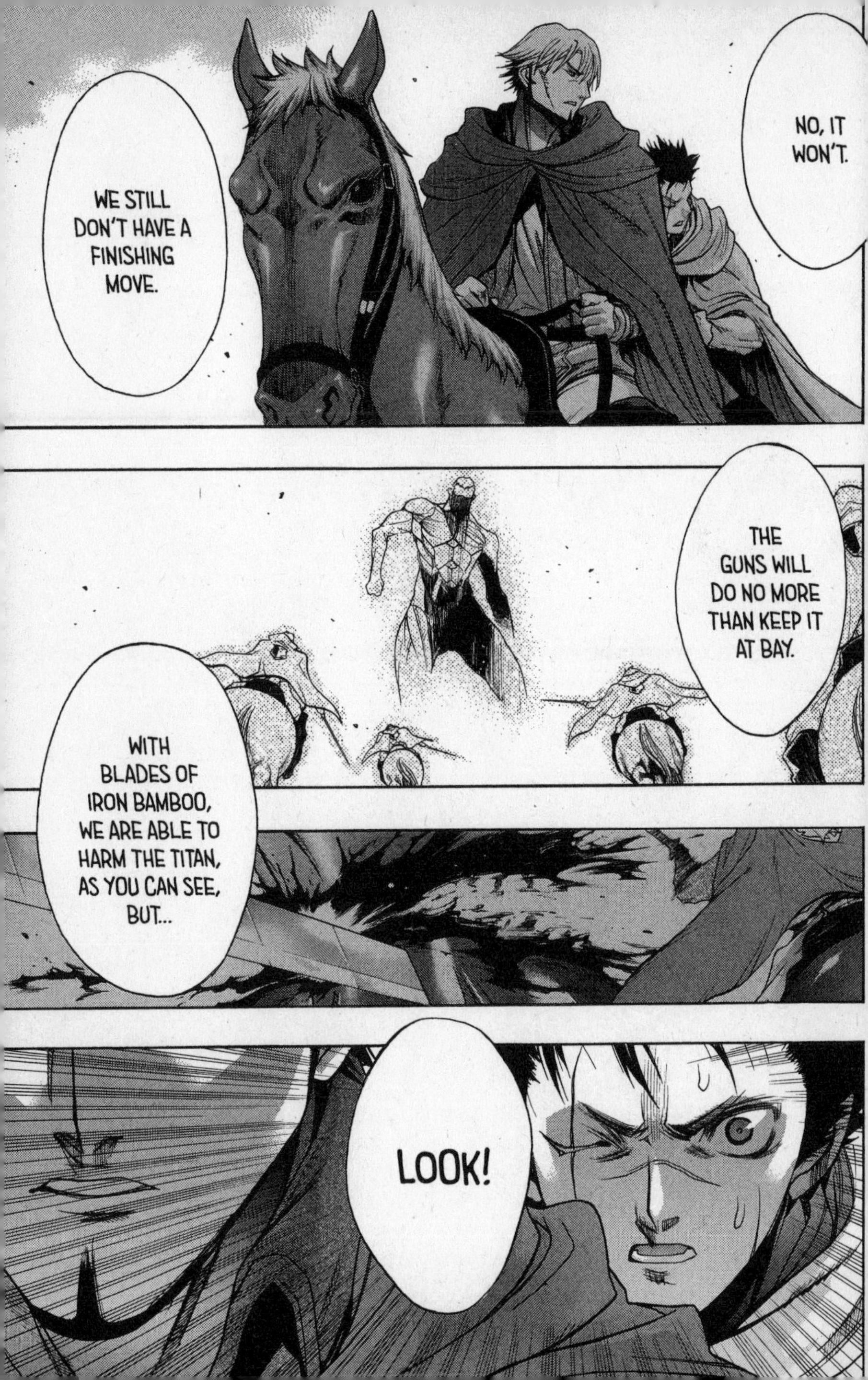
NO, IT WON'T.
WE STILL DON'T HAVE A FINISHING MOVE.
THE GUNS WILL DO NO MORE THAN KEEP IT AT BAY.
WITH BLADES OF IRON BAMBOO, WE ARE ABLE TO HARM THE TITAN, AS YOU CAN SEE, BUT...
LOOK!

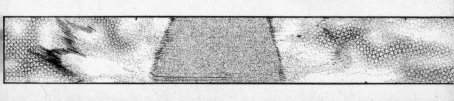

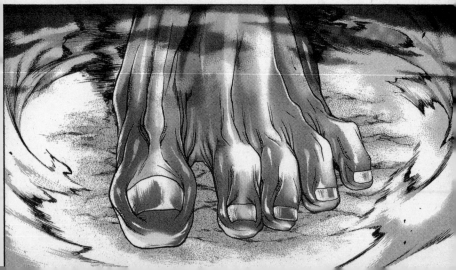

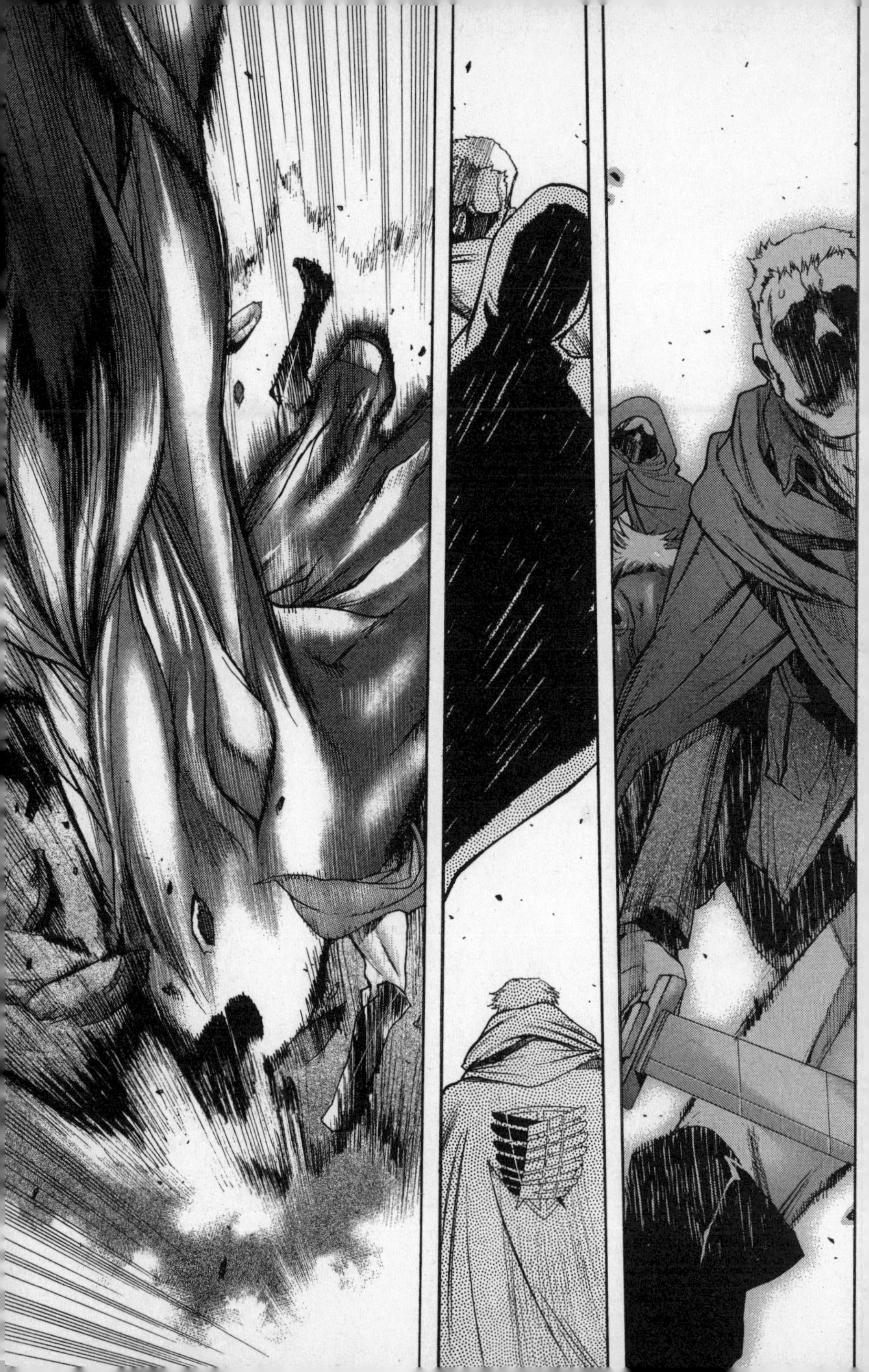

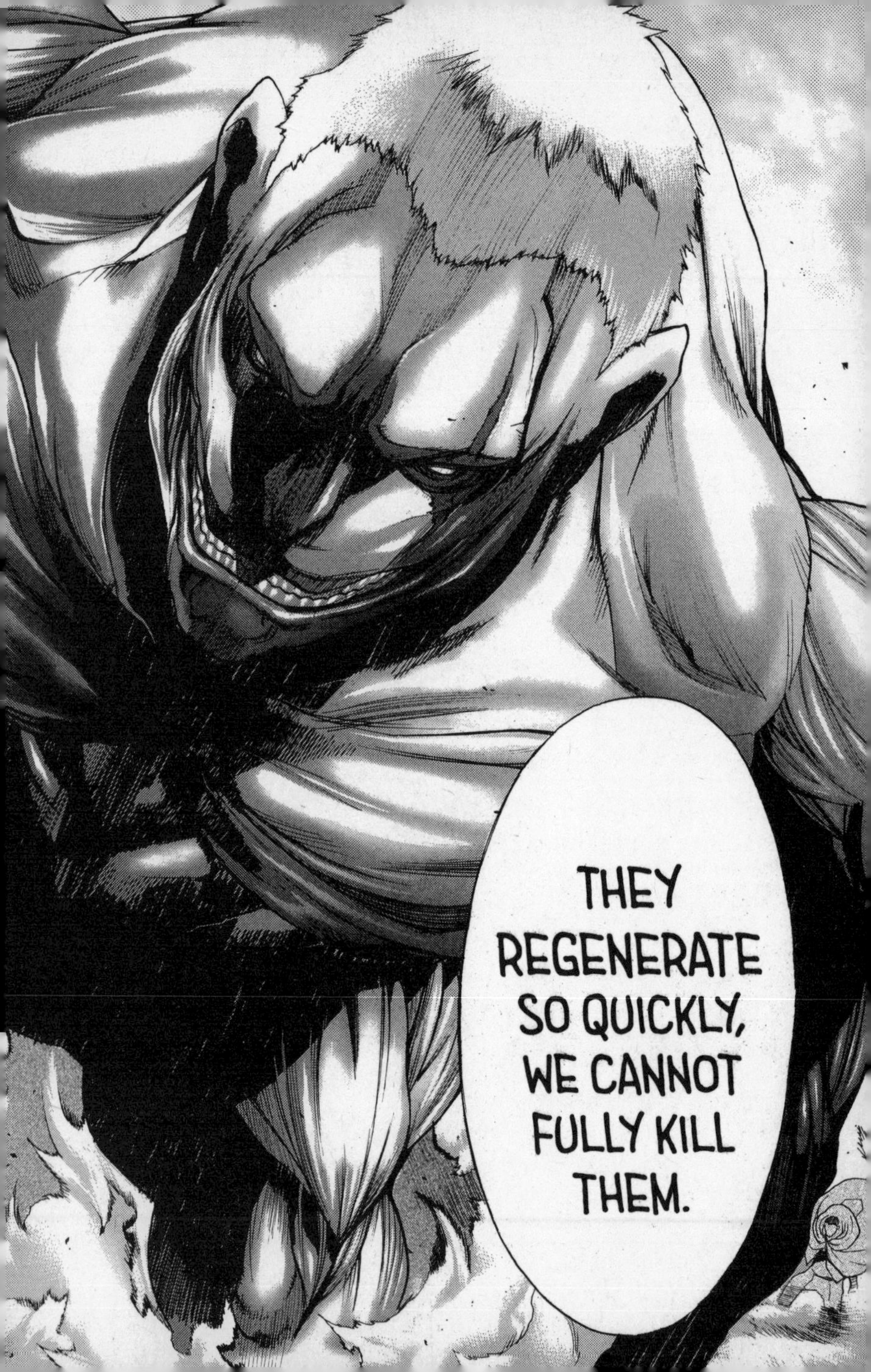
THEY REGENERATE SO QUICKLY, WE CANNOT FULLY KILL THEM.

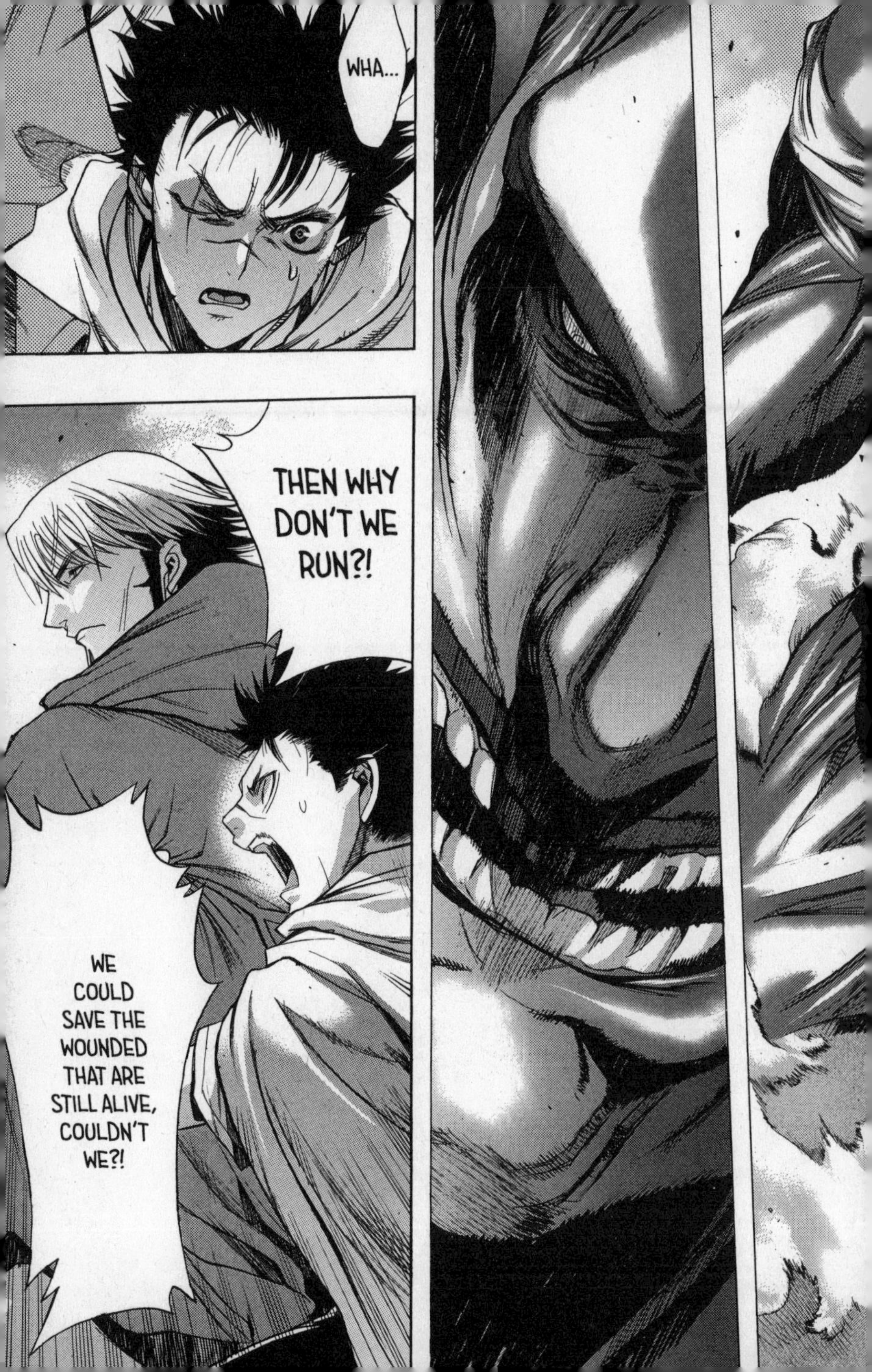
WHA...
THEN WHY DON'T WE RUN?!
WE COULD SAVE THE WOUNDED THAT ARE STILL ALIVE, COULDN'T WE?!

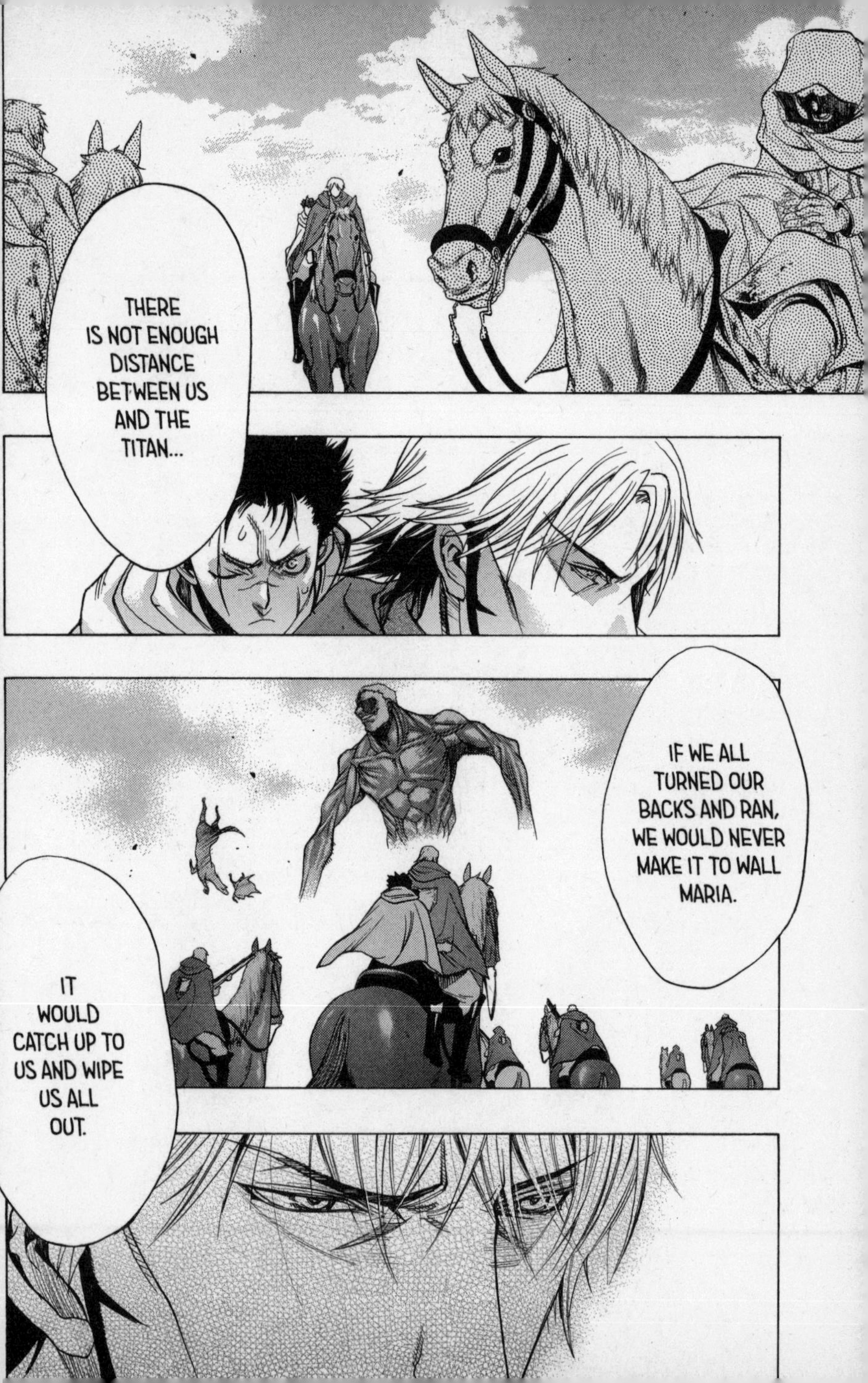
THERE IS NOT ENOUGH DISTANCE BETWEEN US AND THE TITAN...
IF WE ALL TURNED OUR BACKS AND RAN, WE WOULD NEVER MAKE IT TO WALL MARIA.
IT WOULD CATCH UP TO US AND WIPE US ALL OUT.

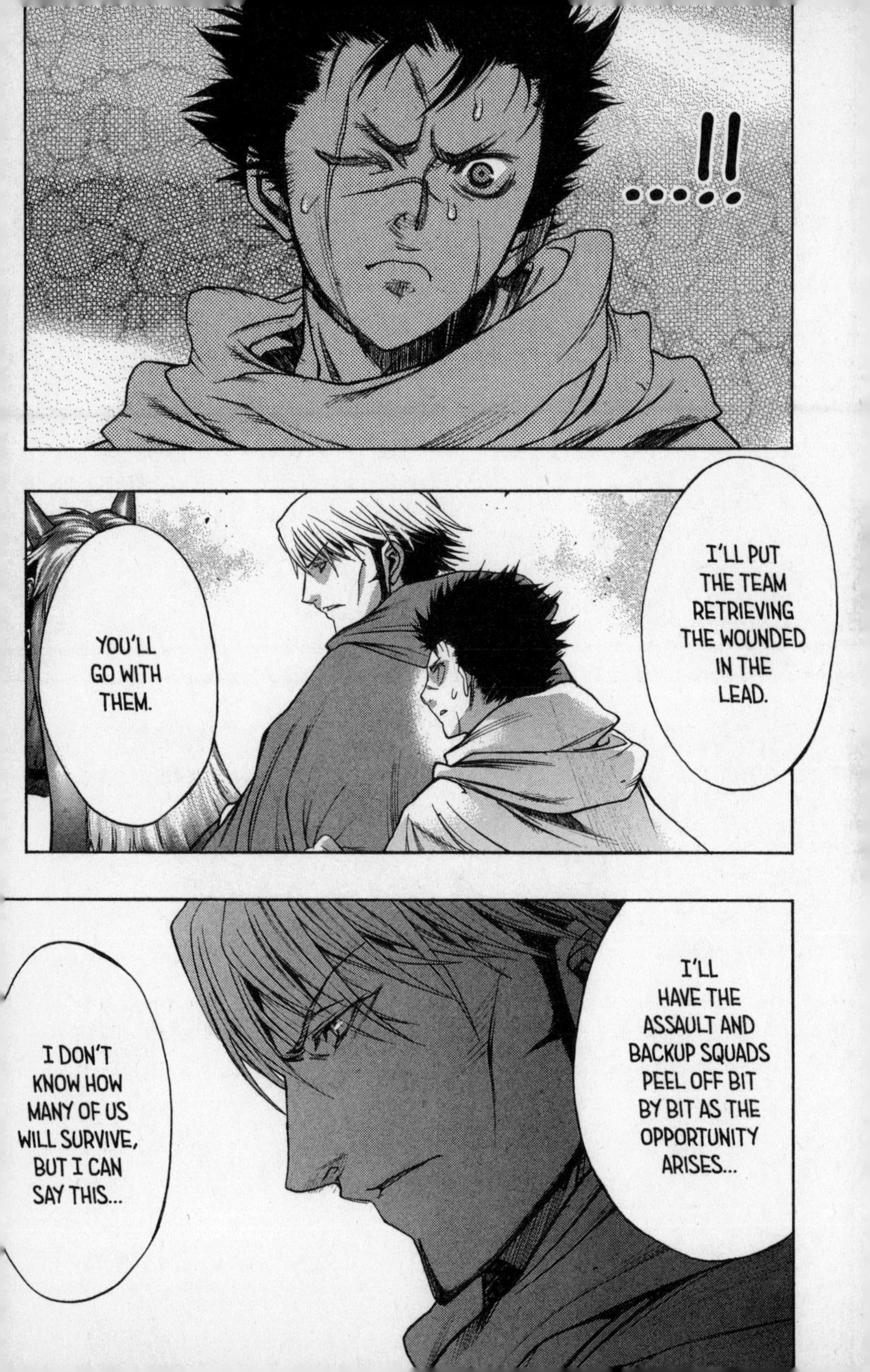
...!!
I'LL PUT THE TEAM RETRIEVING THE WOUNDED IN THE LEAD.
YOU'LL GO WITH THEM.
I'LL HAVE THE ASSAULT AND BACKUP SQUADS PEEL OFF BIT BY BIT AS THE OPPORTUNITY ARISES...
I DON'T KNOW HOW MANY OF US WILL SURVIVE, BUT I CAN SAY THIS...

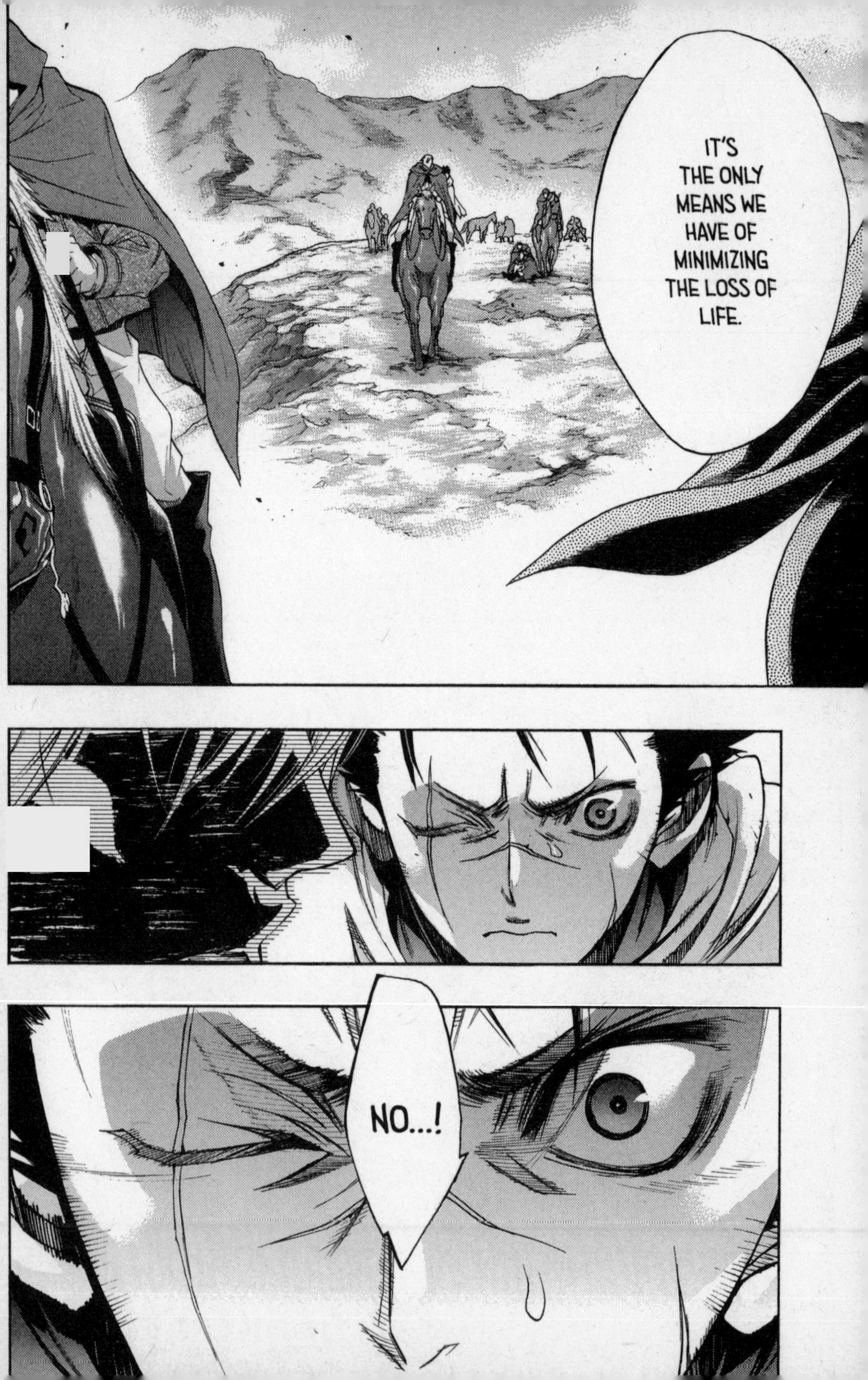
IT'S THE ONLY MEANS WE HAVE OF MINIMIZING THE LOSS OF LIFE.
NO...!

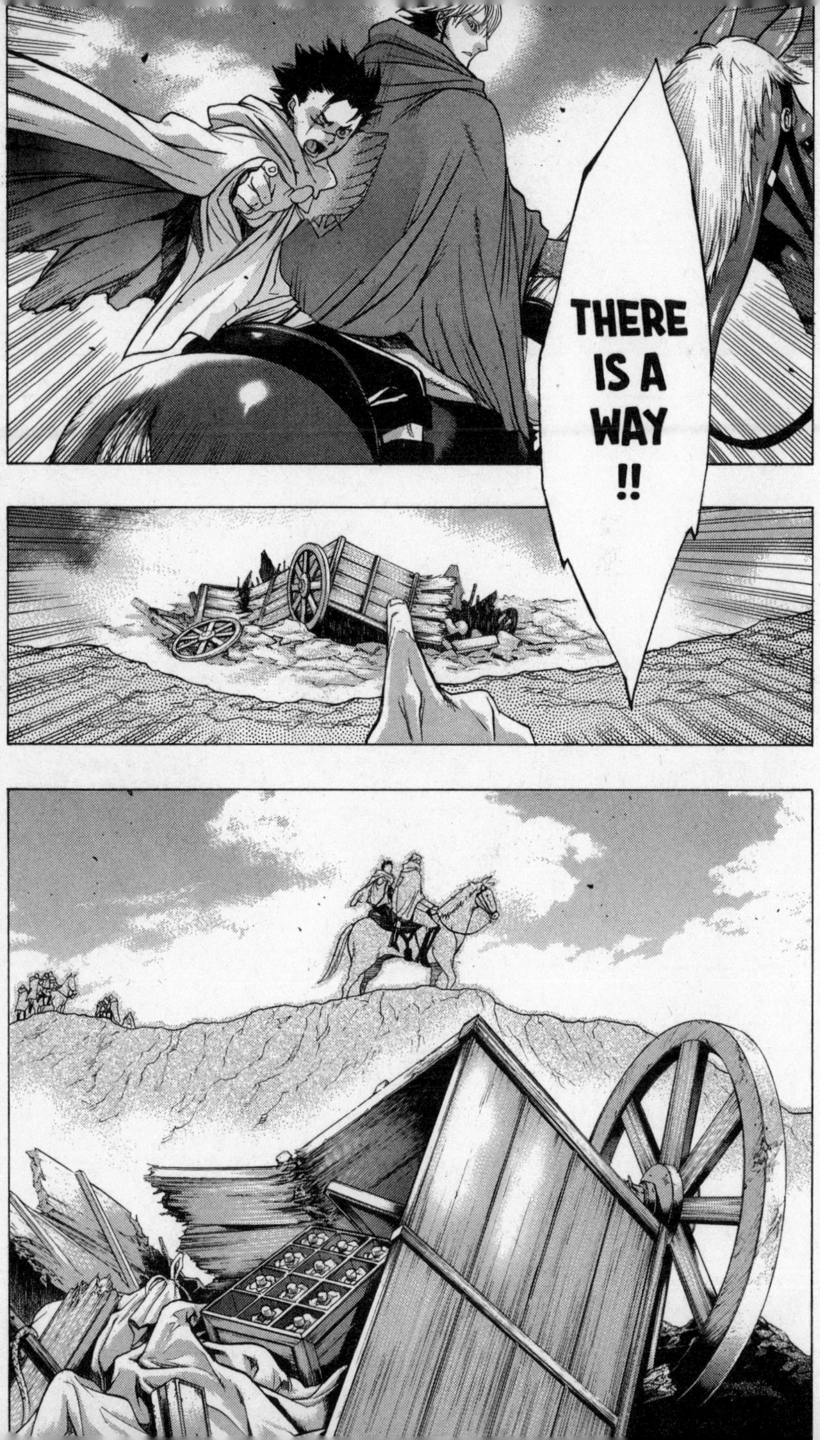
THERE IS A WAY !!

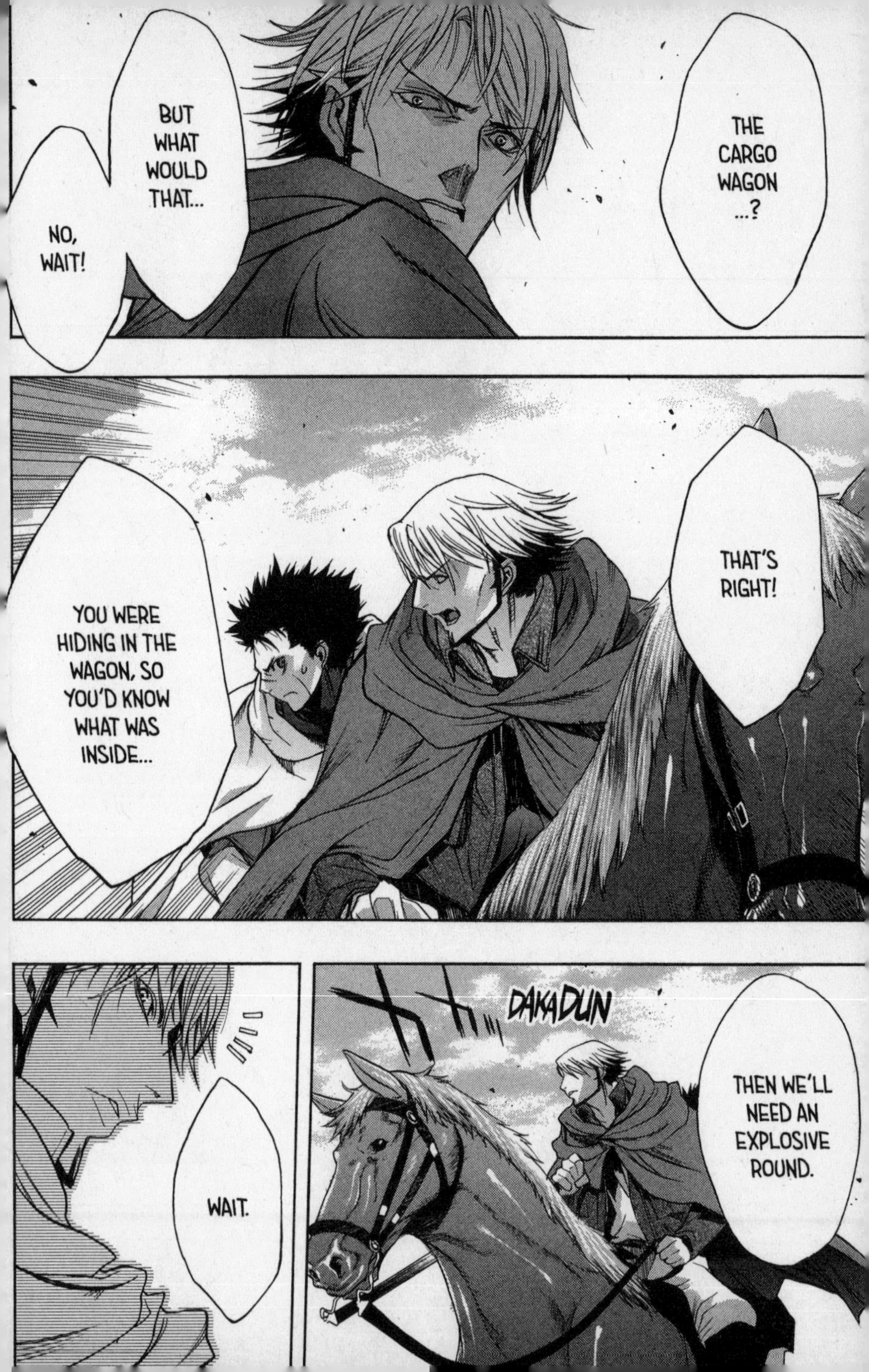
THE CARGO WAGON ...?
BUT WHAT WOULD THAT...
NO, WAIT!
THAT'S RIGHT!
YOU WERE HIDING IN THE WAGON, SO YOU'D KNOW WHAT WAS INSIDE...
THEN WE'LL NEED AN EXPLOSIVE ROUND.
DAKADUN
WAIT.

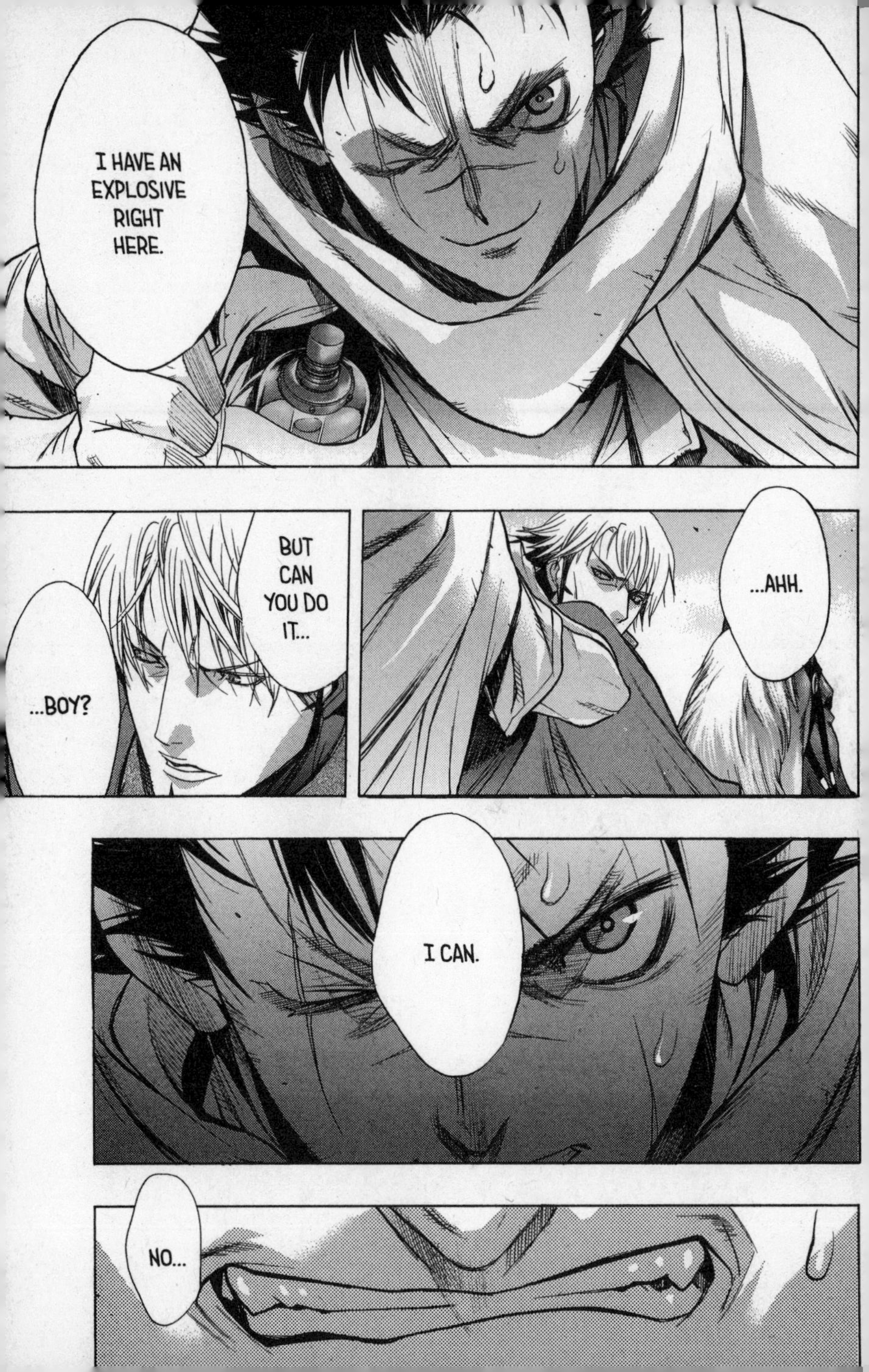
I HAVE AN EXPLOSIVE RIGHT HERE.
...AHH.
BUT CAN YOU DO IT...
...BOY?
I CAN.
NO...

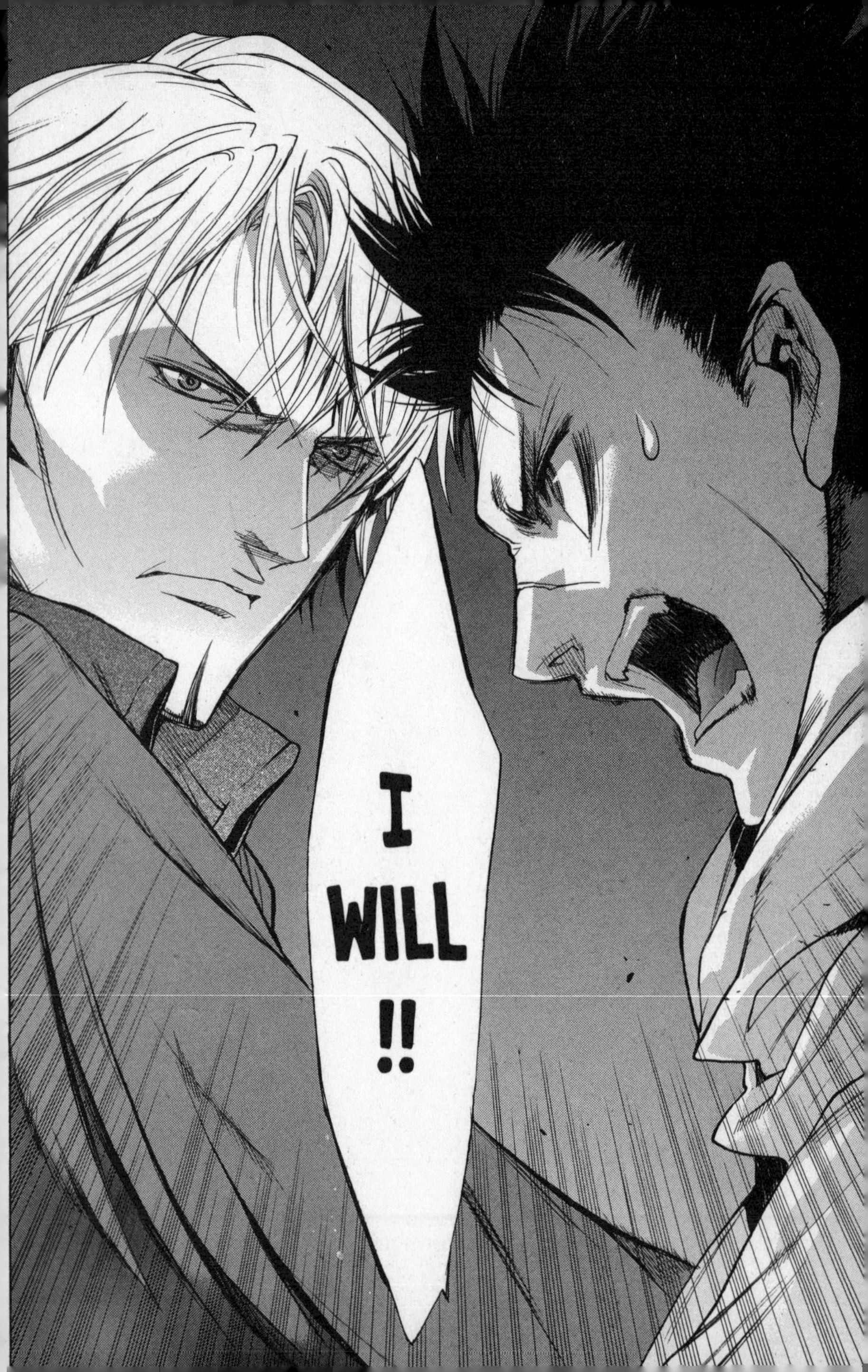
I WILL!!

Chapter 8: Predatory Cycle END

ATTACK on TITAN
BEFORE THE FALL

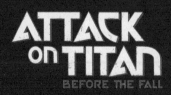

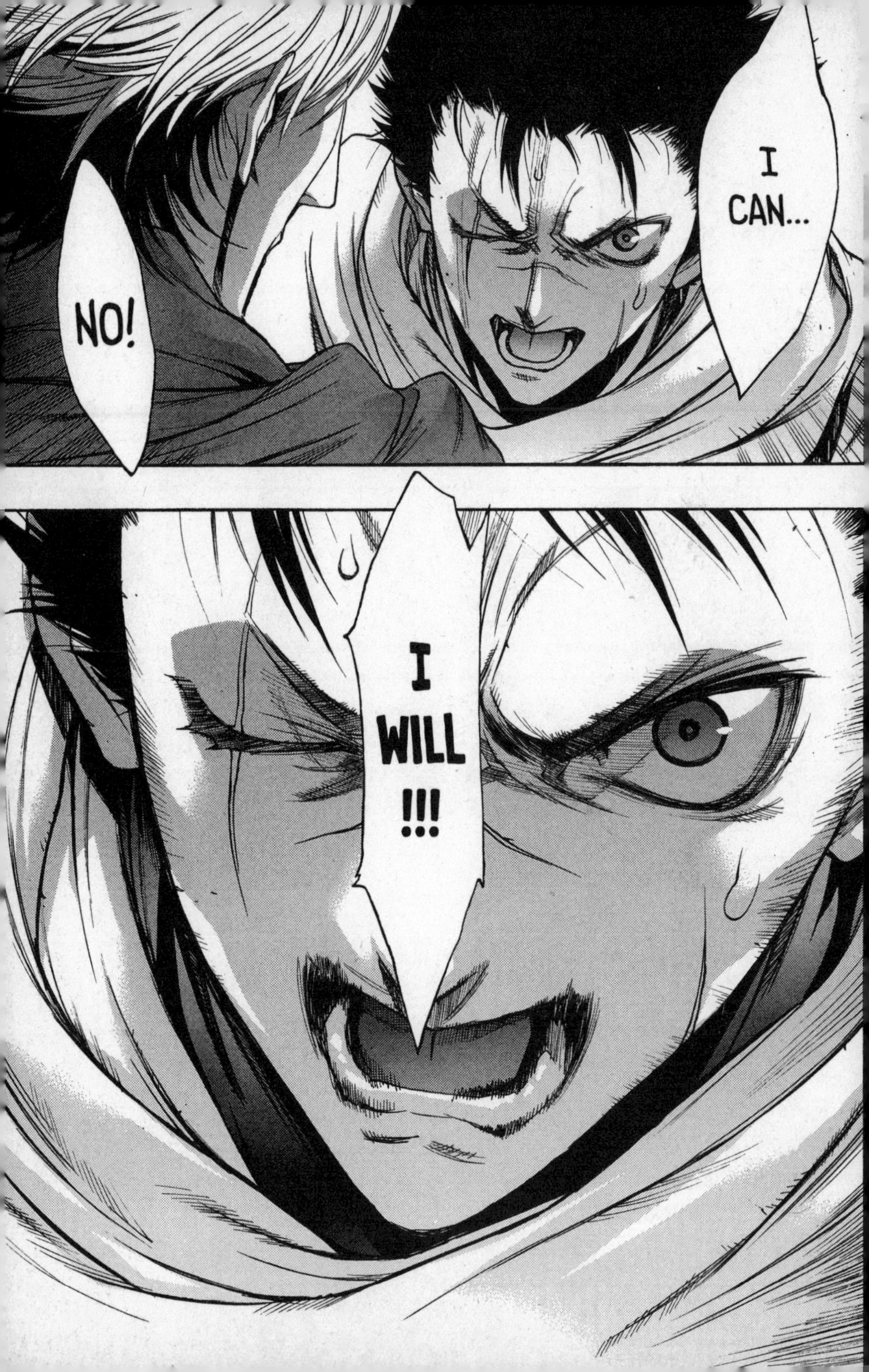
I CAN...
NO!
I WILL!!!

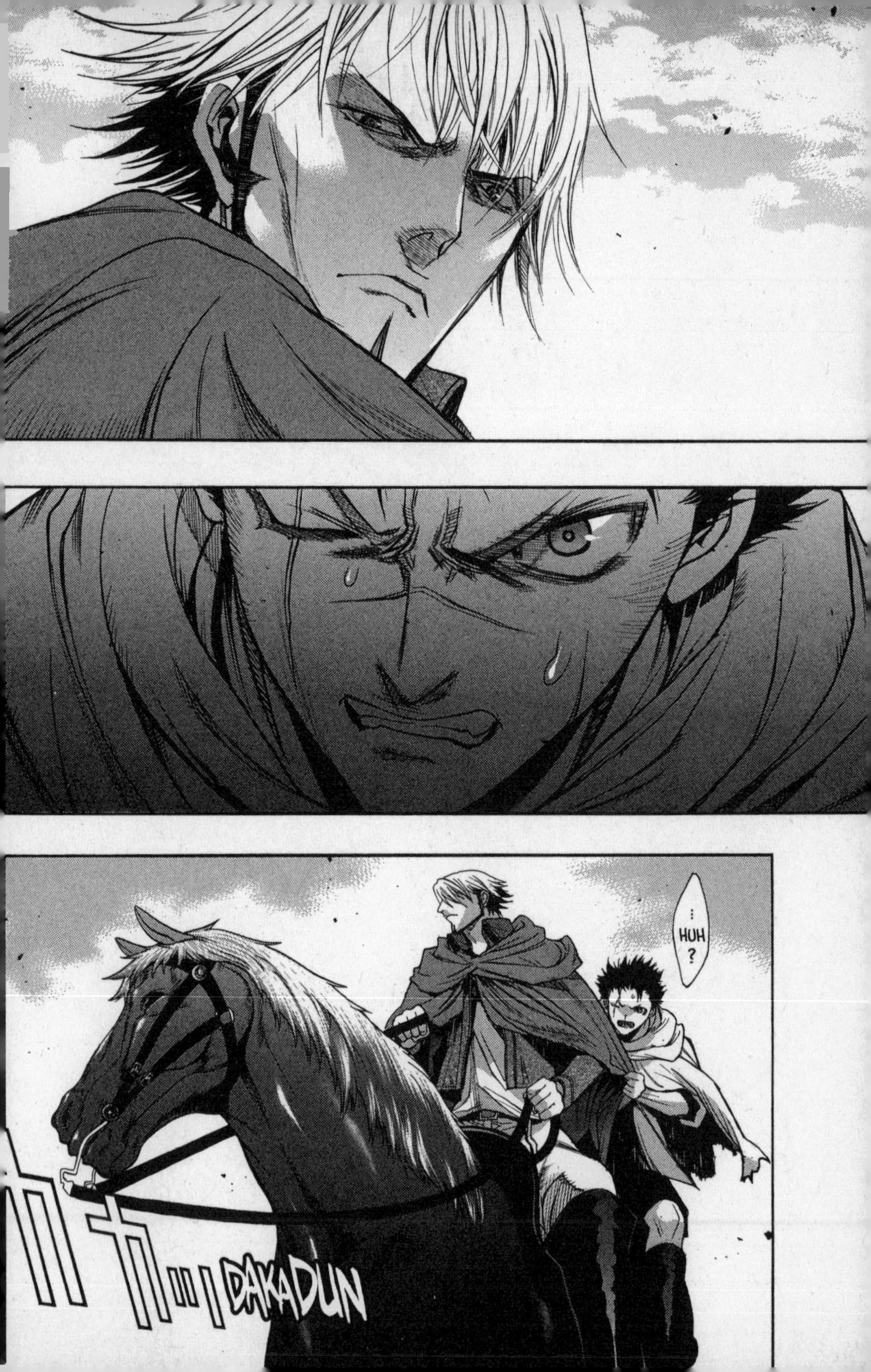
...HUH?
DAKADUN

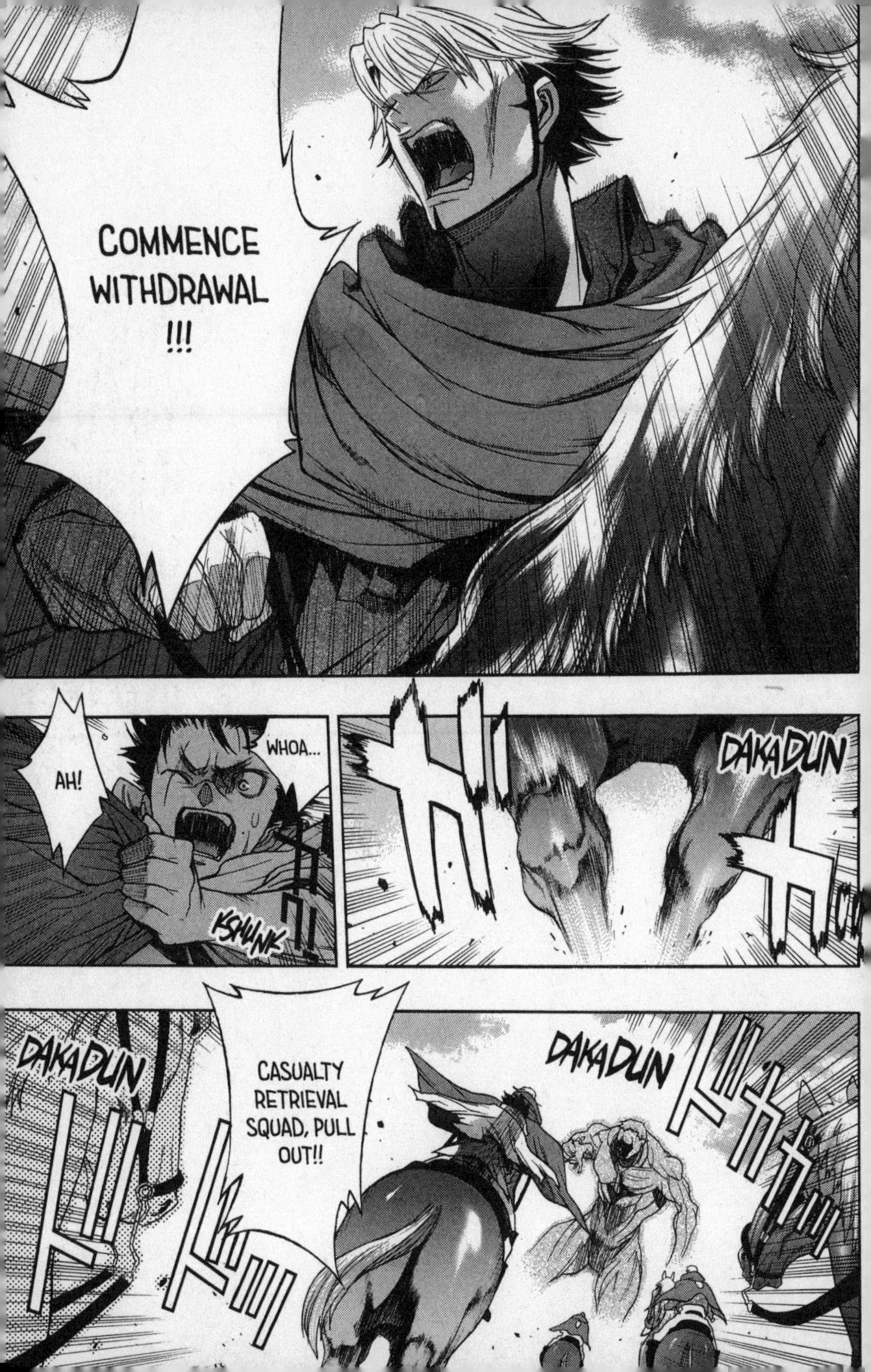
COMMENCE WITHDRAWAL !!!
AH!
WHOA...
KSHUNK
DAKADUN
CASUALTY RETRIEVAL SQUAD, PULL OUT!!
DAKADUN
DAKADUN

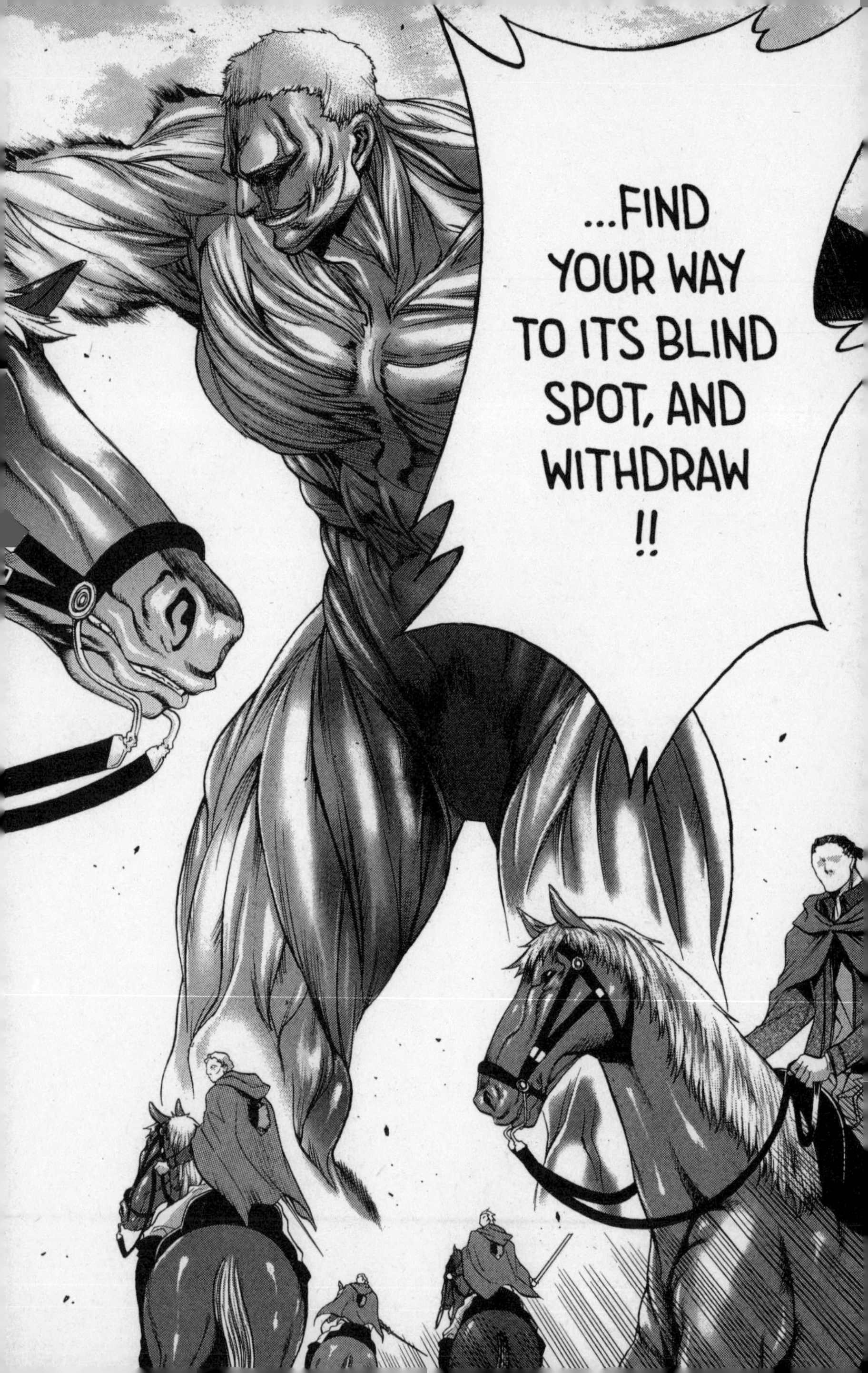
...FIND YOUR WAY TO ITS BLIND SPOT, AND WITHDRAW !!

Chapter 9: The Crimson Tower

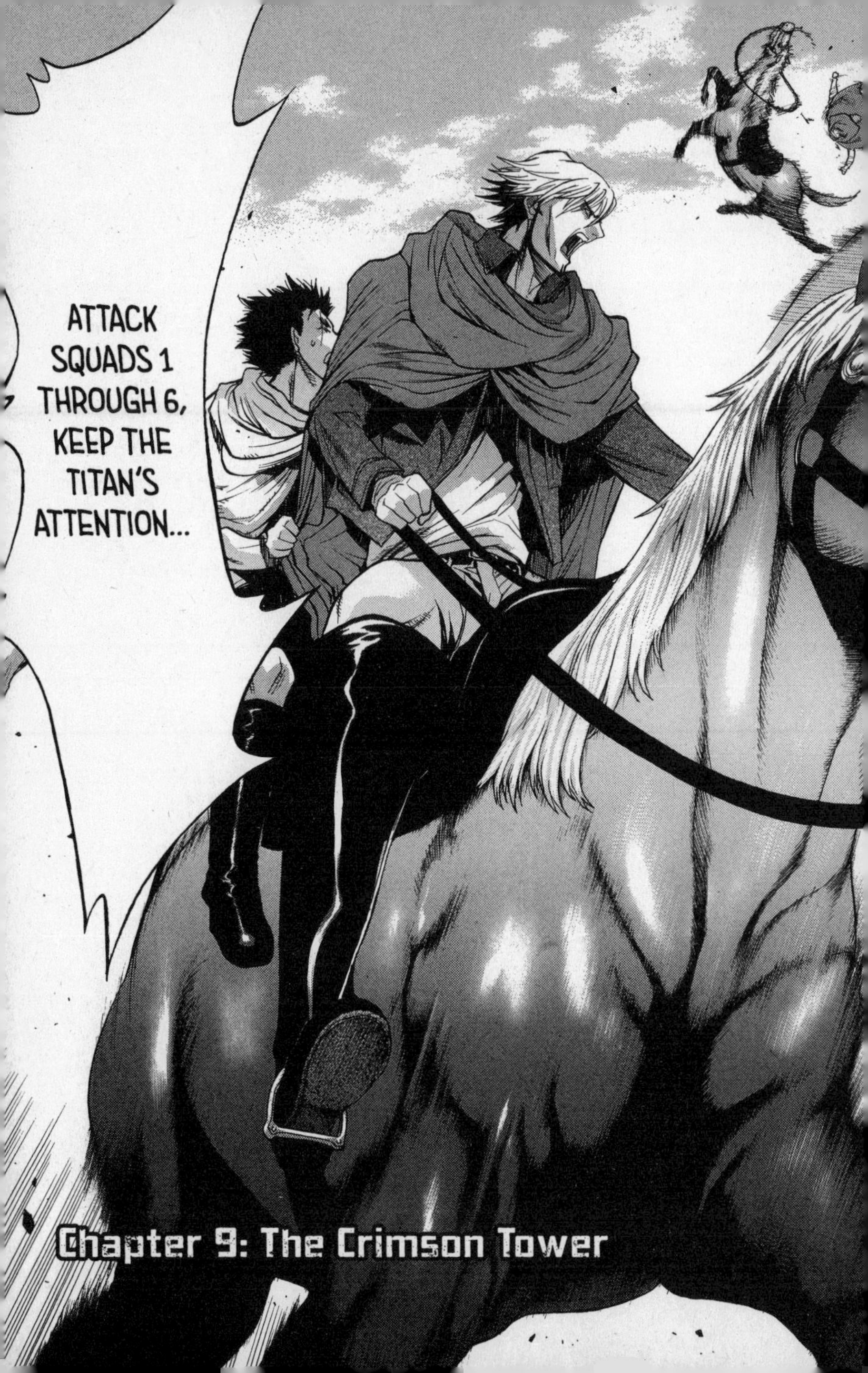
ATTACK SQUADS 1 THROUGH 6, KEEP THE TITAN'S ATTENTION...

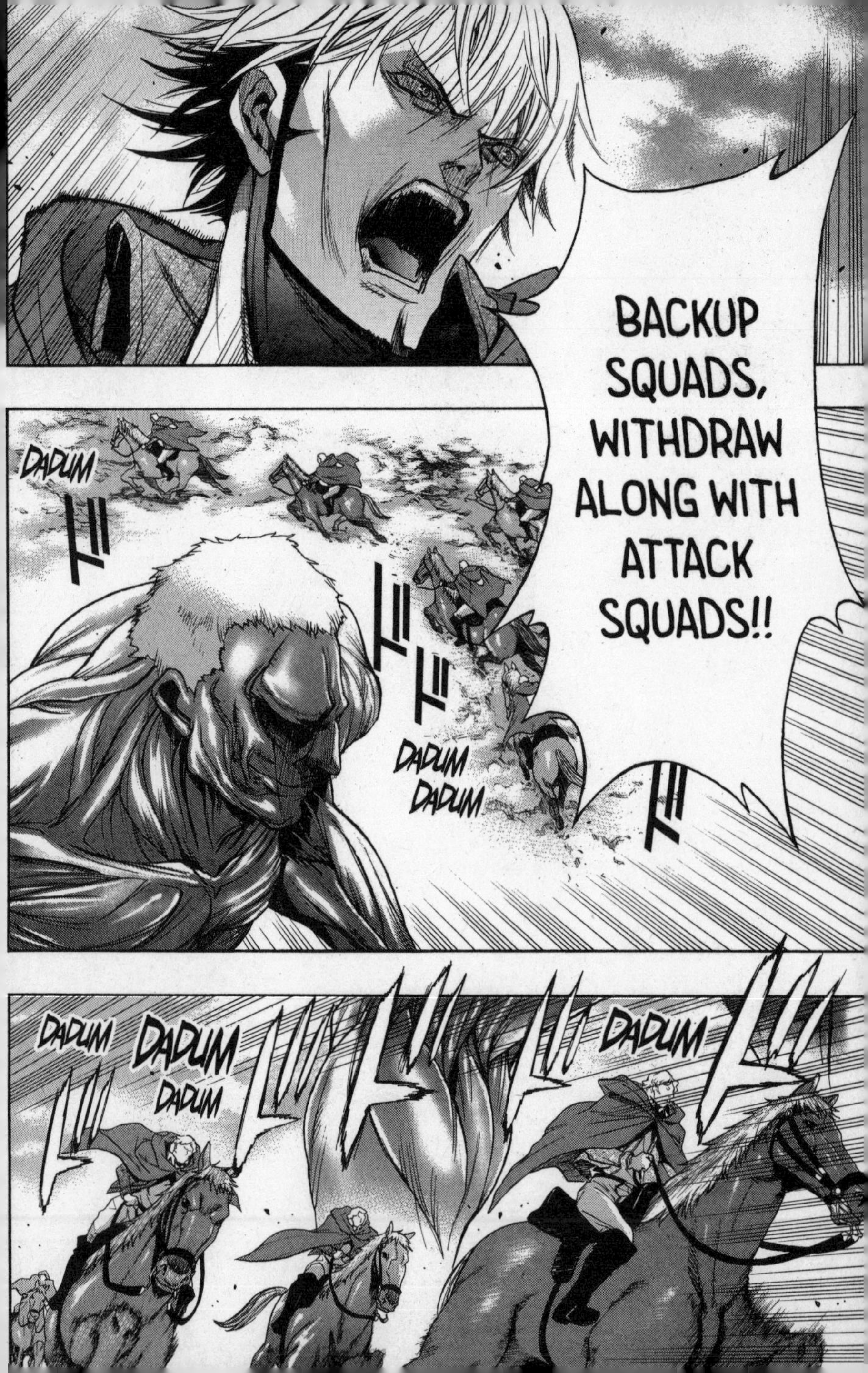
BACKUP SQUADS, WITHDRAW ALONG WITH ATTACK SQUADS!!
DADUM
ド
ドド
DADUM DADUM
ド
DADUM
ドドド
DADUM
DADUM
DADUM
ド
DADUM

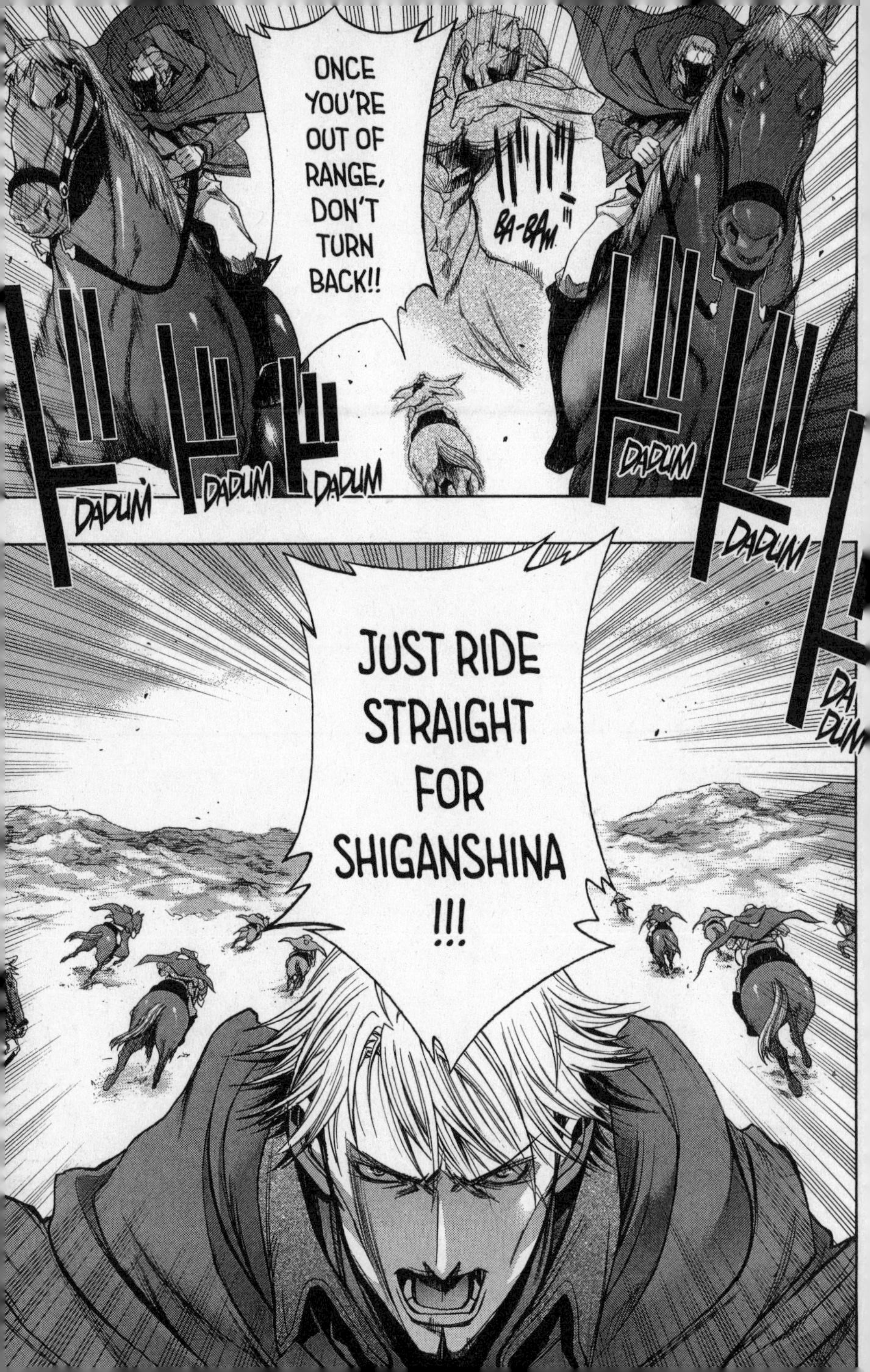
BA-BAM
ONCE YOU'RE OUT OF RANGE, DON'T TURN BACK!!
DADUM
DADUM
DADUM
DADUM
DADUM
DA DUM
JUST RIDE STRAIGHT FOR SHIGANSHINA!!!

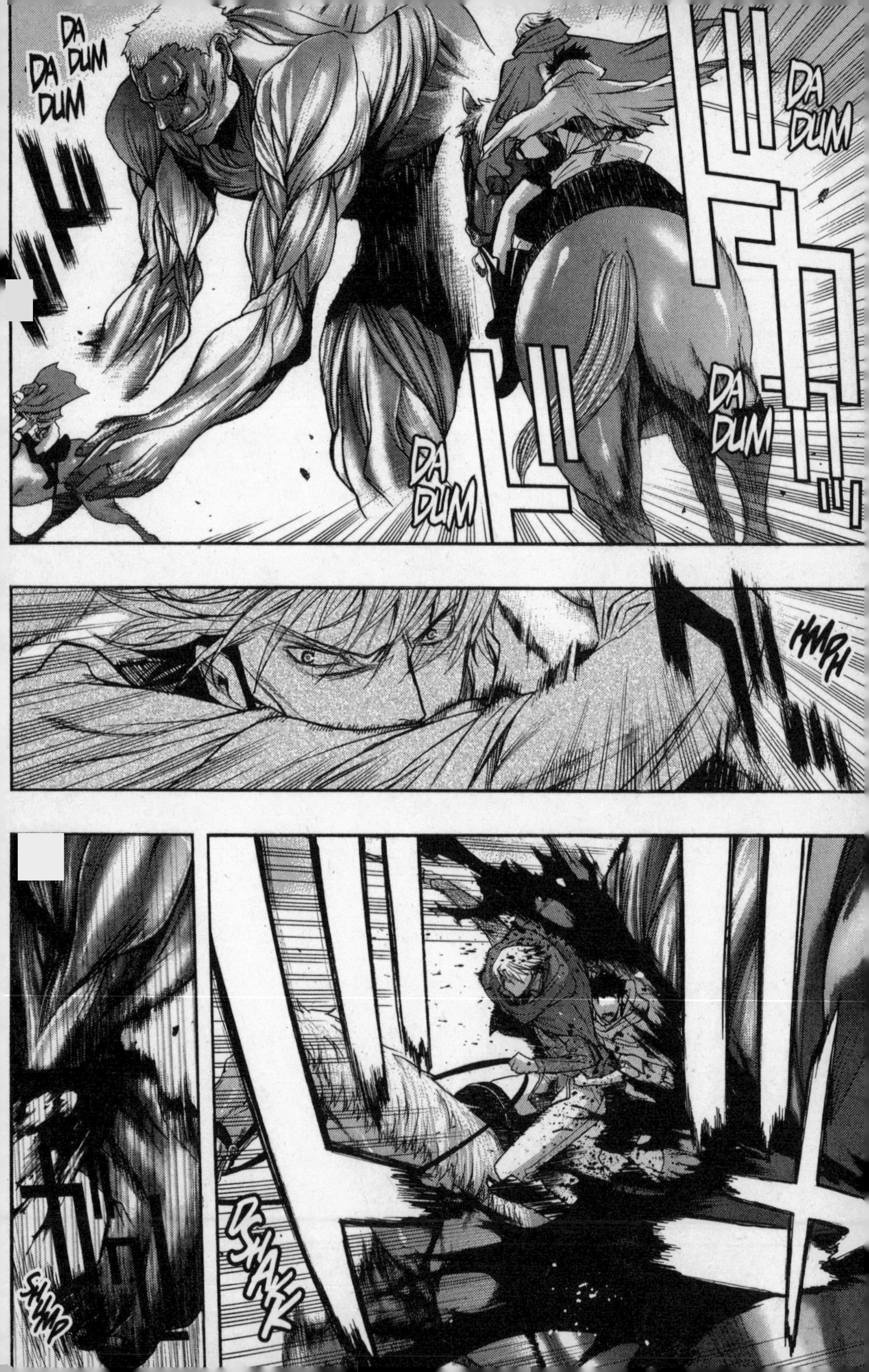
DA DUM
DA DUM
DA DUM
DA DUM
DA DUM
HMPH
DSHAK
SHUNK

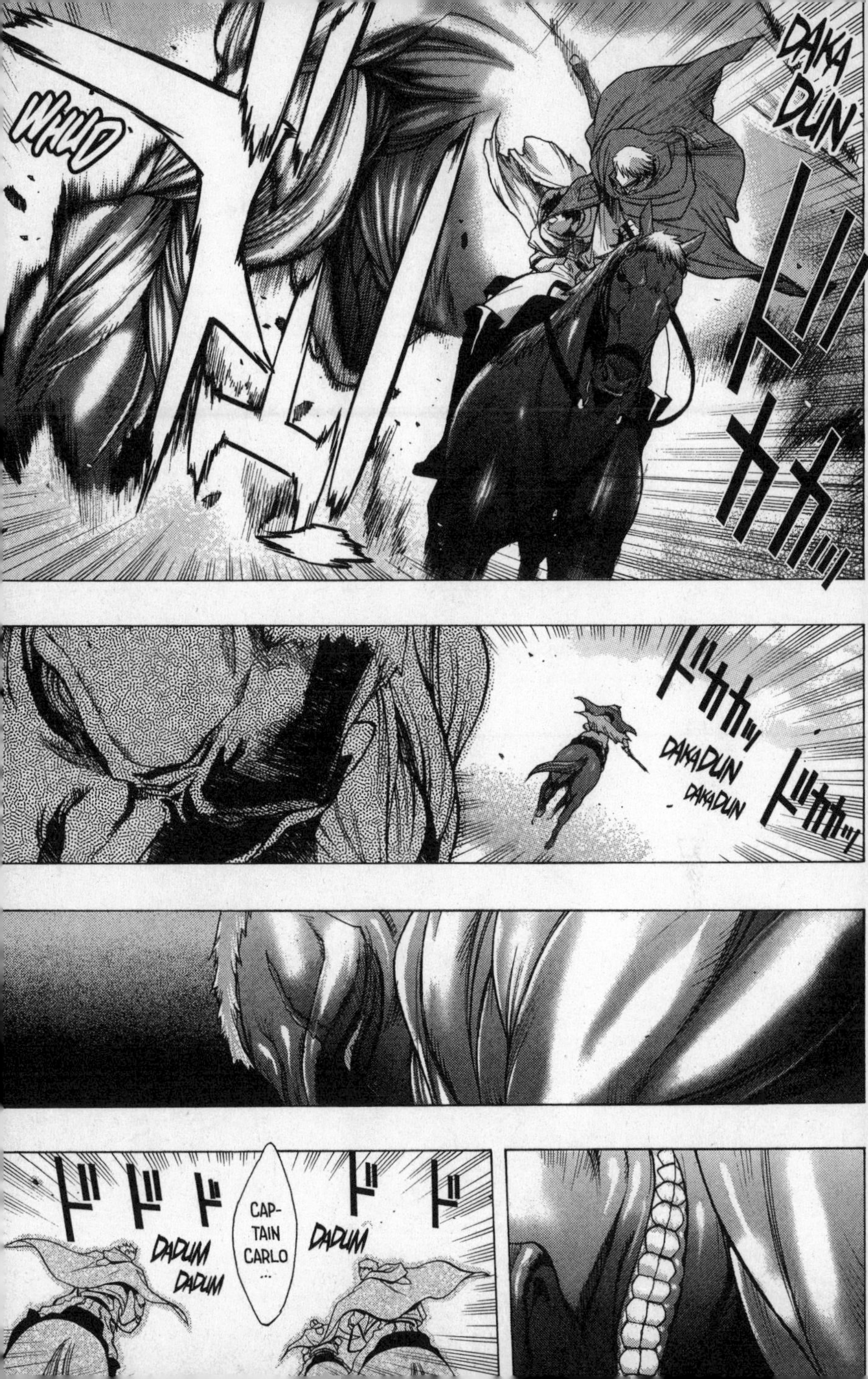
DAKA DUN
WHUD
DAKADUN
DAKADUN
DADUM
CAPTAIN CARLO...
DADUM
DADUM

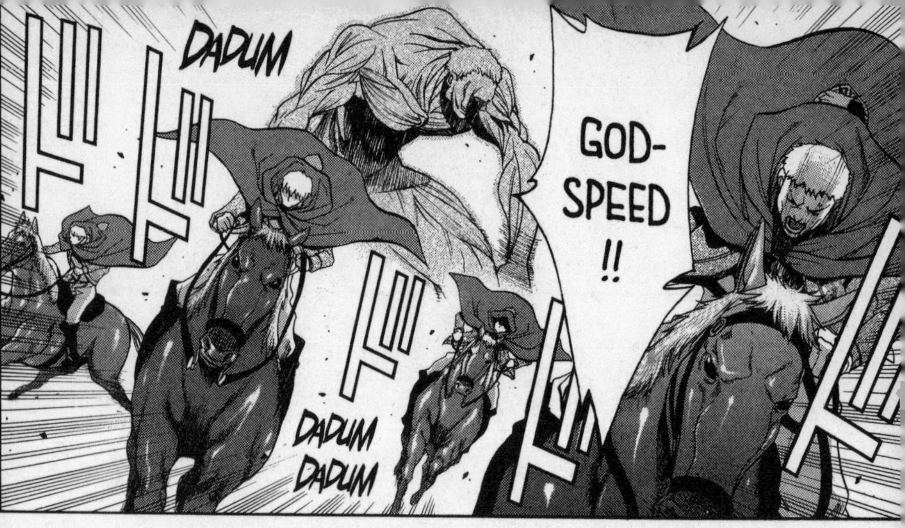
GOD-SPEED!!
DADUM
DADUM DADUM

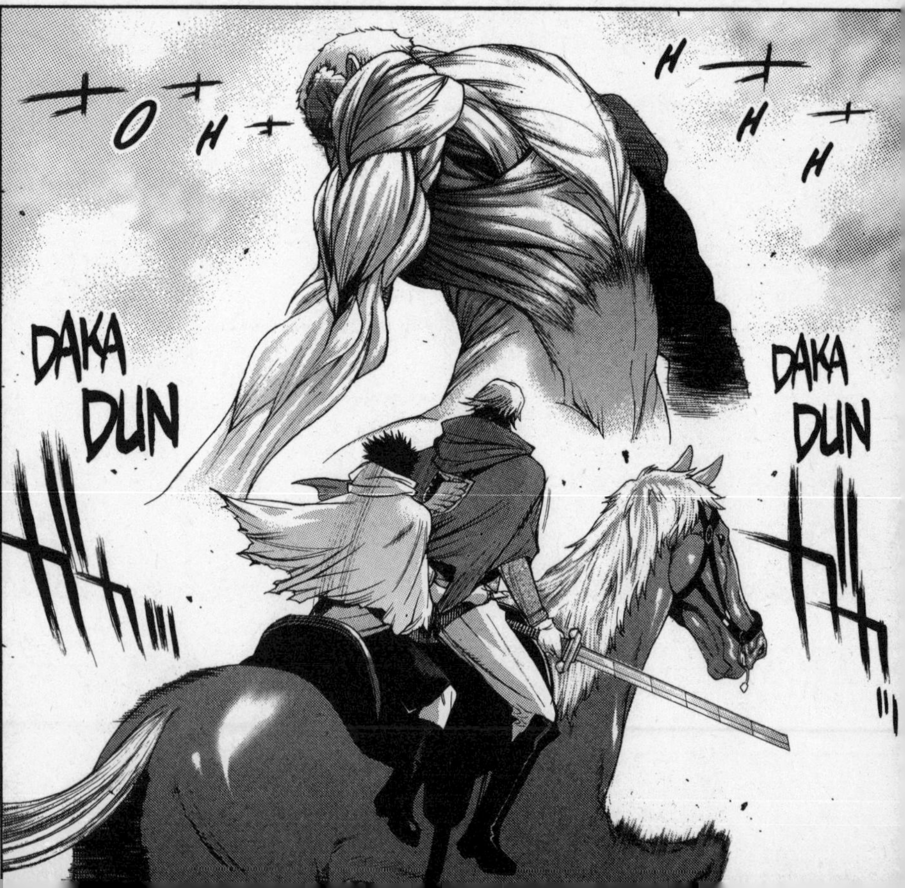
O H
H H H
DAKA DUN
DAKA DUN

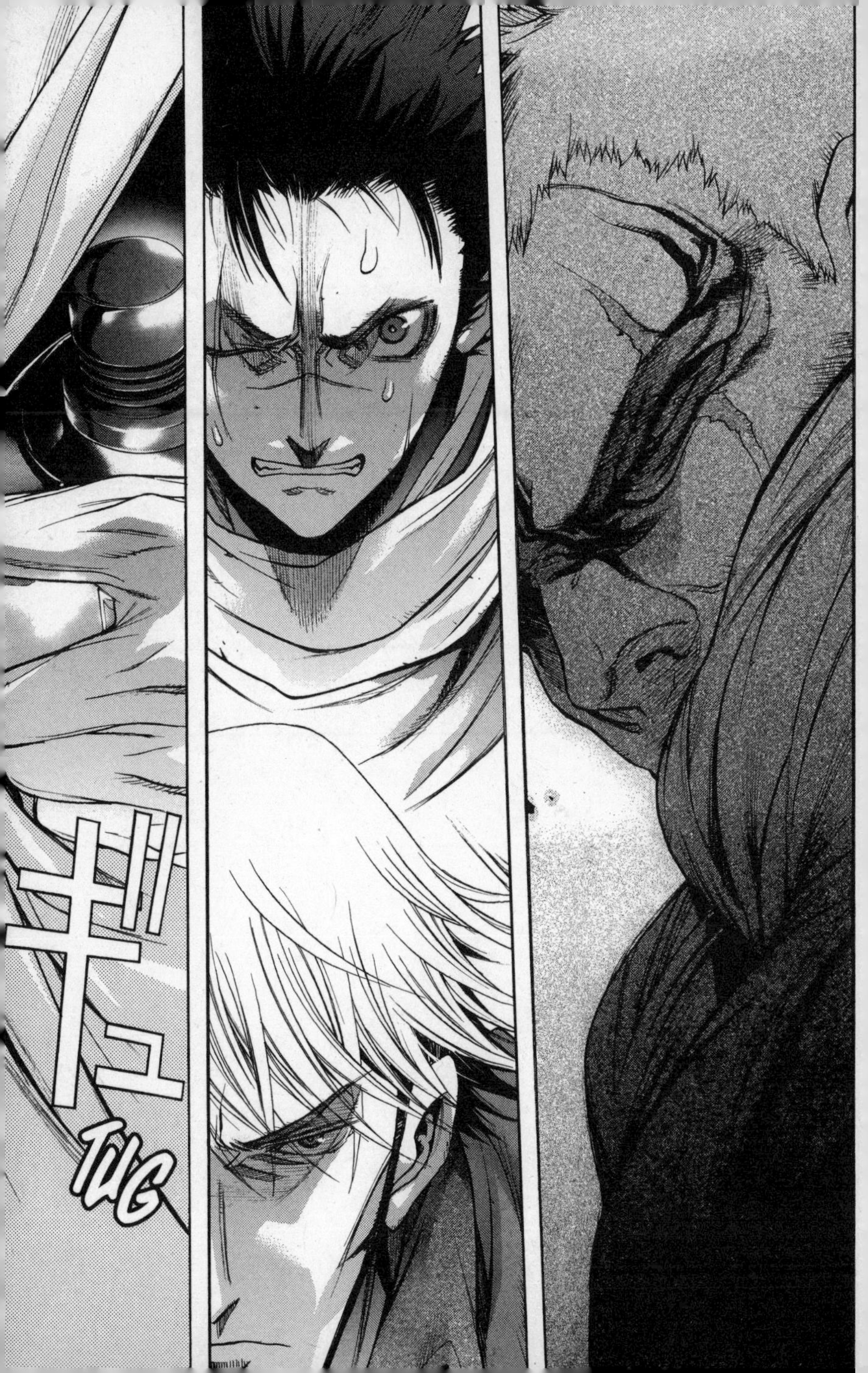
ギュ
TUG

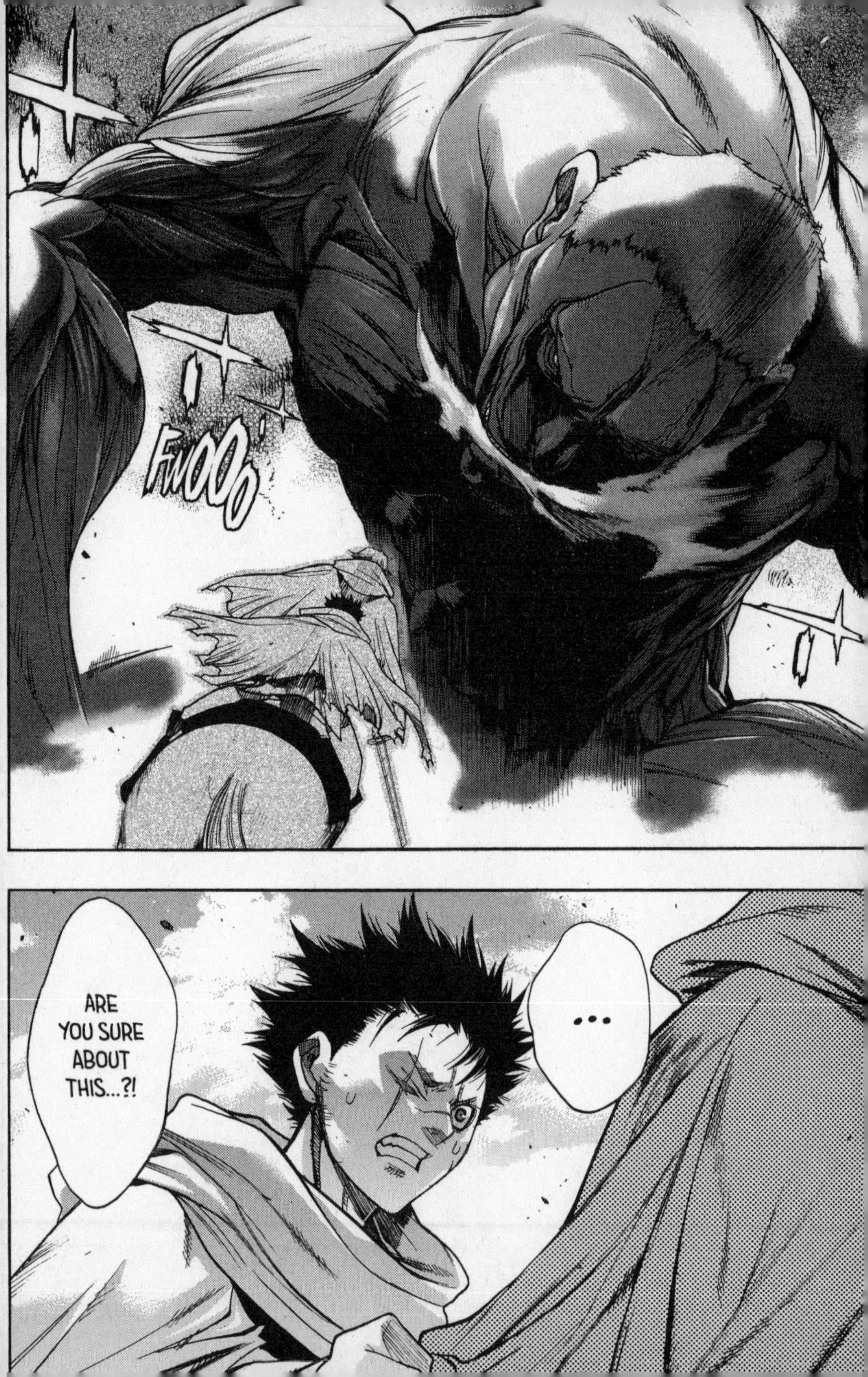
FWOOO
...
ARE YOU SURE ABOUT THIS...?!

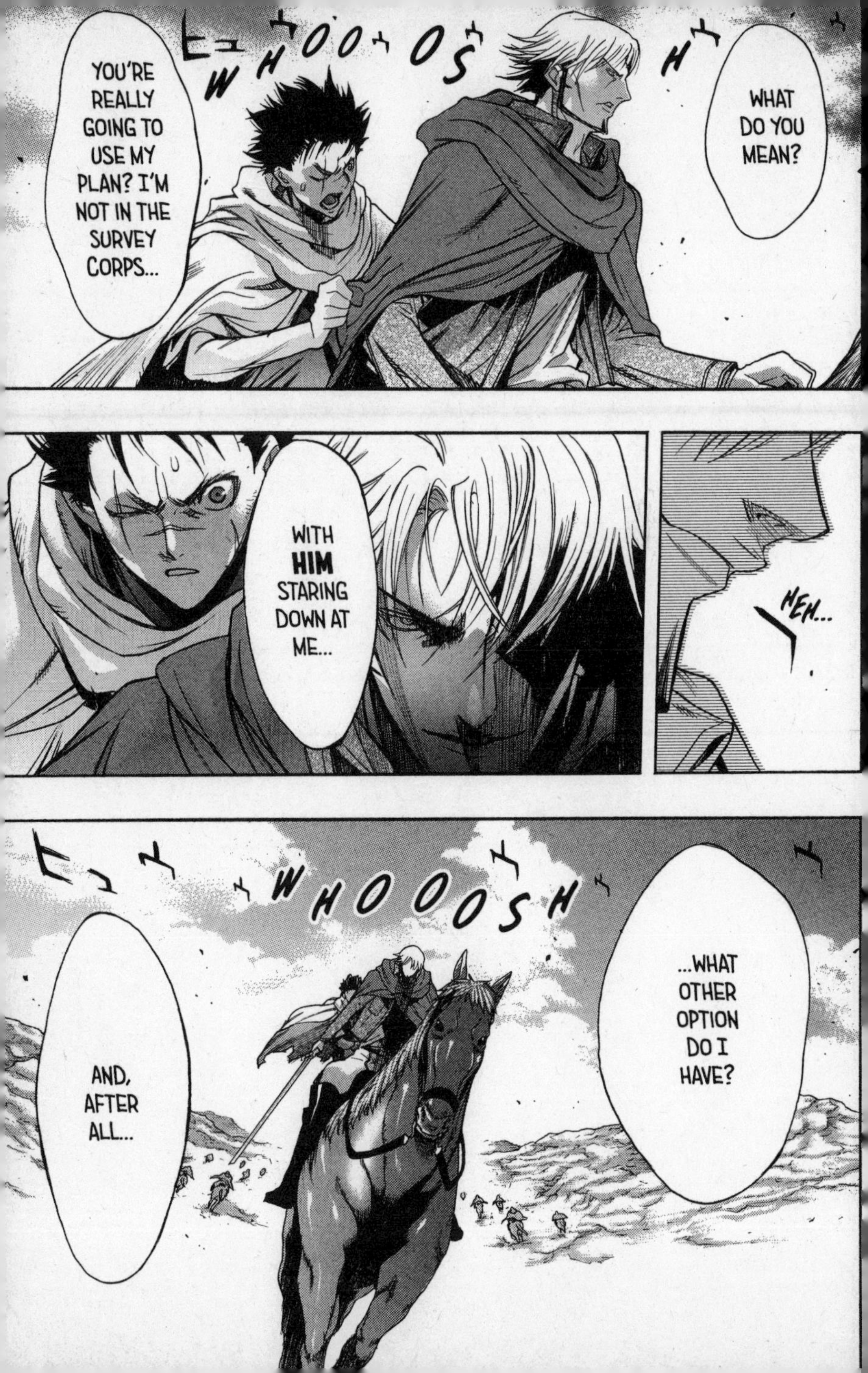
WHOOOSH
WHAT DO YOU MEAN?
YOU'RE REALLY GOING TO USE MY PLAN? I'M NOT IN THE SURVEY CORPS...
HEH...
WITH **HIM** STARING DOWN AT ME...
WHOOOSH
...WHAT OTHER OPTION DO I HAVE?
AND, AFTER ALL...

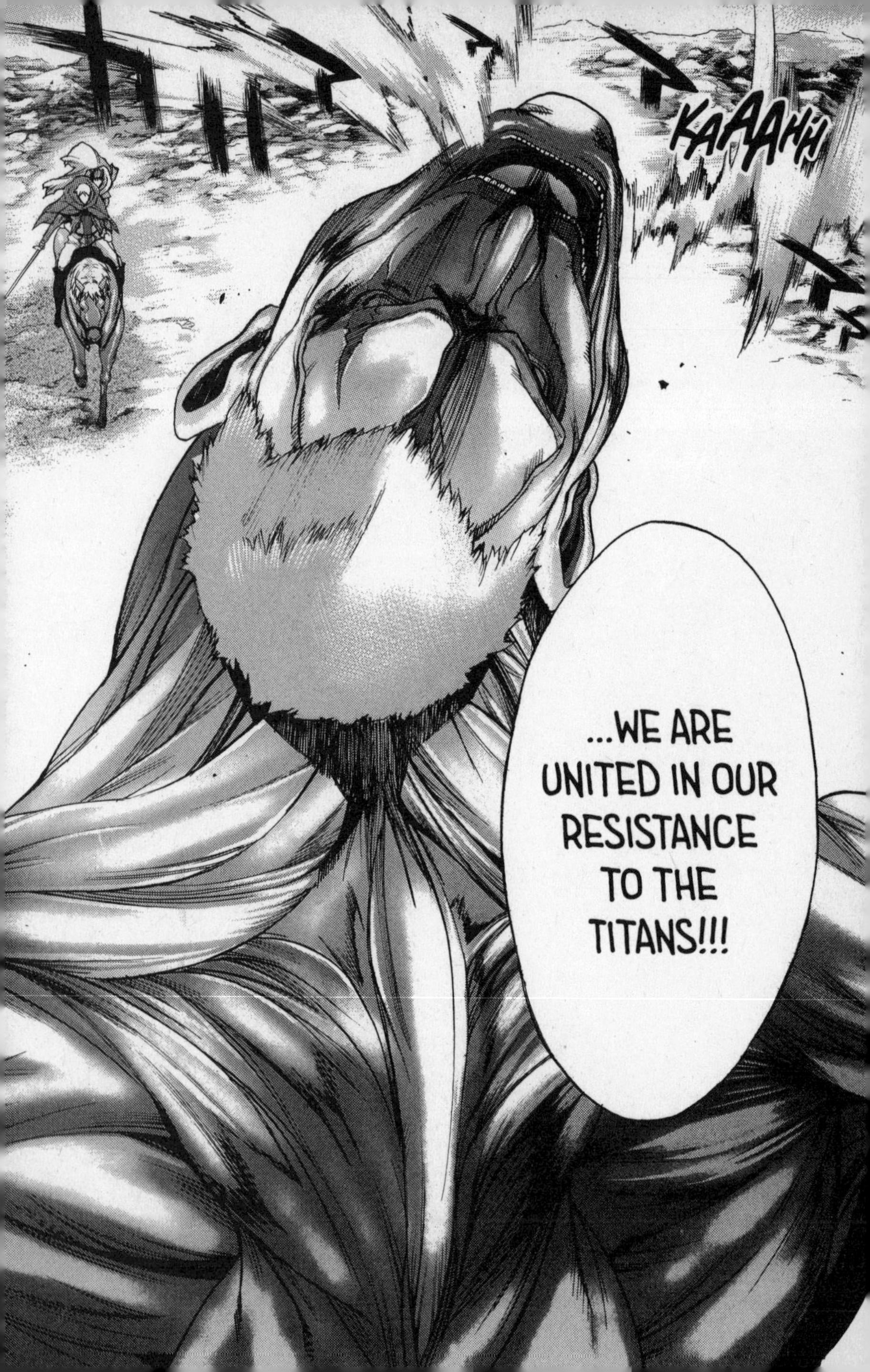
KAAAHH
...WE ARE UNITED IN OUR RESISTANCE TO THE TITANS!!!

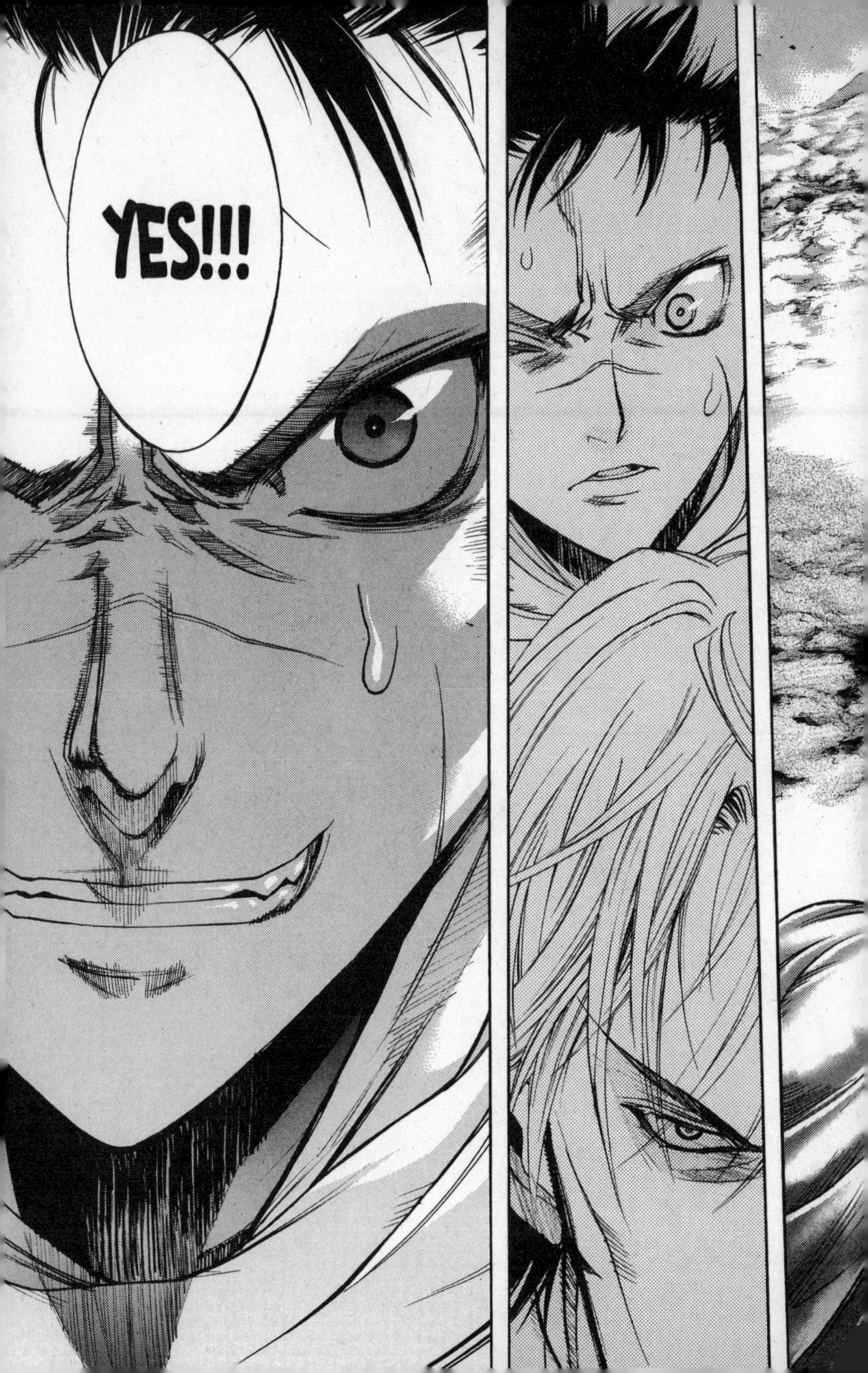
YES!!!

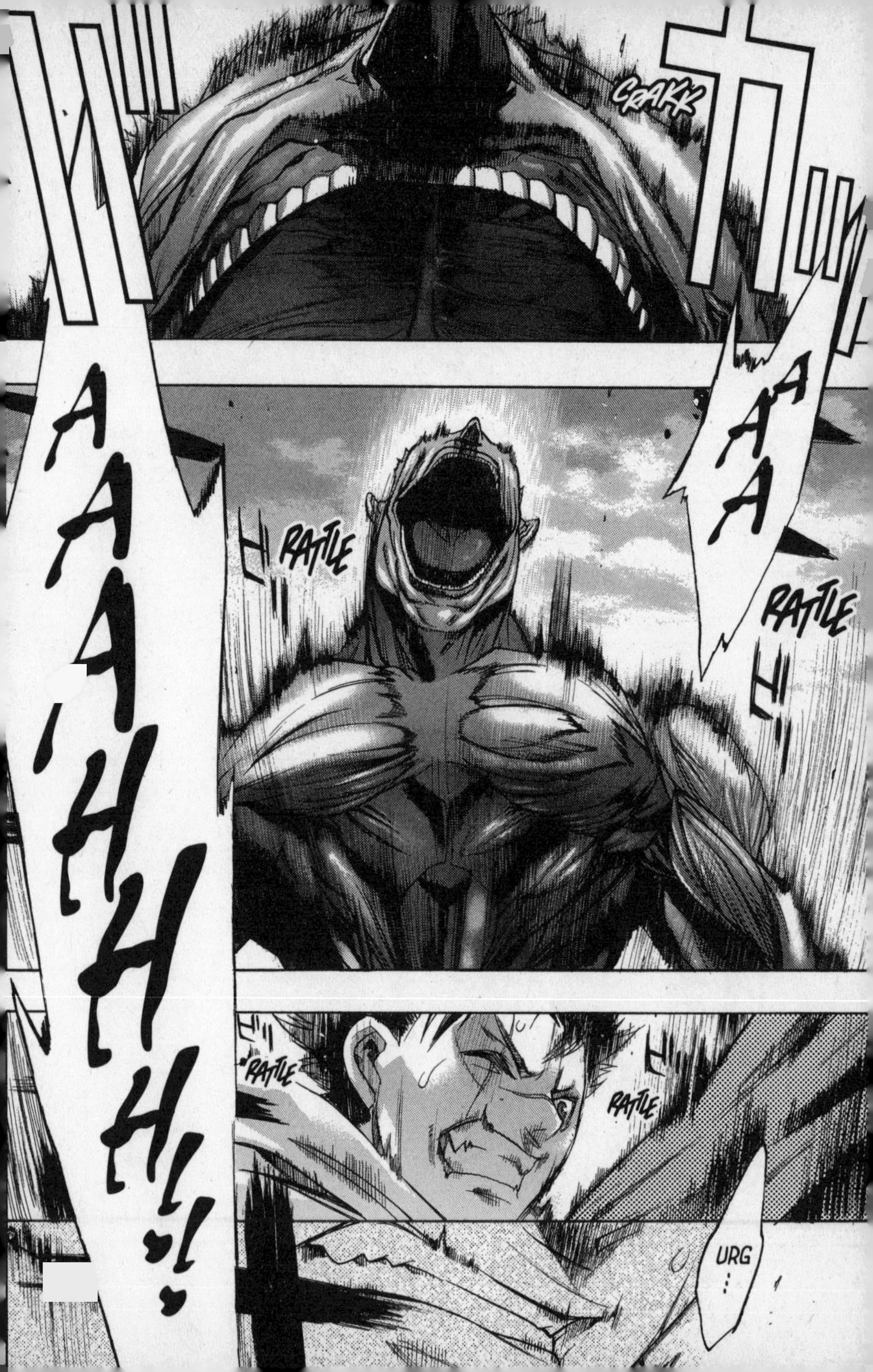
CRAKK
AAAA
AAAAHHHH!!!
RATTLE
RATTLE
RATTLE
RATTLE
URG...

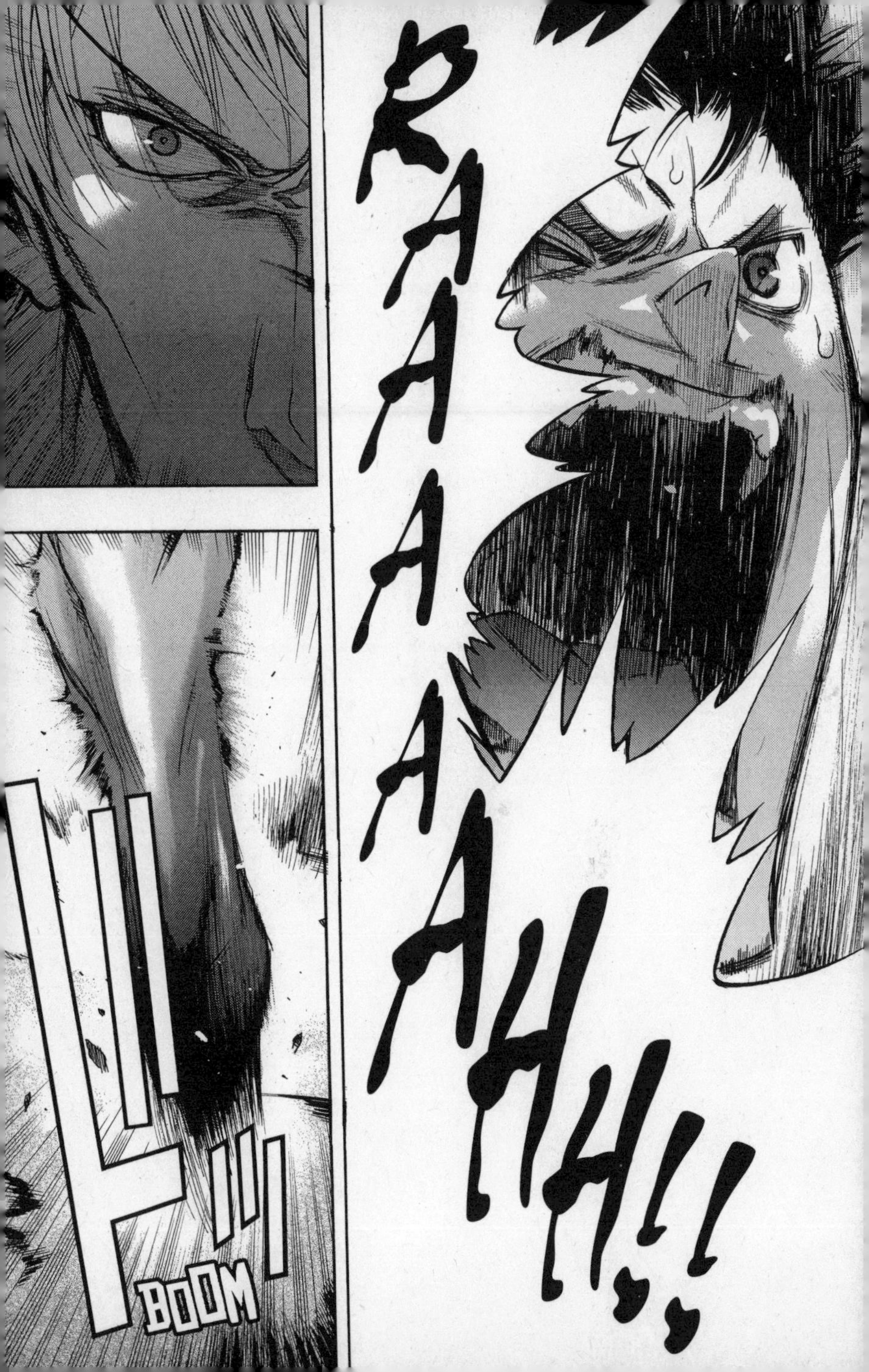
RAAAAAAHH!!
BOOM

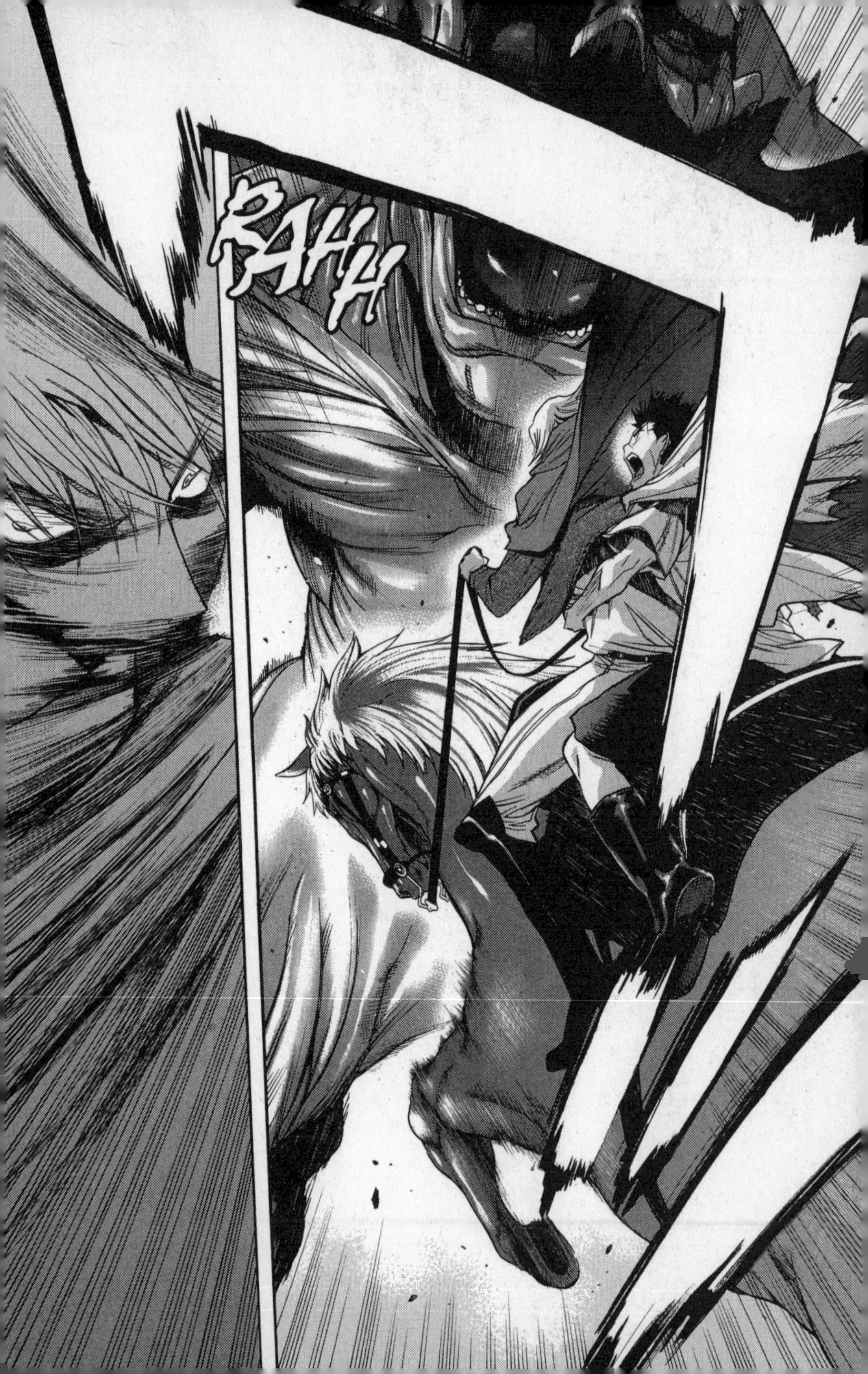
RAHH

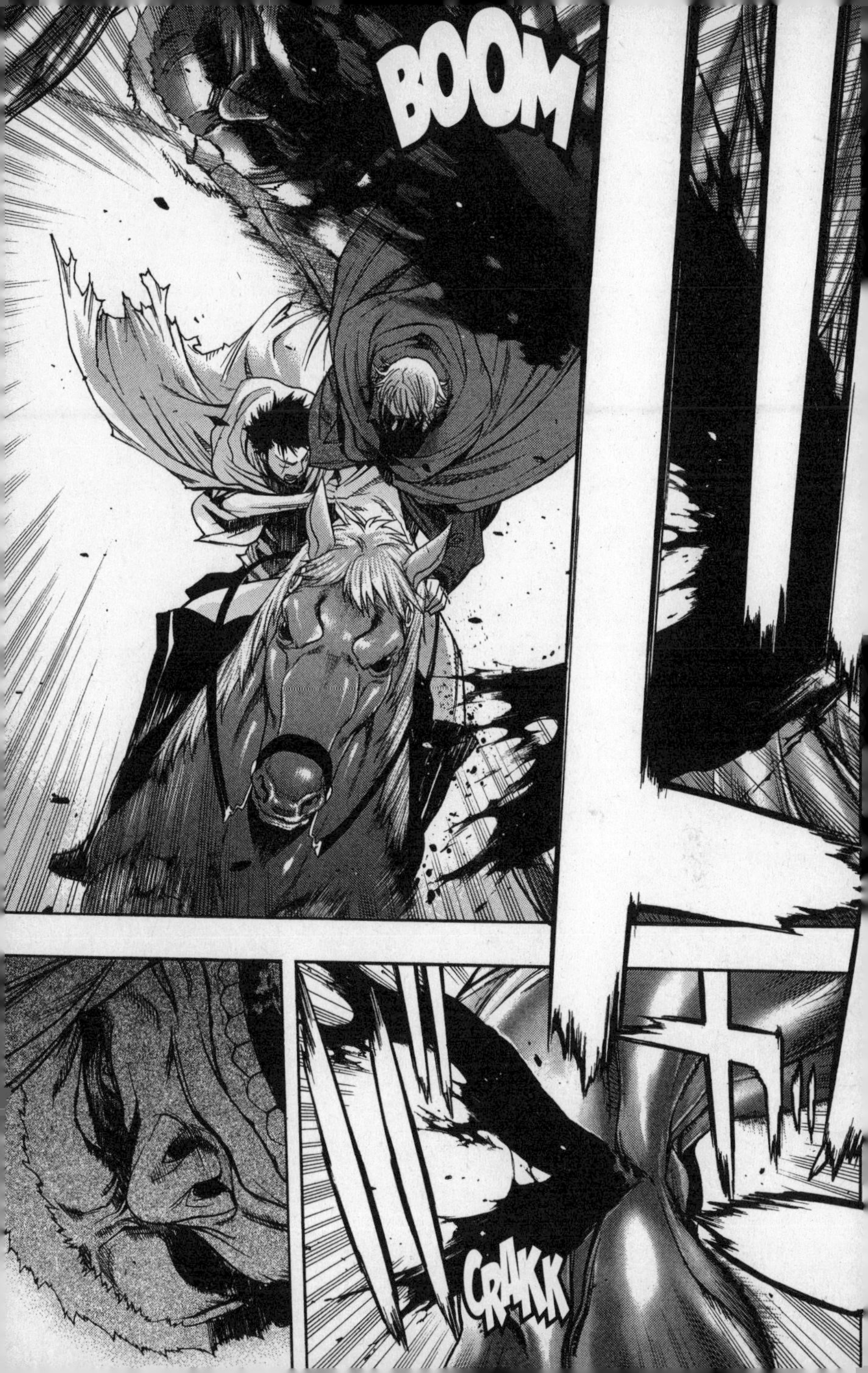
BOOM
CRAKK

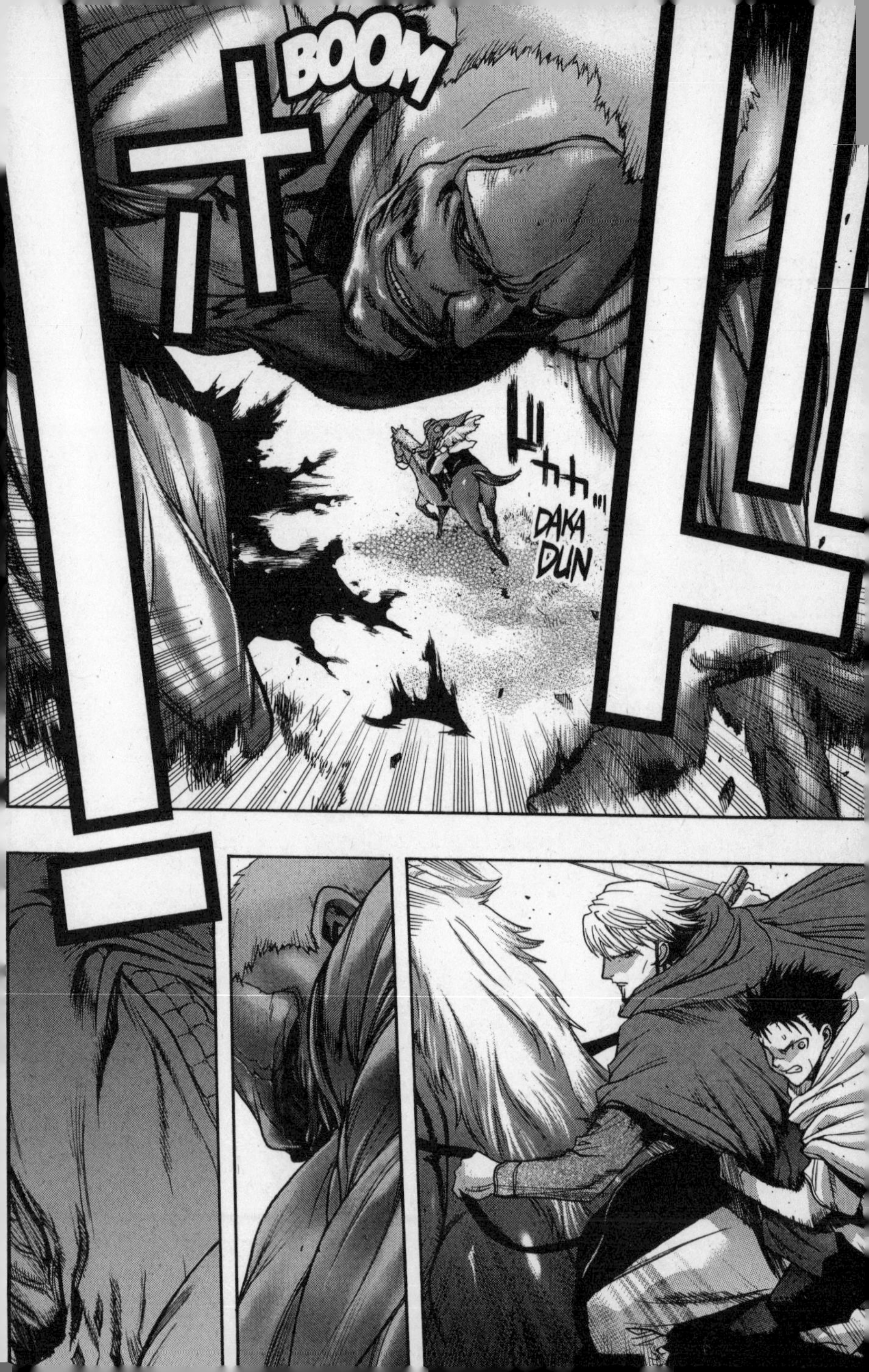
BOOM
DAKA DUN

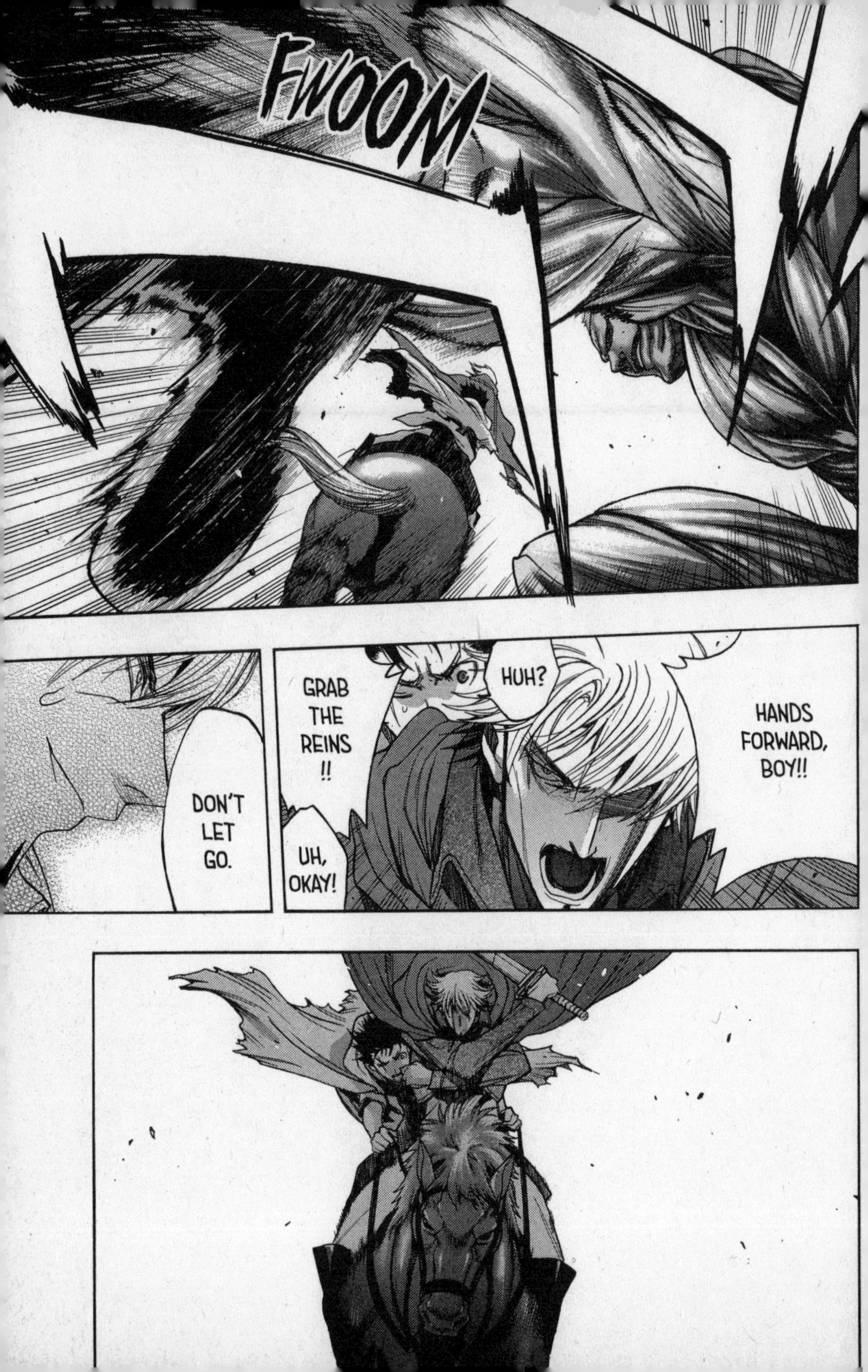
FWOOM
HANDS FORWARD, BOY!!
HUH?
GRAB THE REINS !!
UH, OKAY!
DON'T LET GO.

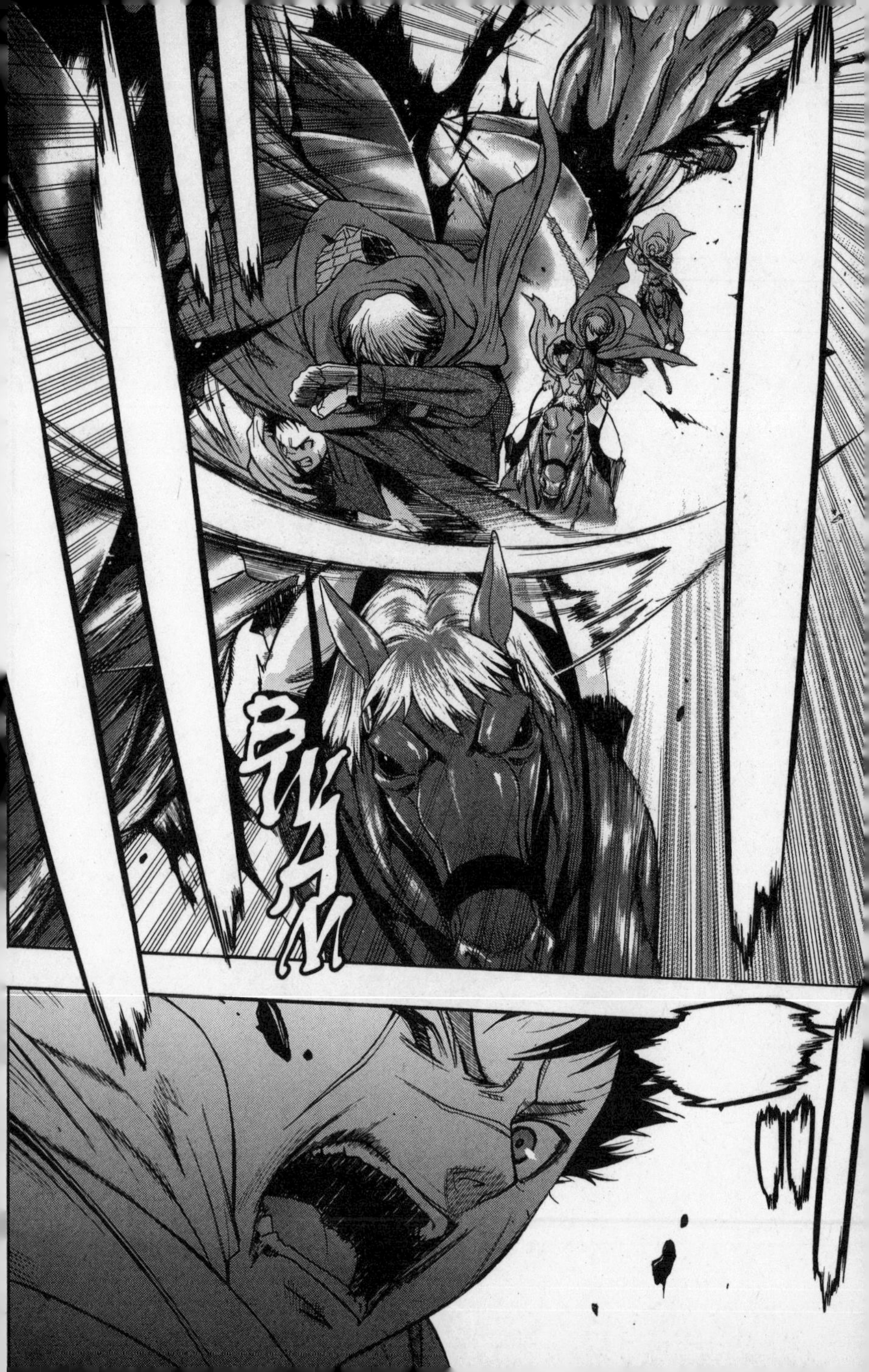
BWAM

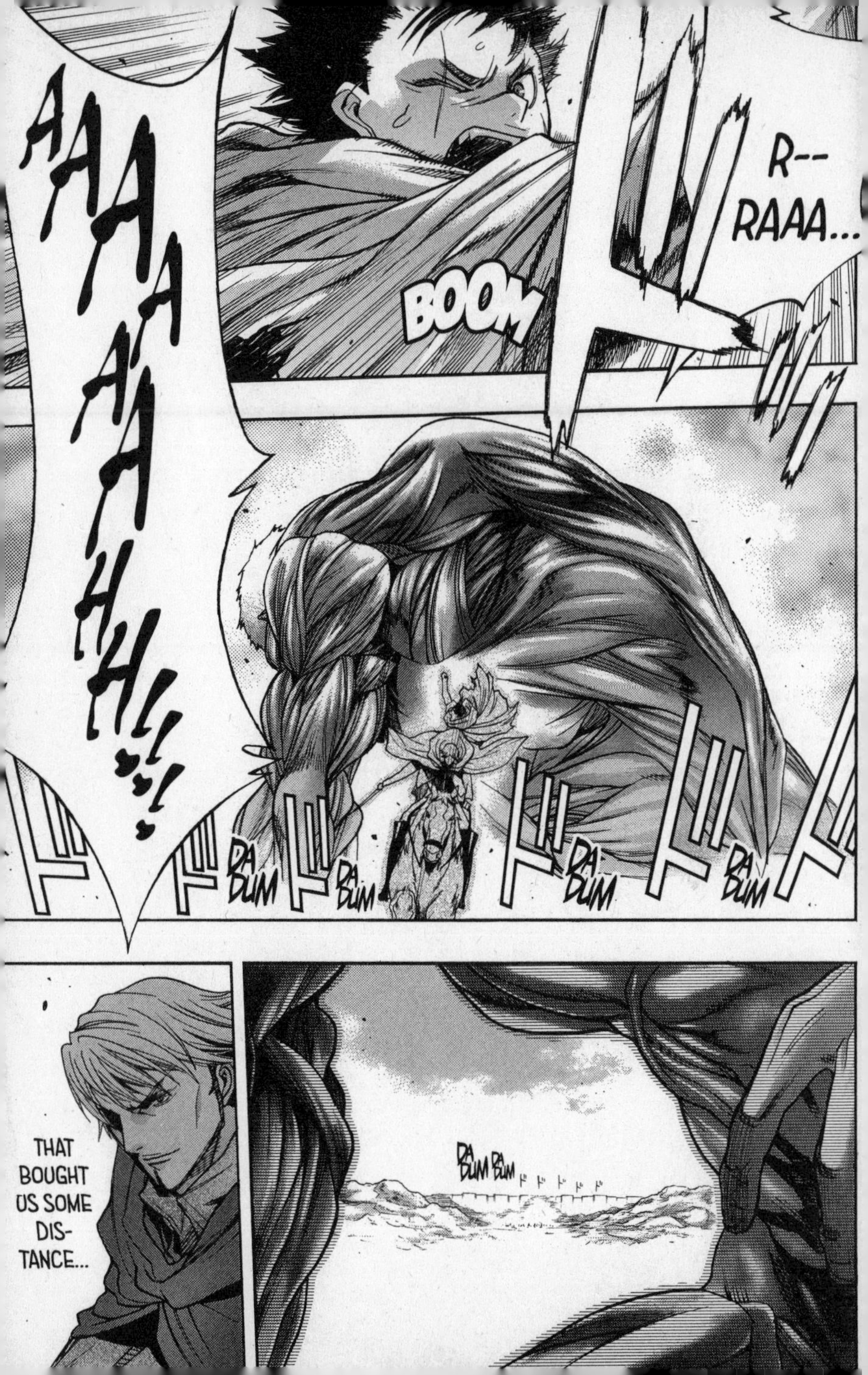
R-- RAAA...
BOOM
AAAAAAHHH!!...!
DA BUM
DA BUM
DA BUM
DA BUM
DA BUM DA BUM
THAT BOUGHT US SOME DIS- TANCE...

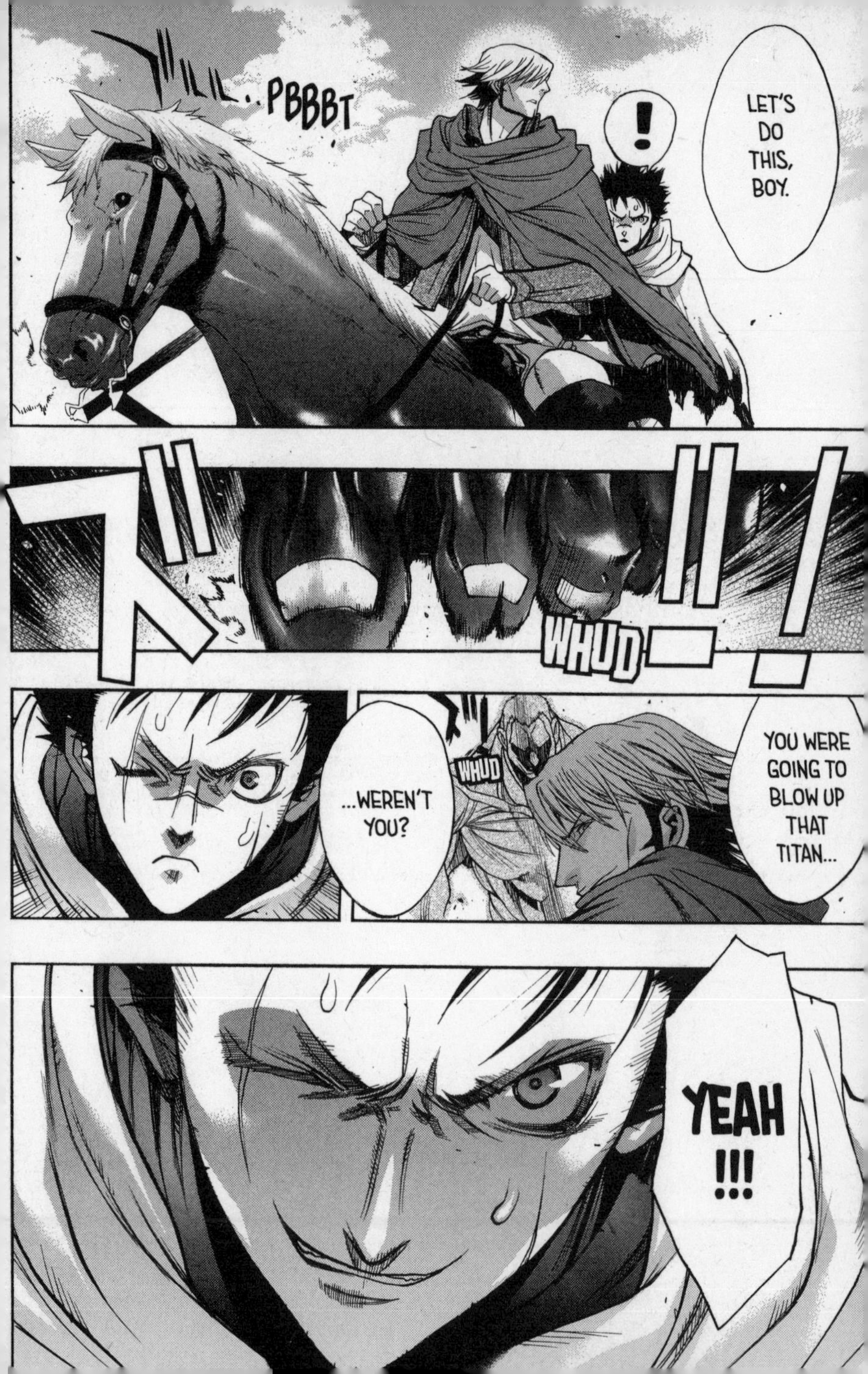
LET'S DO THIS, BOY.
!
...PBBBT
WHUD
YOU WERE GOING TO BLOW UP THAT TITAN...
WHUD
...WEREN'T YOU?
YEAH !!!

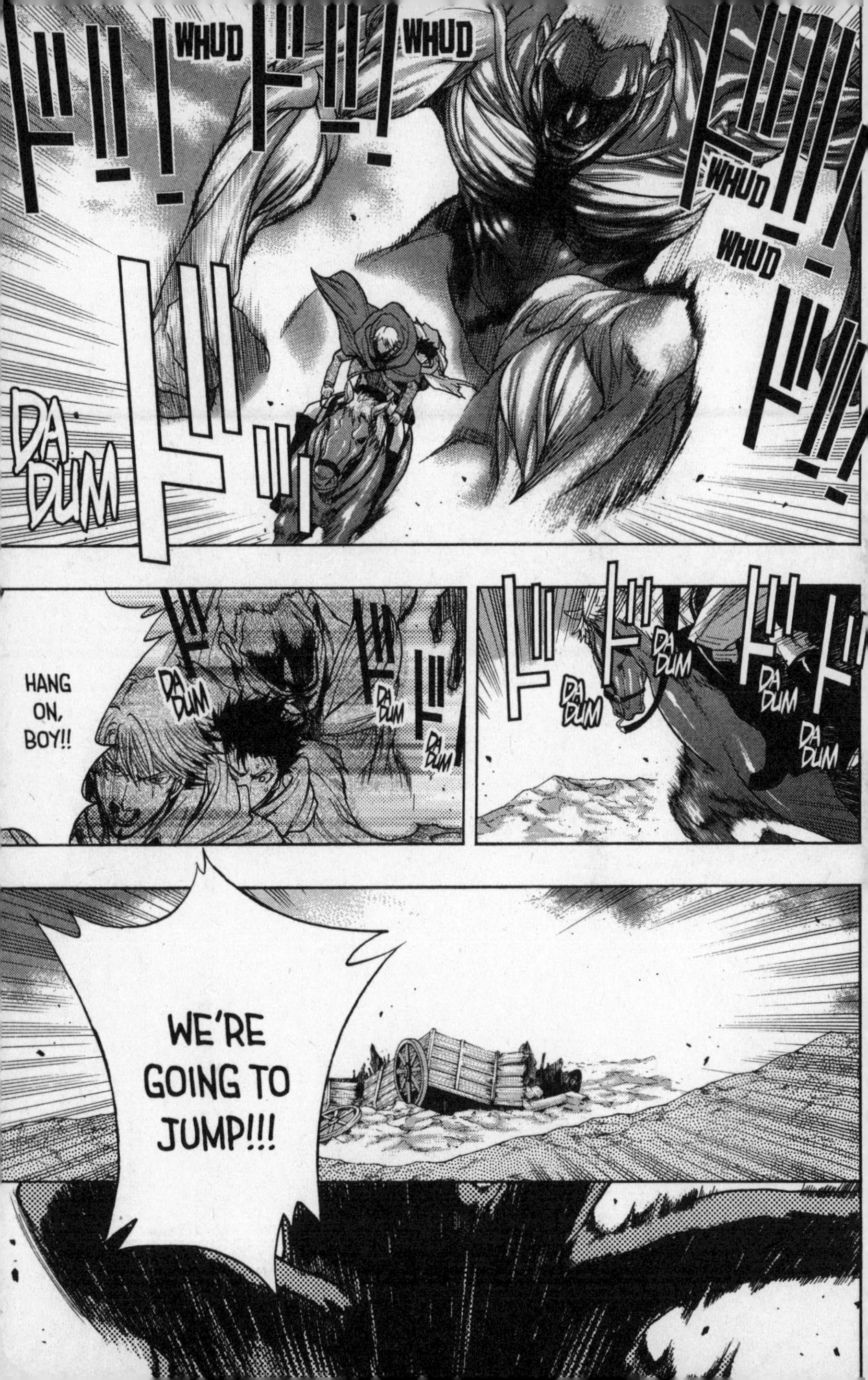
WHUD
WHUD
WHUD
WHUD
DA DUM
DA DUM
DA DUM
DA DUM
DA DUM
DA DUM
DA DUM
DA DUM
HANG ON, BOY!!
WE'RE GOING TO JUMP!!!

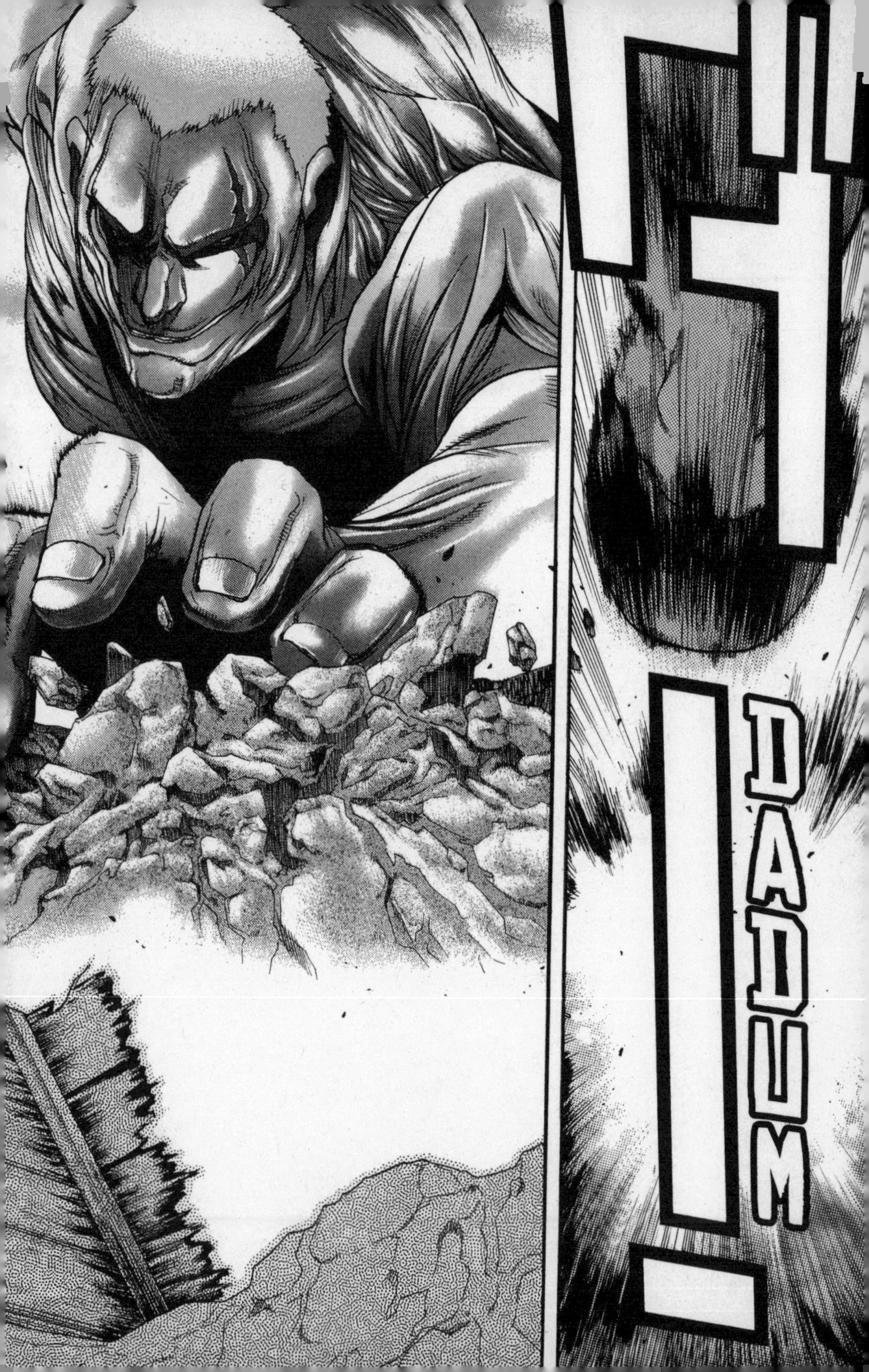
DADUM

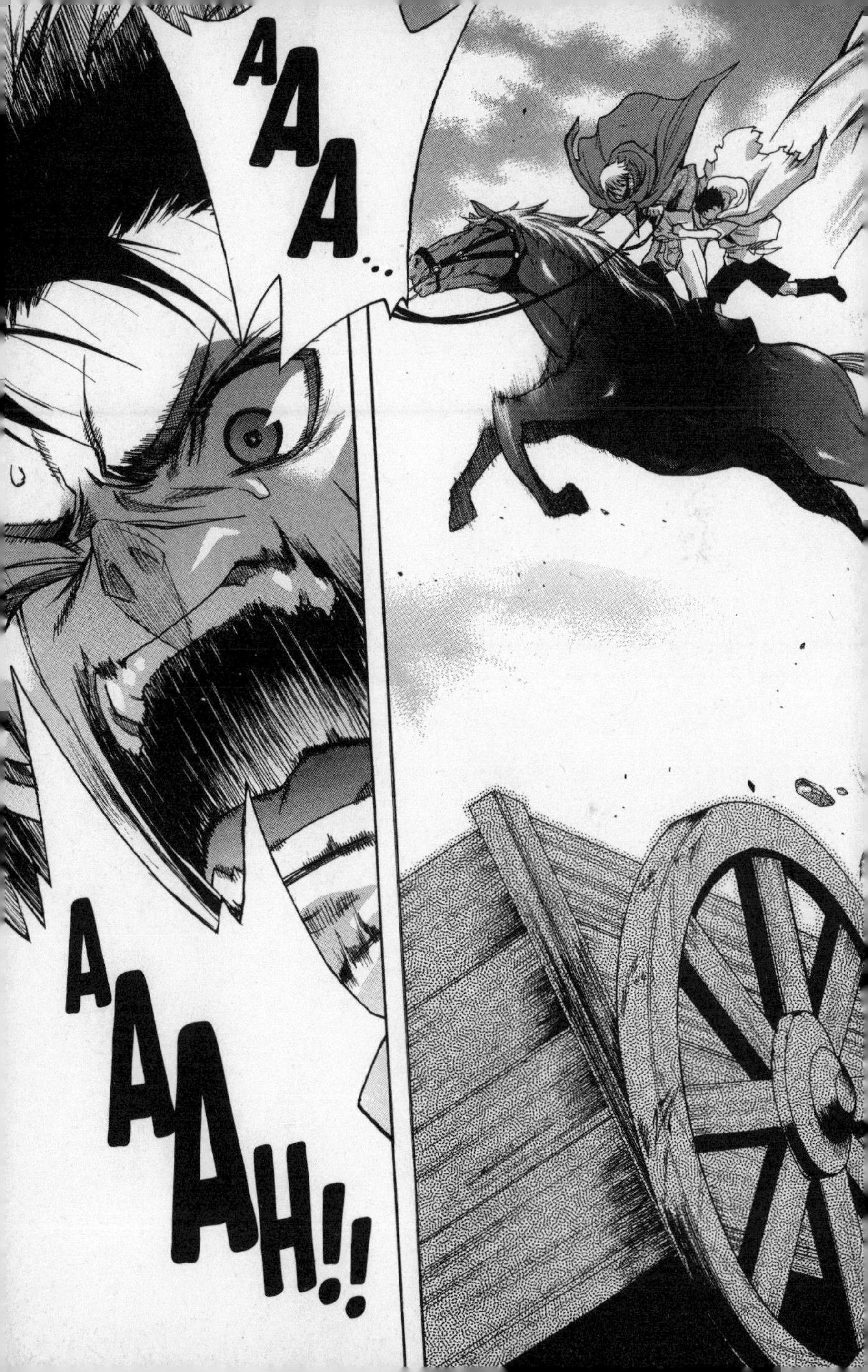
AAAA...
AAAAAH!!

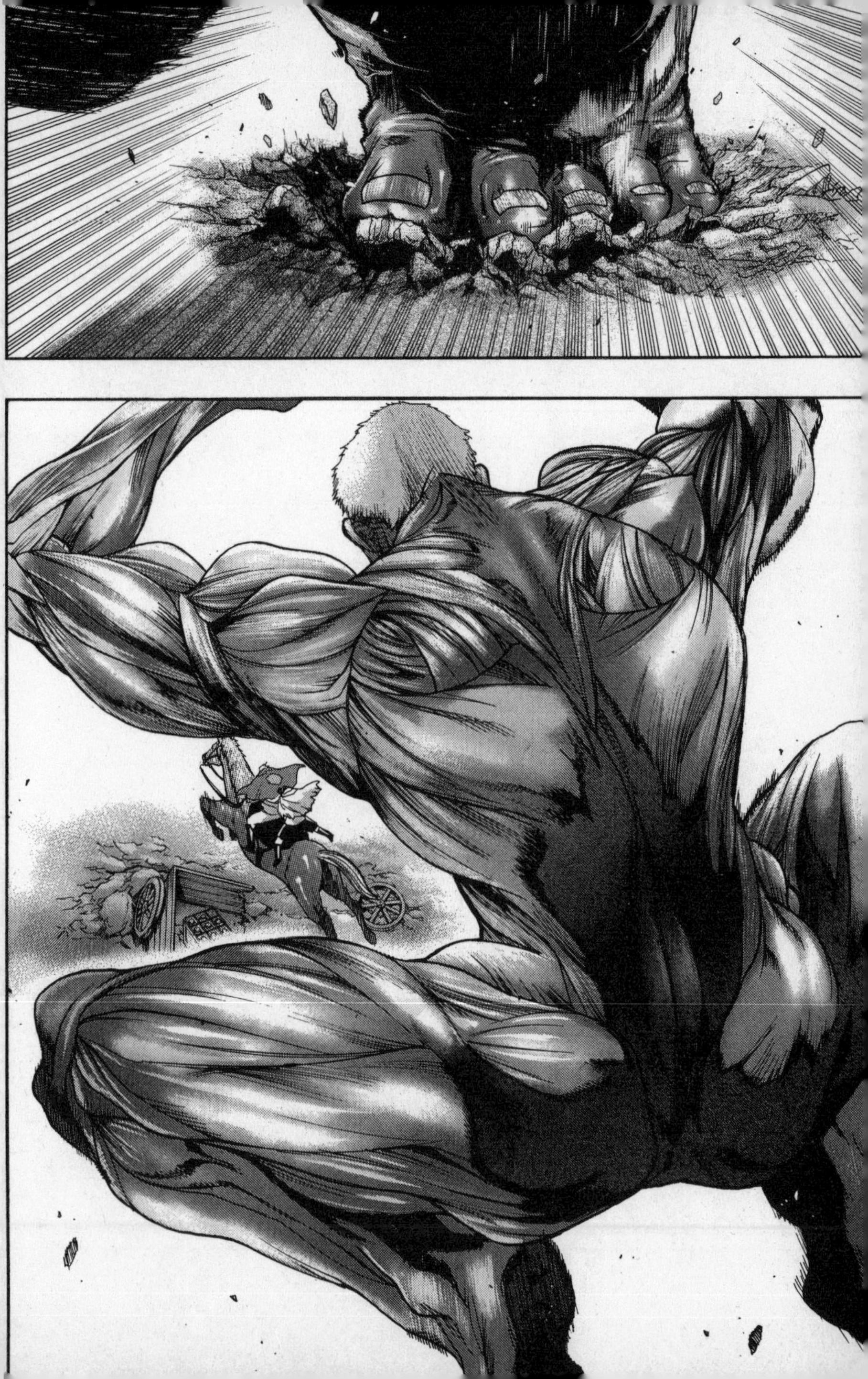

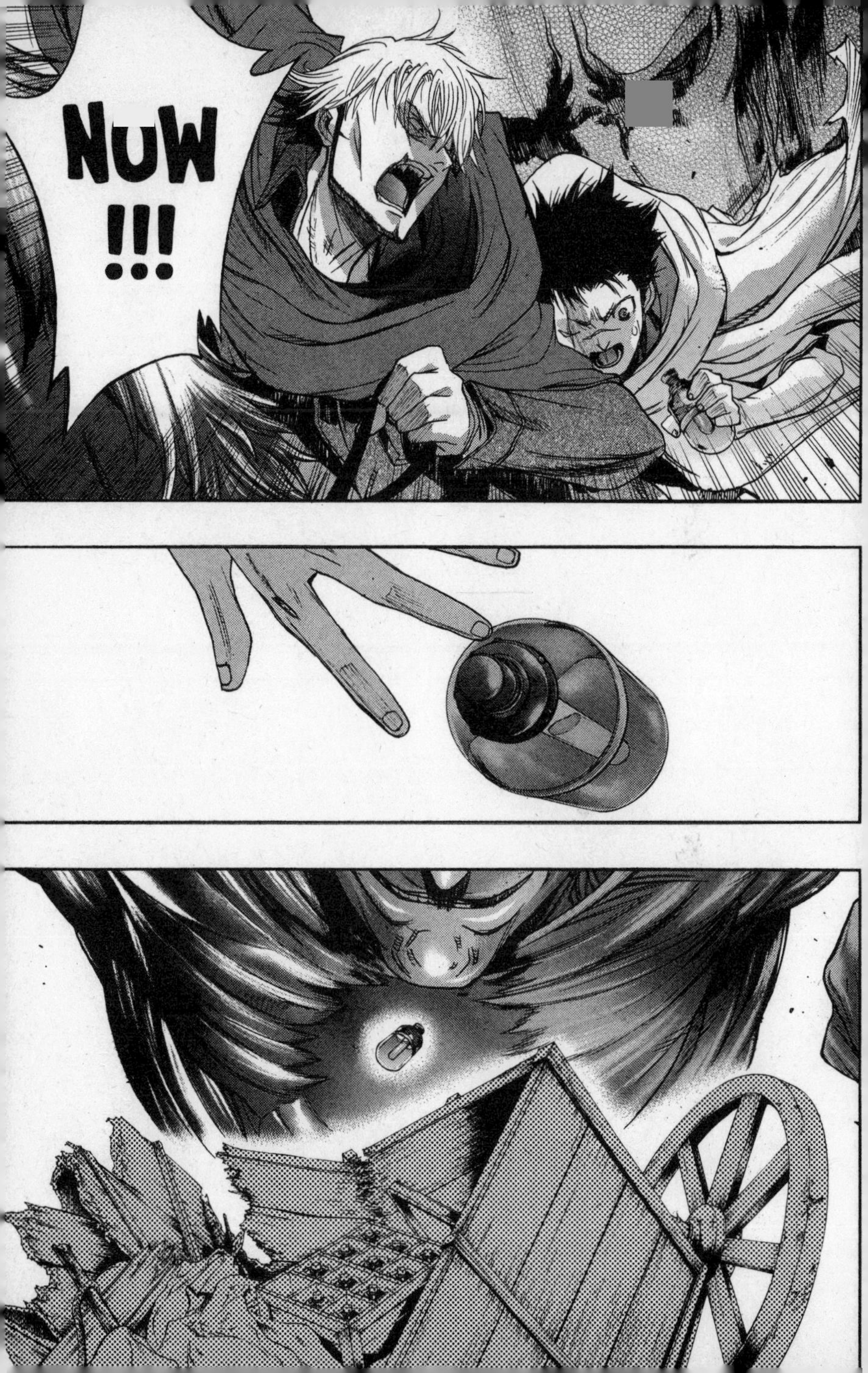
NOW !!!

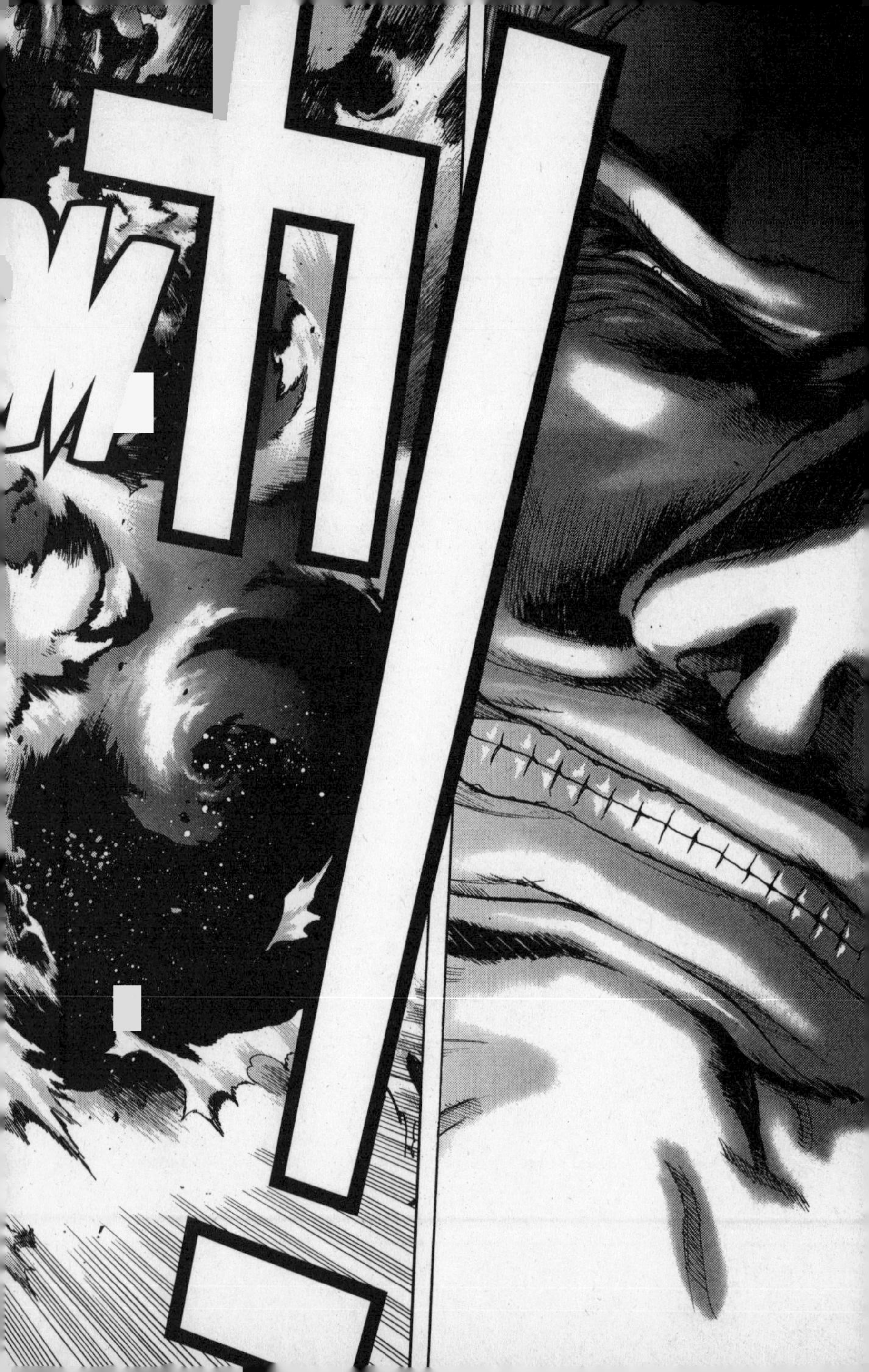

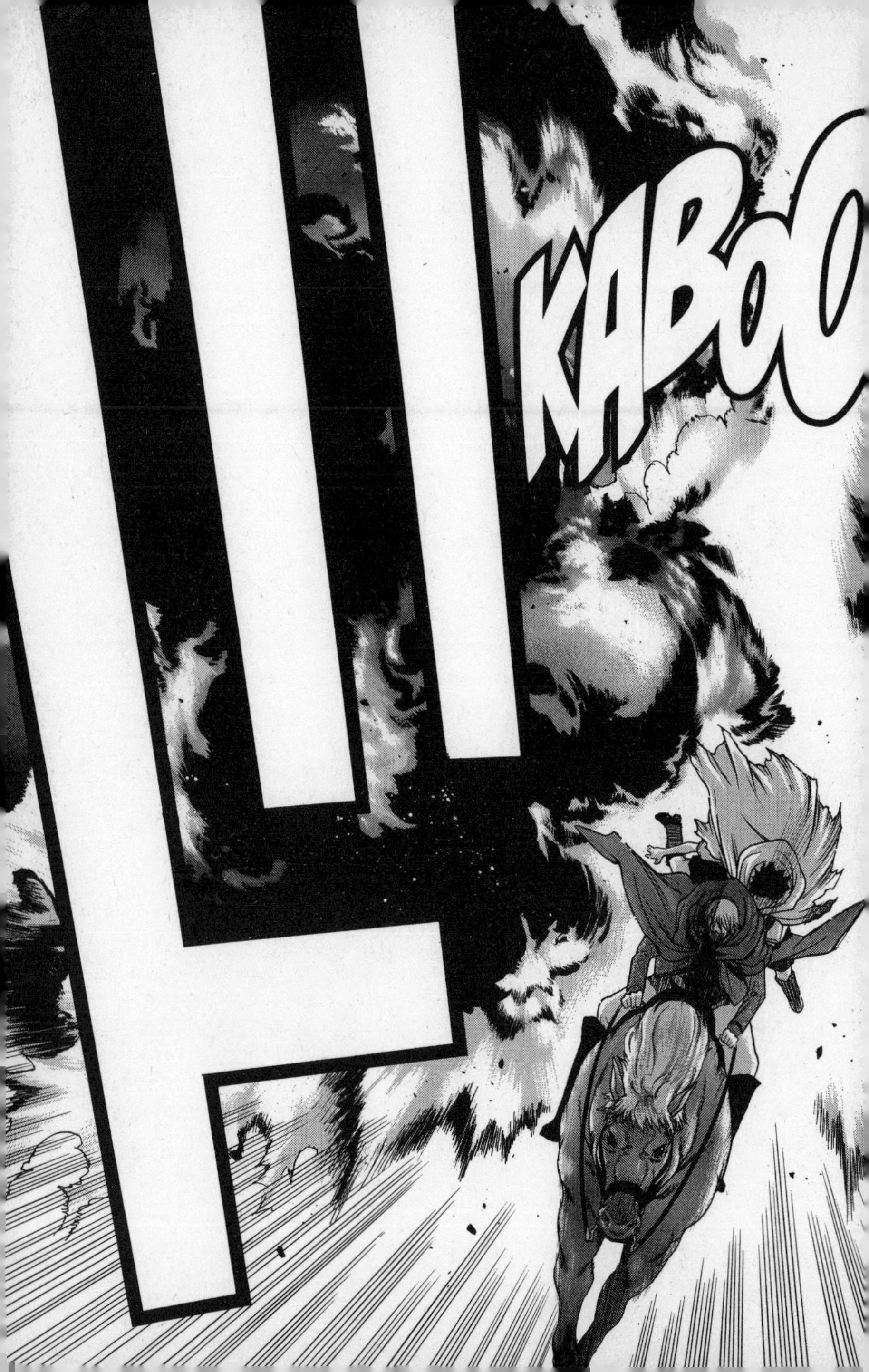
KABOO

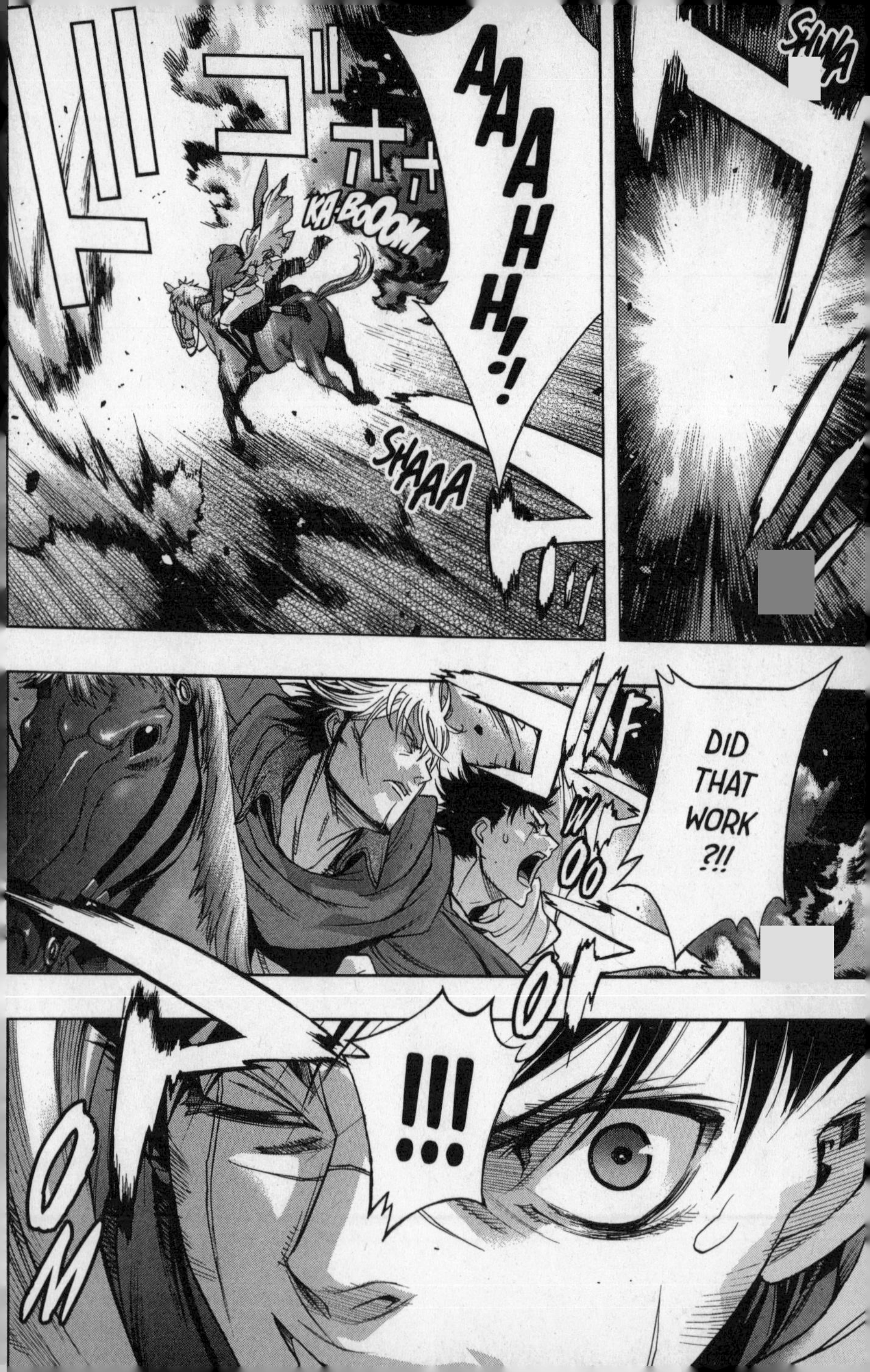
SHWA
AAAAHH!!
KA-BOOOM
SHAAA
DID THAT WORK ?!!
!!!

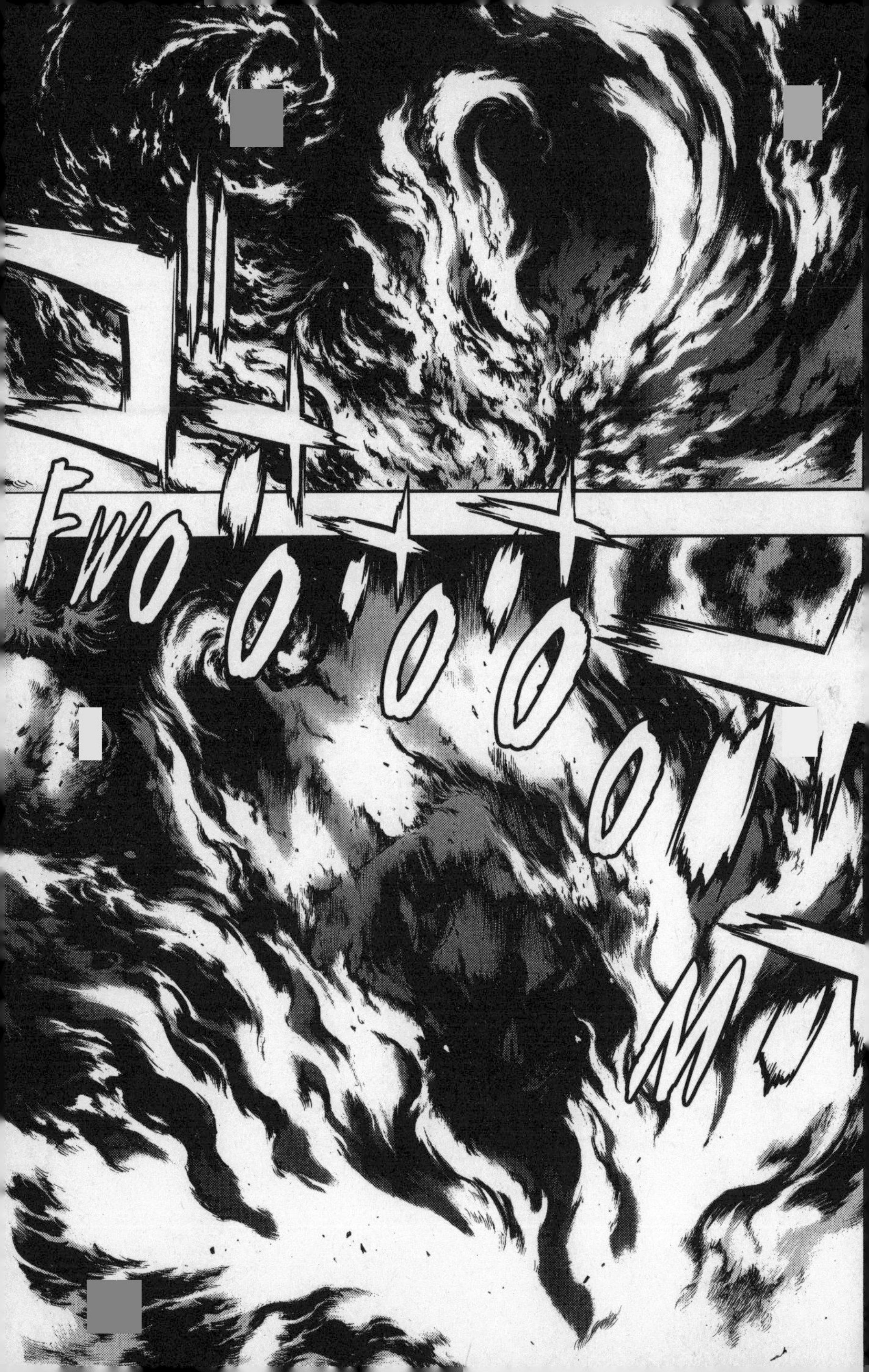
FWOOOOOM

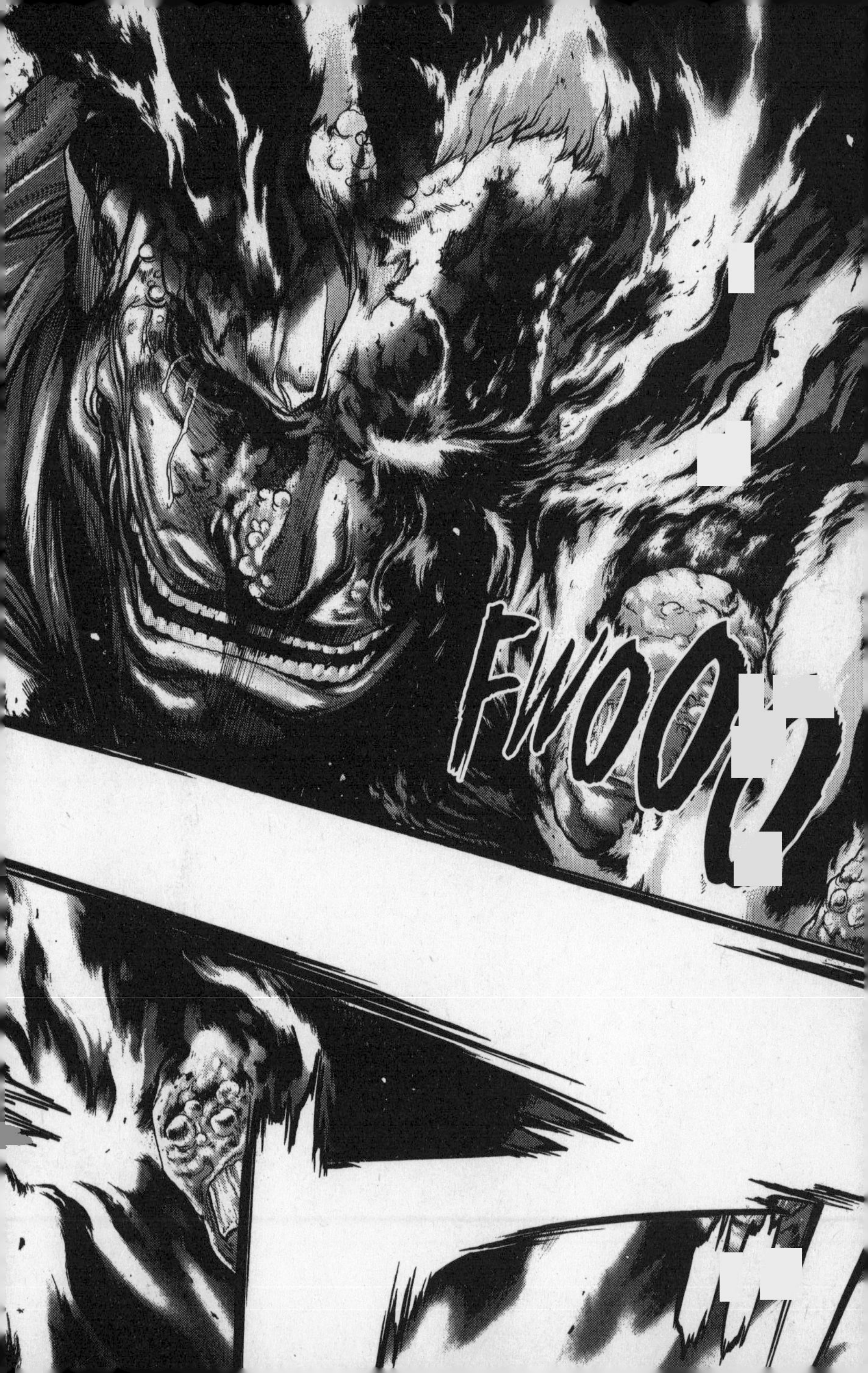
FWOOO

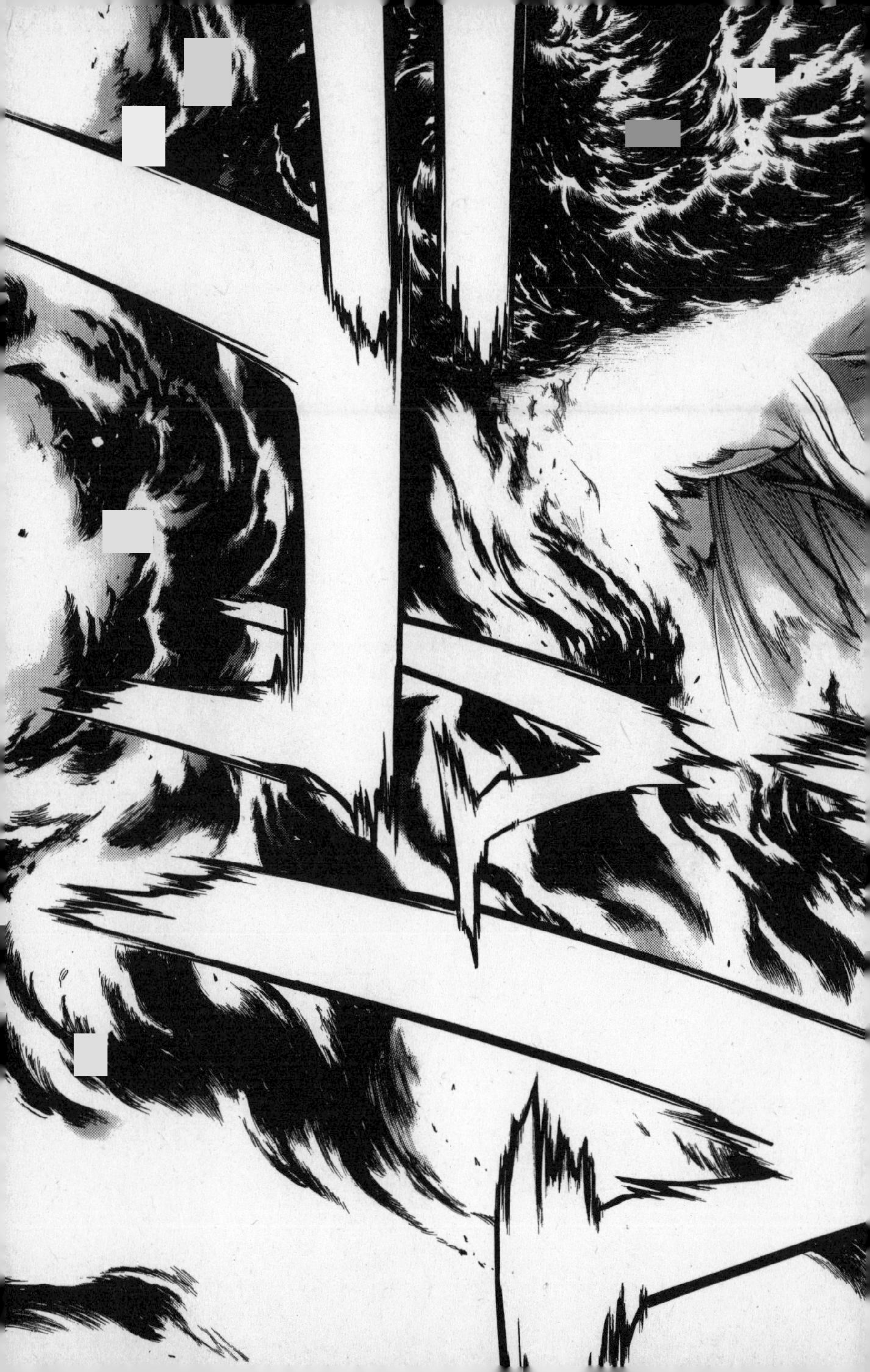

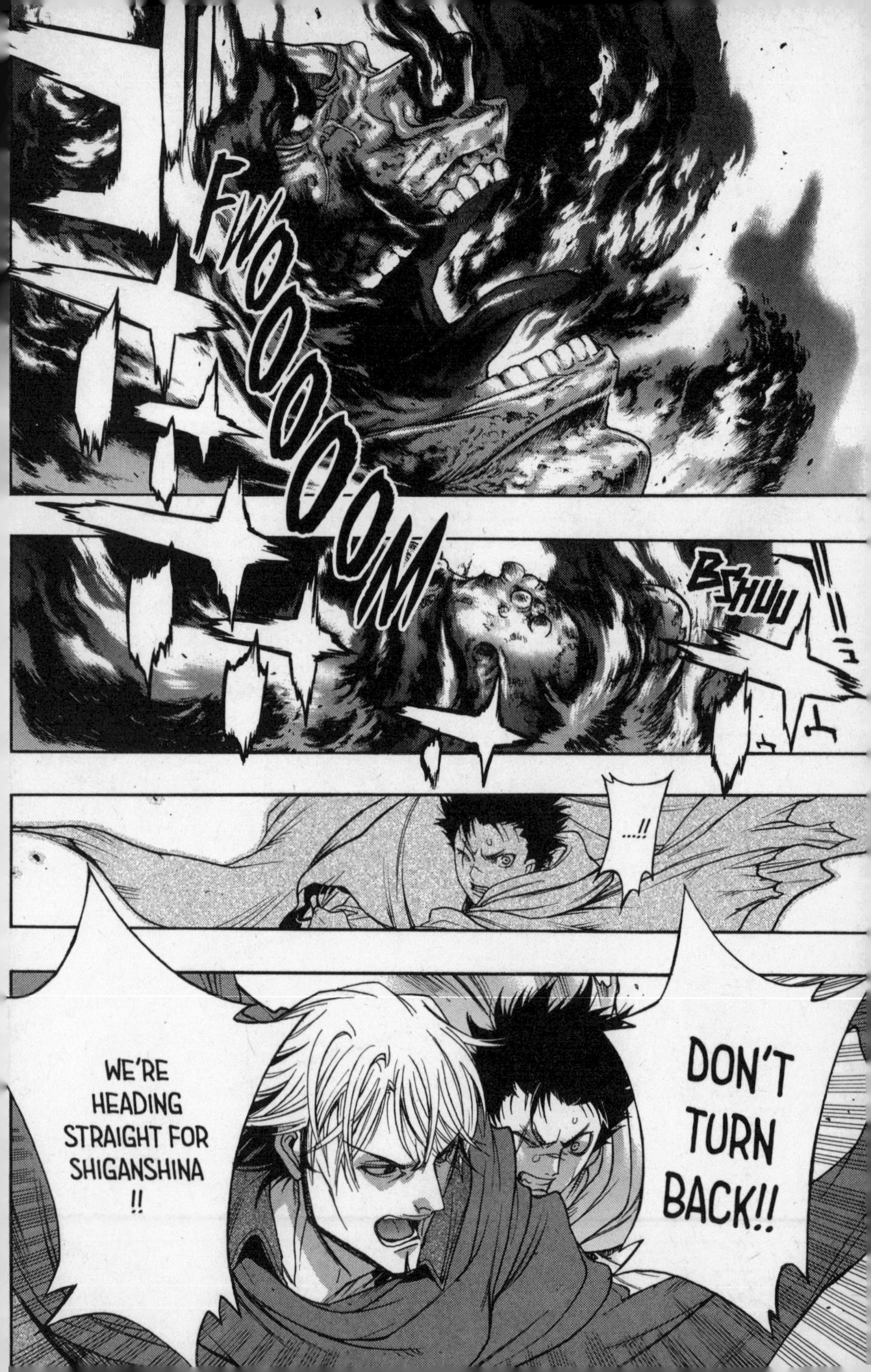
FWOOOOOOOM
BSHUU
...!!
DON'T TURN BACK!!
WE'RE HEADING STRAIGHT FOR SHIGANSHINA!!

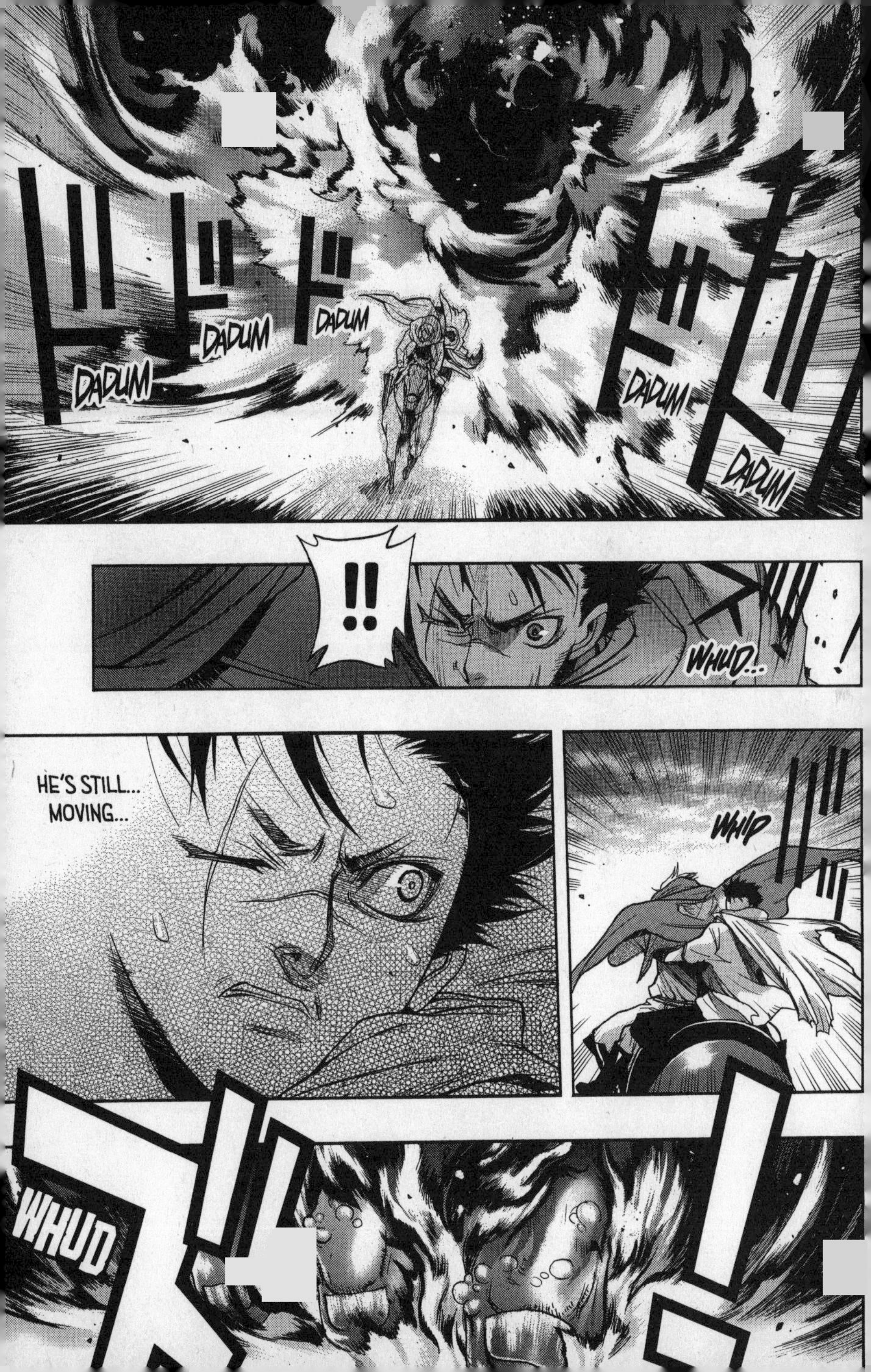
DADUM
DADUM
DADUM
DADUM
DADUM
!!
WHUD...
WHIP
HE'S STILL...
MOVING...
WHUD

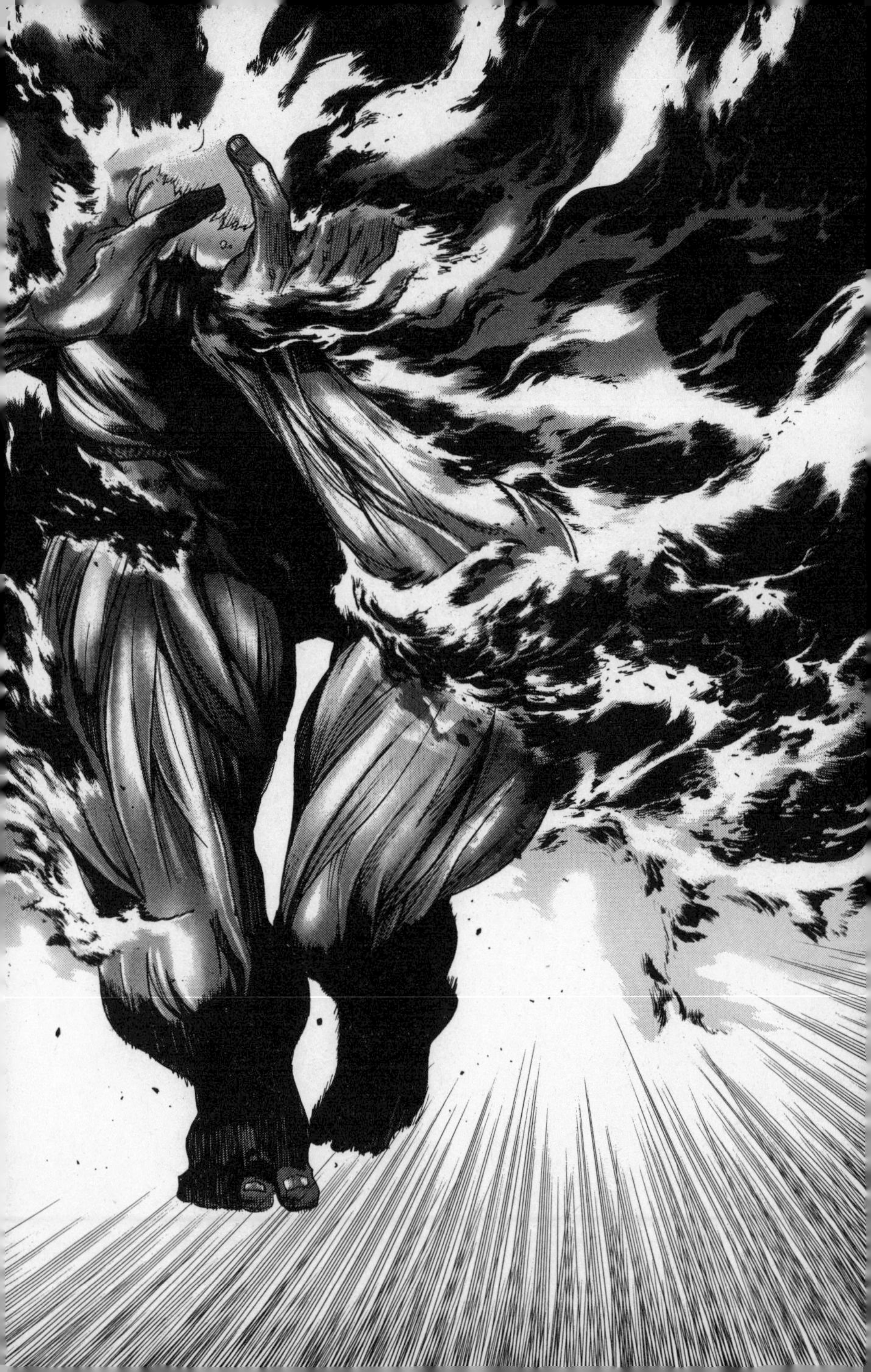

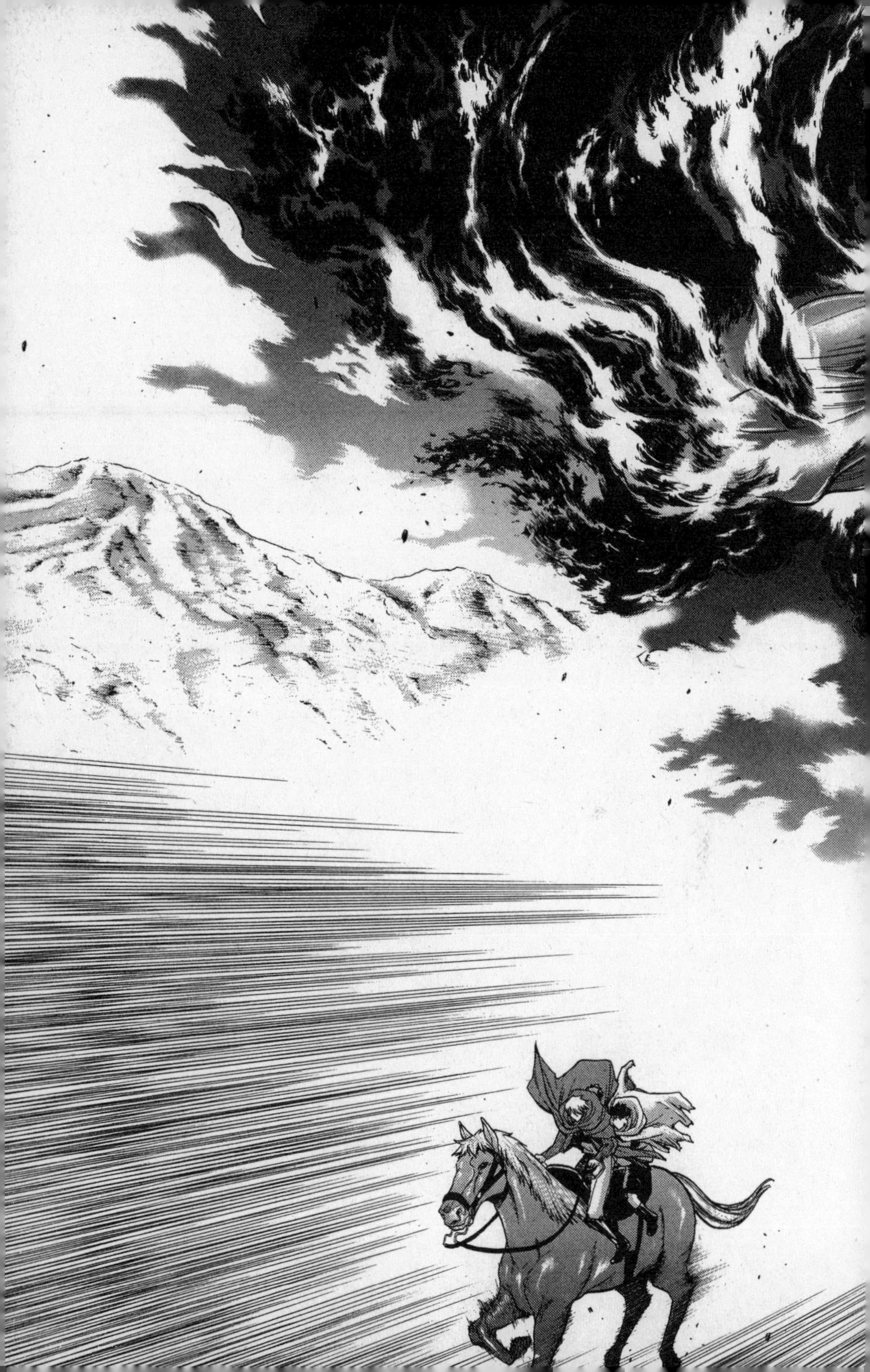

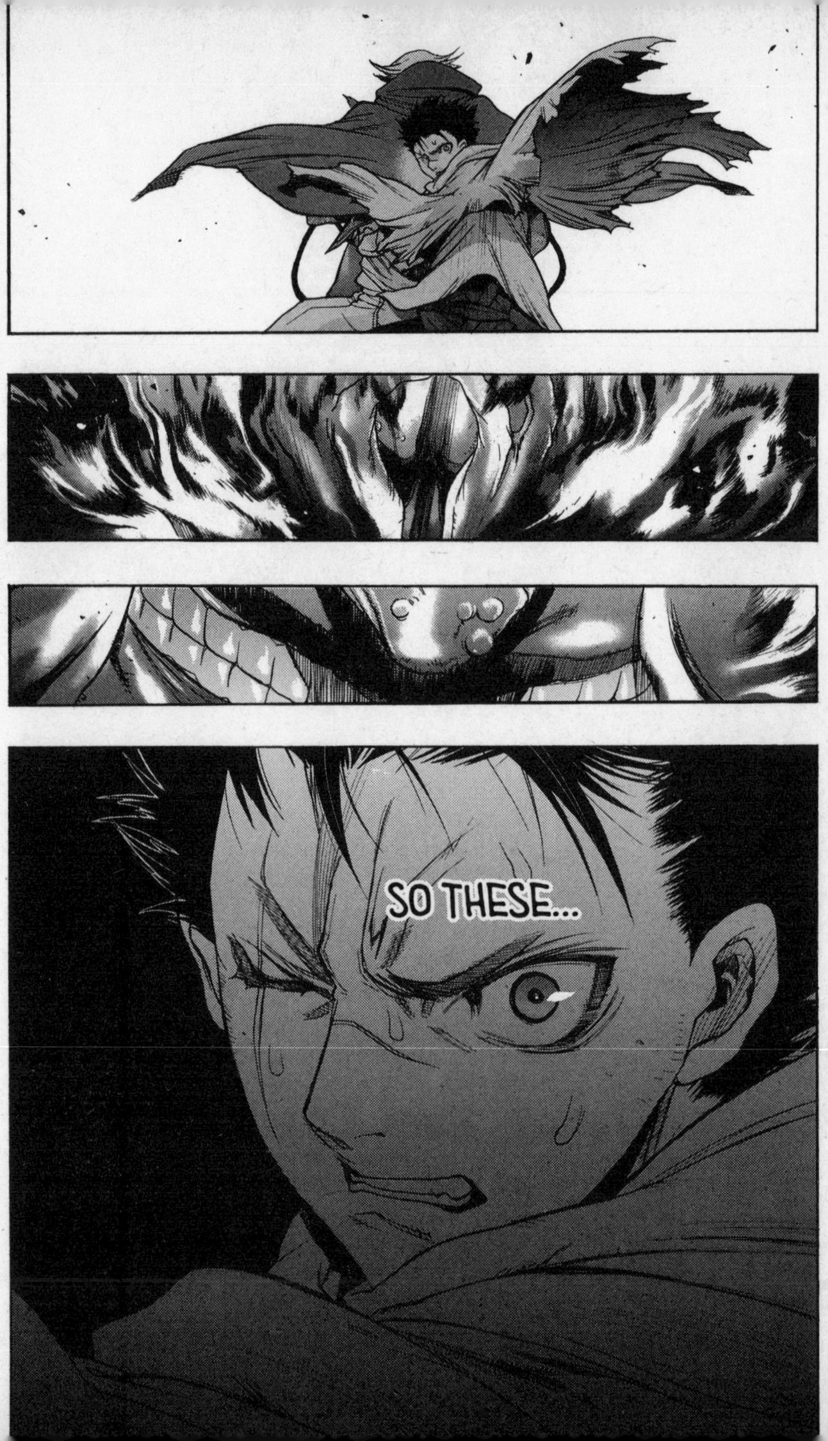
SO THESE...

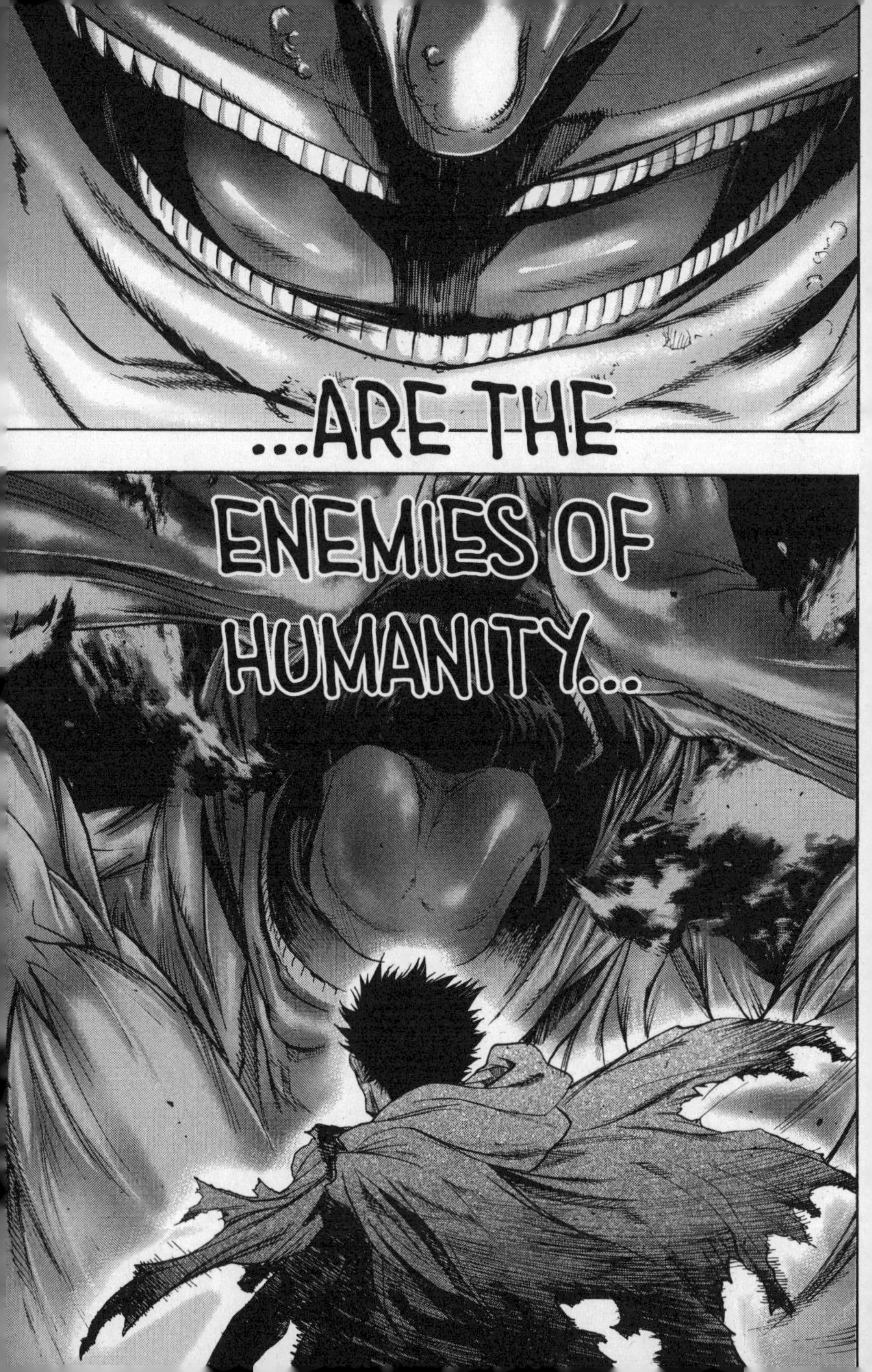
...ARE THE
ENEMIES OF
HUMANITY...

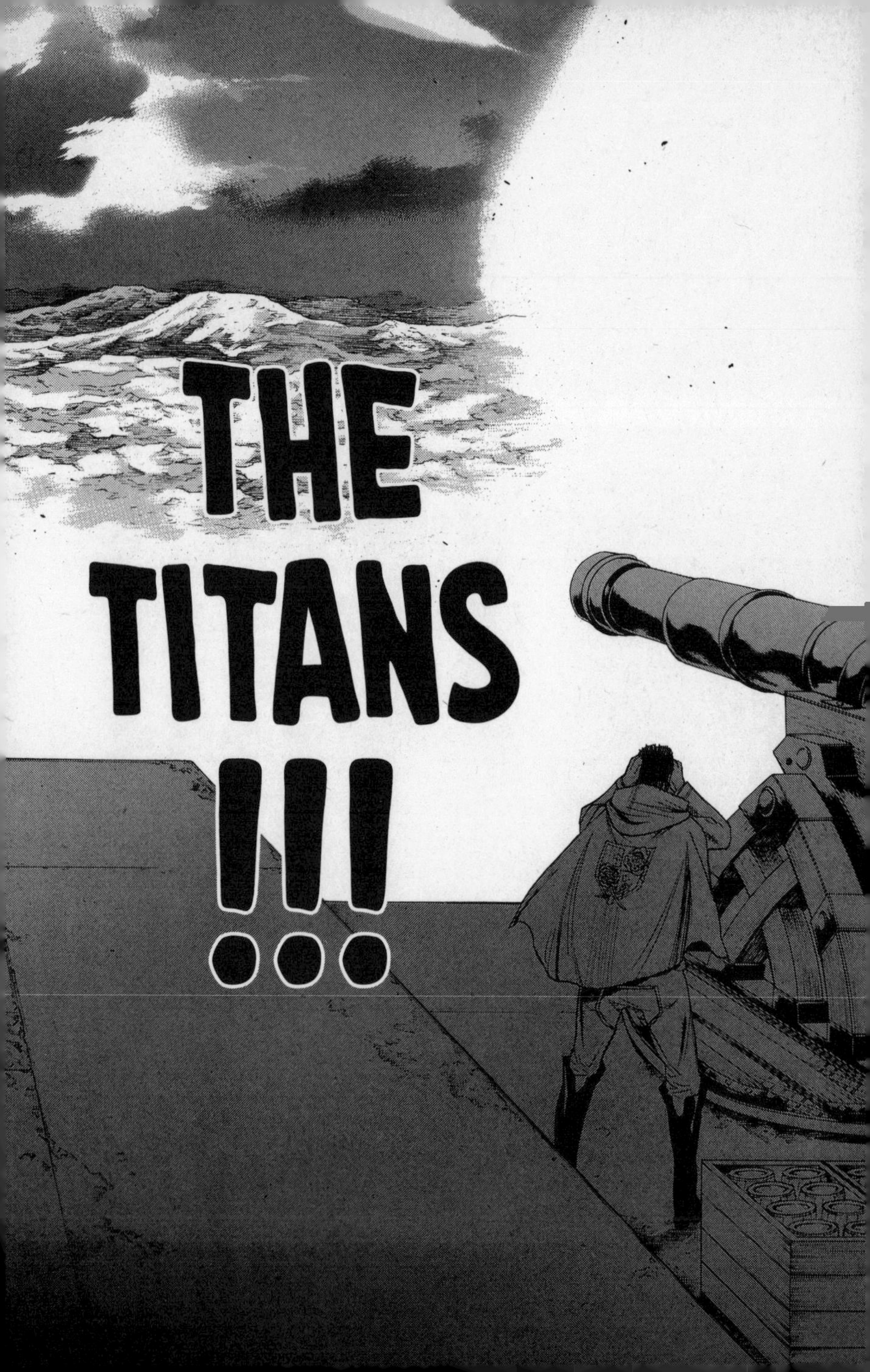
THE TITANS !!!...

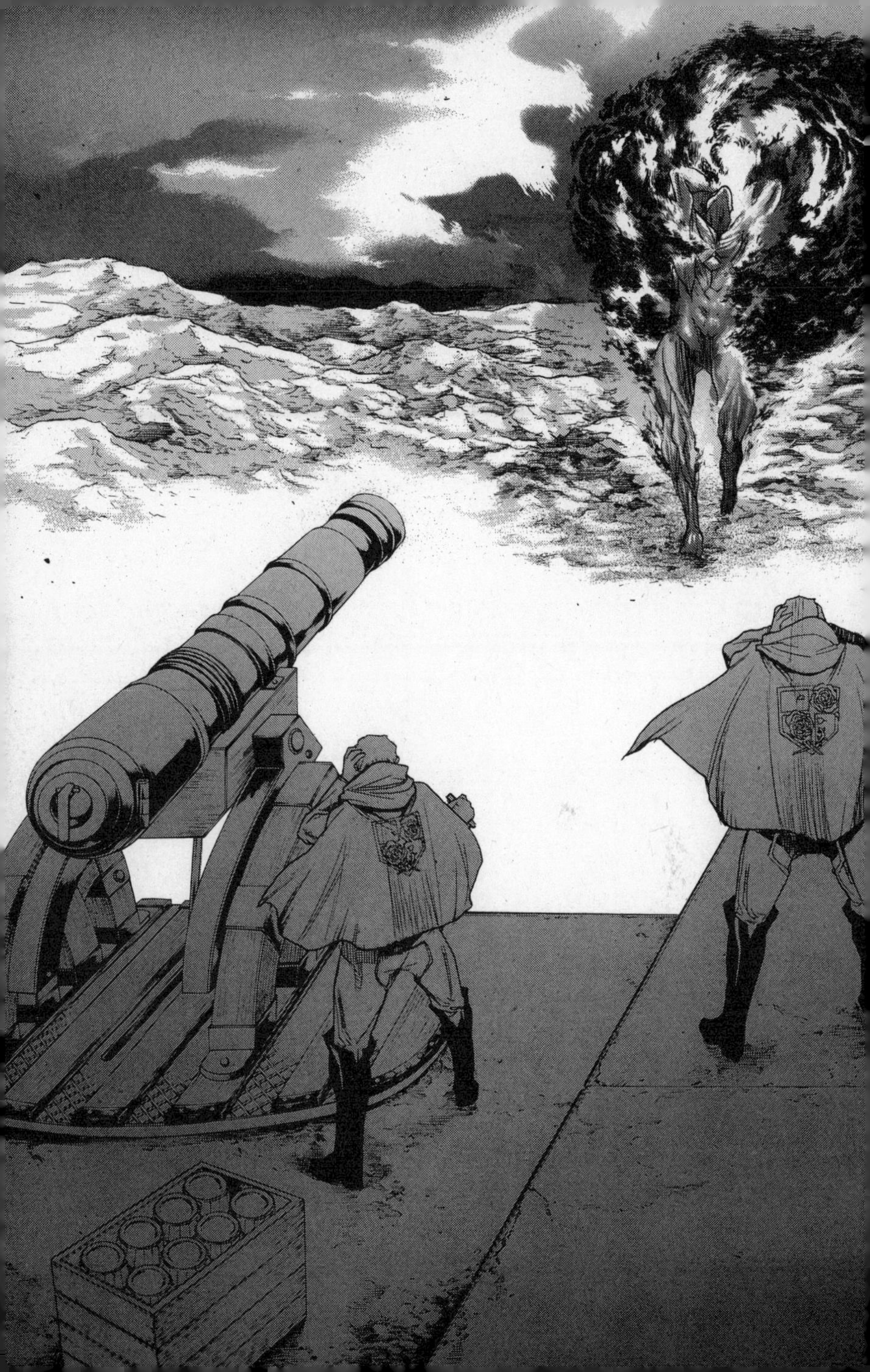

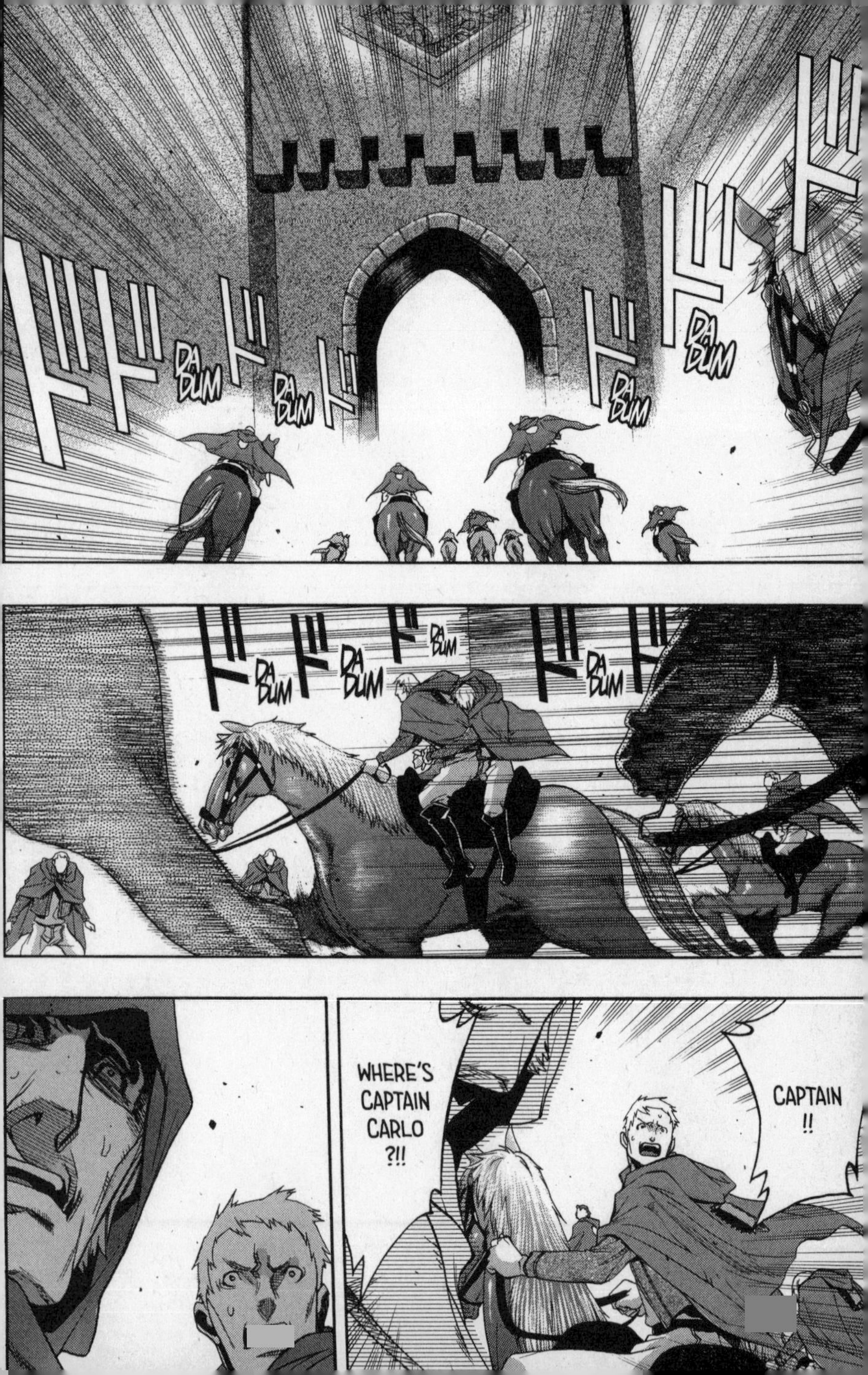
DA DUM
DA DUM
DA DUM
DA DUM
DA DUM
DA DUM
DA DUM
DA DUM
CAPTAIN !!
WHERE'S CAPTAIN CARLO ?!!

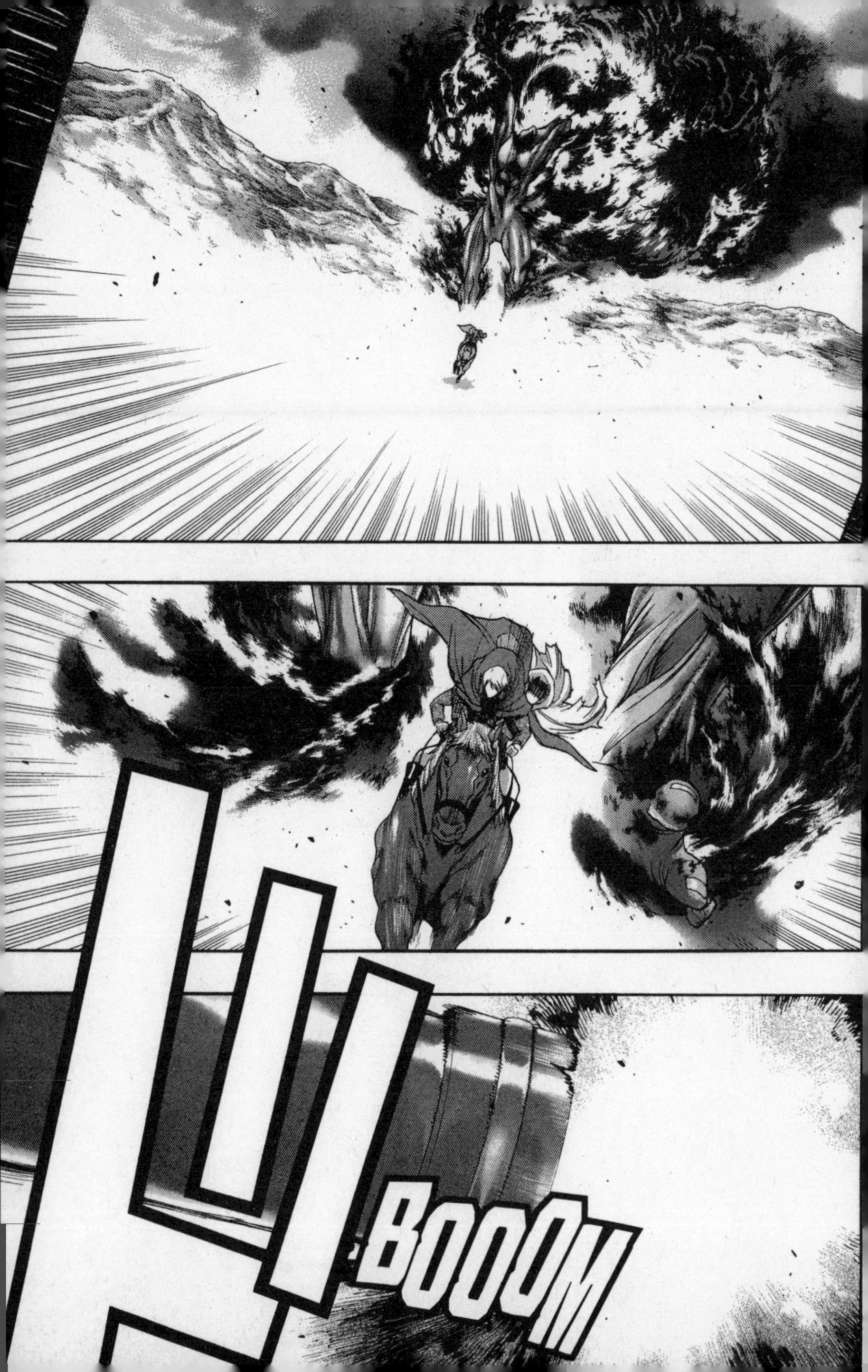
BOOOM

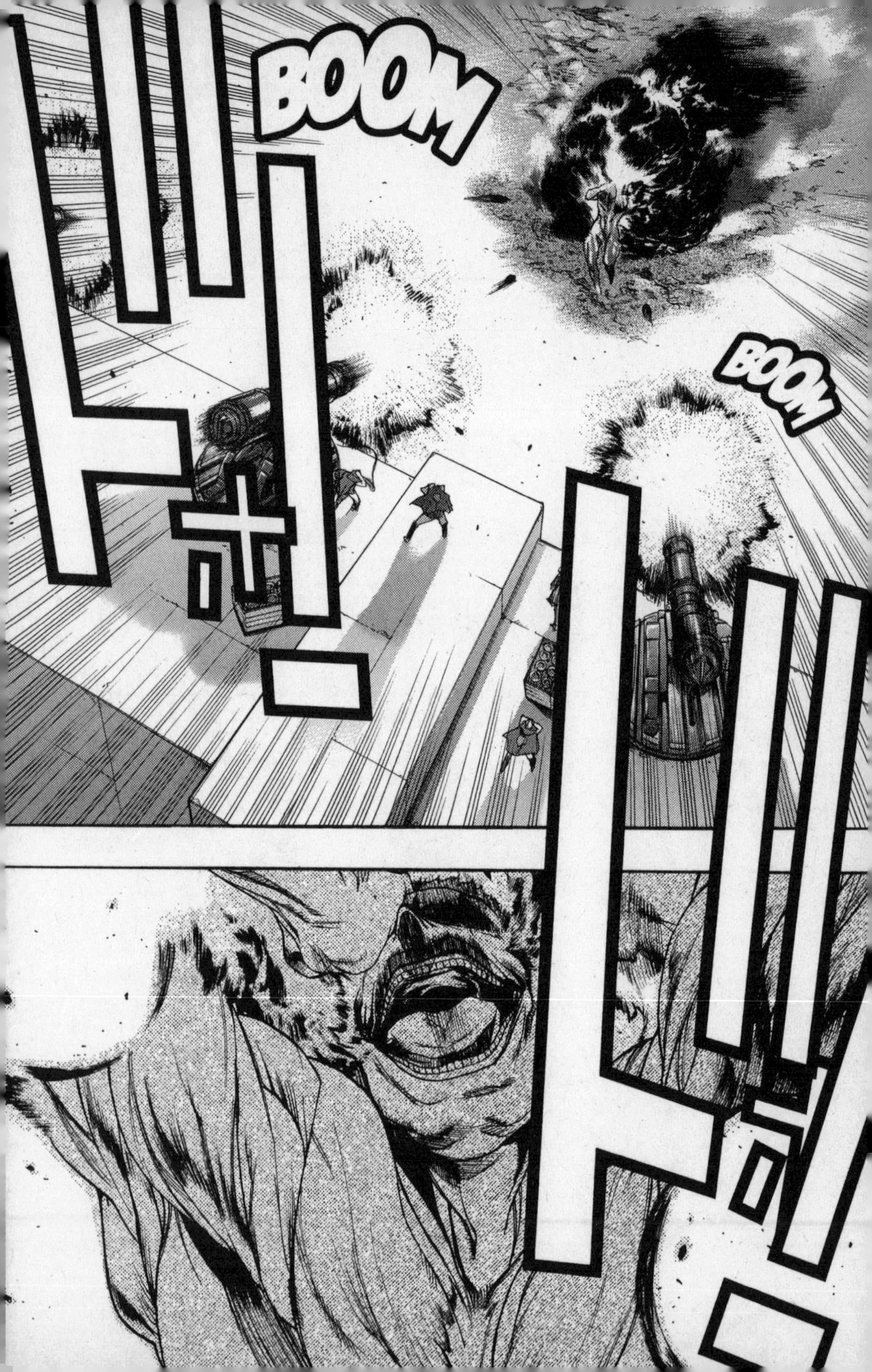
BOOM
BOOM

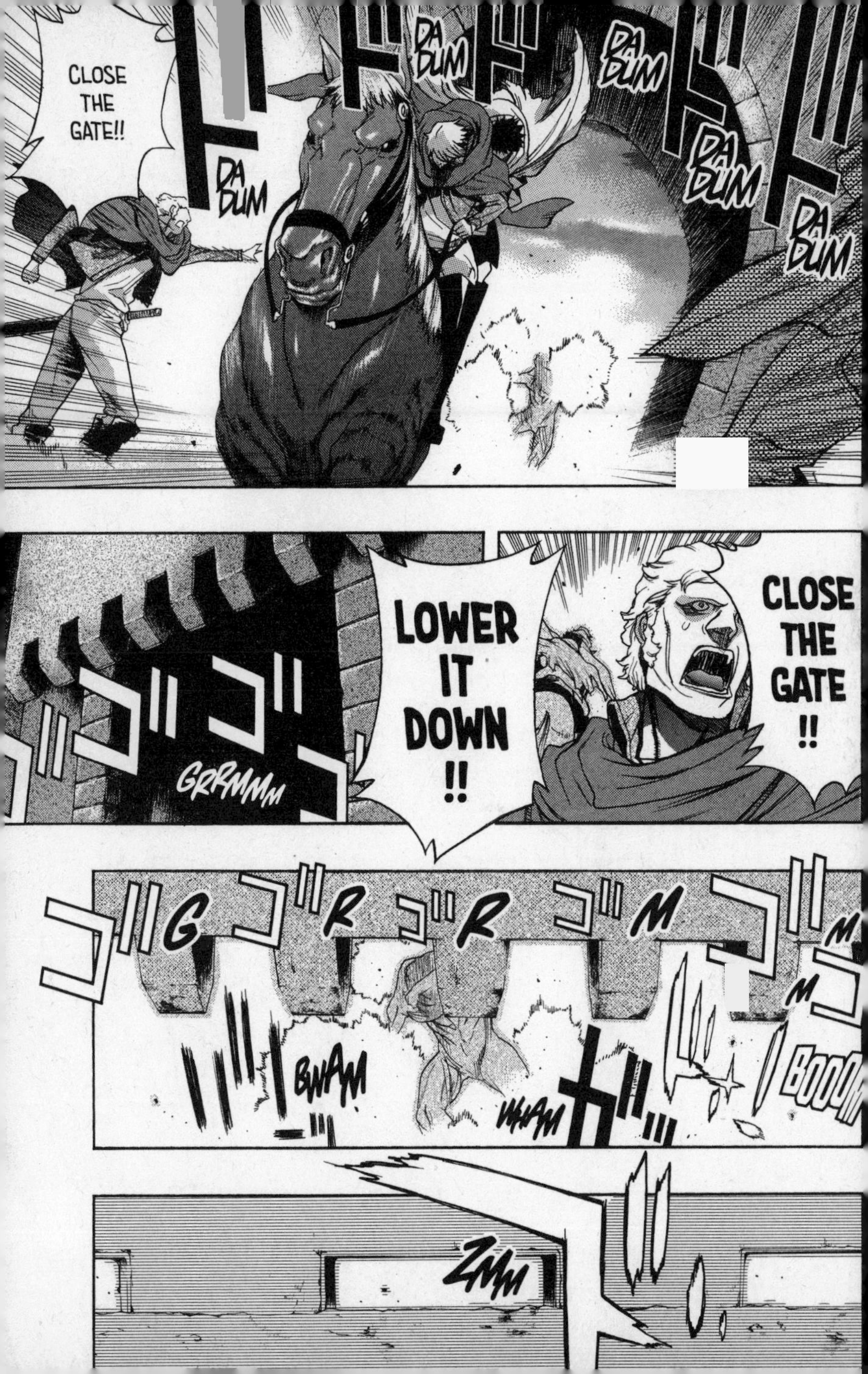
DA DUM
DA DUM
DA DUM
DA DUM
DA DUM
CLOSE THE GATE!!
DA DUM
CLOSE THE GATE !!
LOWER IT DOWN !!
GRRMMM
MM
M
R
R
G
BOOM
WHAM
BWAM
ZMM

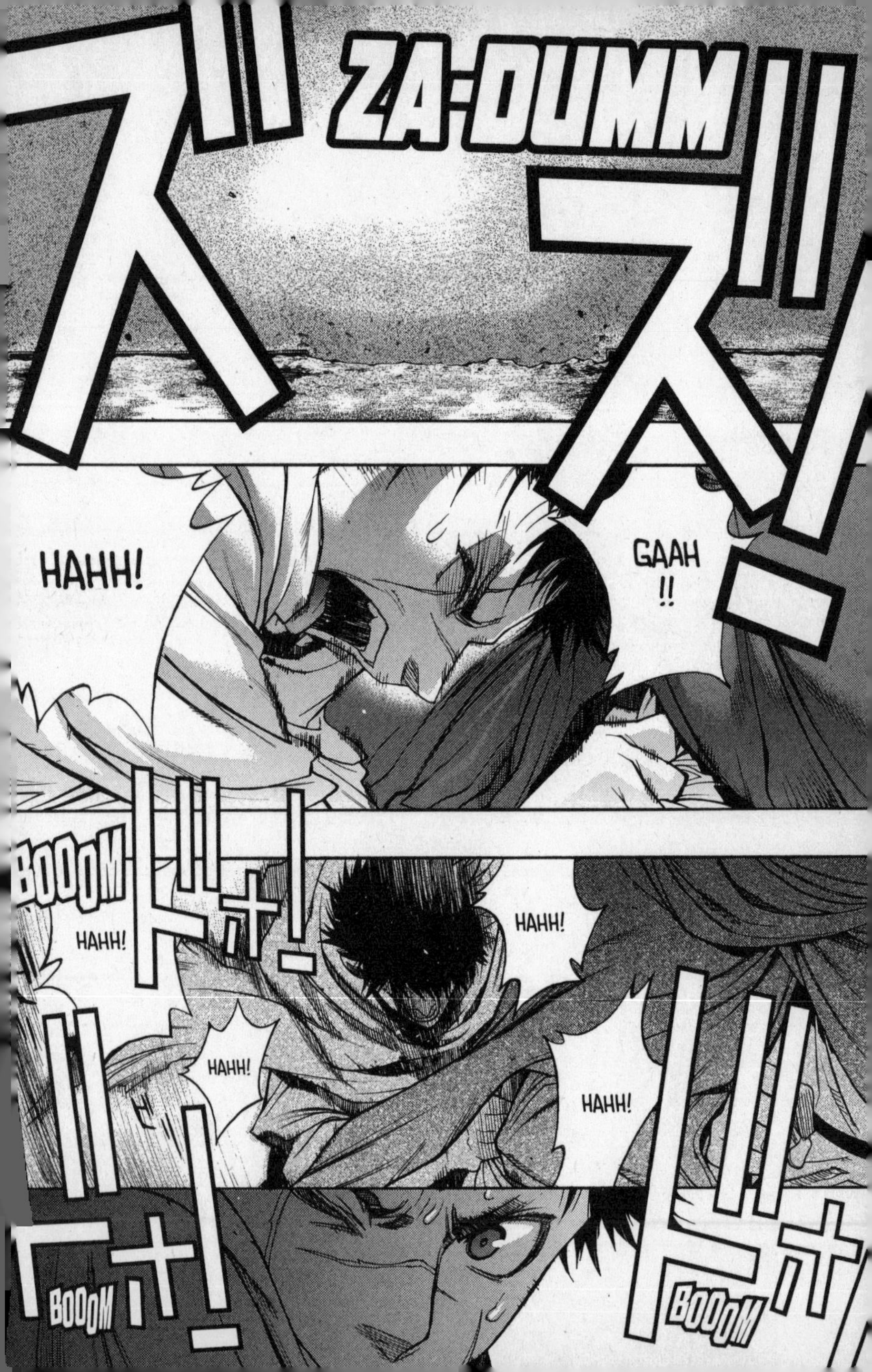
ZA-DUMM!!
GAAH!!
HAHH!
HAHH!
HAHH!
HAHH!
HAHH!
BOOOM
BOOOM
BOOOM

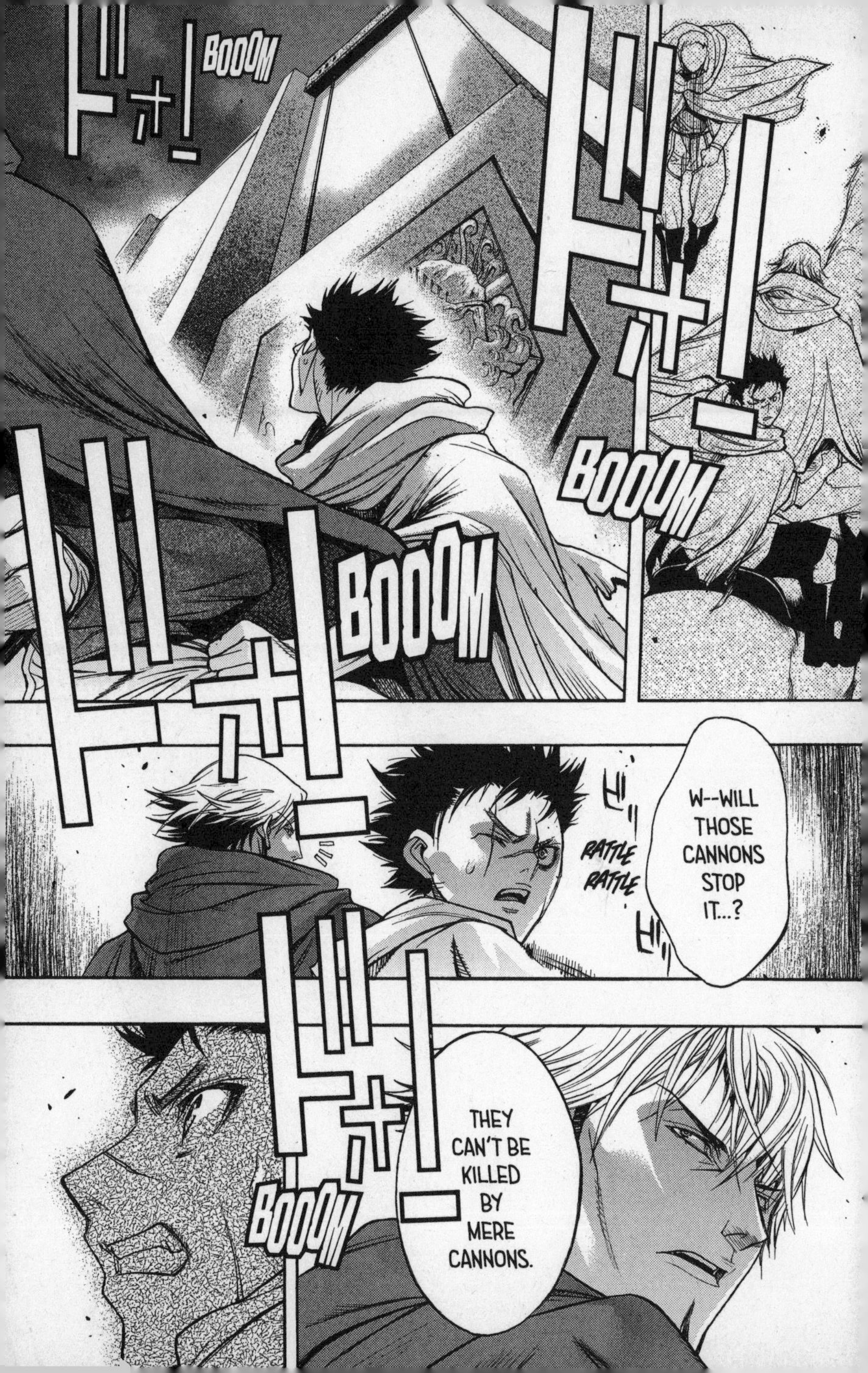
BOOOM
BOOOM
BOOOM
W--WILL THOSE CANNONS STOP IT...?
RATTLE RATTLE
THEY CAN'T BE KILLED BY MERE CANNONS.
BOOOM

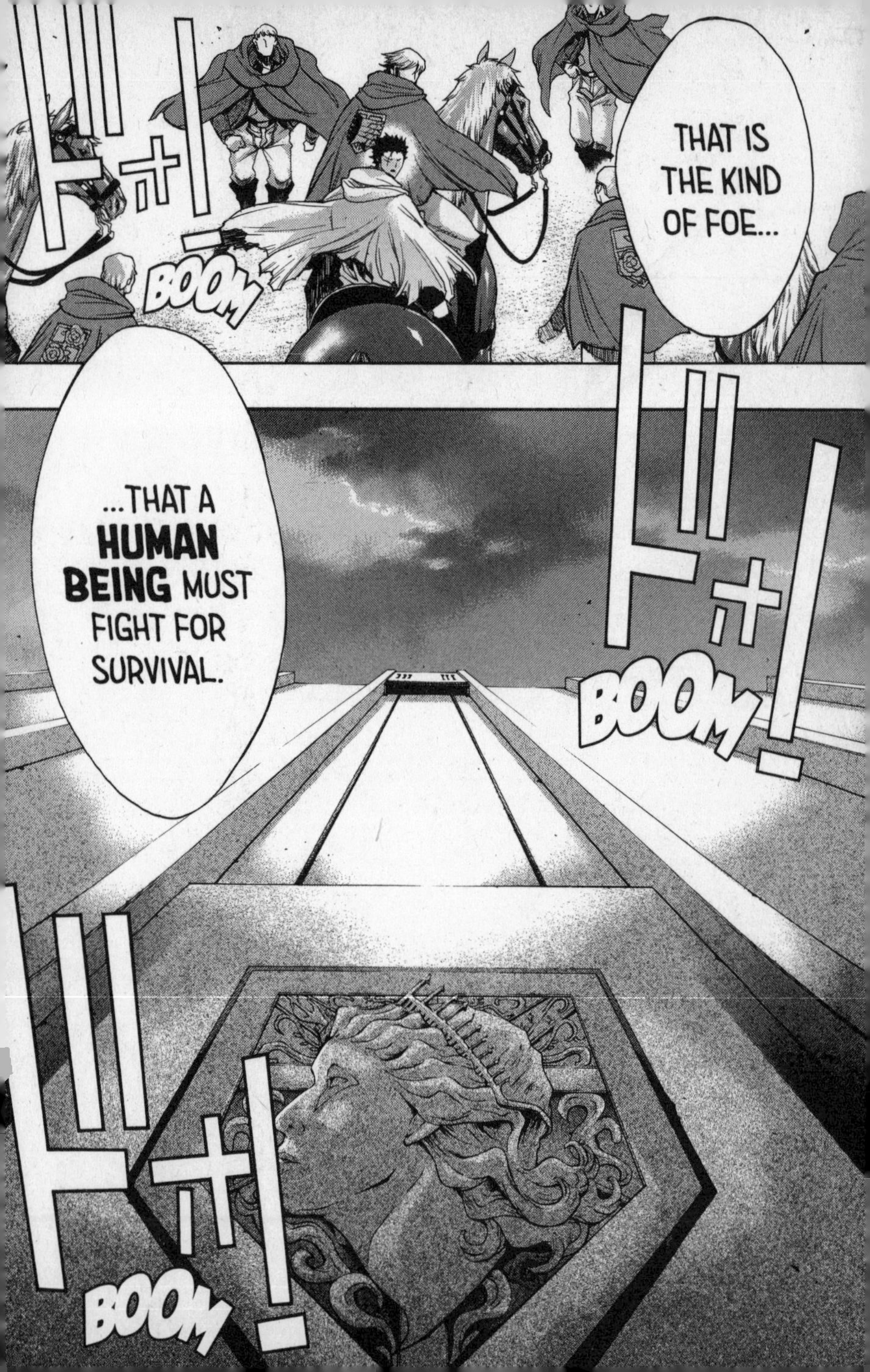
THAT IS THE KIND OF FOE...
BOOM
...THAT A **HUMAN BEING** MUST FIGHT FOR SURVIVAL.
BOOM!
BOOM!

Chapter 9: The Crimson Tower END

ATTACK on TITAN

BEFORE THE FALL

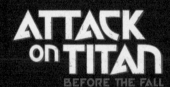

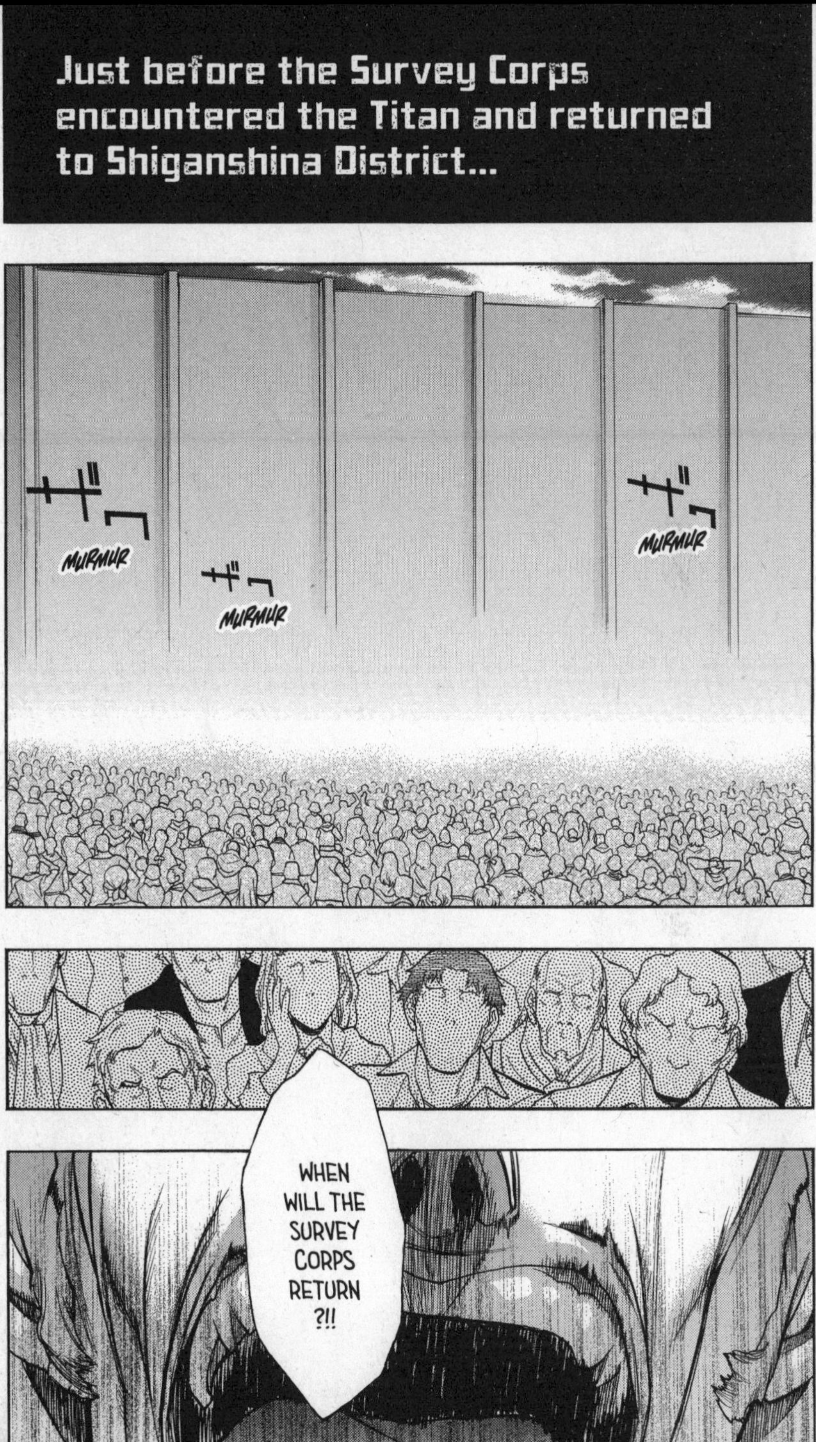
Just before the Survey Corps encountered the Titan and returned to Shiganshina District...
MURMUR
MURMUR
MURMUR
WHEN WILL THE SURVEY CORPS RETURN ?!!

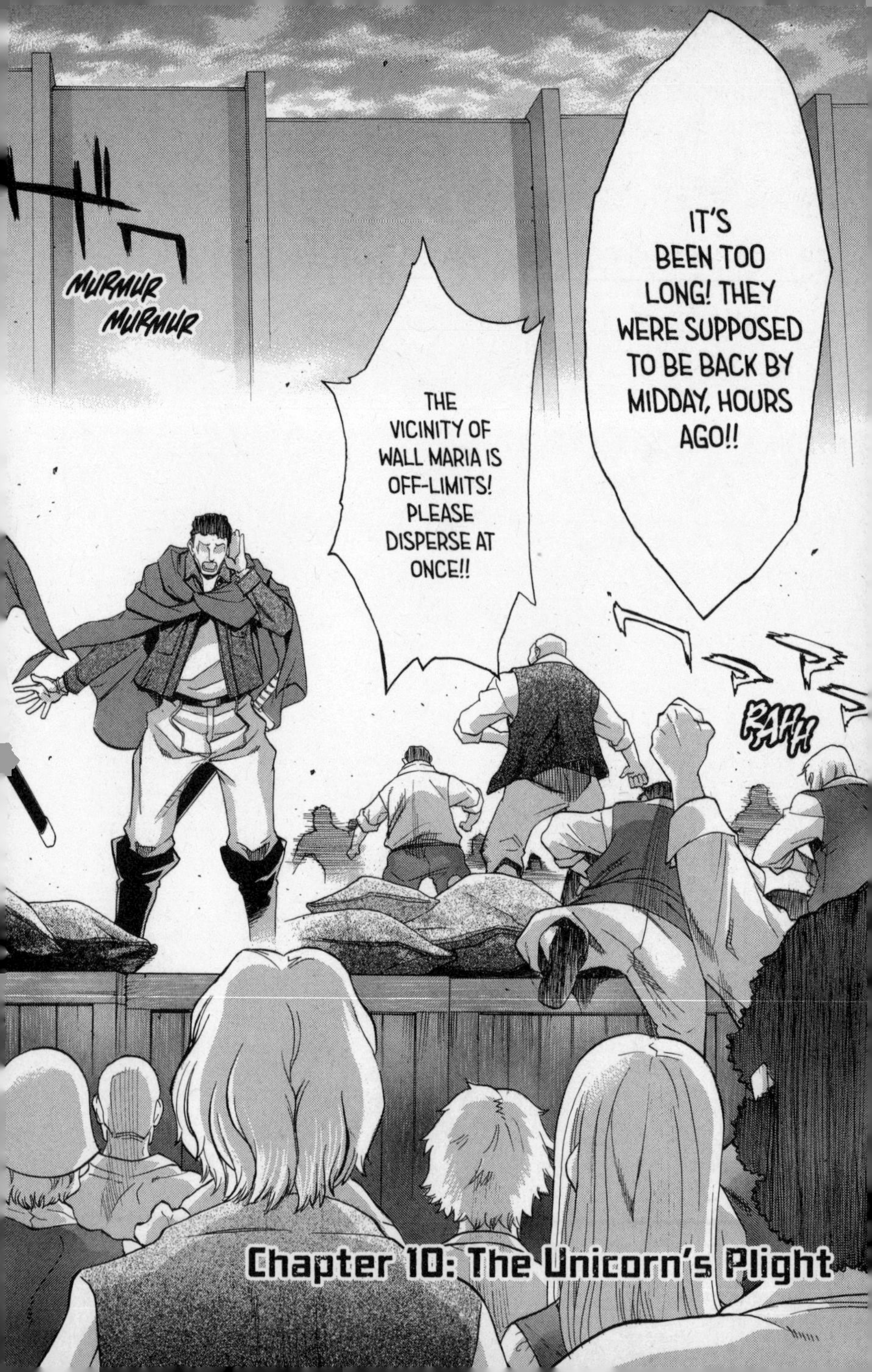
IT'S BEEN TOO LONG! THEY WERE SUPPOSED TO BE BACK BY MIDDAY, HOURS AGO!!
THE VICINITY OF WALL MARIA IS OFF-LIMITS! PLEASE DISPERSE AT ONCE!!
MURMUR MURMUR
RAHH
Chapter 10: The Unicorn's Plight

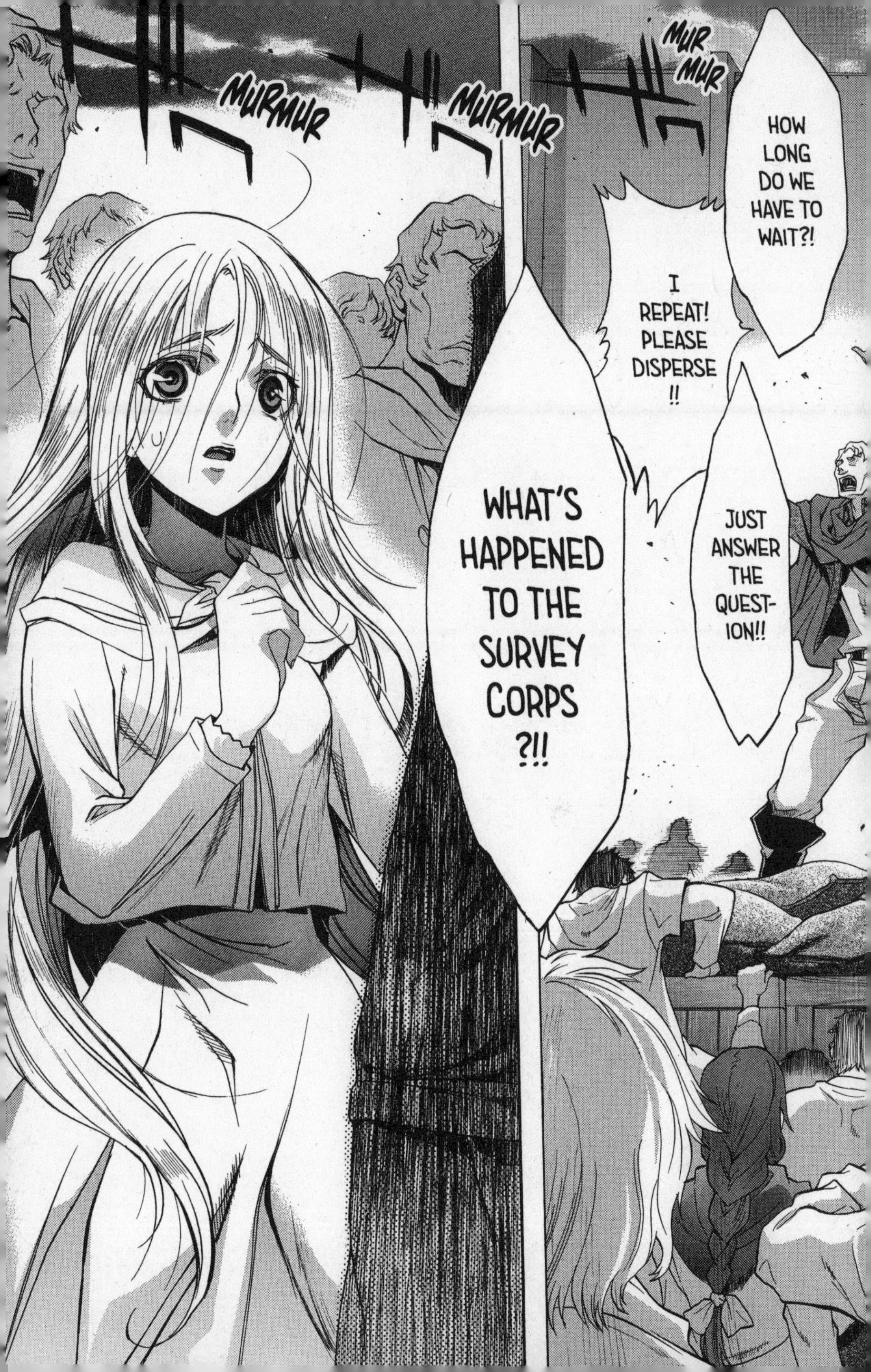
MUR MUR
HOW LONG DO WE HAVE TO WAIT?!
I REPEAT! PLEASE DISPERSE!!
JUST ANSWER THE QUEST-ION!!
WHAT'S HAPPENED TO THE SURVEY CORPS?!!
MURMUR
MURMUR

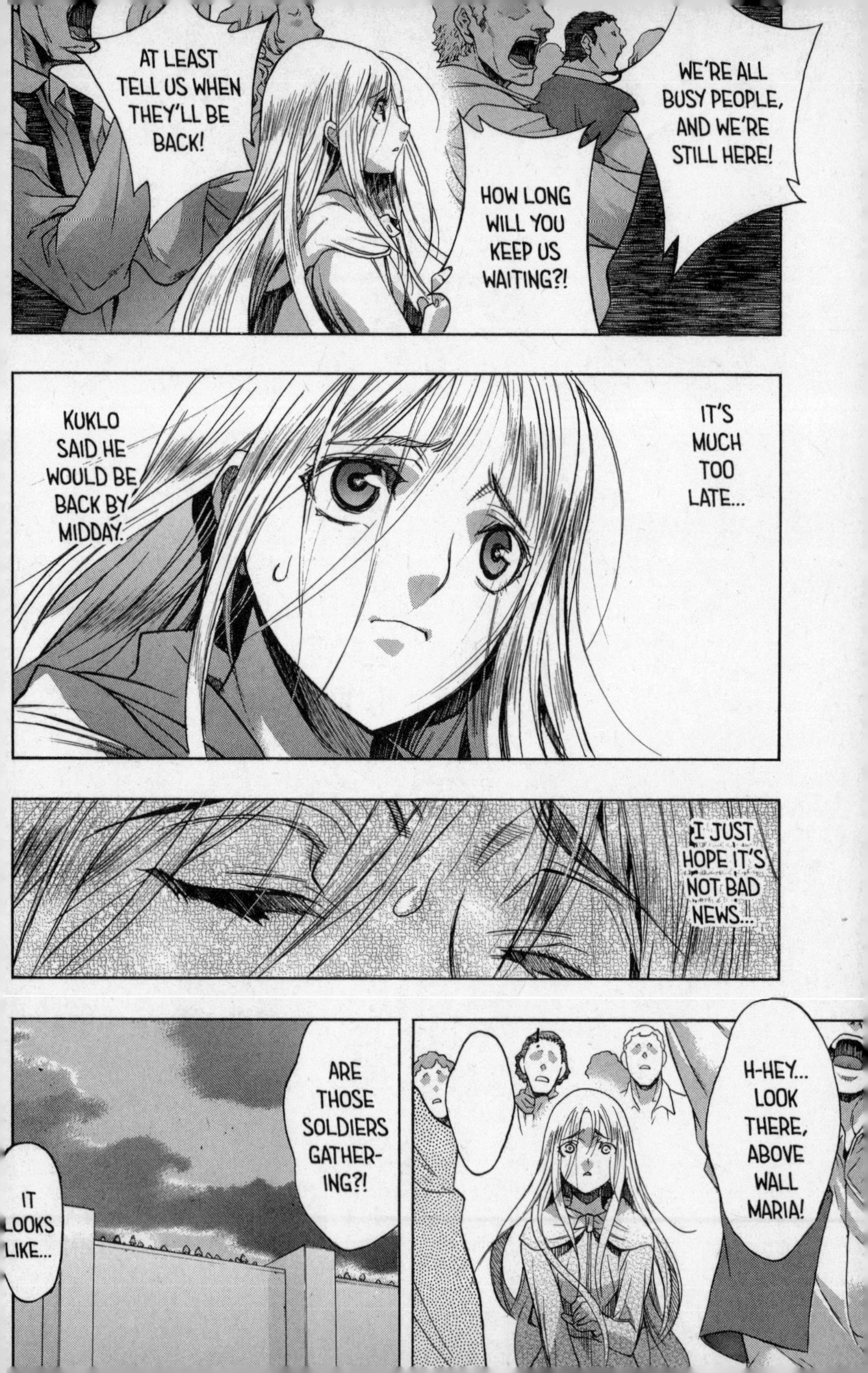
WE'RE ALL BUSY PEOPLE, AND WE'RE STILL HERE!
HOW LONG WILL YOU KEEP US WAITING?!
AT LEAST TELL US WHEN THEY'LL BE BACK!
IT'S MUCH TOO LATE...
KUKLO SAID HE WOULD BE BACK BY MIDDAY.
I JUST HOPE IT'S NOT BAD NEWS...
H-HEY... LOOK THERE, ABOVE WALL MARIA!
ARE THOSE SOLDIERS GATHER-ING?!
IT LOOKS LIKE...

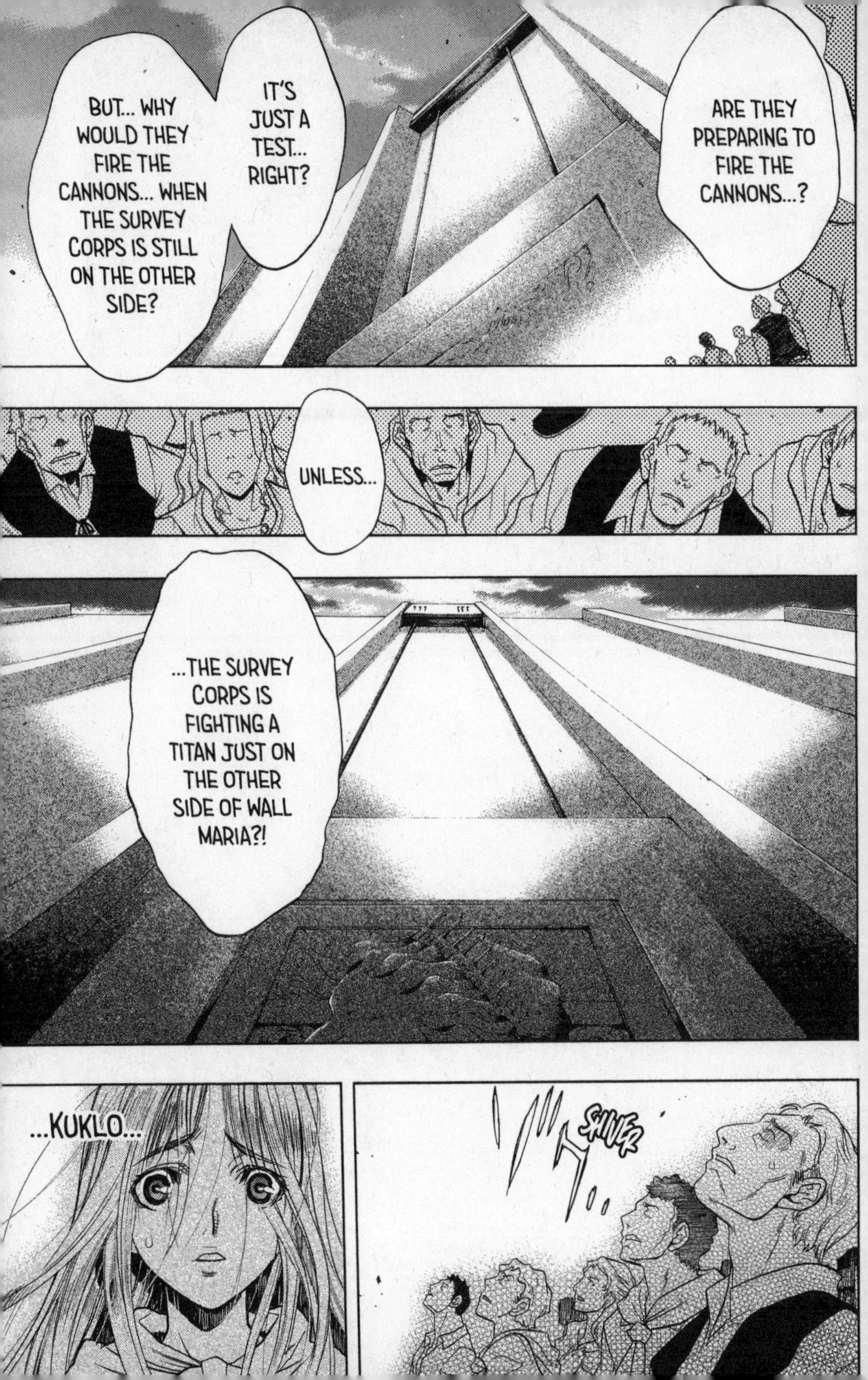
ARE THEY PREPARING TO FIRE THE CANNONS...?
IT'S JUST A TEST... RIGHT?
BUT... WHY WOULD THEY FIRE THE CANNONS... WHEN THE SURVEY CORPS IS STILL ON THE OTHER SIDE?
UNLESS...
...THE SURVEY CORPS IS FIGHTING A TITAN JUST ON THE OTHER SIDE OF WALL MARIA?!
SHIVER
...KUKLO...

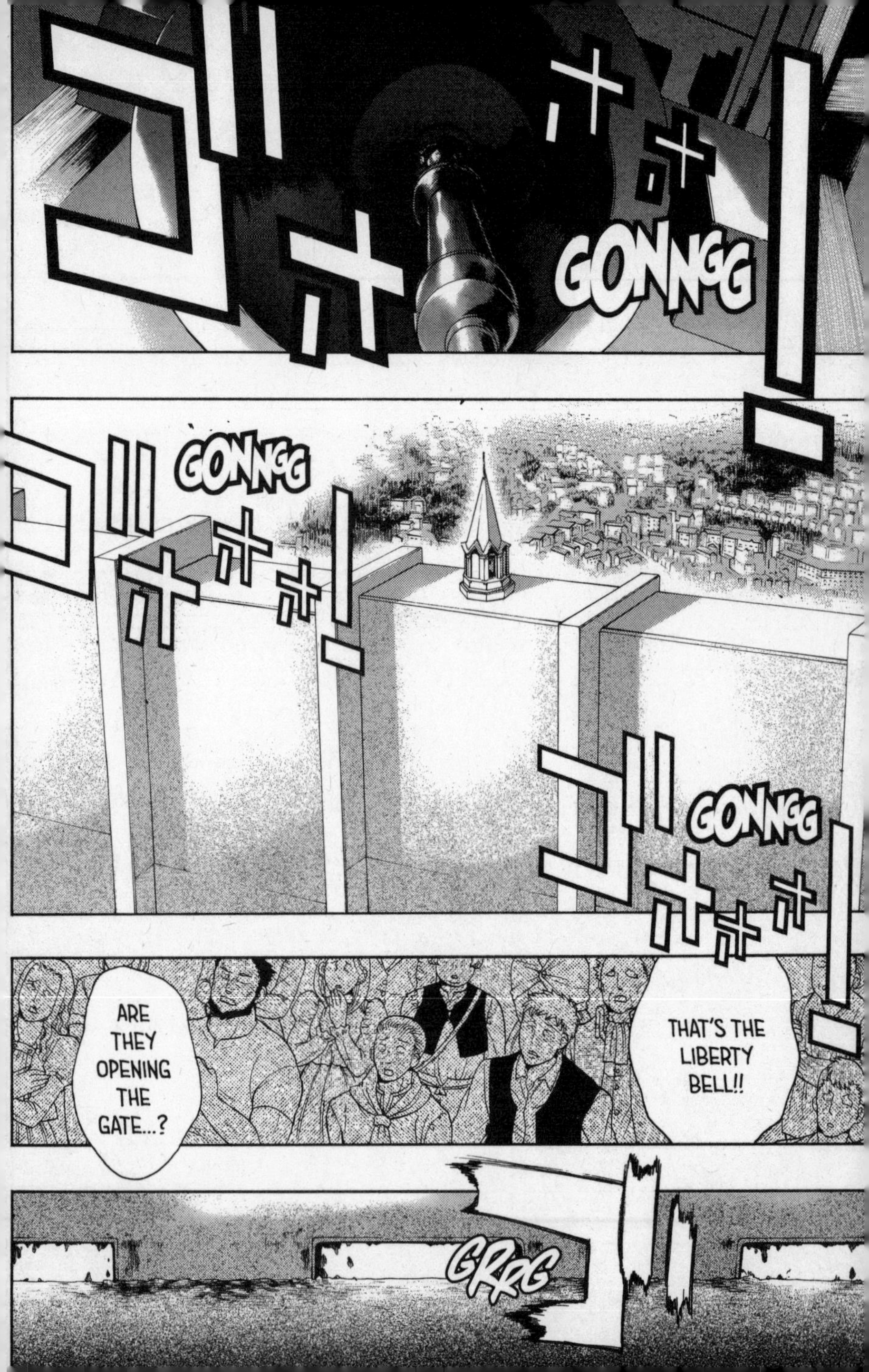
GONNGG
GONNGG
GONNGG
THAT'S THE LIBERTY BELL!!
ARE THEY OPENING THE GATE...?
GRRG

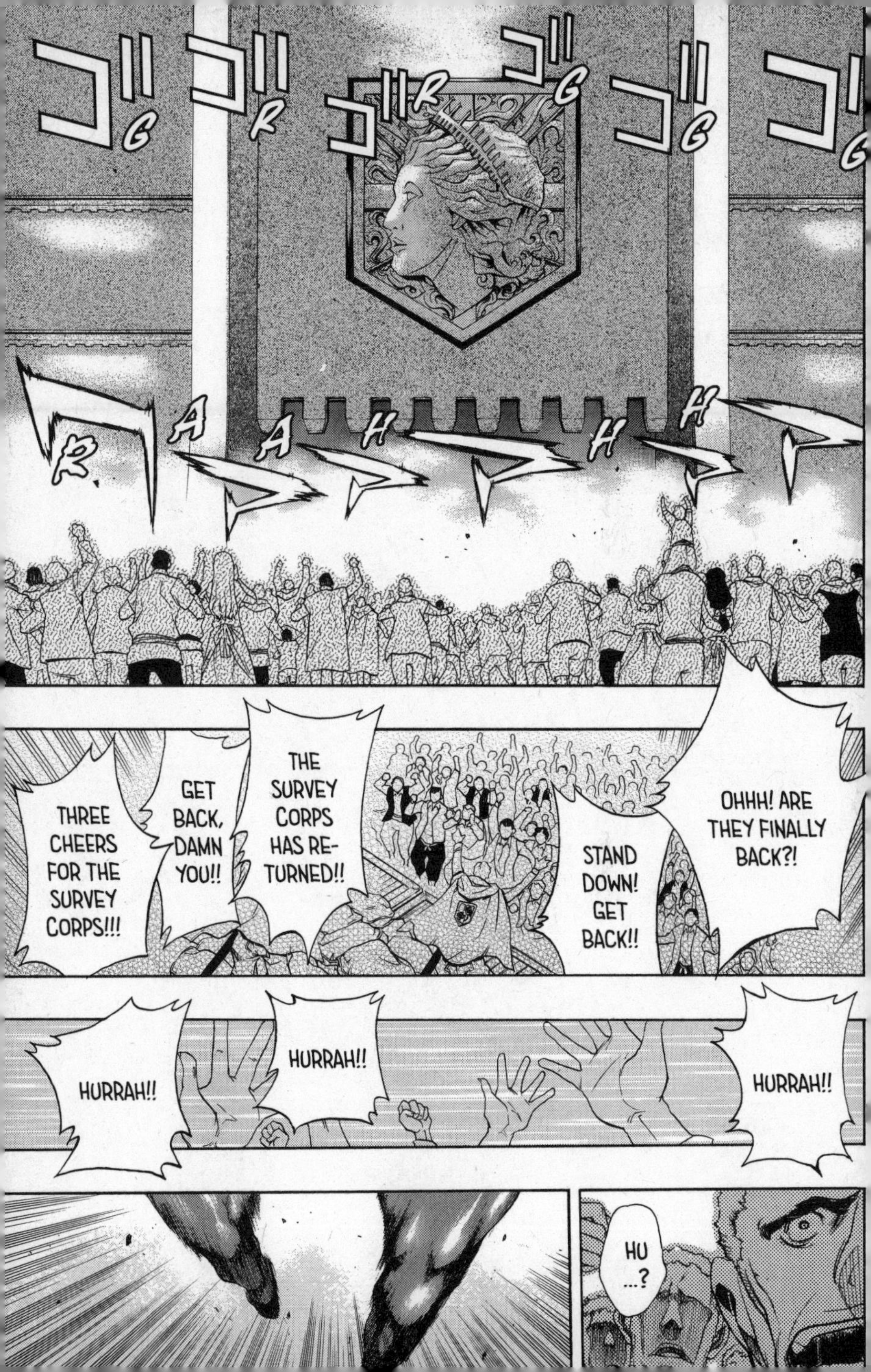
GRRGGG
RAAHHH
OHHH! ARE THEY FINALLY BACK?!
STAND DOWN! GET BACK!!
THE SURVEY CORPS HAS RE-TURNED!!
GET BACK, DAMN YOU!!
THREE CHEERS FOR THE SURVEY CORPS!!!
HURRAH!!
HURRAH!!
HURRAH!!
HU ...?

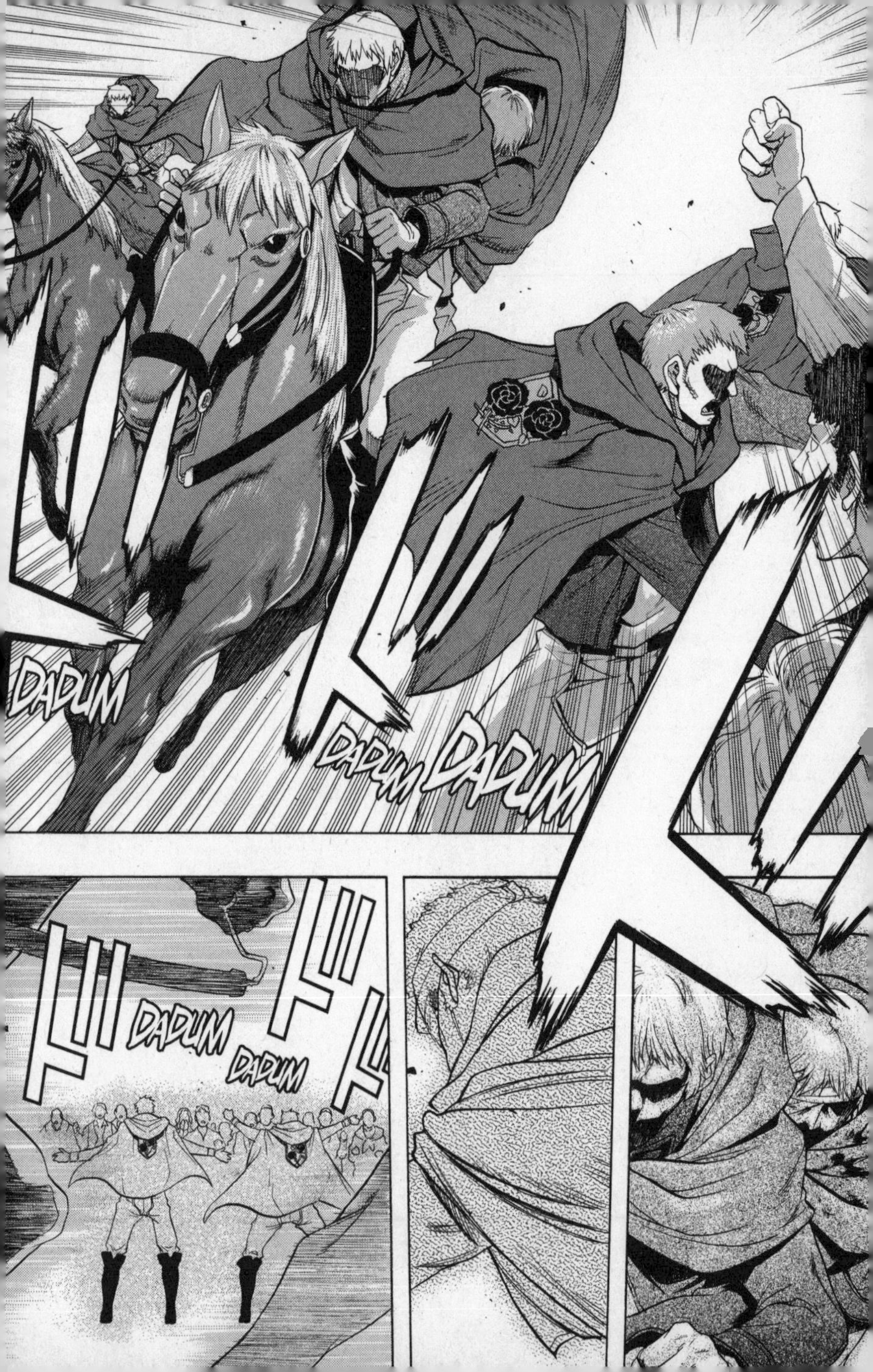
DADUM
DADUM
DADUM
DADUM
DADUM

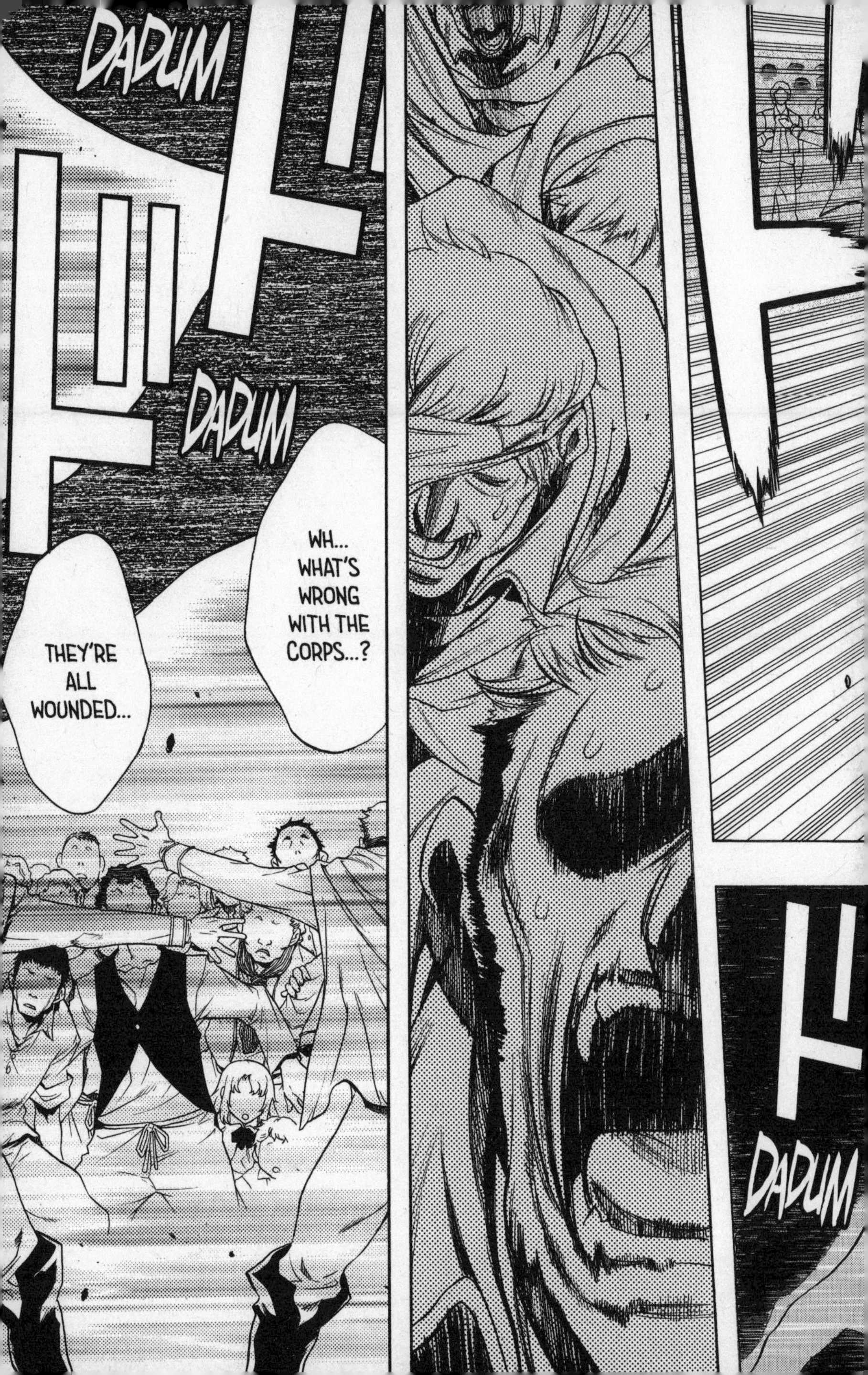
DADUM
DADUM
DADUM
WH... WHAT'S WRONG WITH THE CORPS...?
THEY'RE ALL WOUNDED...

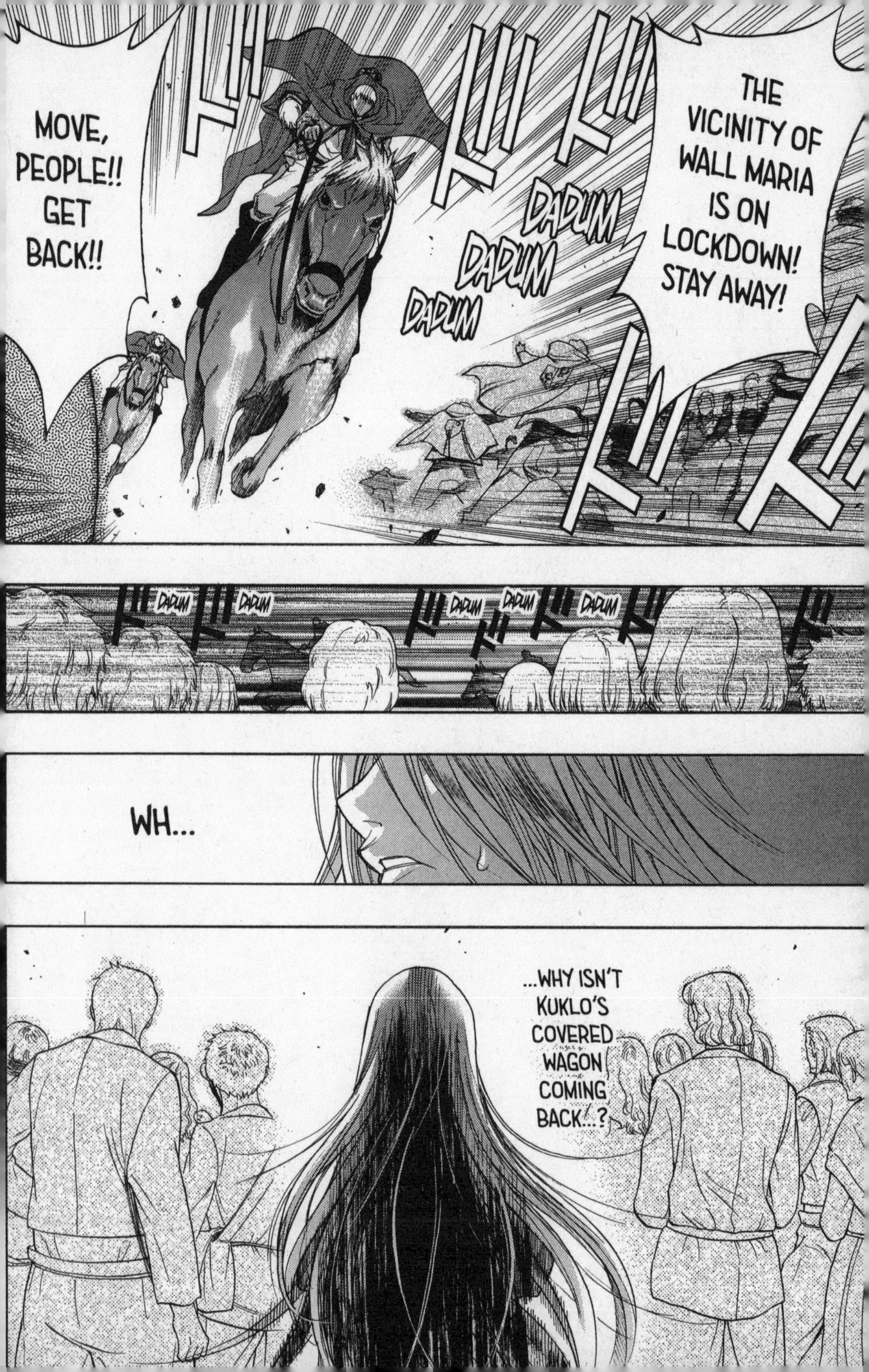
THE VICINITY OF WALL MARIA IS ON LOCKDOWN! STAY AWAY!
DADUM
DADUM
DADUM
MOVE, PEOPLE!! GET BACK!!
DADUM
DADUM
DADUM
DADUM
DADUM
WH...
...WHY ISN'T KUKLO'S COVERED WAGON COMING BACK...?

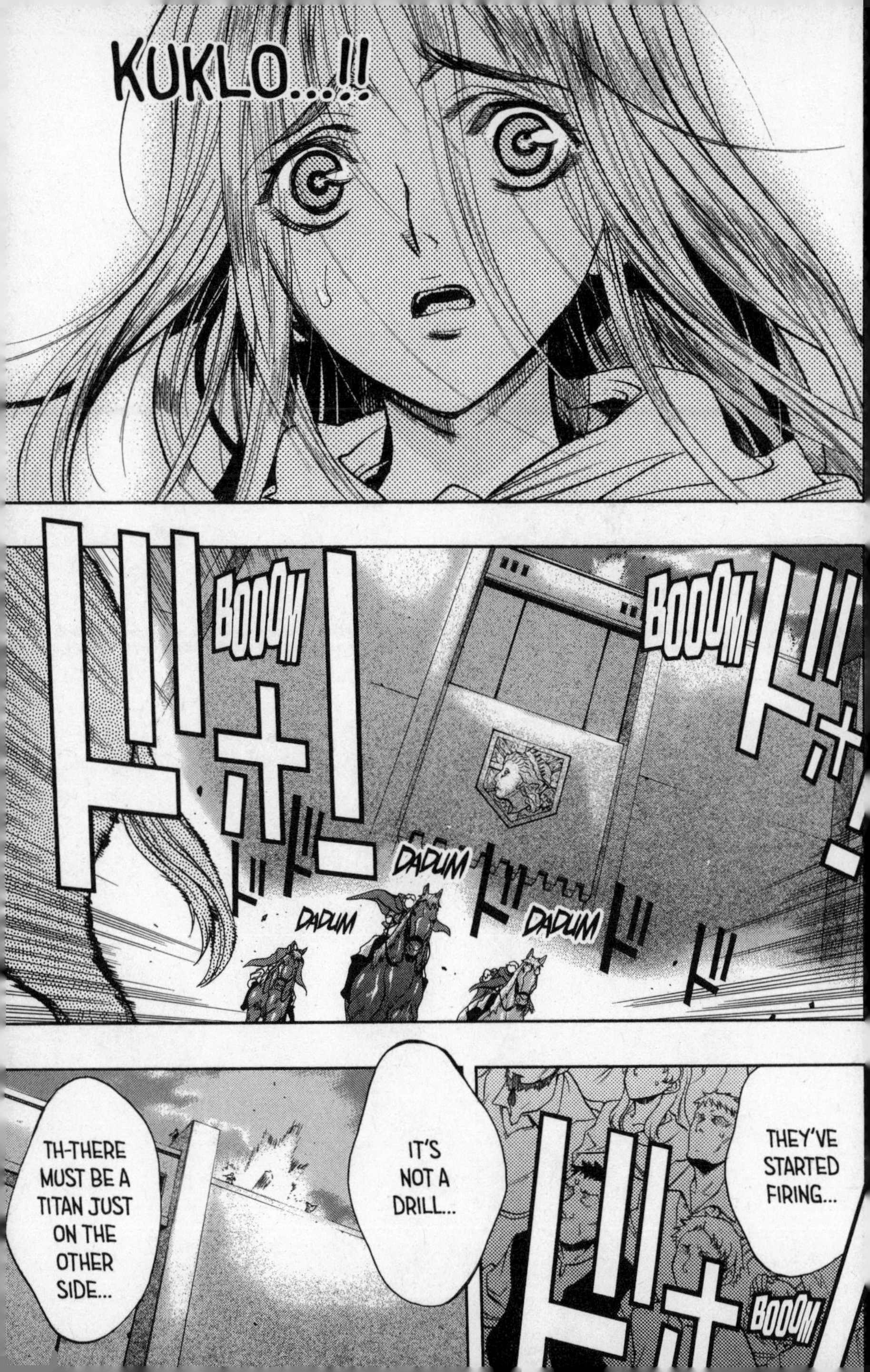
KUKLO...!!
BOOOM
BOOOM
DADUM
DADUM
DADUM
THEY'VE STARTED FIRING...
BOOOM
IT'S NOT A DRILL...
TH-THERE MUST BE A TITAN JUST ON THE OTHER SIDE...

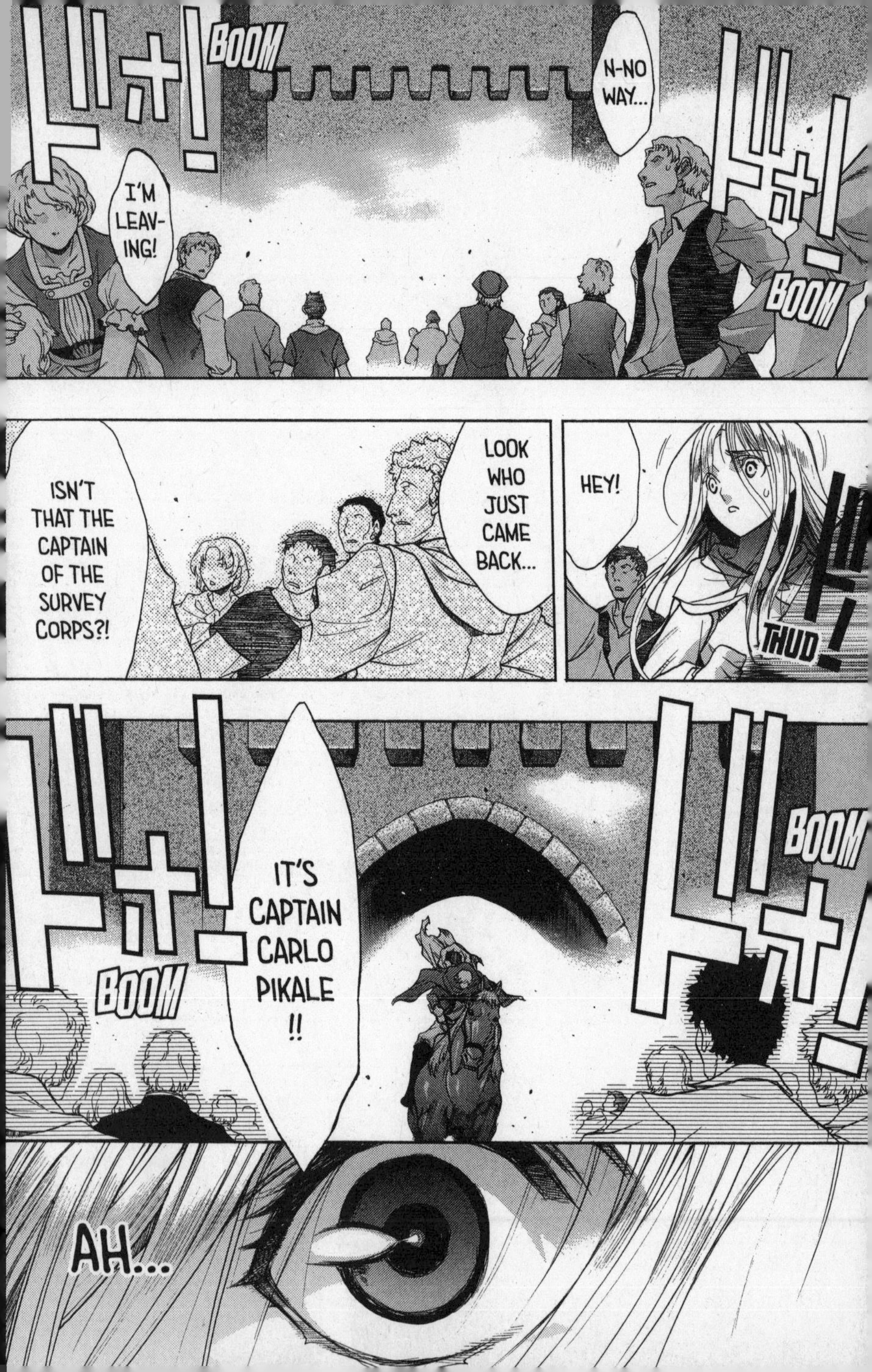
N-NO WAY...
BOOM
BOOM
I'M LEAV-ING!
HEY!
THUD!
LOOK WHO JUST CAME BACK...
ISN'T THAT THE CAPTAIN OF THE SURVEY CORPS?!
BOOM
IT'S CAPTAIN CARLO PIKALE!!
BOOM
AH...

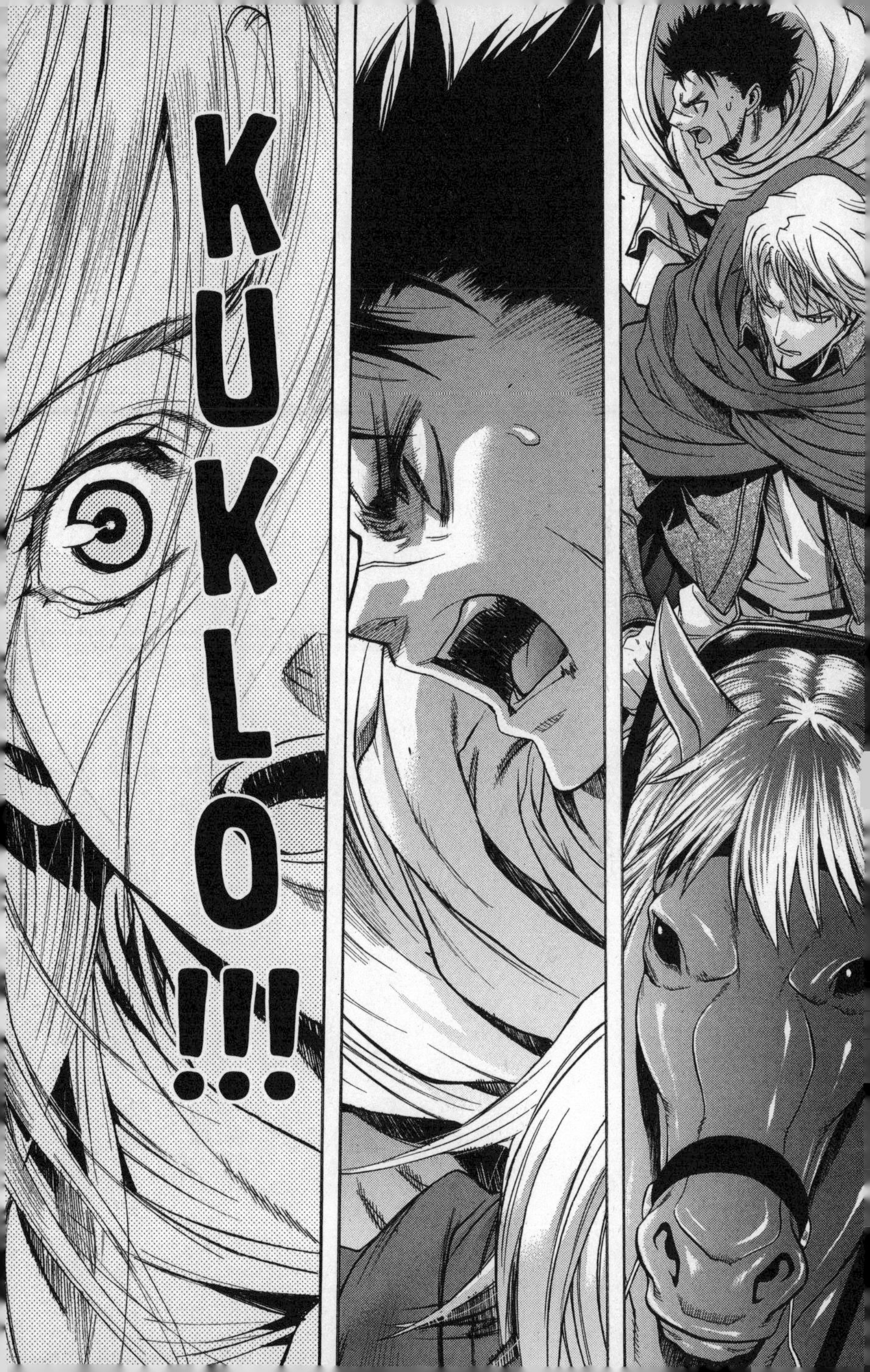
KUKLO!!!

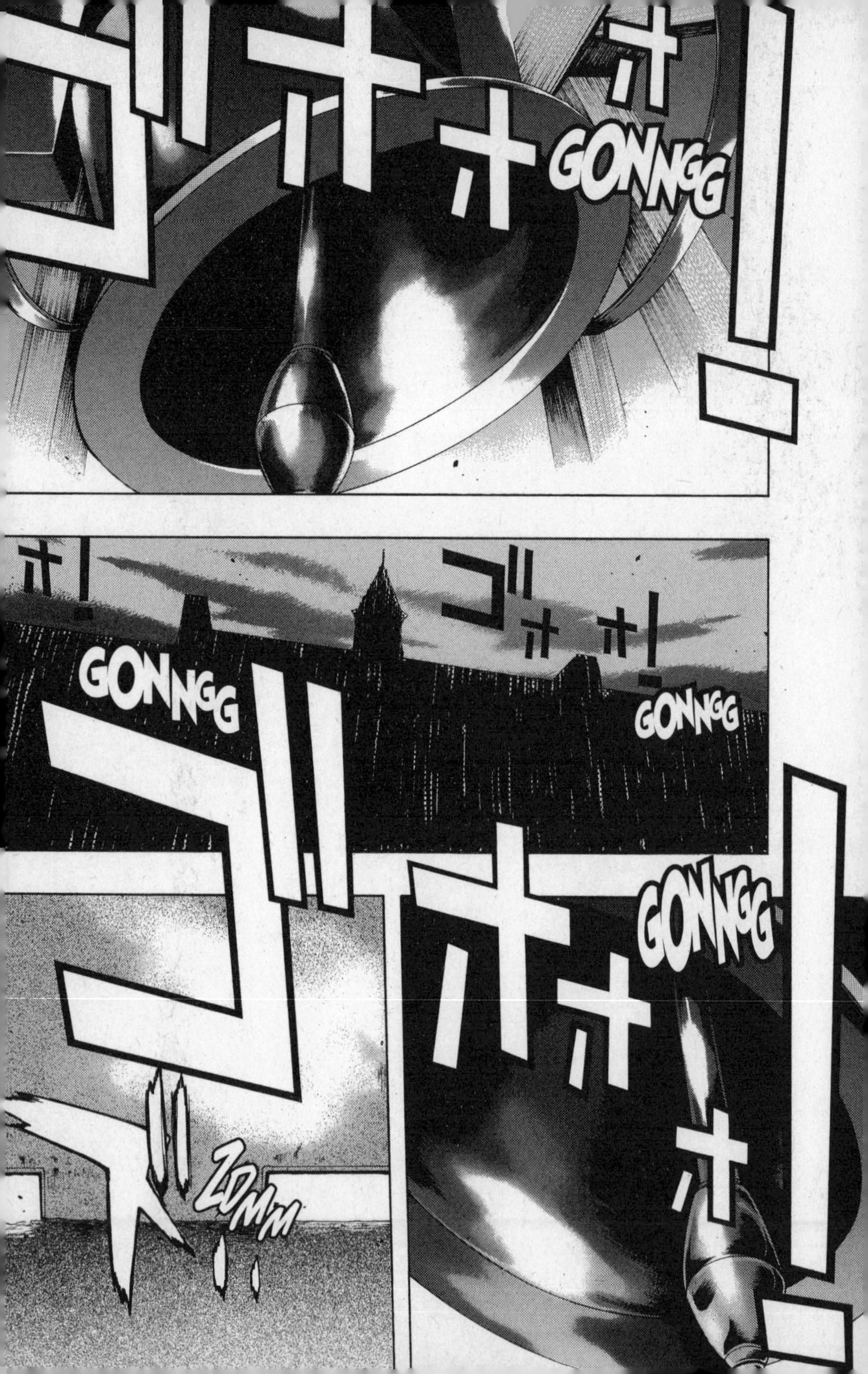
GONNGG
GONNGG
GONNGG
GONNGG
ZOMM

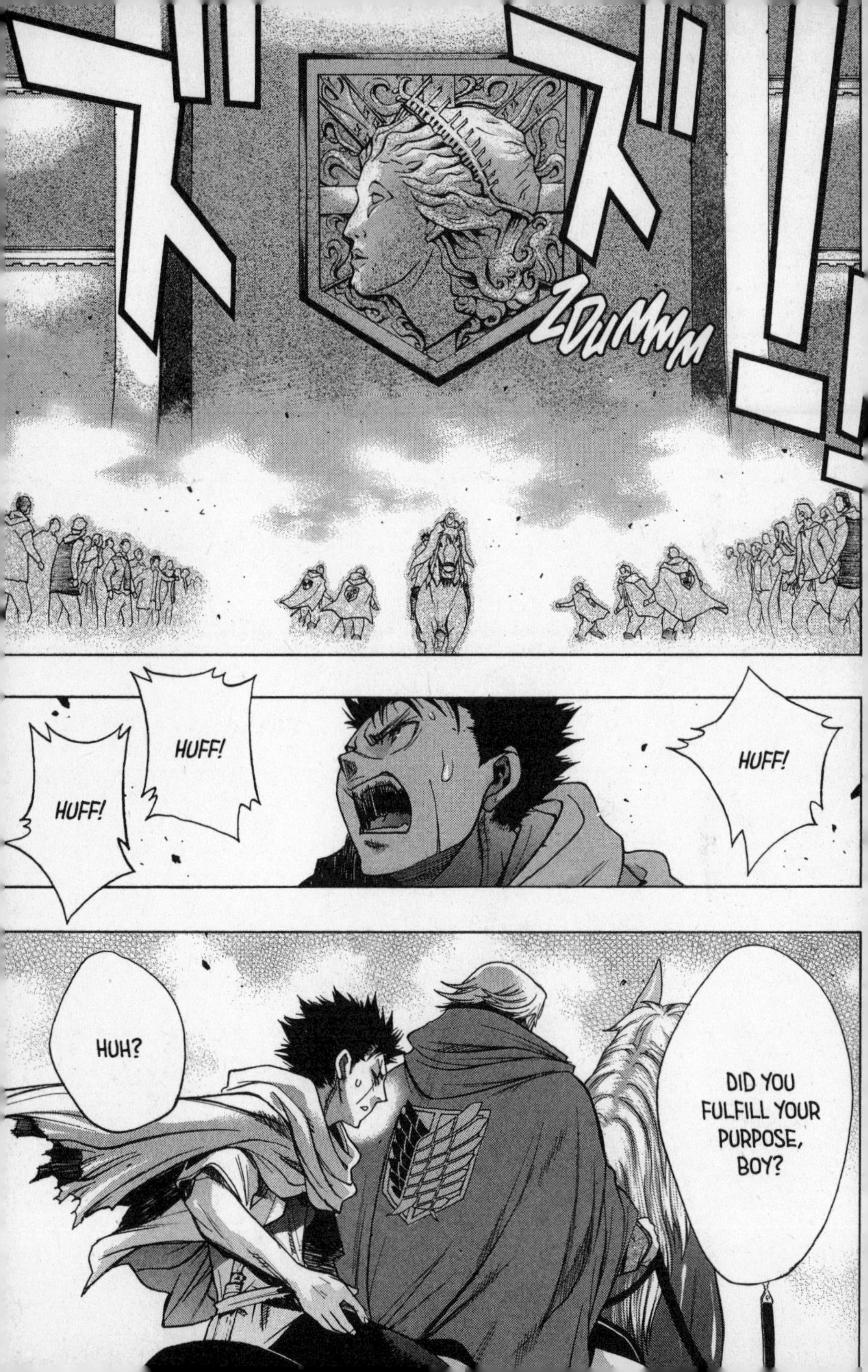
ズズ!!
ZOUMMM
HUFF!
HUFF!
HUFF!
DID YOU FULFILL YOUR PURPOSE, BOY?
HUH?

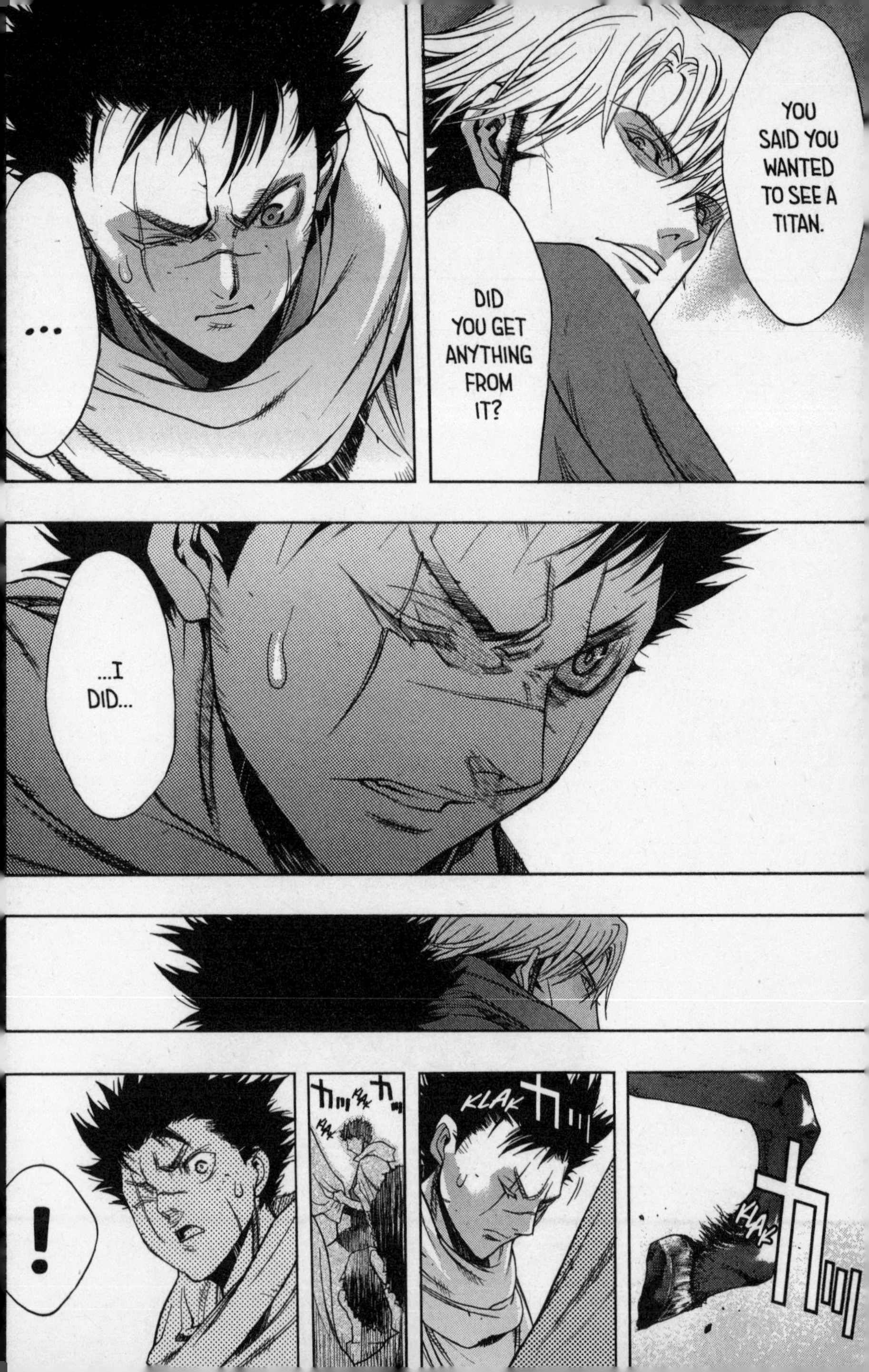
YOU SAID YOU WANTED TO SEE A TITAN.
DID YOU GET ANYTHING FROM IT?
...
...I DID...
KLAK
カッ
KLAK
カッ
カッ
KLAK
KLAK
カッ
!

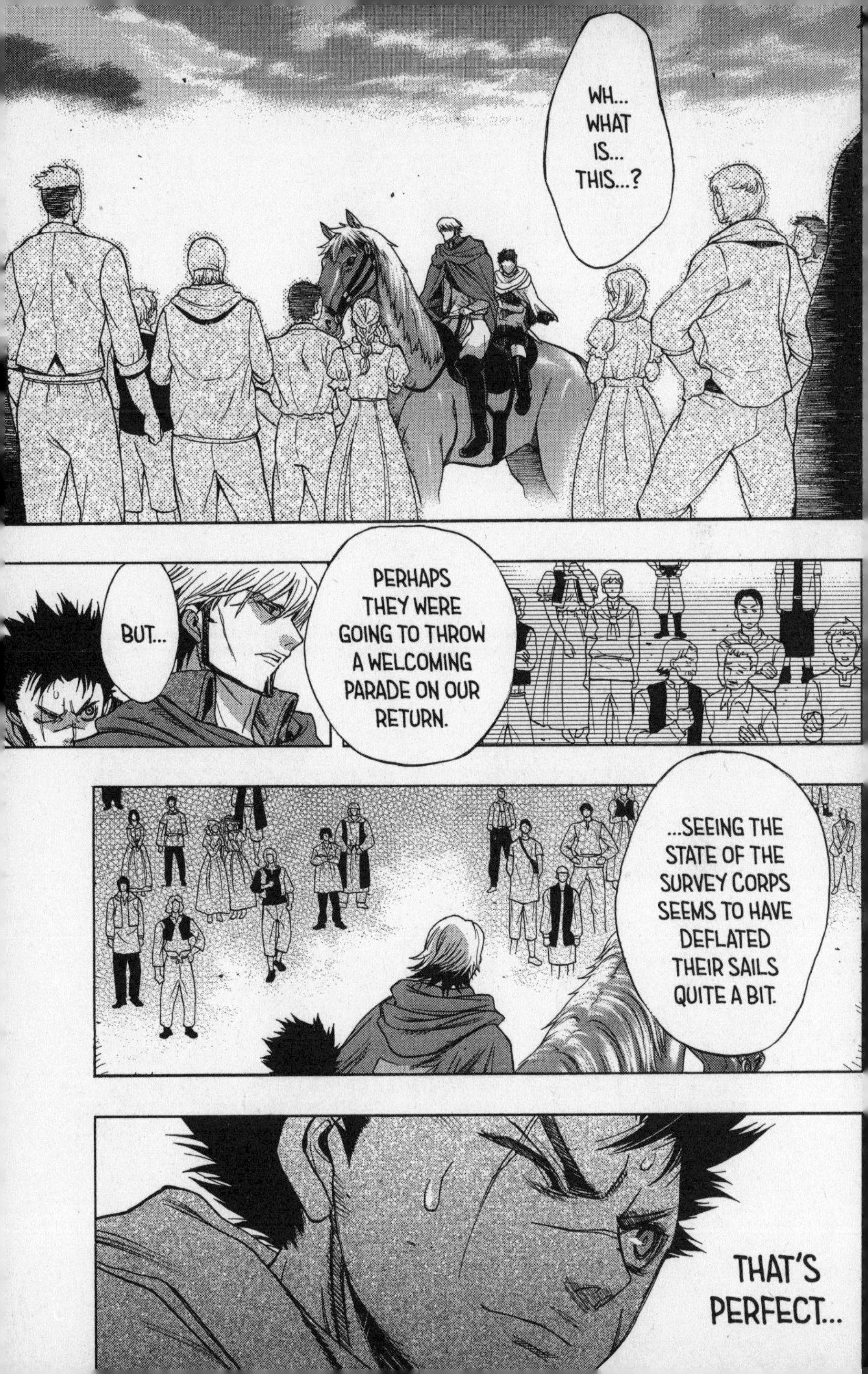
WH... WHAT IS... THIS...?
PERHAPS THEY WERE GOING TO THROW A WELCOMING PARADE ON OUR RETURN.
BUT...
...SEEING THE STATE OF THE SURVEY CORPS SEEMS TO HAVE DEFLATED THEIR SAILS QUITE A BIT.
THAT'S PERFECT...

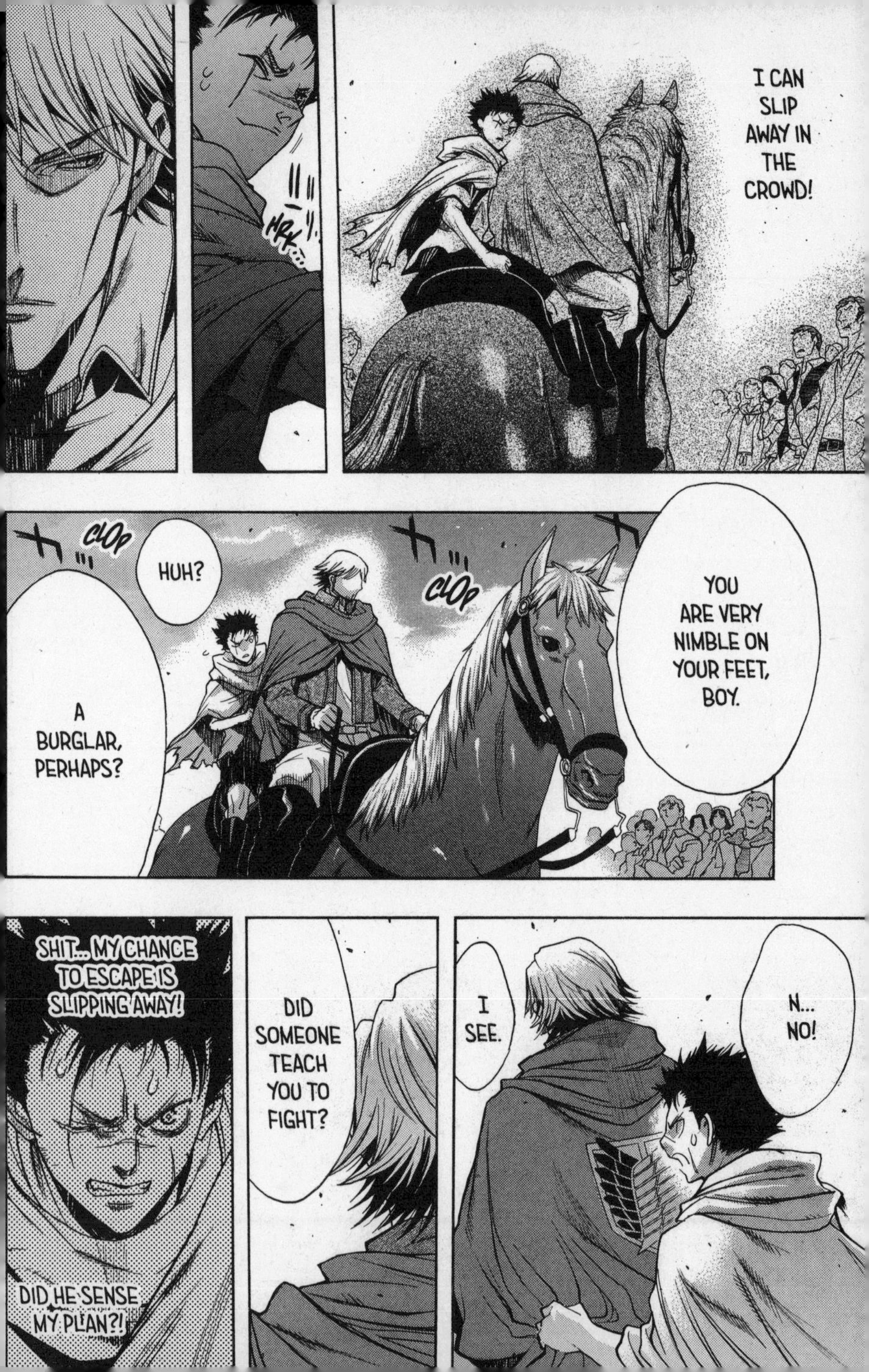
I CAN SLIP AWAY IN THE CROWD!
HRK...
YOU ARE VERY NIMBLE ON YOUR FEET, BOY.
CLOP
HUH?
CLOP
A BURGLAR, PERHAPS?
N... NO!
I SEE.
DID SOMEONE TEACH YOU TO FIGHT?
SHIT... MY CHANCE TO ESCAPE IS SLIPPING AWAY!
DID HE SENSE MY PLAN?!

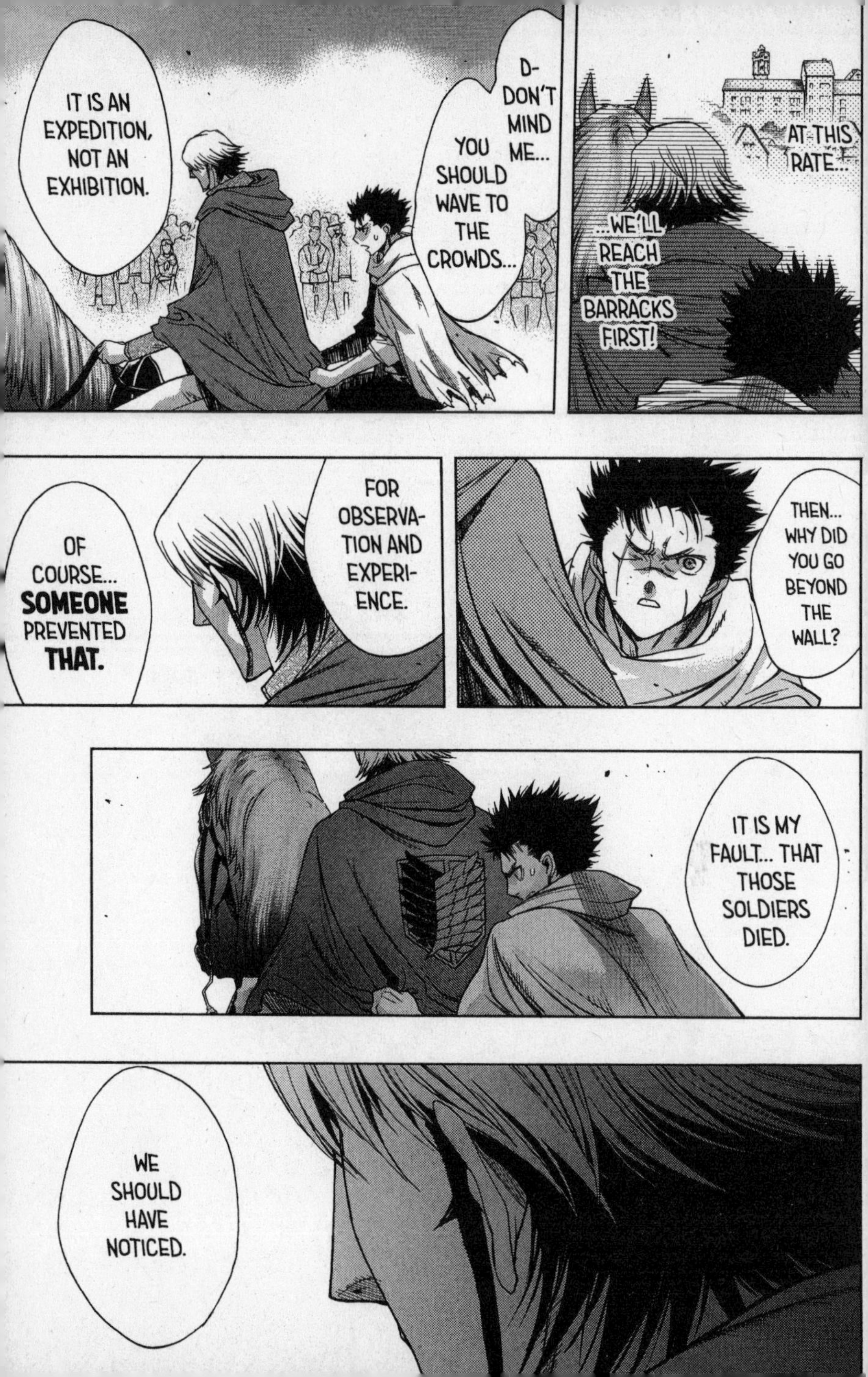
AT THIS RATE...
...WE'LL REACH THE BARRACKS FIRST!
D-DON'T MIND ME... YOU SHOULD WAVE TO THE CROWDS...
IT IS AN EXPEDITION, NOT AN EXHIBITION.
THEN... WHY DID YOU GO BEYOND THE WALL?
FOR OBSERVATION AND EXPERIENCE.
OF COURSE... **SOMEONE** PREVENTED **THAT.**
IT IS MY FAULT... THAT THOSE SOLDIERS DIED.
WE SHOULD HAVE NOTICED.

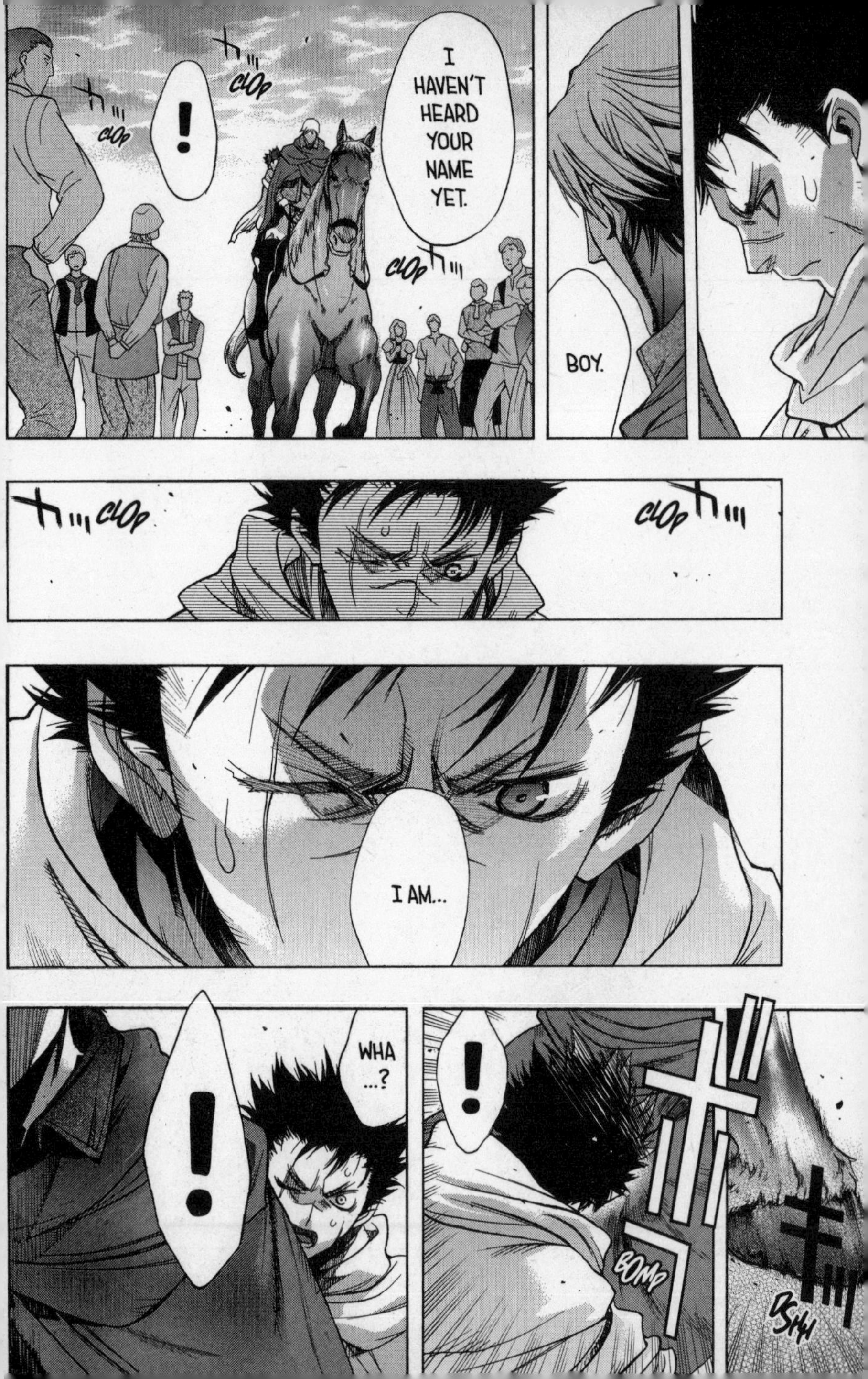
BOY.
CLOP
CLOP
!
I HAVEN'T HEARD YOUR NAME YET.
CLOP
CLOP
CLOP
I AM...
!
BOMP
DSHH
!
WHA ...?

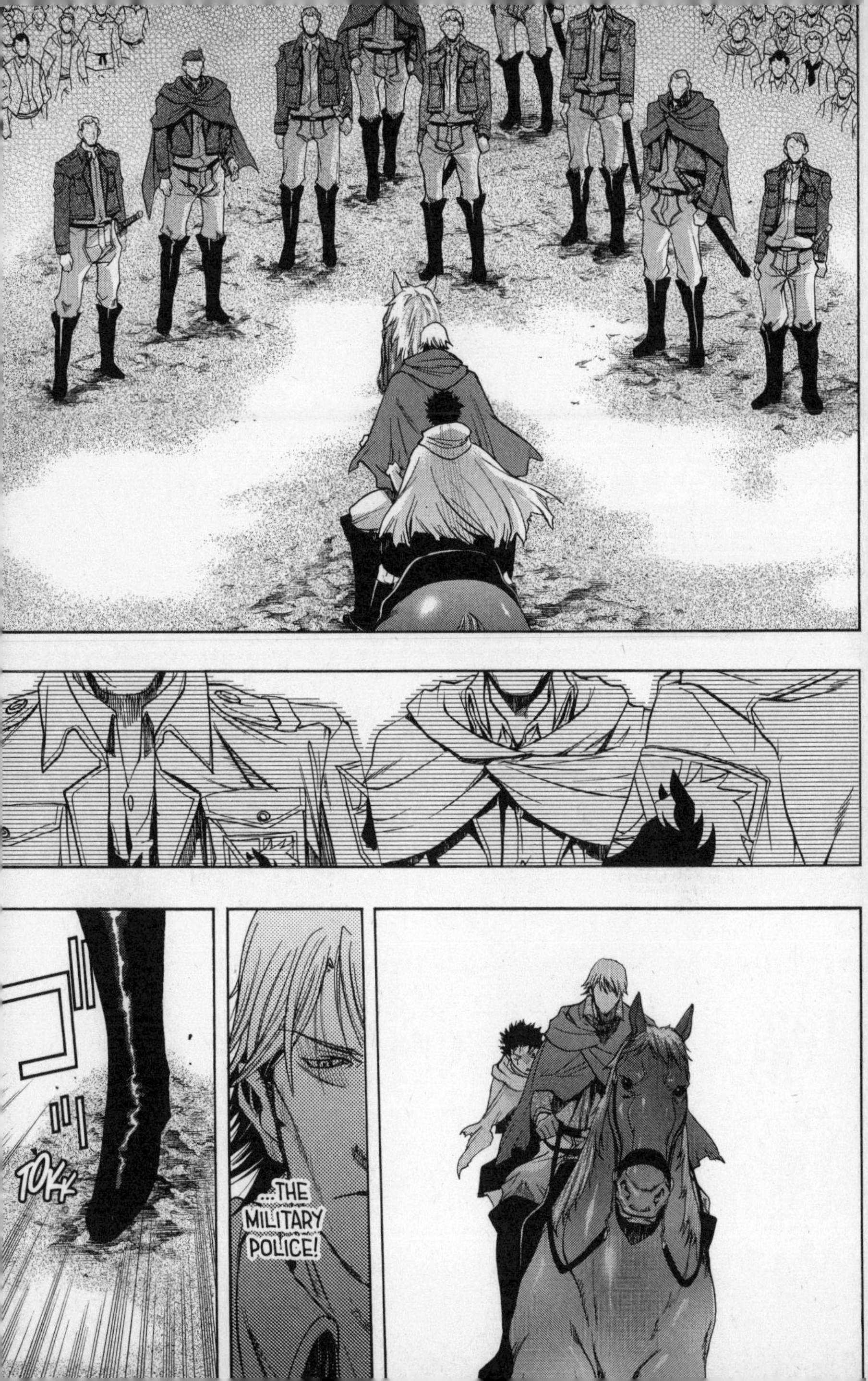
...THE MILITARY POLICE!
TOKK

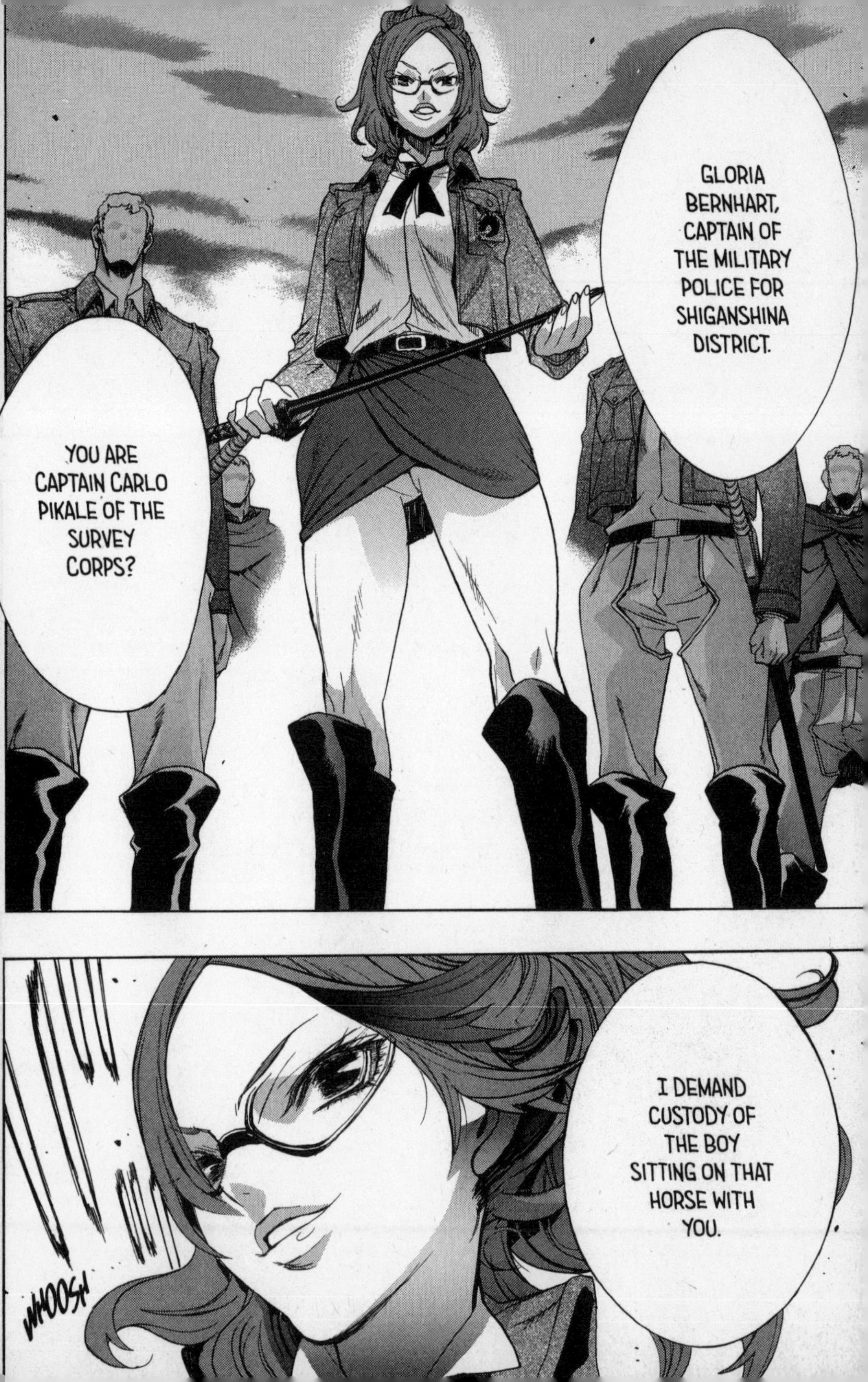
GLORIA BERNHART, CAPTAIN OF THE MILITARY POLICE FOR SHIGANSHINA DISTRICT.
YOU ARE CAPTAIN CARLO PIKALE OF THE SURVEY CORPS?
I DEMAND CUSTODY OF THE BOY SITTING ON THAT HORSE WITH YOU.
WHOOSH

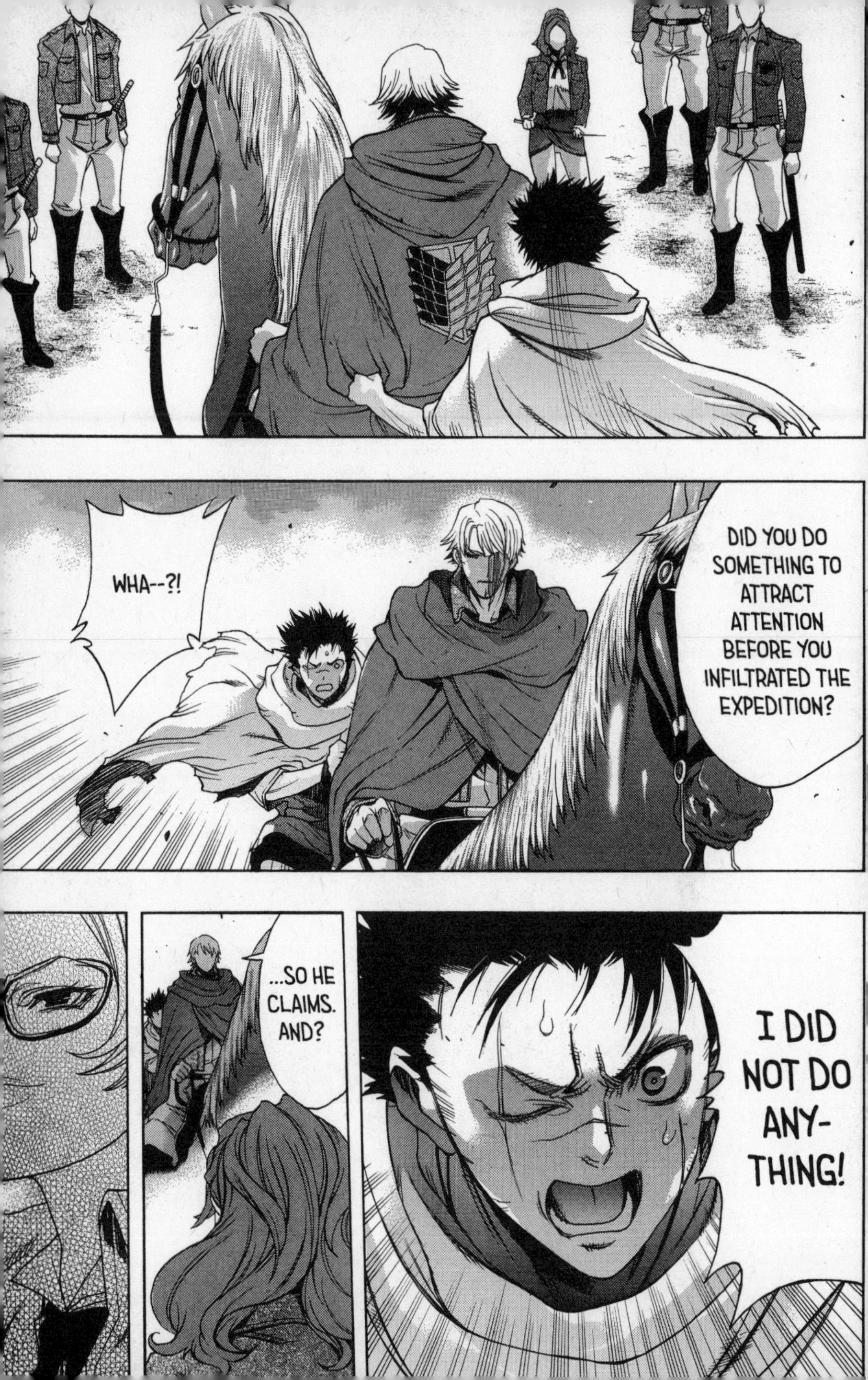
DID YOU DO SOMETHING TO ATTRACT ATTENTION BEFORE YOU INFILTRATED THE EXPEDITION?
WHA--?!
I DID NOT DO ANY-THING!
...SO HE CLAIMS. AND?

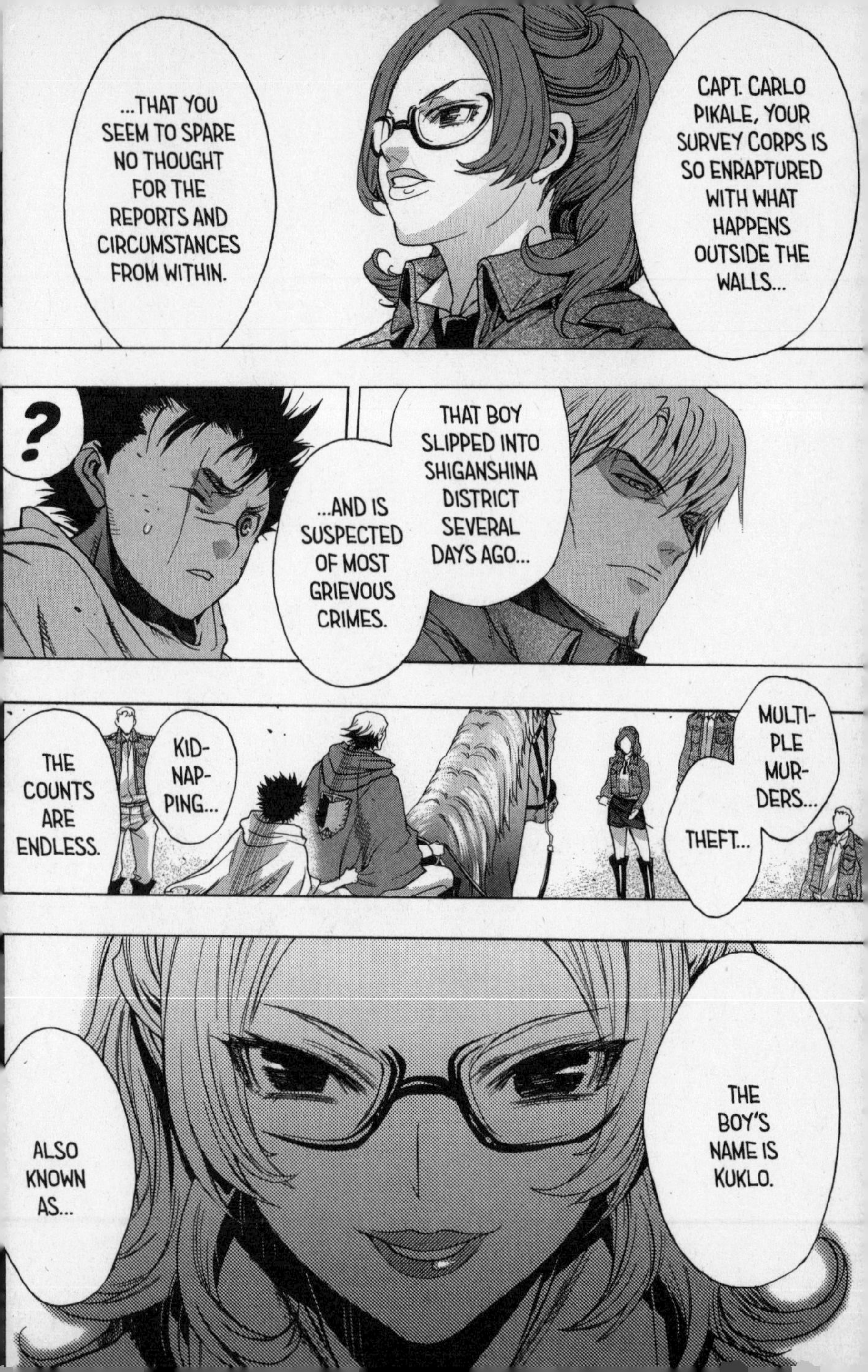
CAPT. CARLO PIKALE, YOUR SURVEY CORPS IS SO ENRAPTURED WITH WHAT HAPPENS OUTSIDE THE WALLS...
...THAT YOU SEEM TO SPARE NO THOUGHT FOR THE REPORTS AND CIRCUMSTANCES FROM WITHIN.
THAT BOY SLIPPED INTO SHIGANSHINA DISTRICT SEVERAL DAYS AGO...
...AND IS SUSPECTED OF MOST GRIEVOUS CRIMES.
?
MULTIPLE MURDERS...
THEFT...
KIDNAPPING...
THE COUNTS ARE ENDLESS.
THE BOY'S NAME IS KUKLO.
ALSO KNOWN AS...

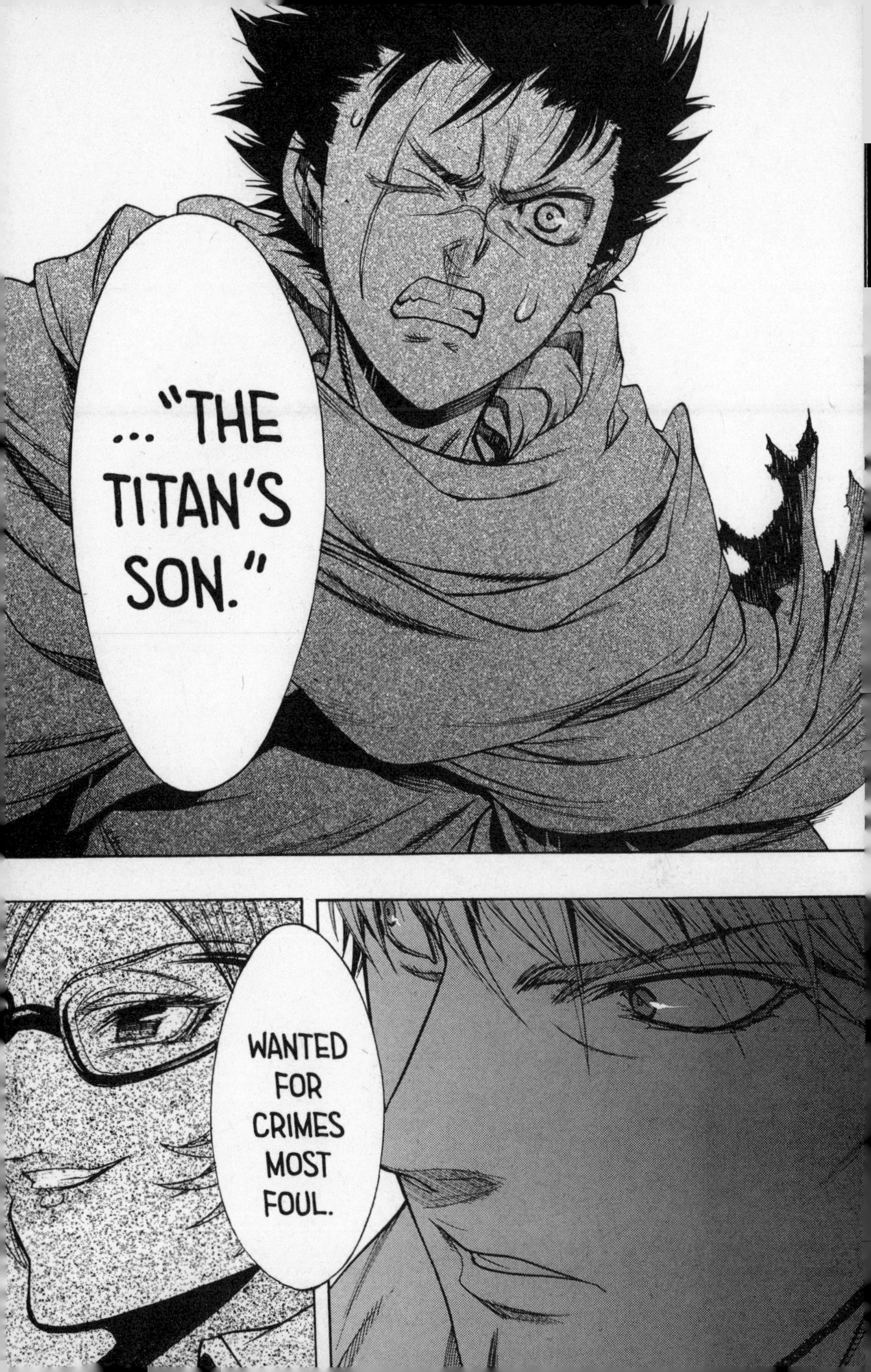
..."THE TITAN'S SON."
WANTED FOR CRIMES MOST FOUL.

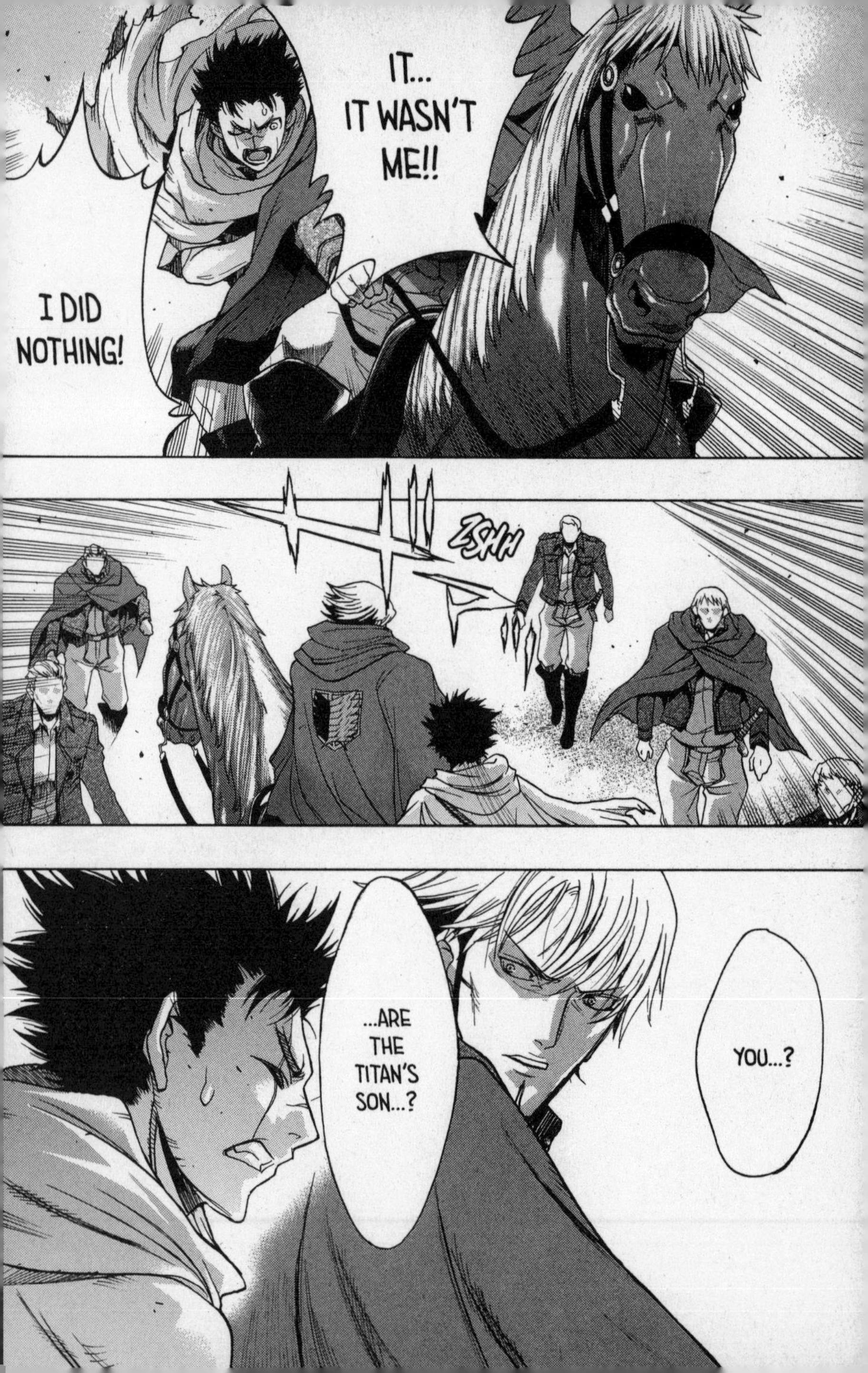
IT... IT WASN'T ME!!
I DID NOTHING!
ZSHH
YOU...?
...ARE THE TITAN'S SON...?

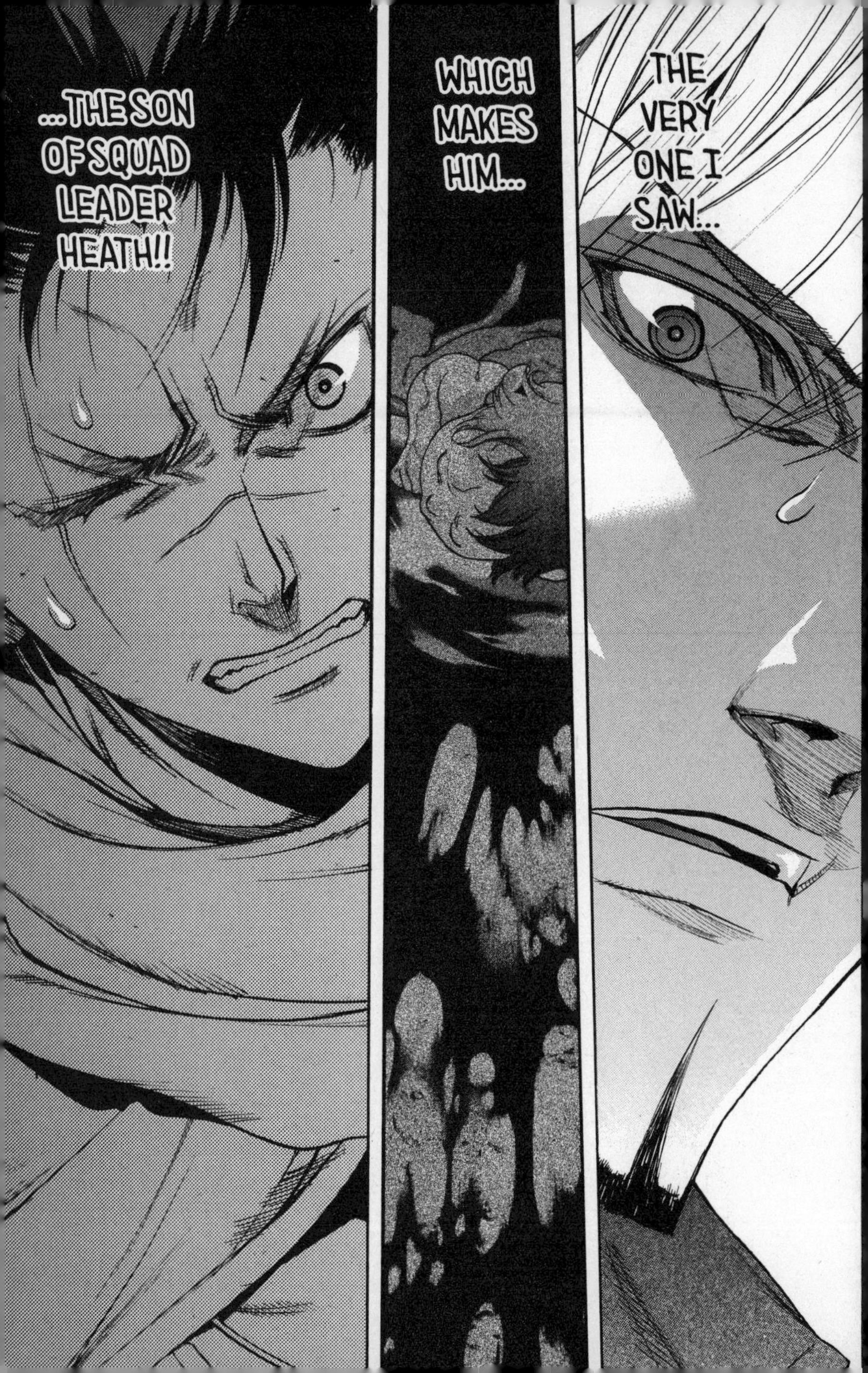
THE VERY ONE I SAW...
WHICH MAKES HIM...
...THE SON OF SQUAD LEADER HEATH!!

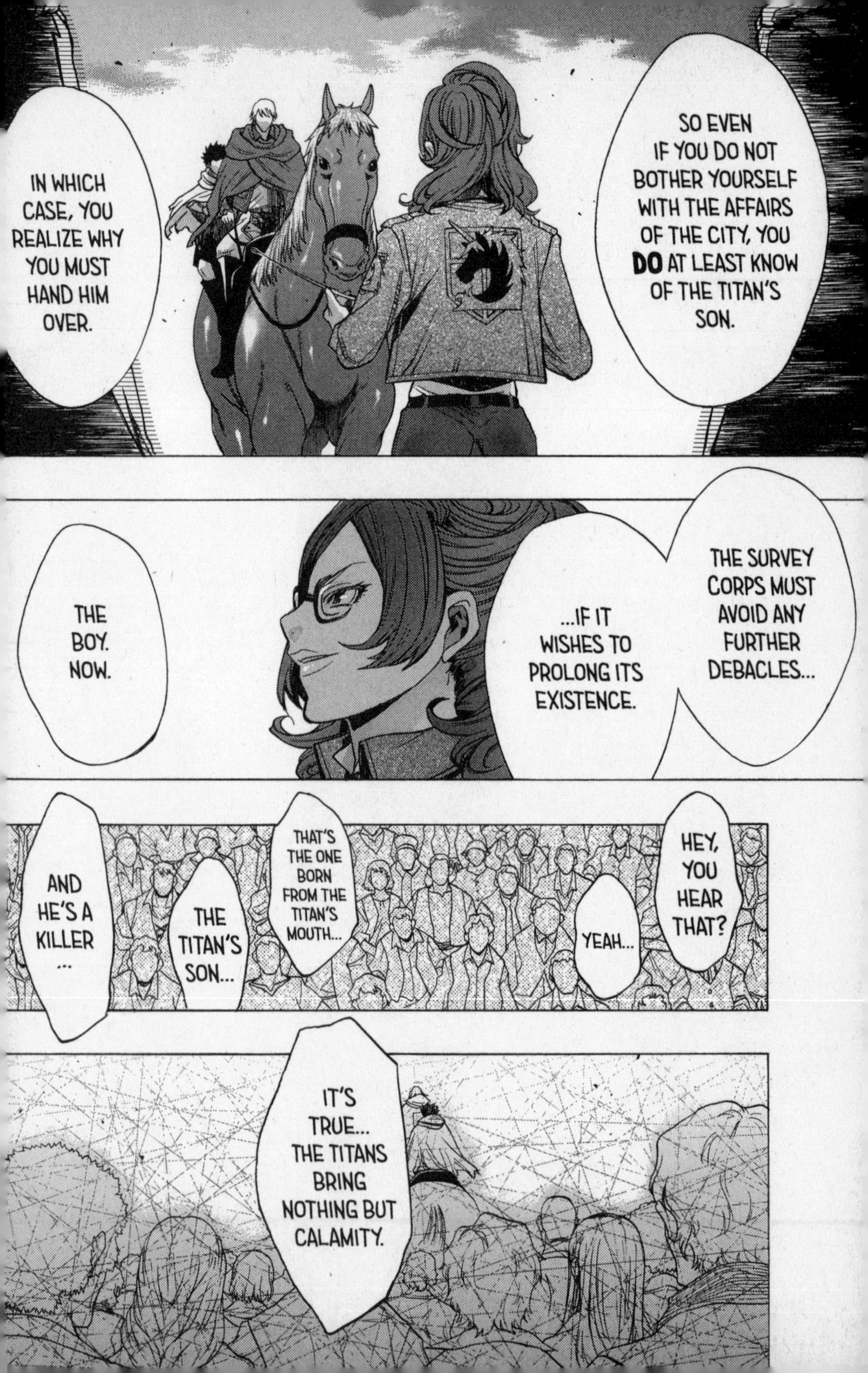
SO EVEN IF YOU DO NOT BOTHER YOURSELF WITH THE AFFAIRS OF THE CITY, YOU **DO** AT LEAST KNOW OF THE TITAN'S SON.
IN WHICH CASE, YOU REALIZE WHY YOU MUST HAND HIM OVER.
THE SURVEY CORPS MUST AVOID ANY FURTHER DEBACLES...
...IF IT WISHES TO PROLONG ITS EXISTENCE.
THE BOY. NOW.
HEY, YOU HEAR THAT?
YEAH...
THAT'S THE ONE BORN FROM THE TITAN'S MOUTH...
THE TITAN'S SON...
AND HE'S A KILLER ...
IT'S TRUE... THE TITANS BRING NOTHING BUT CALAMITY.

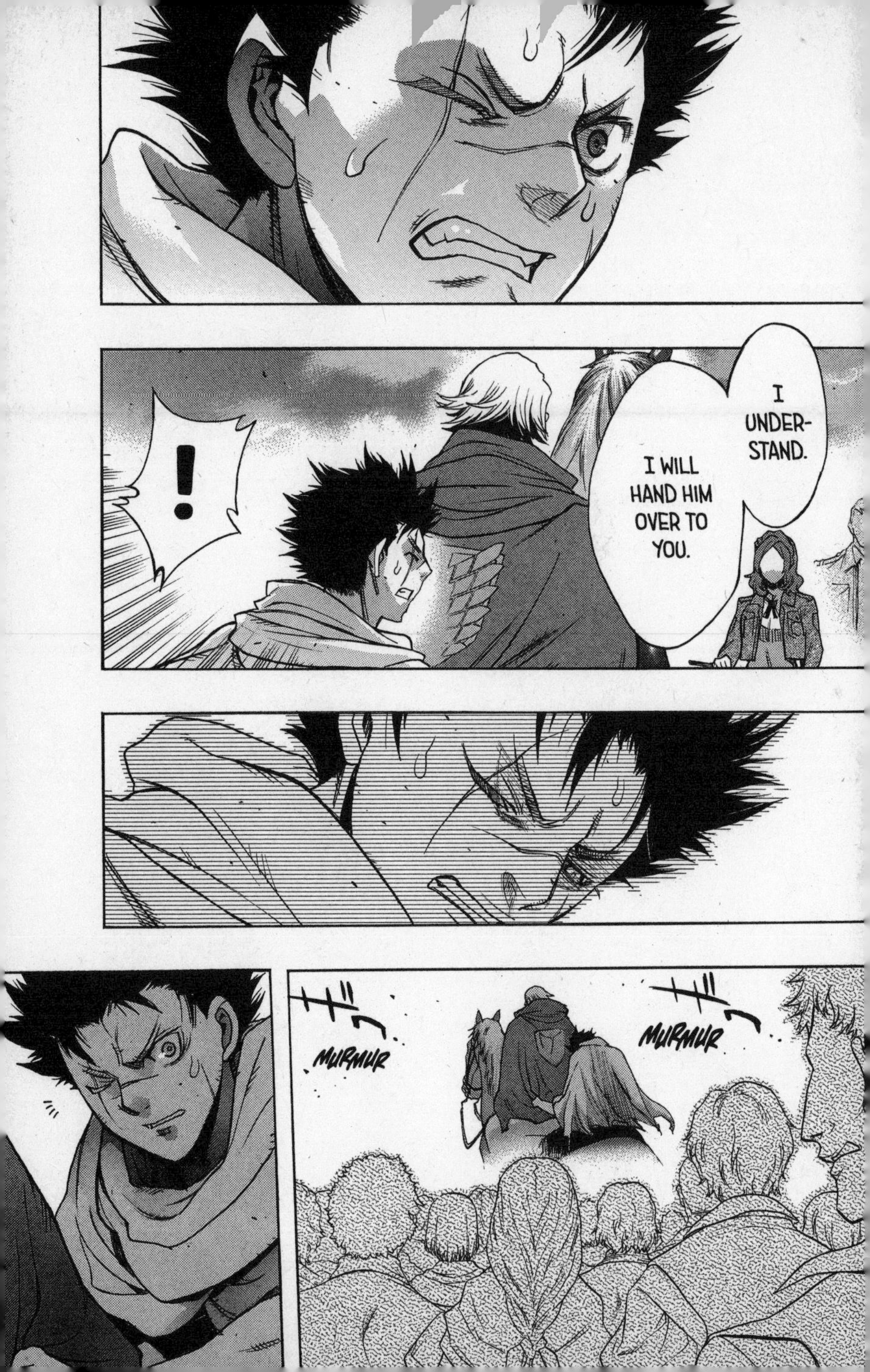
I UNDER-STAND.
I WILL HAND HIM OVER TO YOU.
!
MURMUR
MURMUR

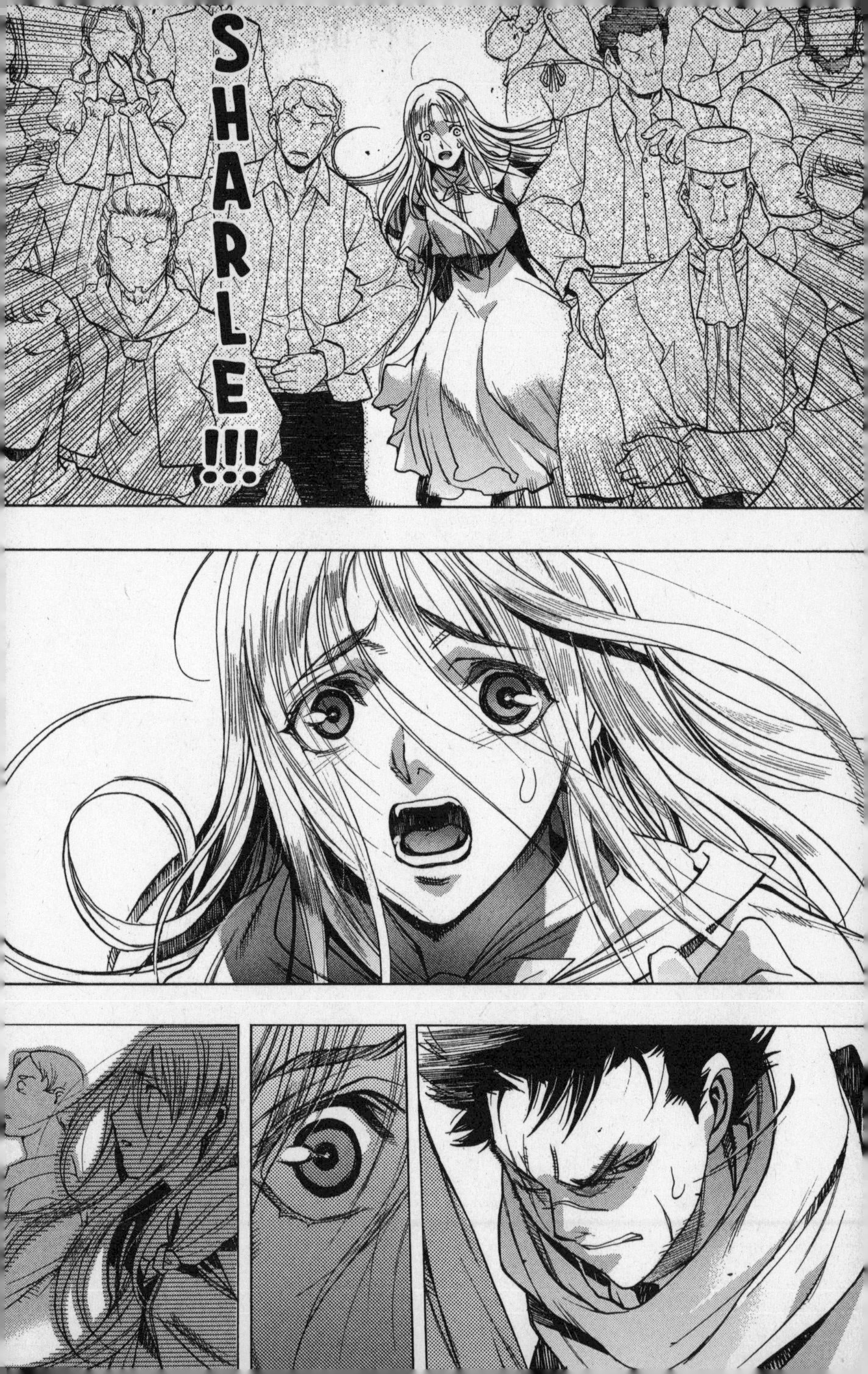
SHARLE!!!

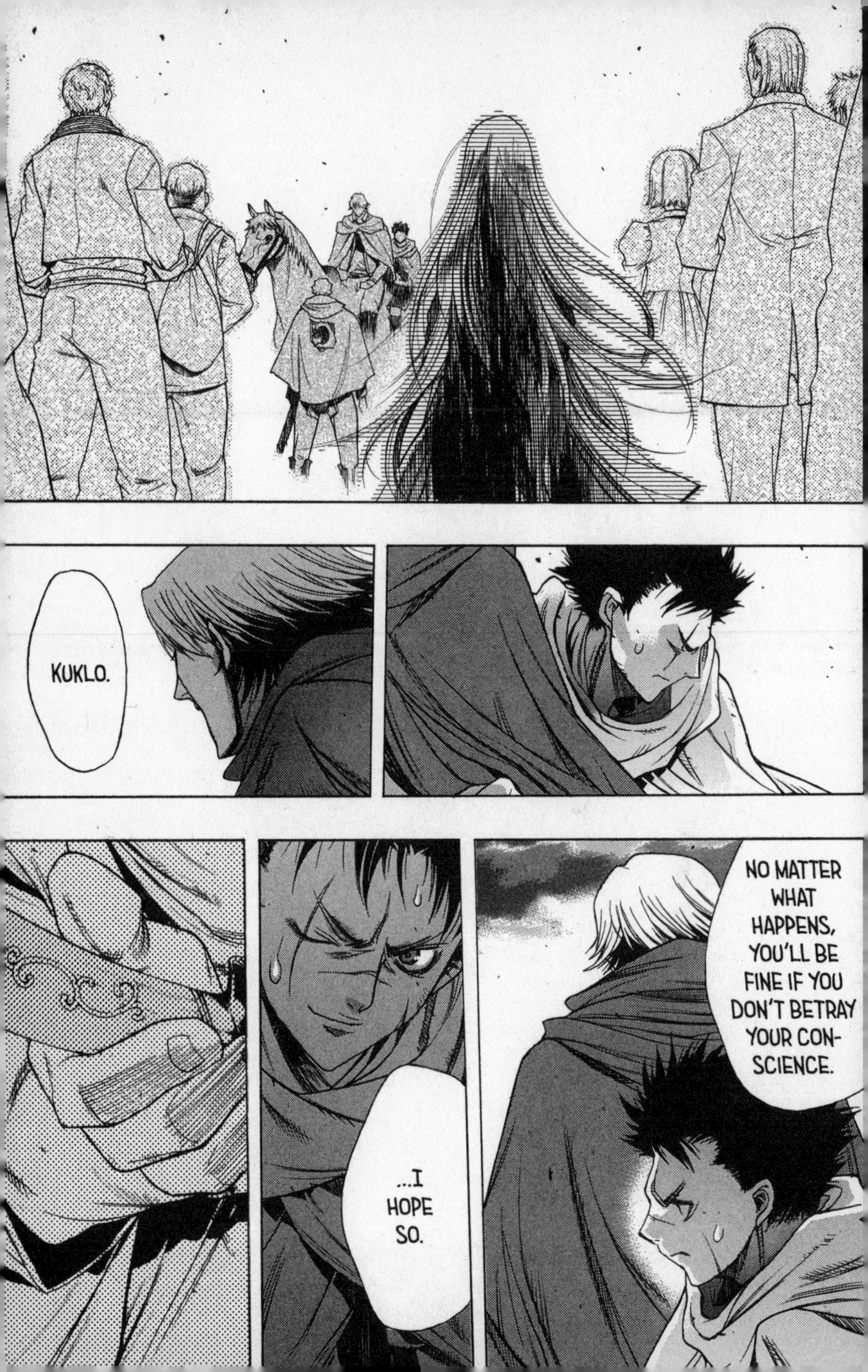
KUKLO.
NO MATTER WHAT HAPPENS, YOU'LL BE FINE IF YOU DON'T BETRAY YOUR CON-SCIENCE.
...I HOPE SO.

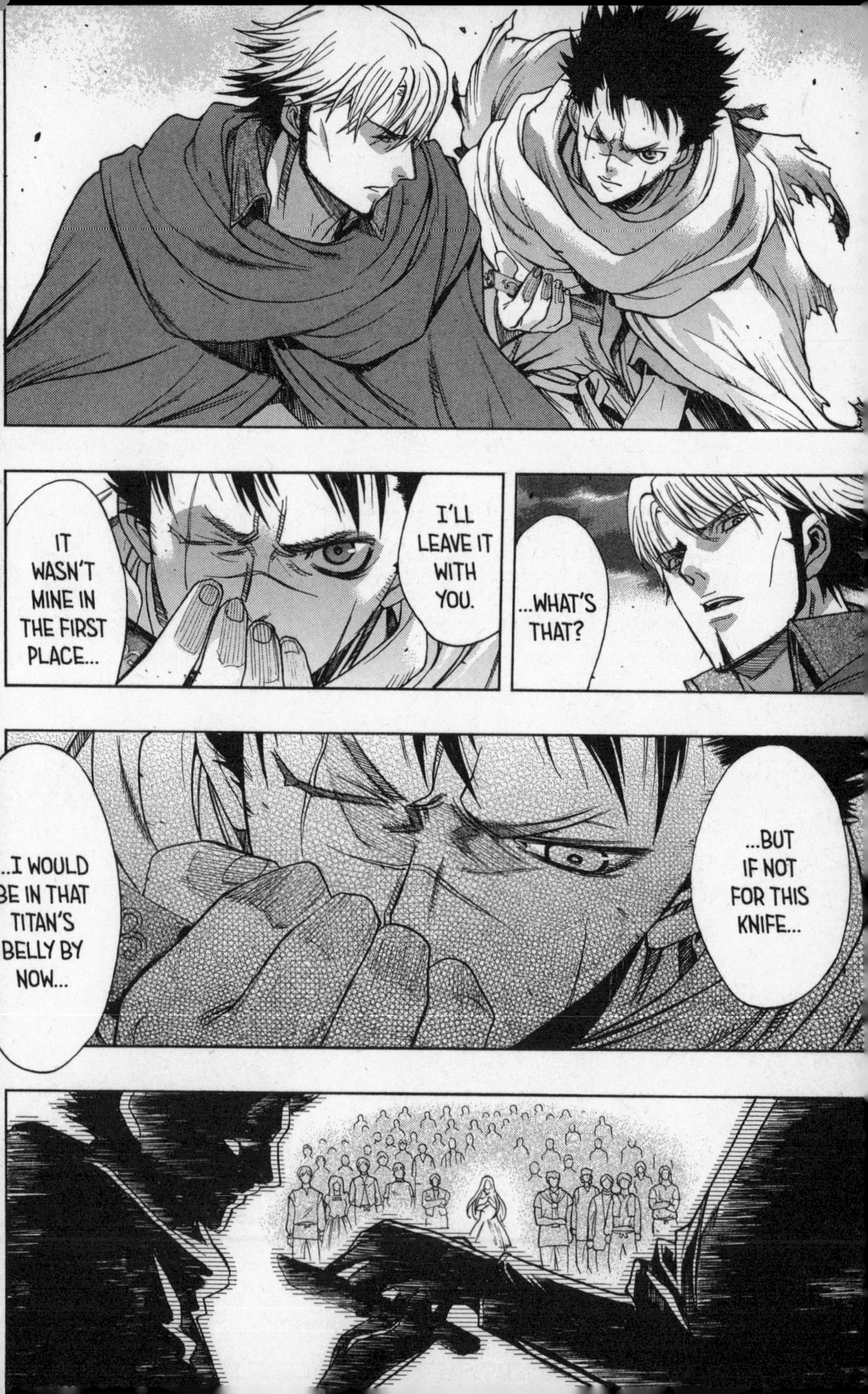
...WHAT'S THAT?
I'LL LEAVE IT WITH YOU.
IT WASN'T MINE IN THE FIRST PLACE...
...BUT IF NOT FOR THIS KNIFE...
...I WOULD BE IN THAT TITAN'S BELLY BY NOW...

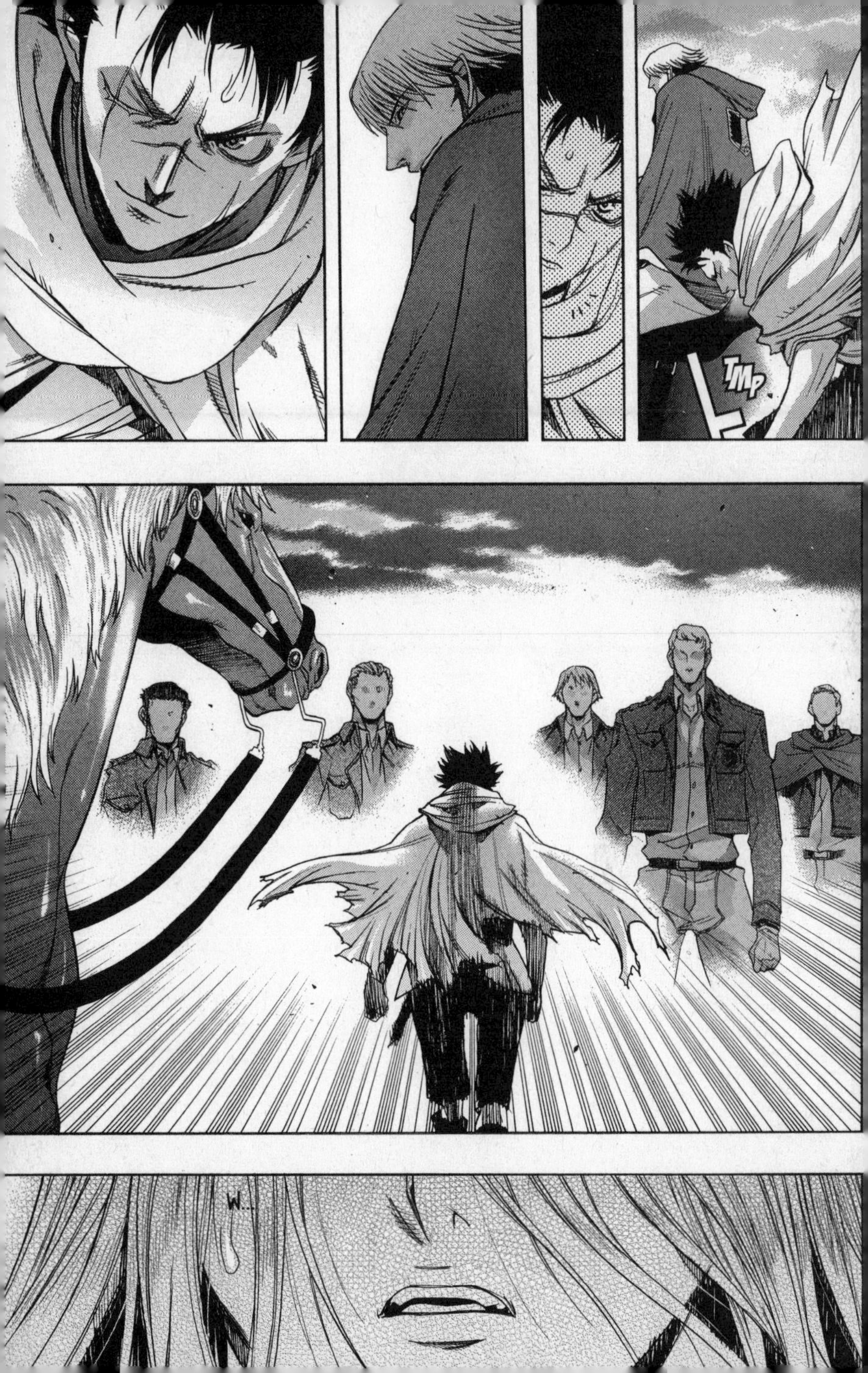
TMP
W...

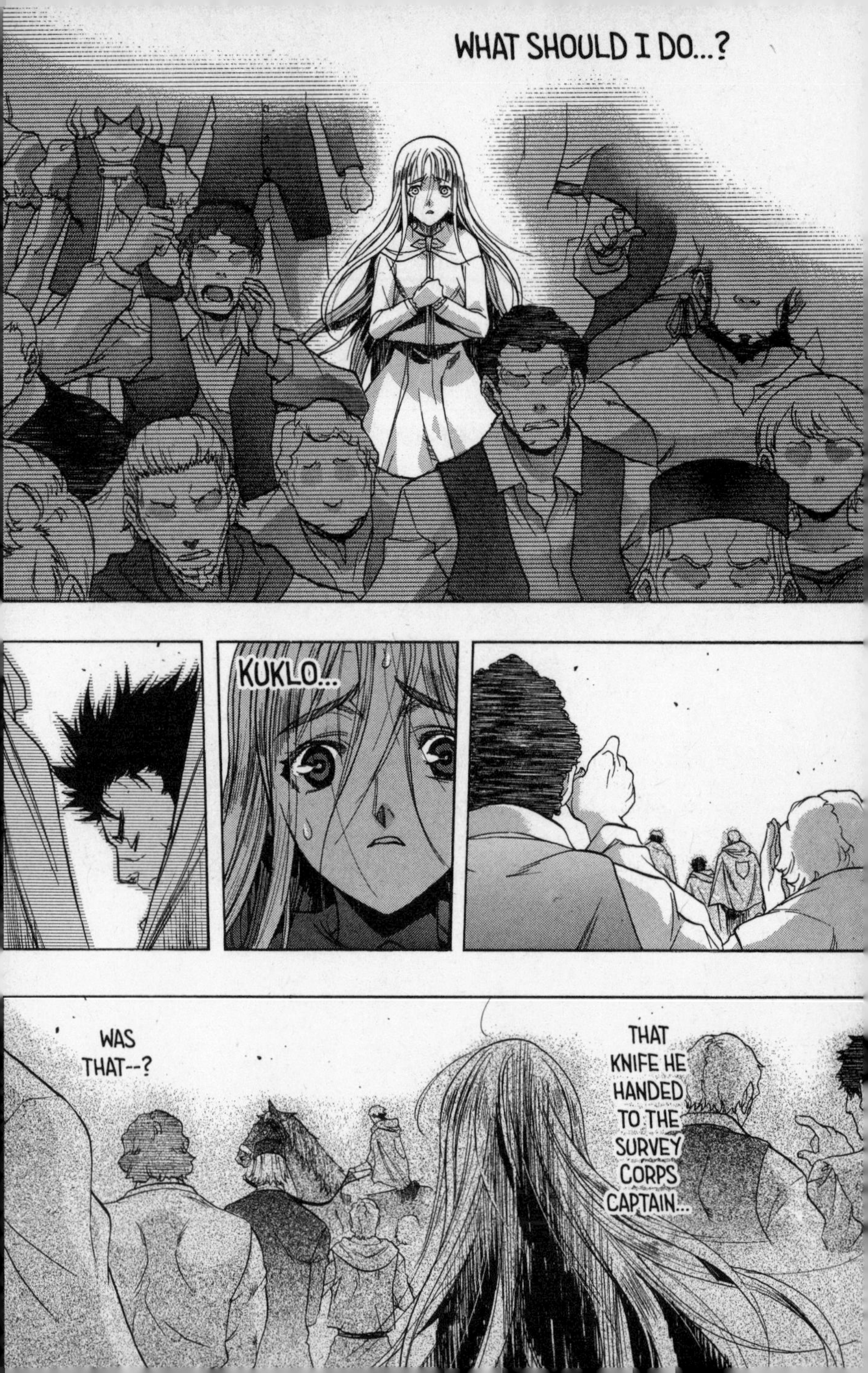
WHAT SHOULD I DO...?
KUKLO...
THAT KNIFE HE HANDED TO THE SURVEY CORPS CAPTAIN...
WAS THAT--?

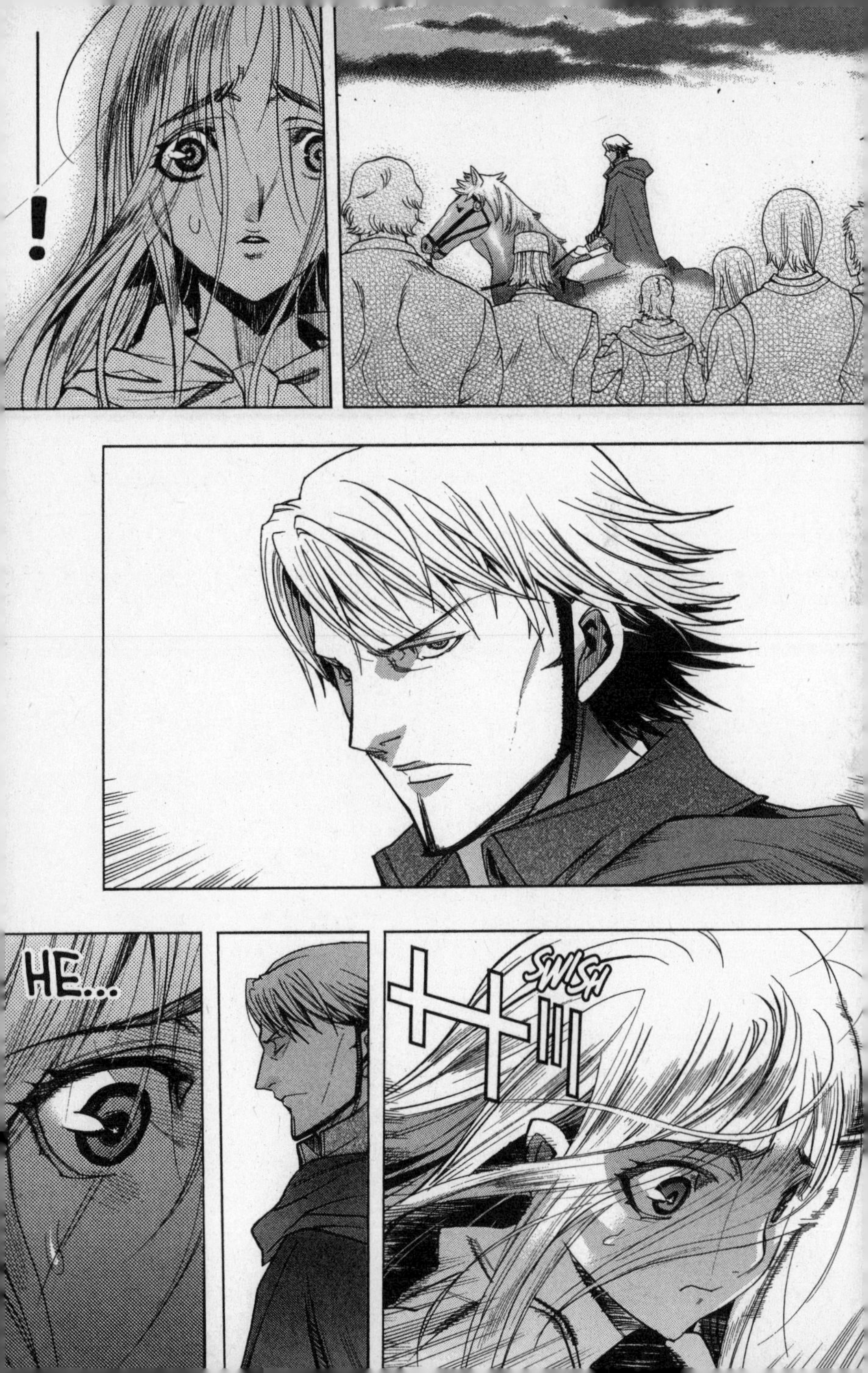
!
SWISH
HE...

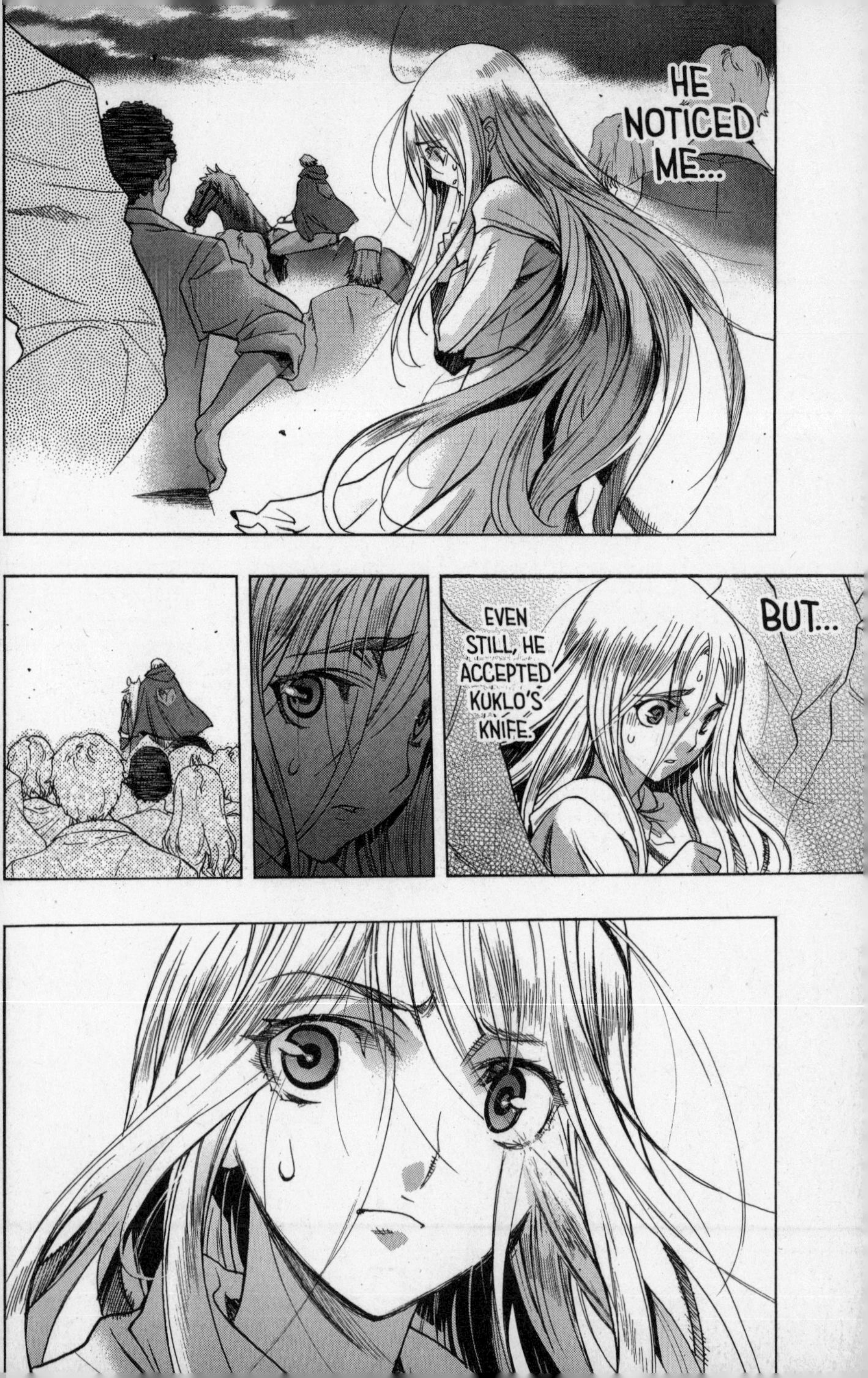
HE NOTICED ME...
BUT...
EVEN STILL, HE ACCEPTED KUKLO'S KNIFE.

...WHICH
MEANS...

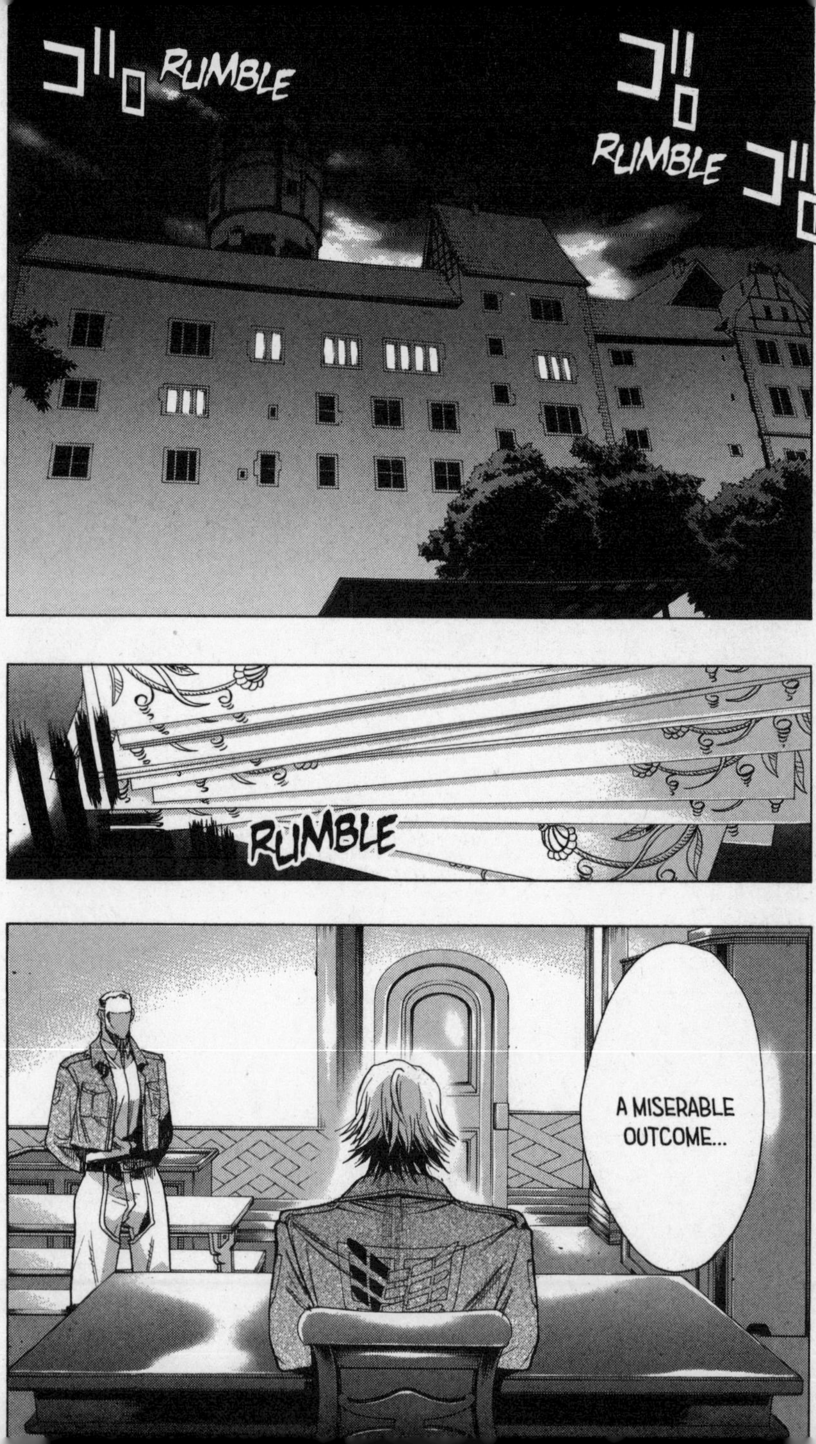
RUMBLE
RUMBLE
RUMBLE
A MISERABLE OUTCOME...

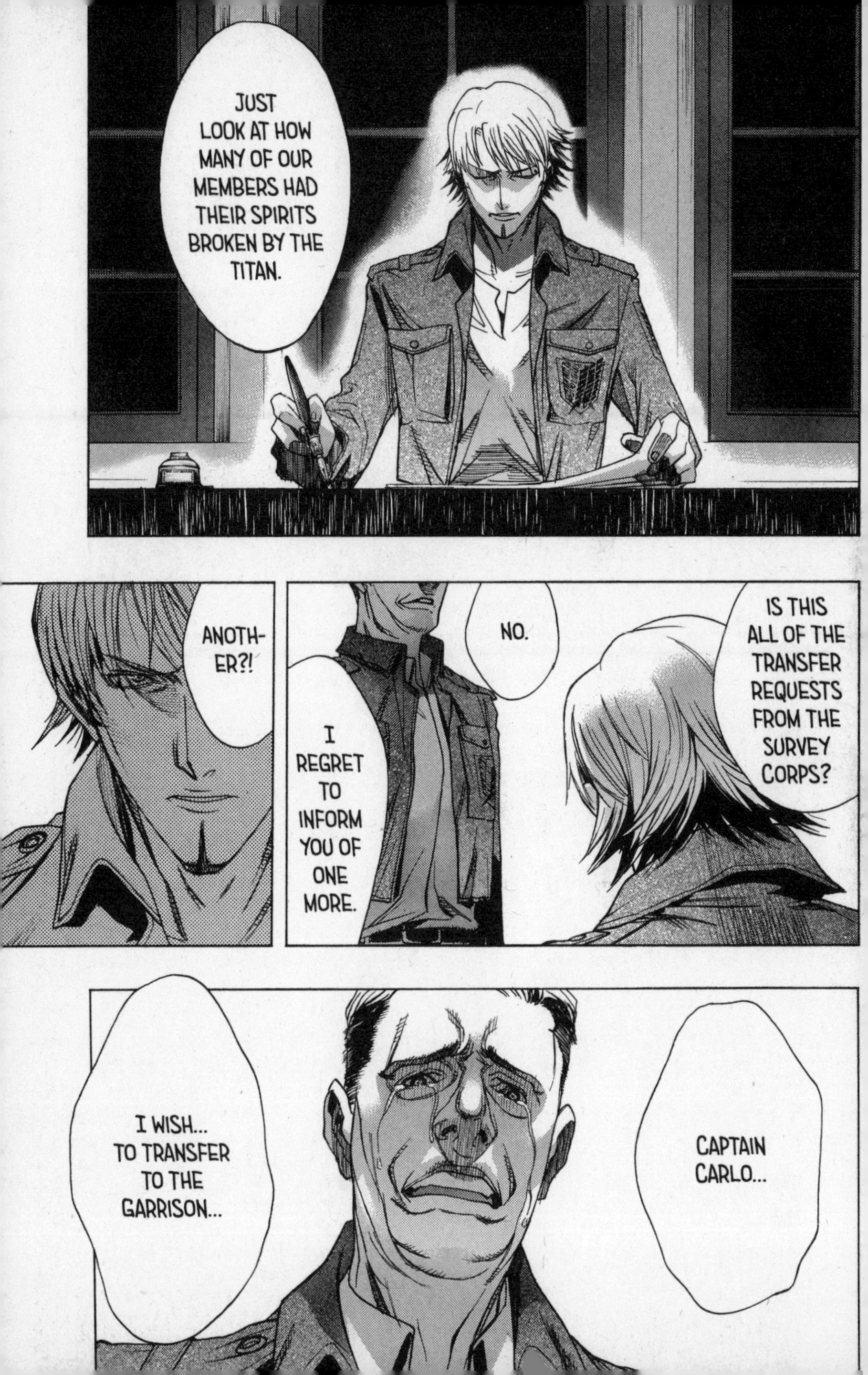
JUST LOOK AT HOW MANY OF OUR MEMBERS HAD THEIR SPIRITS BROKEN BY THE TITAN.
IS THIS ALL OF THE TRANSFER REQUESTS FROM THE SURVEY CORPS?
NO.
I REGRET TO INFORM YOU OF ONE MORE.
ANOTH-ER?!
CAPTAIN CARLO...
I WISH... TO TRANSFER TO THE GARRISON...

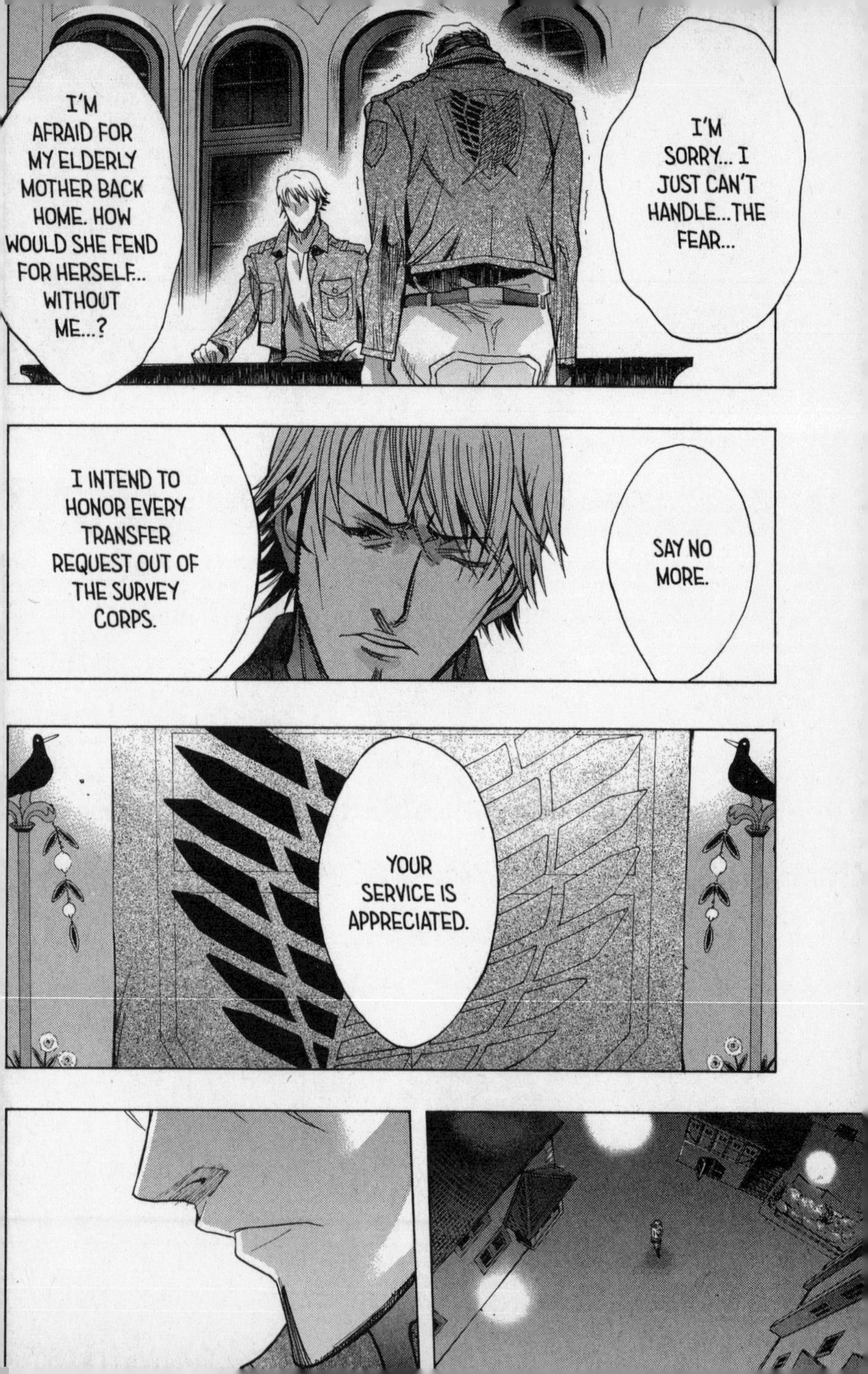
I'M SORRY... I JUST CAN'T HANDLE...THE FEAR...
I'M AFRAID FOR MY ELDERLY MOTHER BACK HOME. HOW WOULD SHE FEND FOR HERSELF... WITHOUT ME...?
SAY NO MORE.
I INTEND TO HONOR EVERY TRANSFER REQUEST OUT OF THE SURVEY CORPS.
YOUR SERVICE IS APPRECIATED.

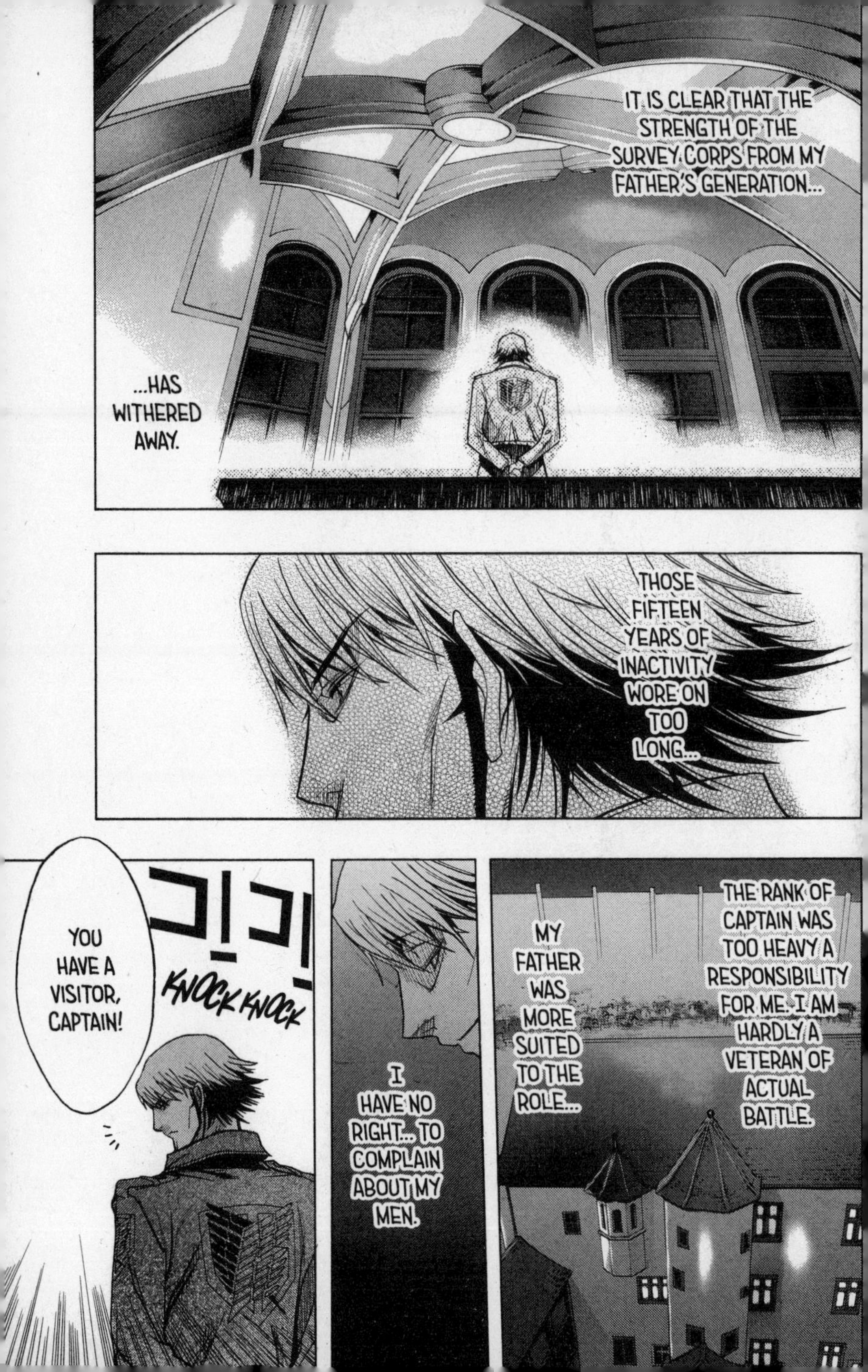
IT IS CLEAR THAT THE STRENGTH OF THE SURVEY CORPS FROM MY FATHER'S GENERATION...
...HAS WITHERED AWAY.
THOSE FIFTEEN YEARS OF INACTIVITY WORE ON TOO LONG...
THE RANK OF CAPTAIN WAS TOO HEAVY A RESPONSIBILITY FOR ME. I AM HARDLY A VETERAN OF ACTUAL BATTLE.
MY FATHER WAS MORE SUITED TO THE ROLE...
I HAVE NO RIGHT... TO COMPLAIN ABOUT MY MEN.
KNOCK KNOCK
YOU HAVE A VISITOR, CAPTAIN!

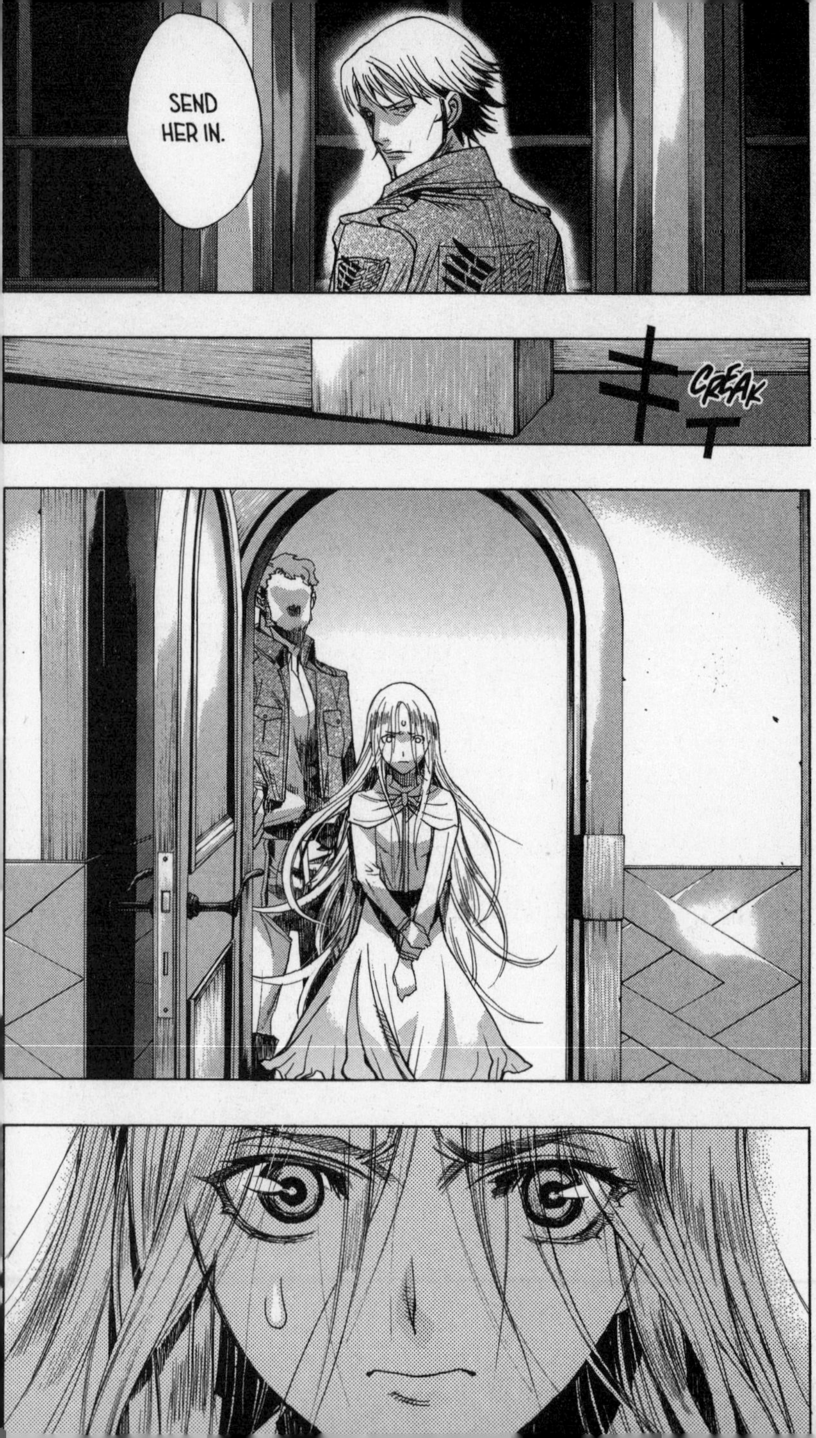
SEND HER IN.
CREAK

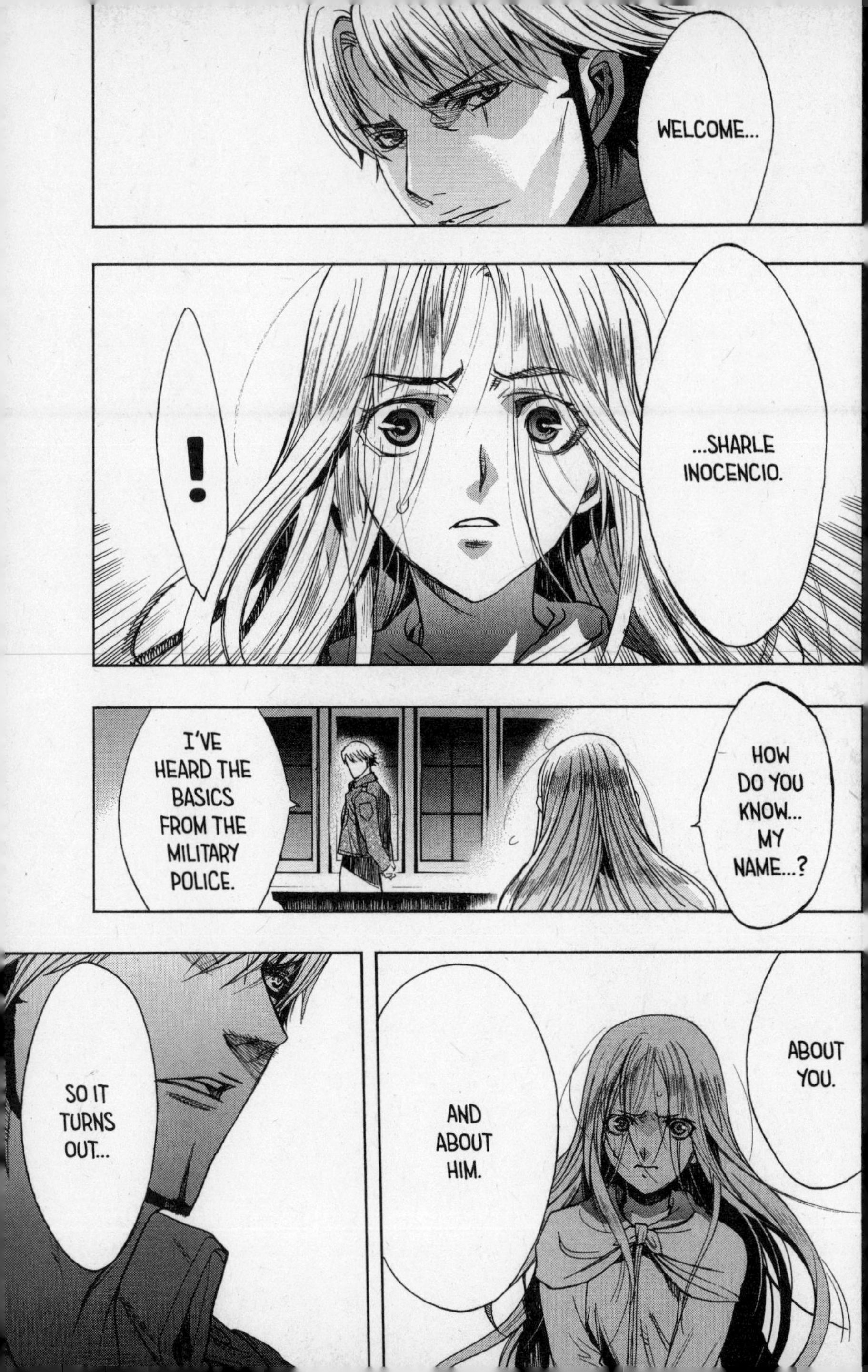
WELCOME...
...SHARLE INOCENCIO.
!
HOW DO YOU KNOW... MY NAME...?
I'VE HEARD THE BASICS FROM THE MILITARY POLICE.
ABOUT YOU.
AND ABOUT HIM.
SO IT TURNS OUT...

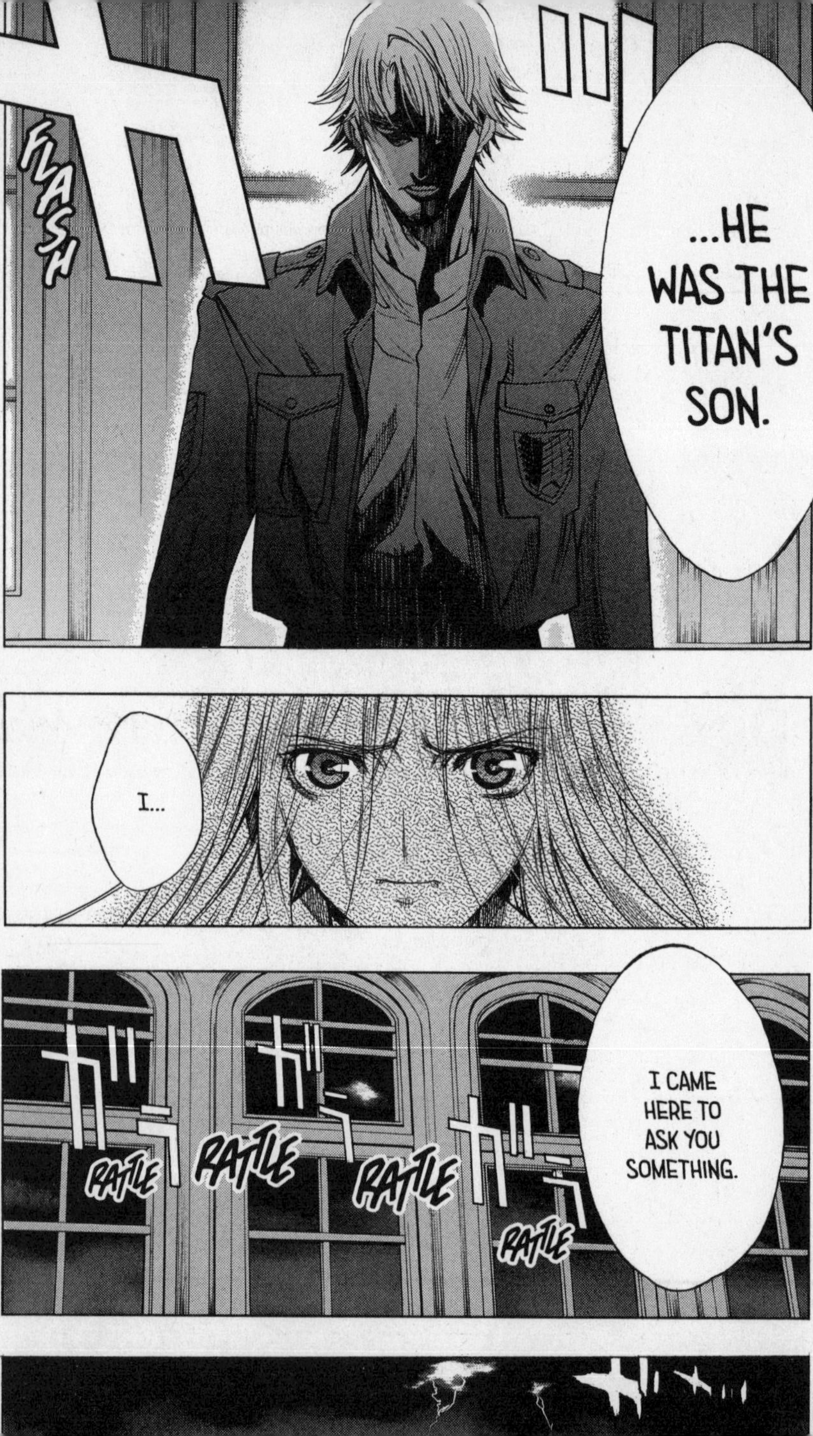
FLASH
...HE WAS THE TITAN'S SON.
I...
I CAME HERE TO ASK YOU SOMETHING.
RATTLE
RATTLE
RATTLE
RATTLE

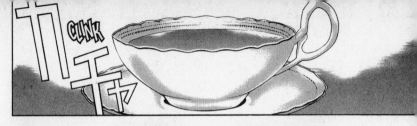

カチャ
CLINK
IT'S MY FAVORITE TEA.
VERY RARE LEAVES. I HAD TO CALL IN A FAVOR FROM A MERCHANT I KNOW TO GET THEM.
THEY HELP EASE TENSION AND ANXIETY.
IS... IS THAT SO?
カチャッ
CLINK

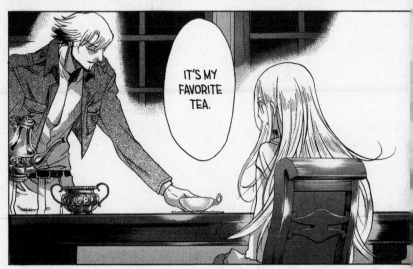

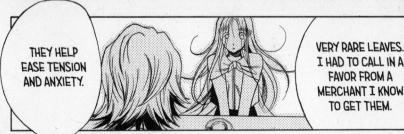

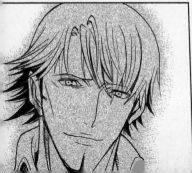

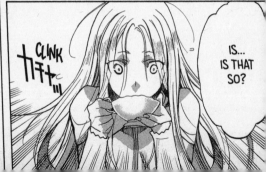

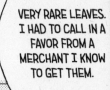

WHAT IS HE...

RUMBLE RUMBLE

WHAT IS KUKLO DOING NOW?

TO WALL SHEENA ...?

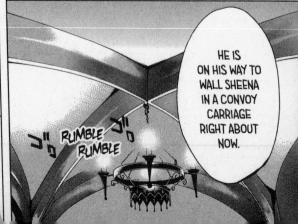

HE IS ON HIS WAY TO WALL SHEENA IN A CONVOY CARRIAGE RIGHT ABOUT NOW.

RUMBLE RUMBLE

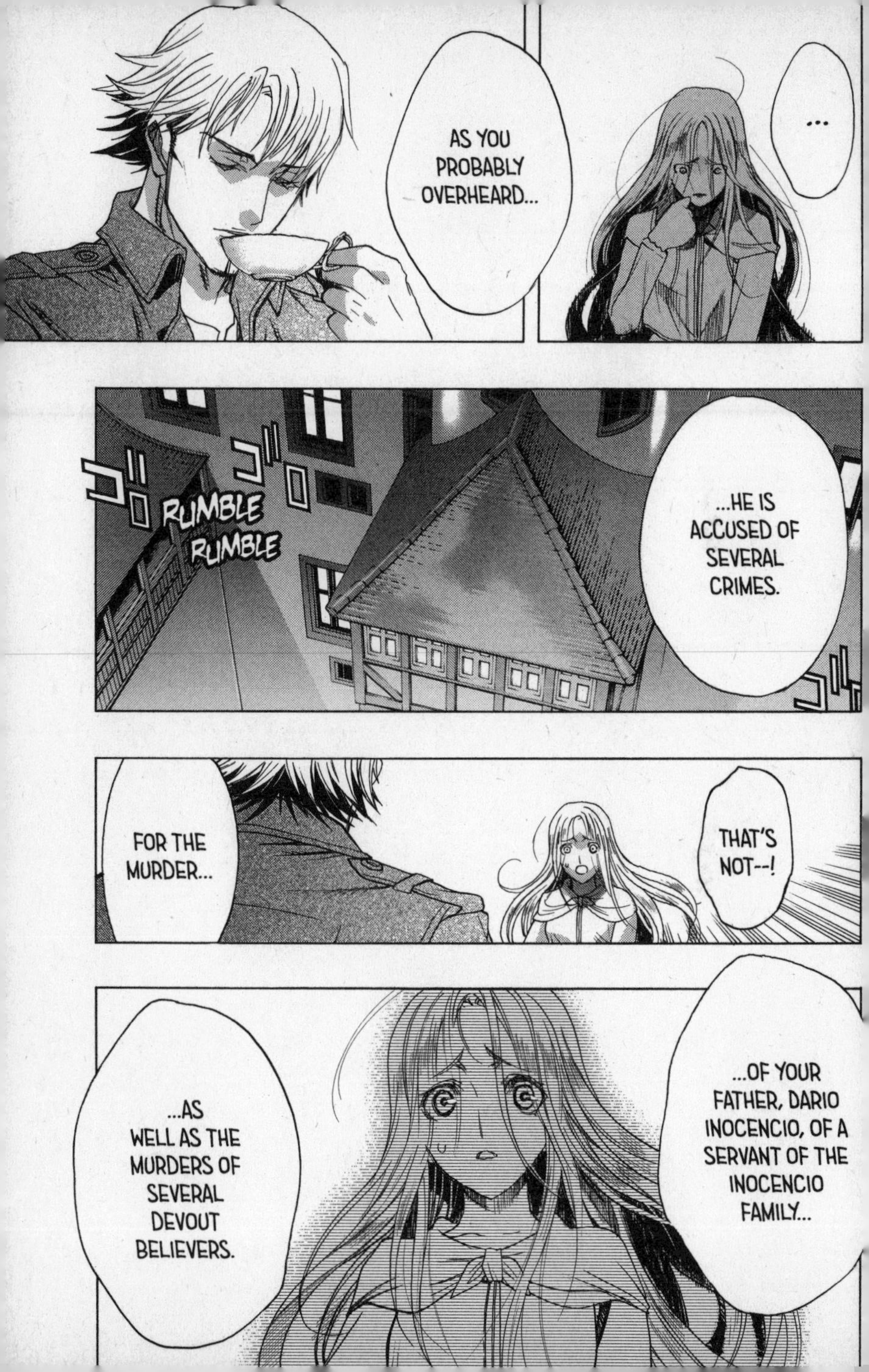
...
AS YOU PROBABLY OVERHEARD...
...HE IS ACCUSED OF SEVERAL CRIMES.
RUMBLE RUMBLE
THAT'S NOT--!
FOR THE MURDER...
...OF YOUR FATHER, DARIO INOCENCIO, OF A SERVANT OF THE INOCENCIO FAMILY...
...AS WELL AS THE MURDERS OF SEVERAL DEVOUT BELIEVERS.

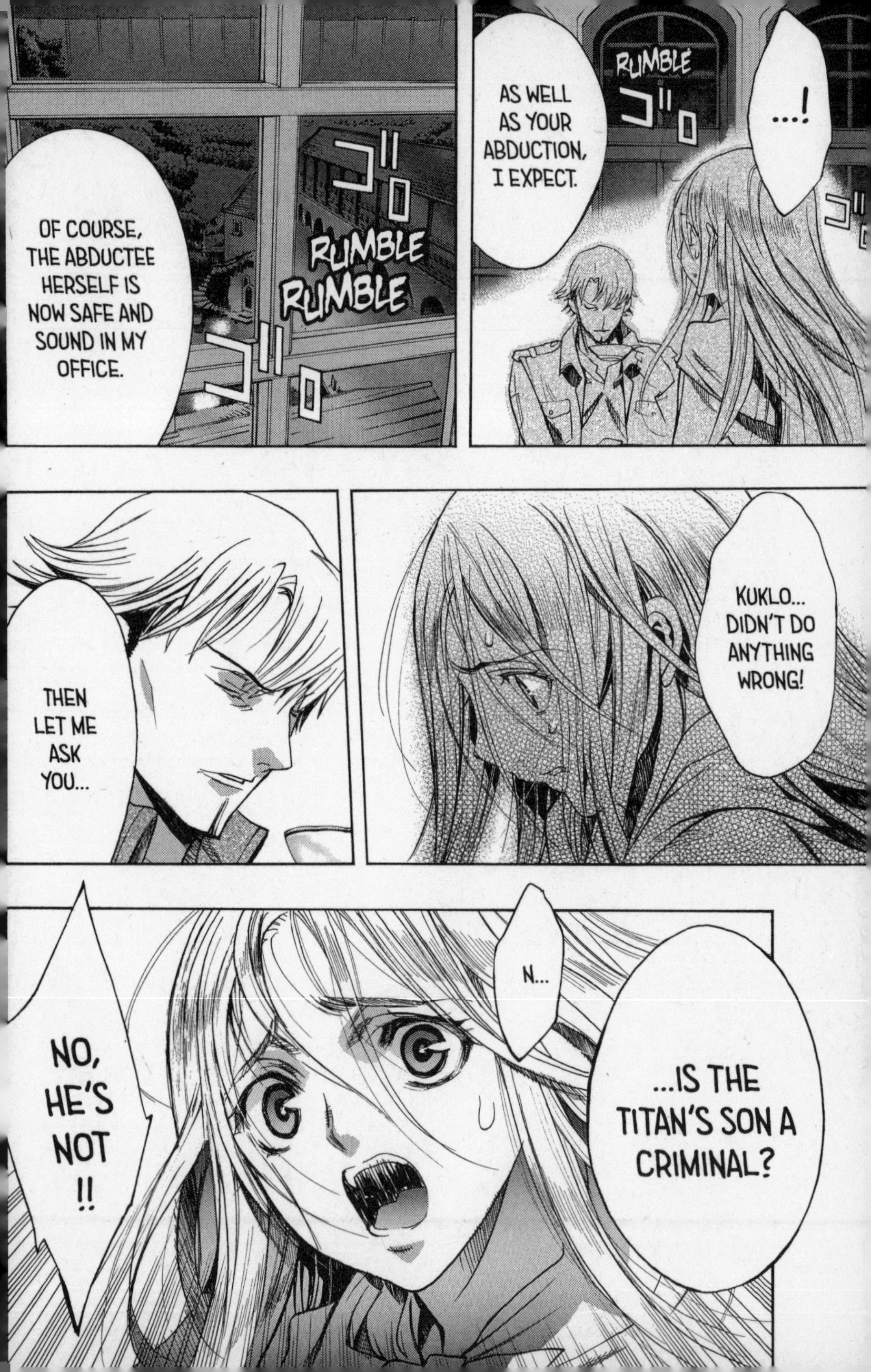
...!
RUMBLE
ゴロ
AS WELL AS YOUR ABDUCTION, I EXPECT.
ゴロ
RUMBLE
RUMBLE
ゴロ
OF COURSE, THE ABDUCTEE HERSELF IS NOW SAFE AND SOUND IN MY OFFICE.
KUKLO... DIDN'T DO ANYTHING WRONG!
THEN LET ME ASK YOU...
...IS THE TITAN'S SON A CRIMINAL?
N...
NO, HE'S NOT !!

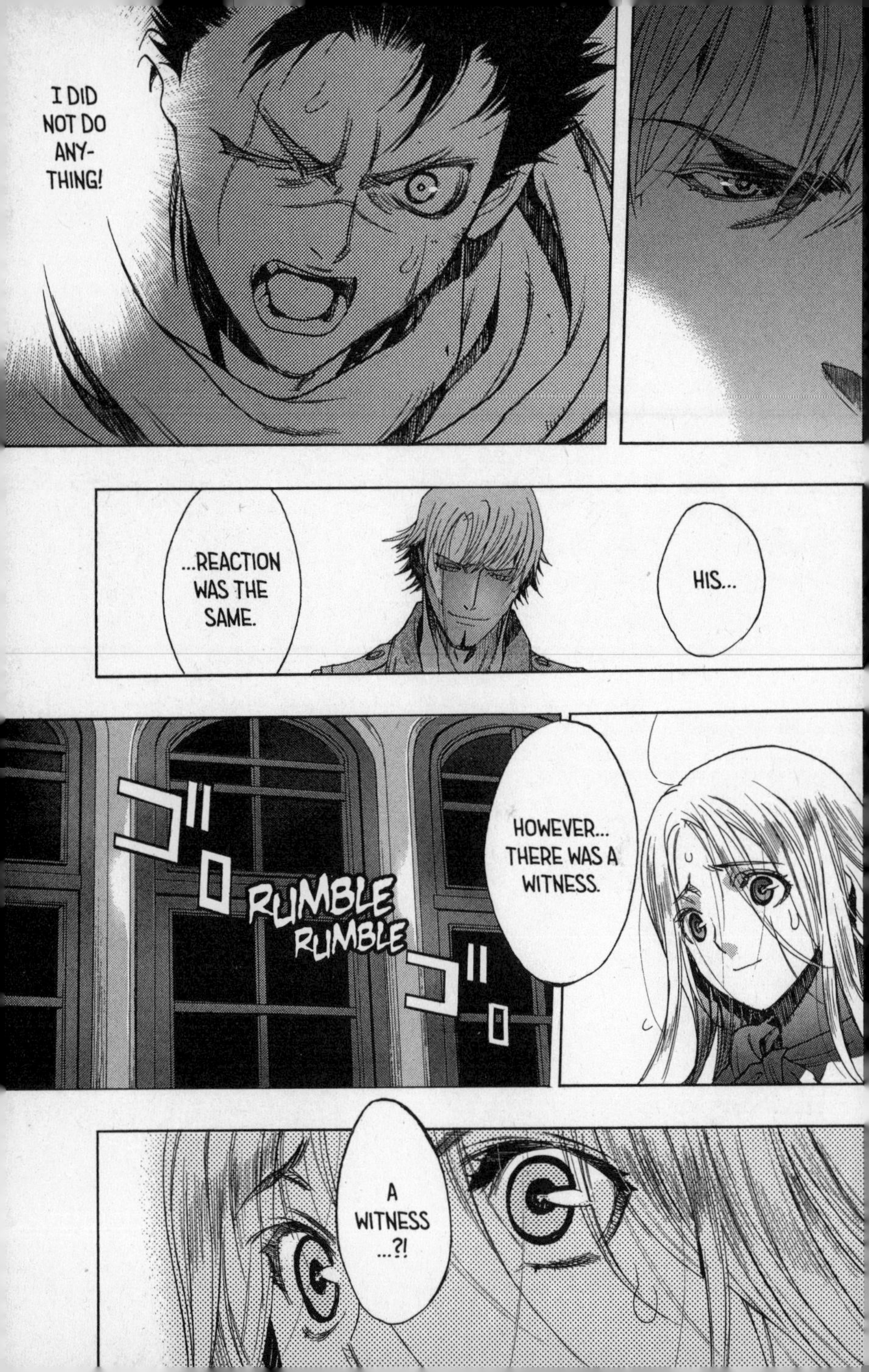
I DID NOT DO ANY-THING!
HIS...
...REACTION WAS THE SAME.
HOWEVER... THERE WAS A WITNESS.
ゴロ
RUMBLE RUMBLE
ゴロ
A WITNESS ...?!

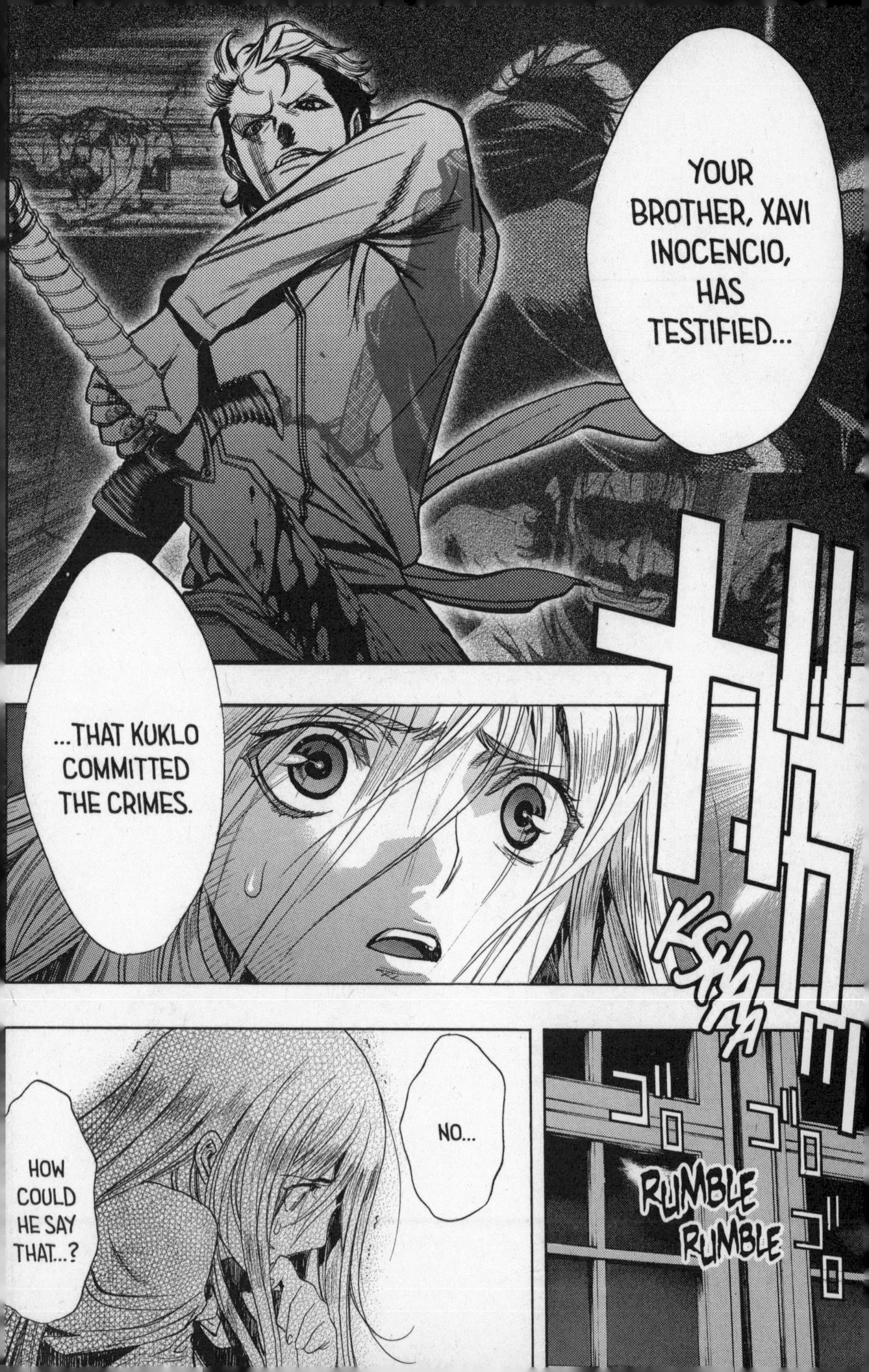
YOUR BROTHER, XAVI INOCENCIO, HAS TESTIFIED...
...THAT KUKLO COMMITTED THE CRIMES.
KSHAA
RUMBLE RUMBLE
NO...
HOW COULD HE SAY THAT...?

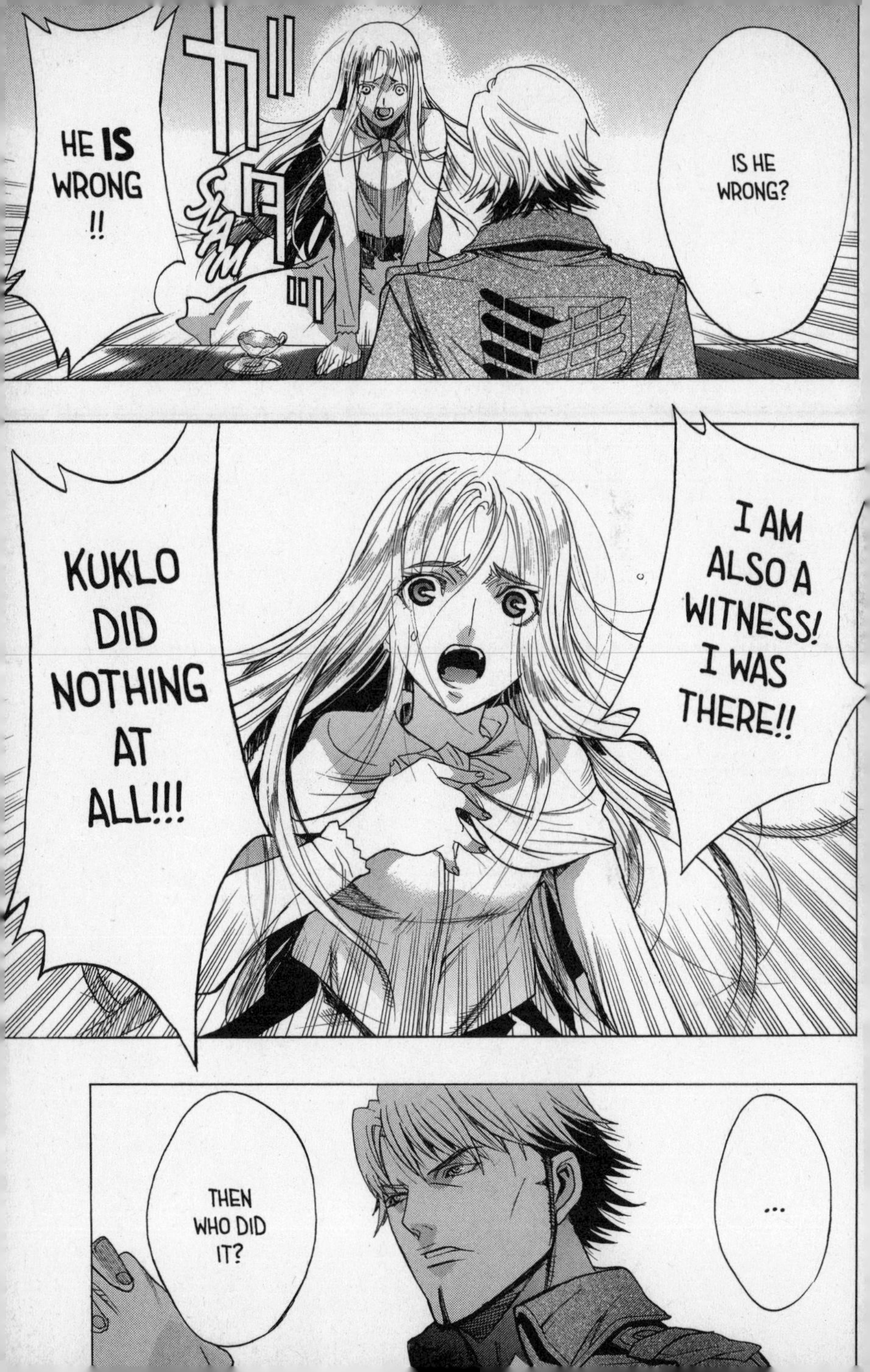
IS HE WRONG?
HE **IS** WRONG !!
SLAM
I AM ALSO A WITNESS! I WAS THERE!!
KUKLO DID NOTHING AT ALL!!!
...
THEN WHO DID IT?

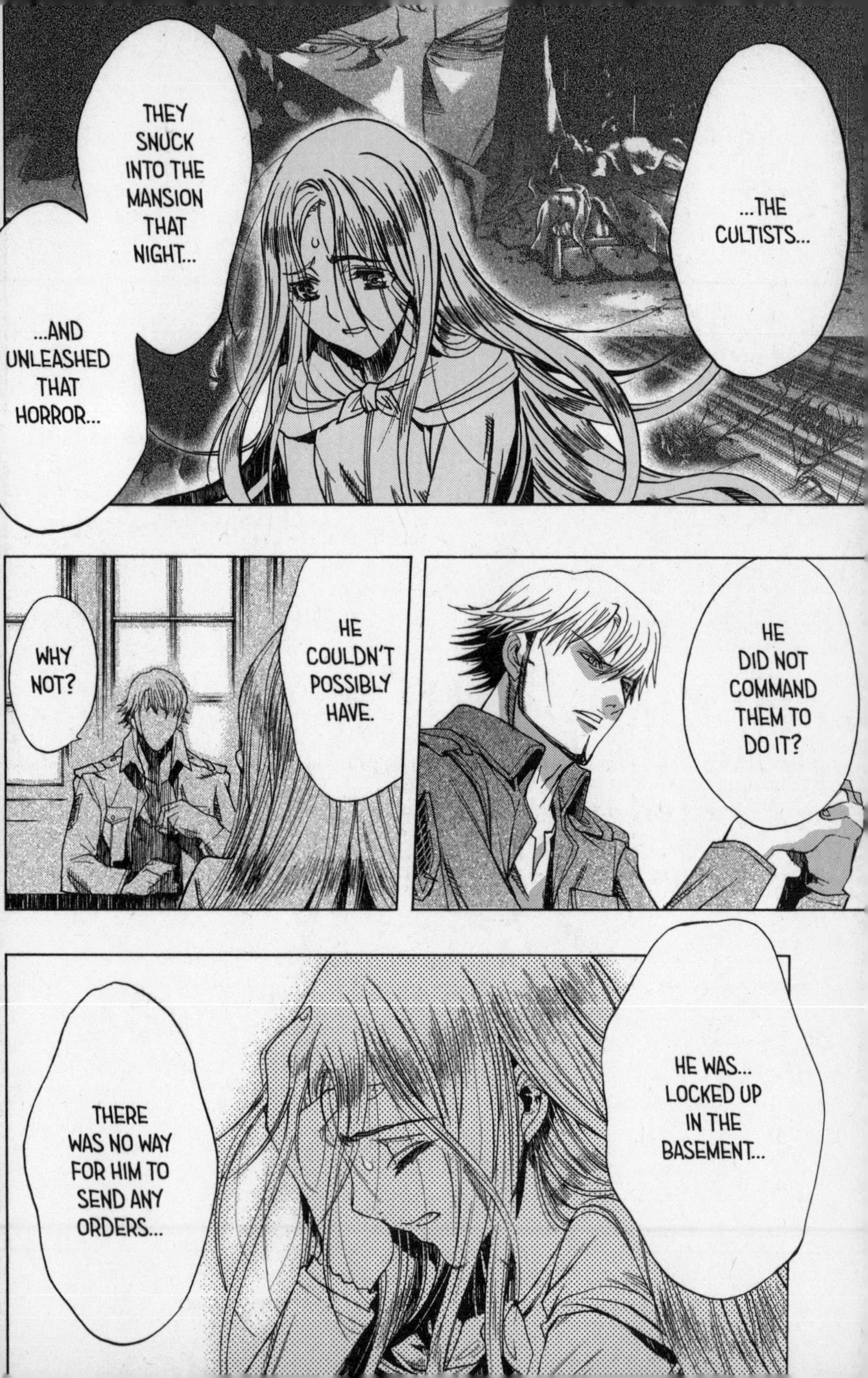
...THE CULTISTS...
THEY SNUCK INTO THE MANSION THAT NIGHT...
...AND UNLEASHED THAT HORROR...
HE DID NOT COMMAND THEM TO DO IT?
HE COULDN'T POSSIBLY HAVE.
WHY NOT?
HE WAS... LOCKED UP IN THE BASEMENT...
THERE WAS NO WAY FOR HIM TO SEND ANY ORDERS...

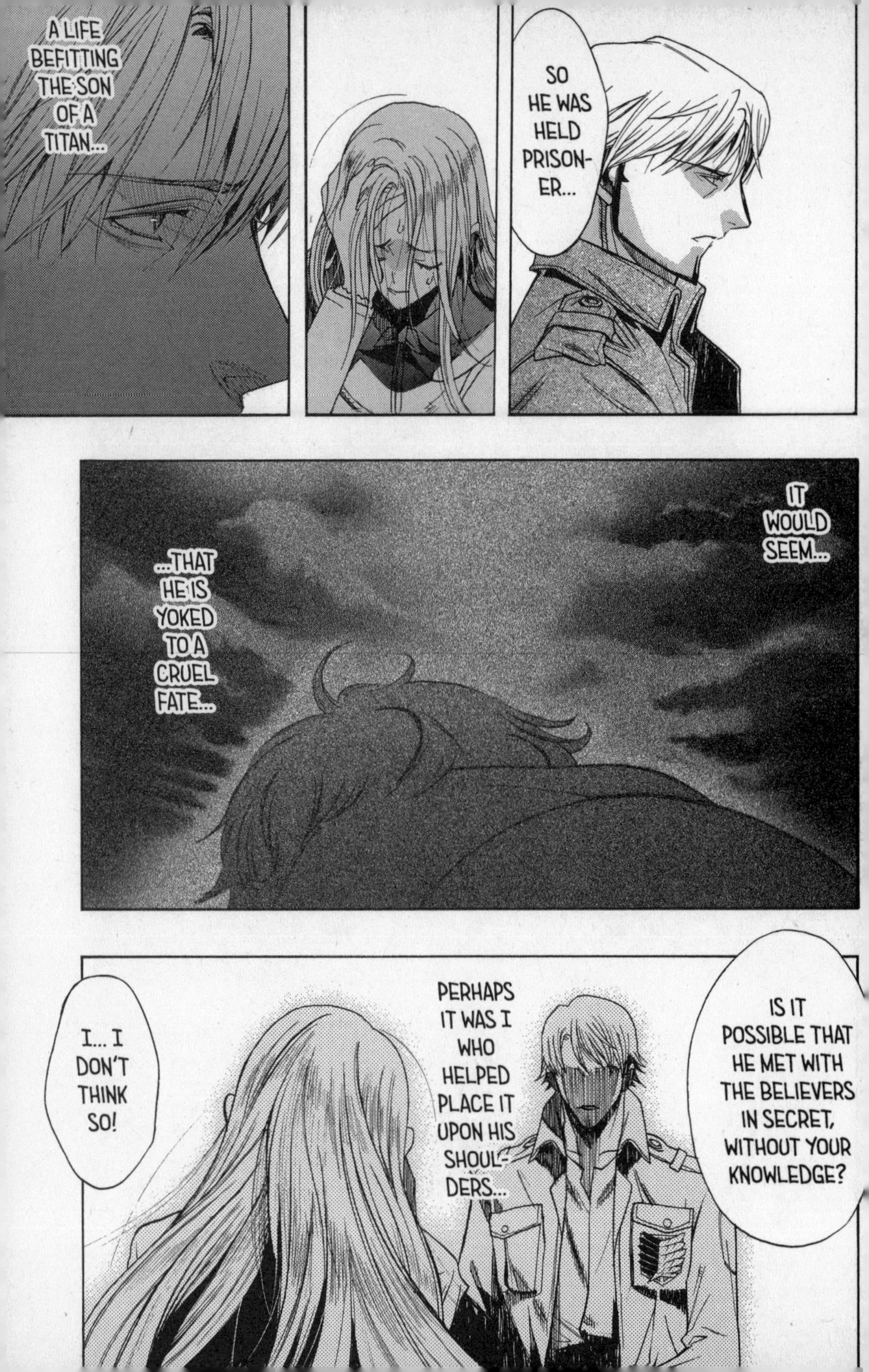
SO HE WAS HELD PRISONER...
A LIFE BEFITTING THE SON OF A TITAN...
IT WOULD SEEM...
...THAT HE IS YOKED TO A CRUEL FATE...
IS IT POSSIBLE THAT HE MET WITH THE BELIEVERS IN SECRET, WITHOUT YOUR KNOWLEDGE?
PERHAPS IT WAS I WHO HELPED PLACE IT UPON HIS SHOULDERS...
I... I DON'T THINK SO!

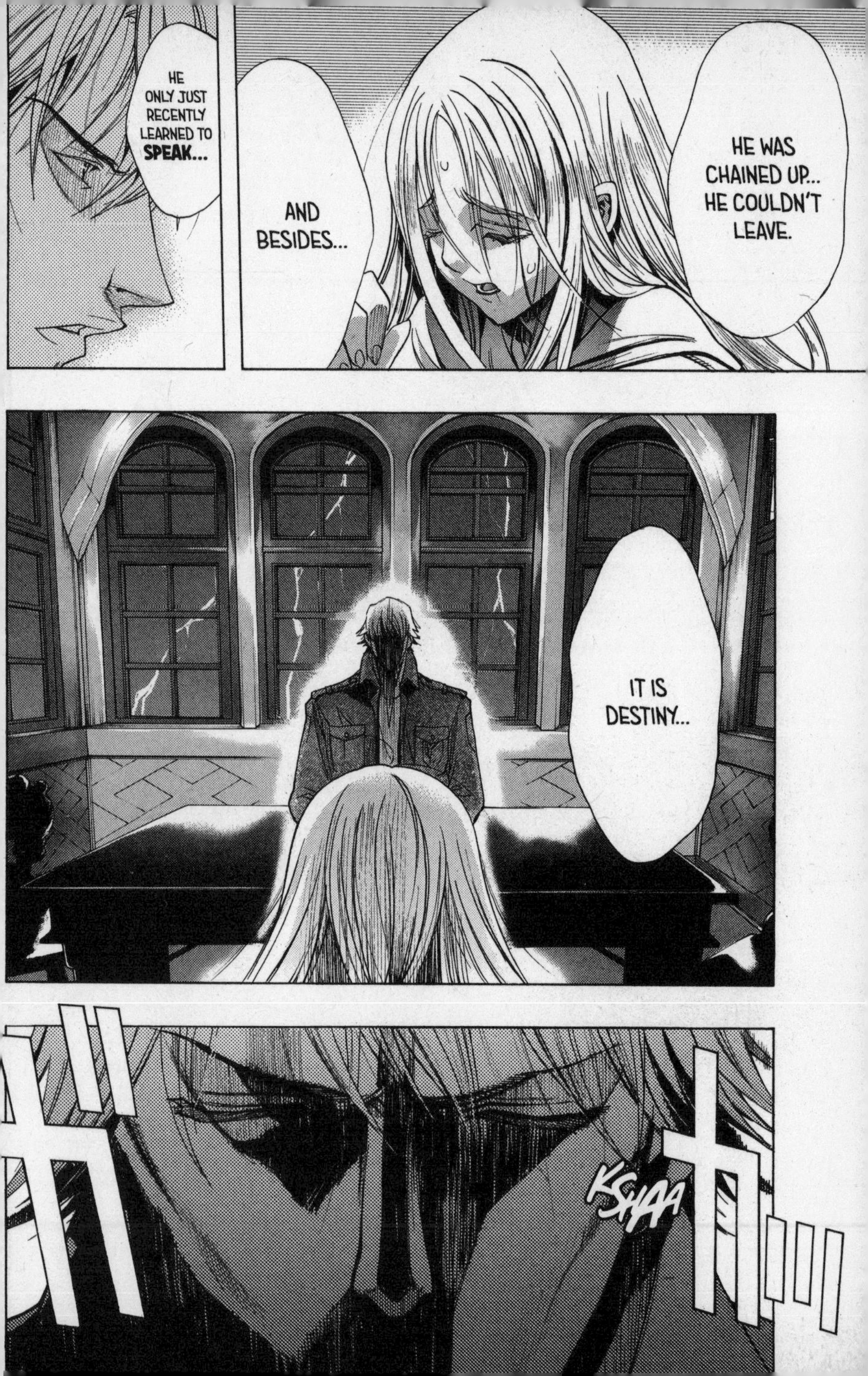
HE WAS CHAINED UP... HE COULDN'T LEAVE.
AND BESIDES...
HE ONLY JUST RECENTLY LEARNED TO SPEAK...
IT IS DESTINY...
KSHAA

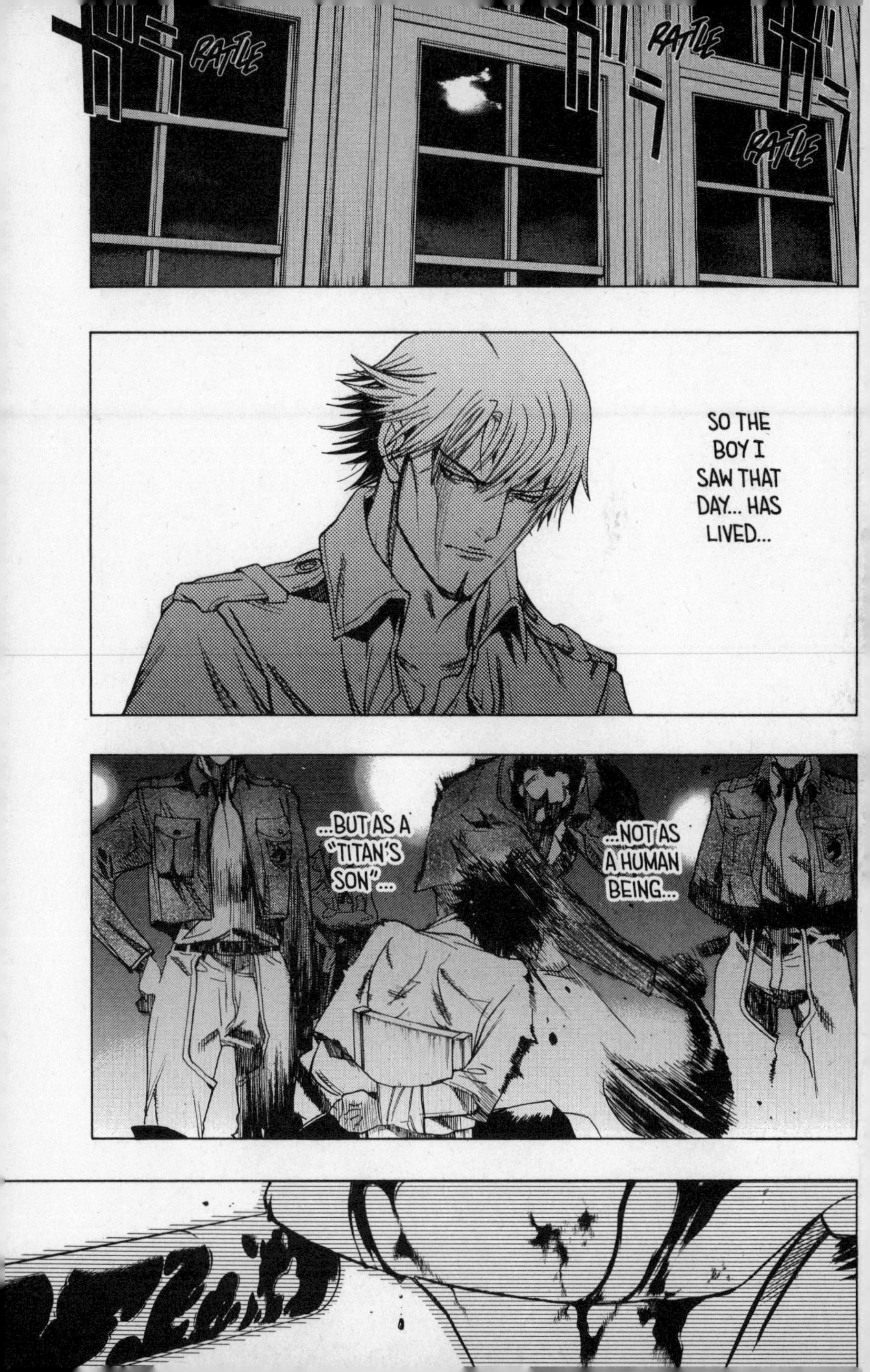
RATTLE
RATTLE
RATTLE
SO THE BOY I SAW THAT DAY... HAS LIVED...
...NOT AS A HUMAN BEING...
...BUT AS A "TITAN'S SON"...

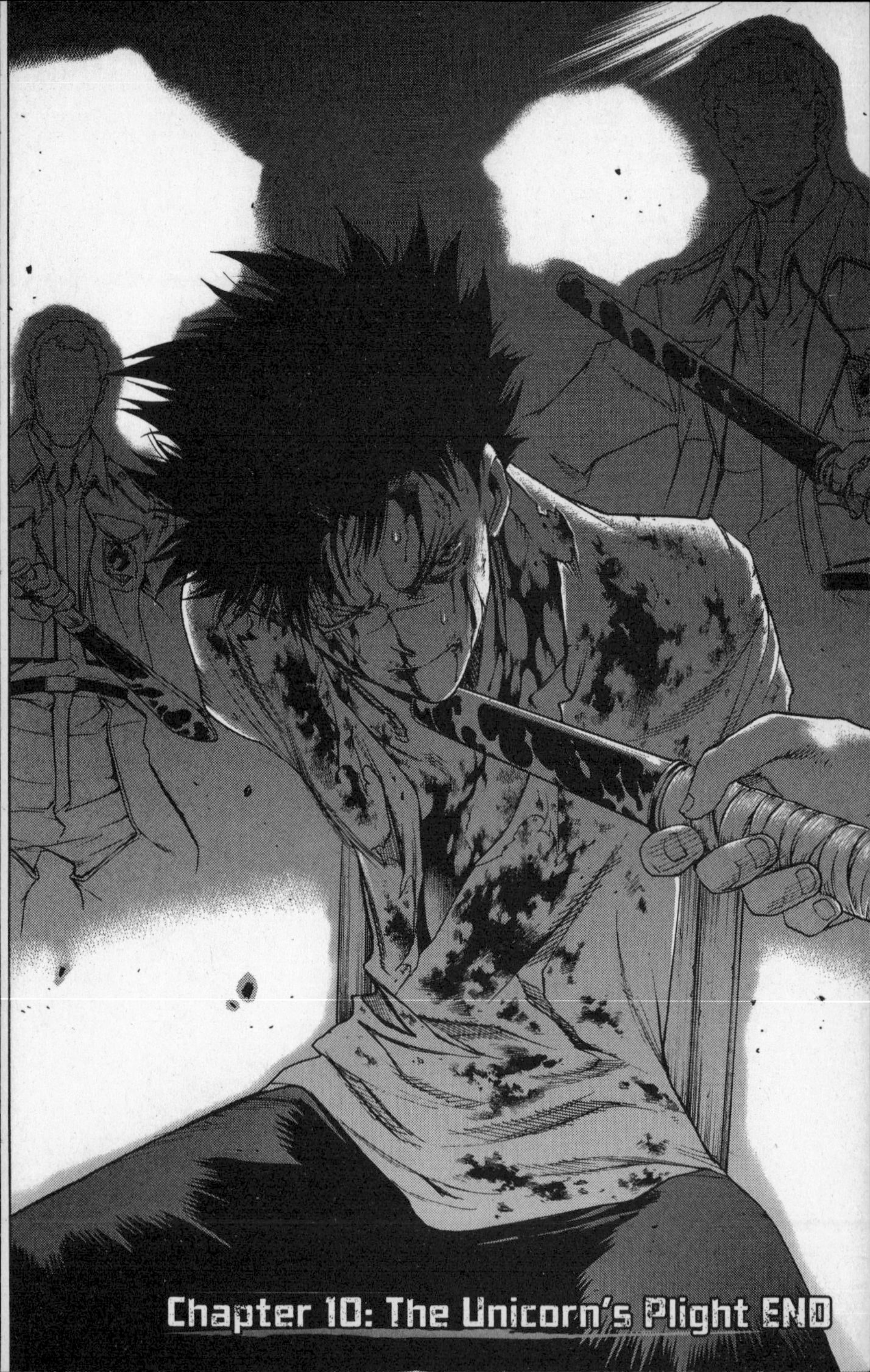
Chapter 10: The Unicorn's Plight END

ATTACK ON TITAN
—BEFORE THE FALL

TO BE CONTINUED

ATTACK ON TITAN
BEFORE THE FALL

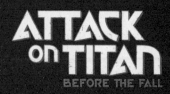

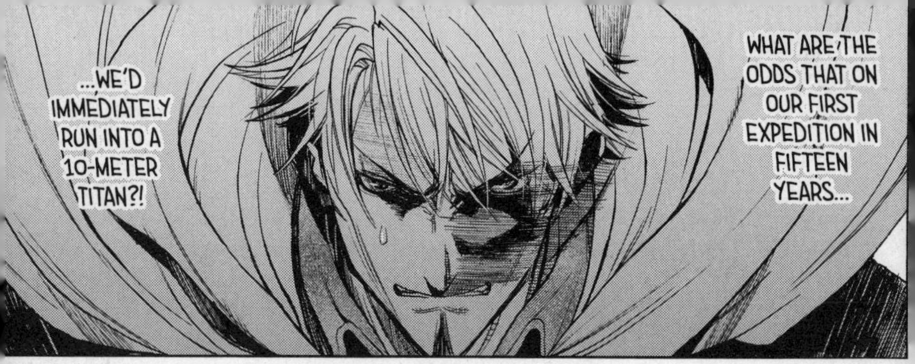
WHAT ARE THE ODDS THAT ON OUR FIRST EXPEDITION IN FIFTEEN YEARS...
...WE'D IMMEDIATELY RUN INTO A 10-METER TITAN?!

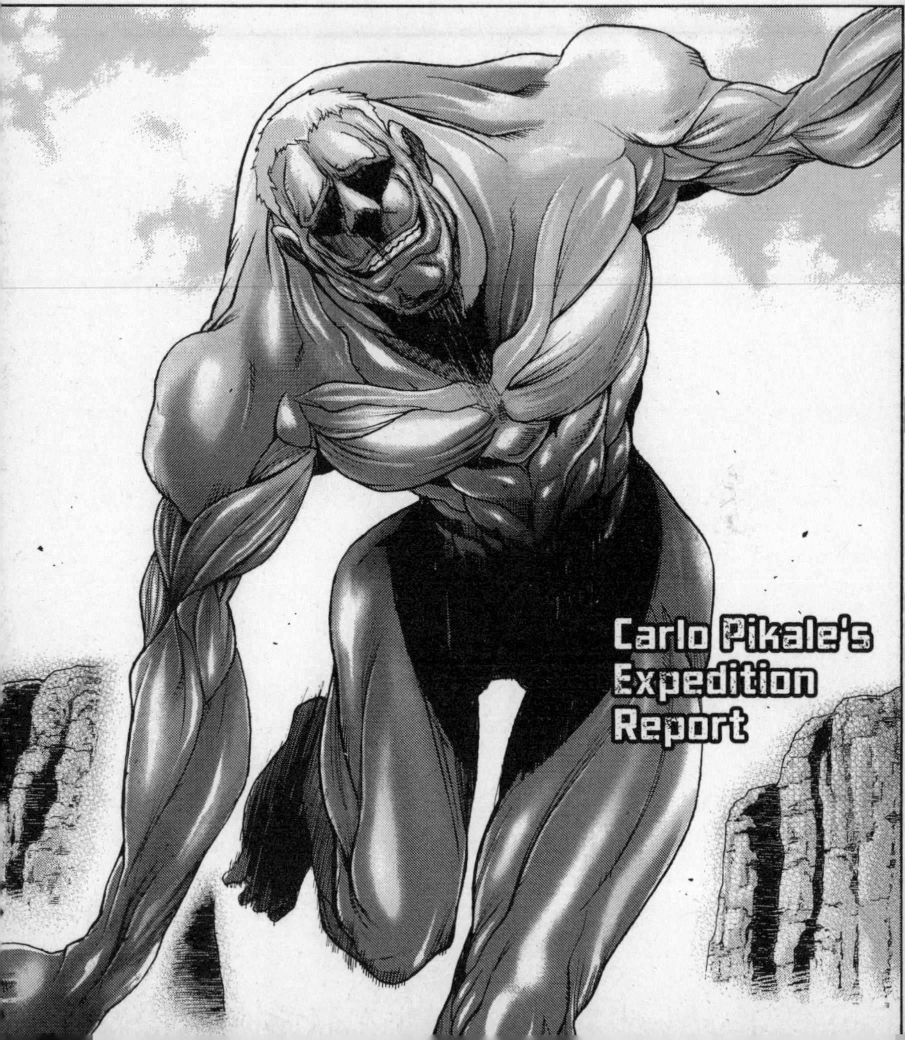
Carlo Pikale's Expedition Report

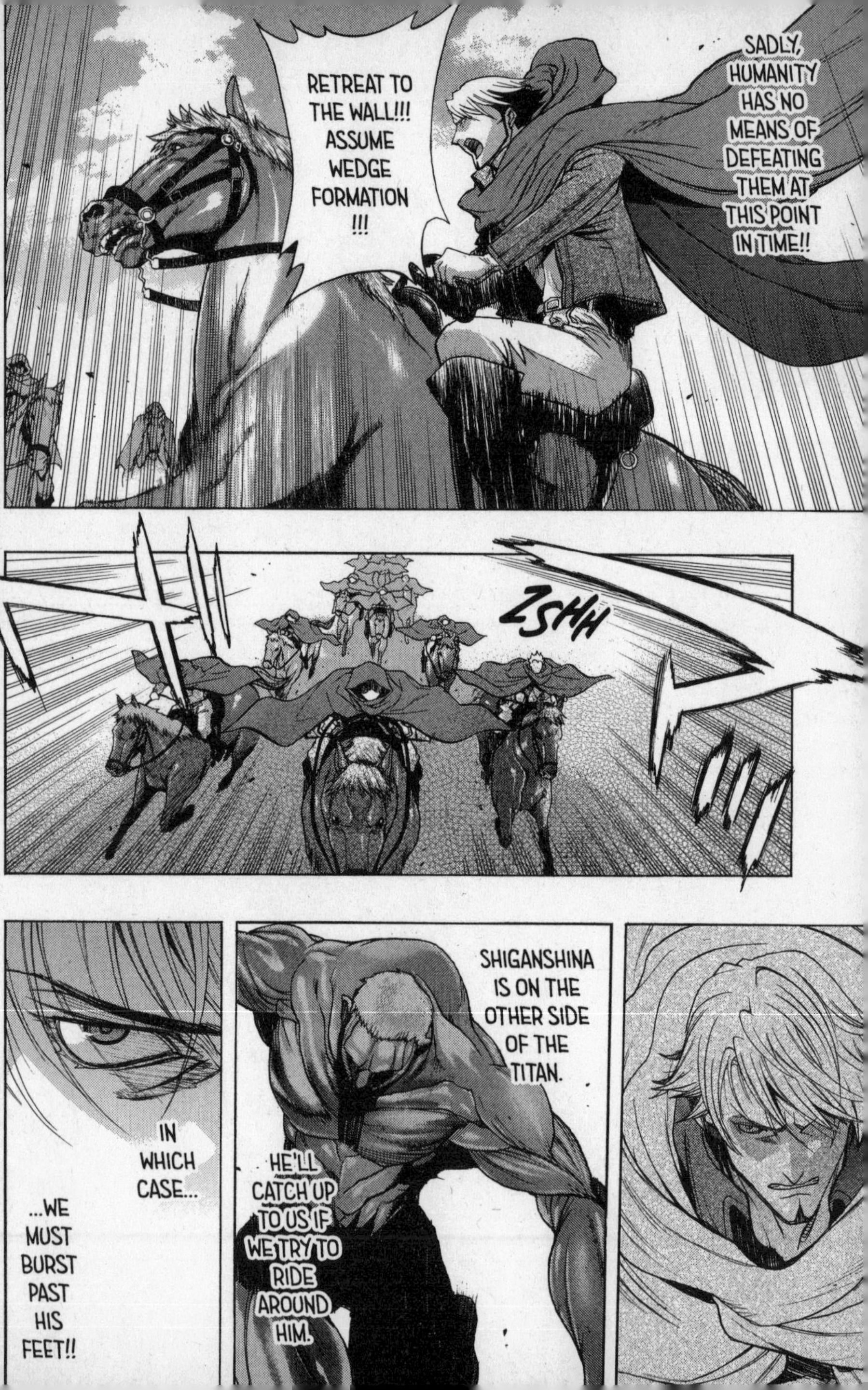
SADLY, HUMANITY HAS NO MEANS OF DEFEATING THEM AT THIS POINT IN TIME!!
RETREAT TO THE WALL!!! ASSUME WEDGE FORMATION!!!
ZSHH
SHIGANSHINA IS ON THE OTHER SIDE OF THE TITAN.
HE'LL CATCH UP TO US IF WE TRY TO RIDE AROUND HIM.
IN WHICH CASE...
...WE MUST BURST PAST HIS FEET!!

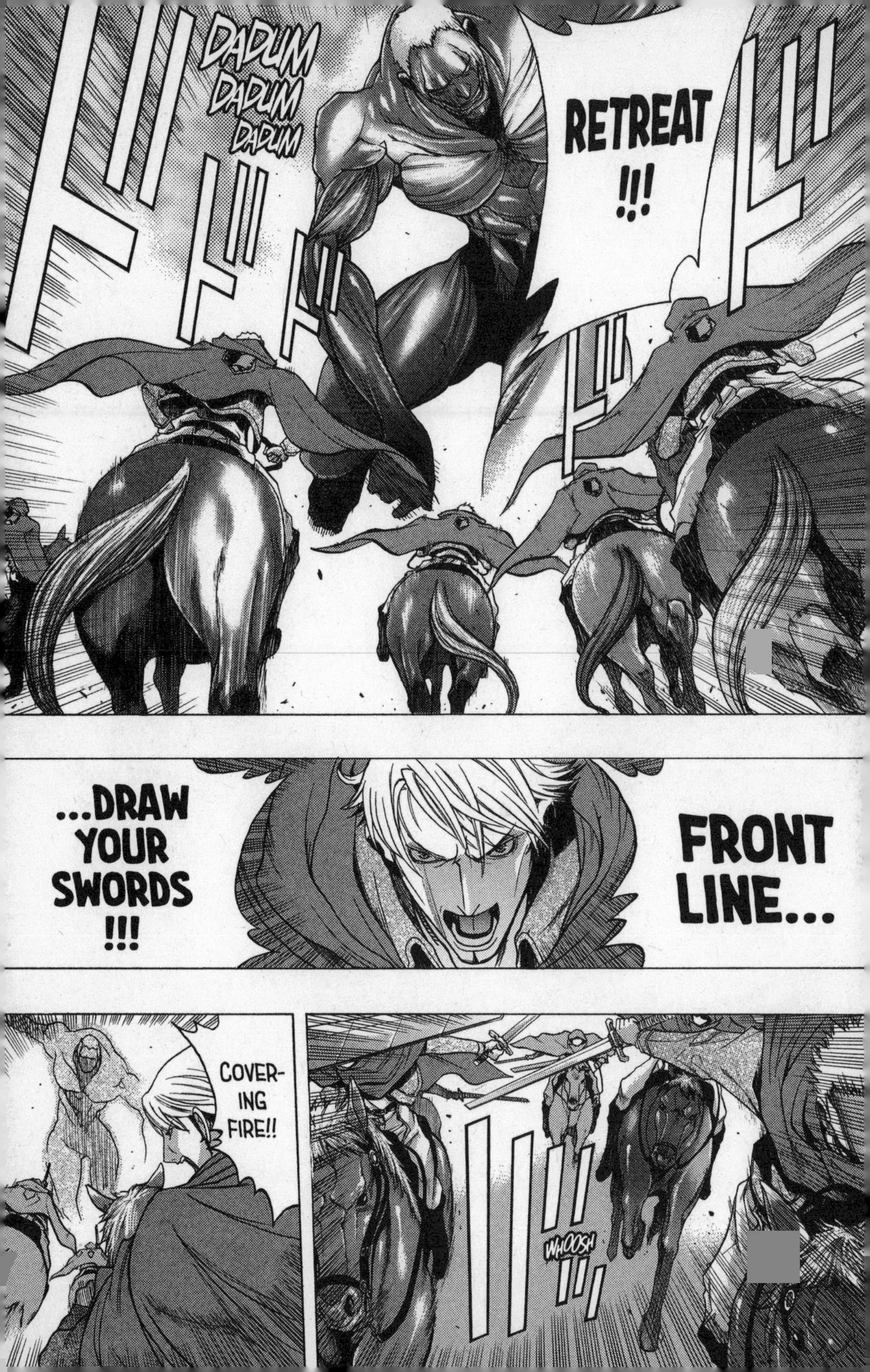
RETREAT!!!
DADUM DADUM DADUM
FRONT LINE...
...DRAW YOUR SWORDS!!!
WHOOSH
COVERING FIRE!!

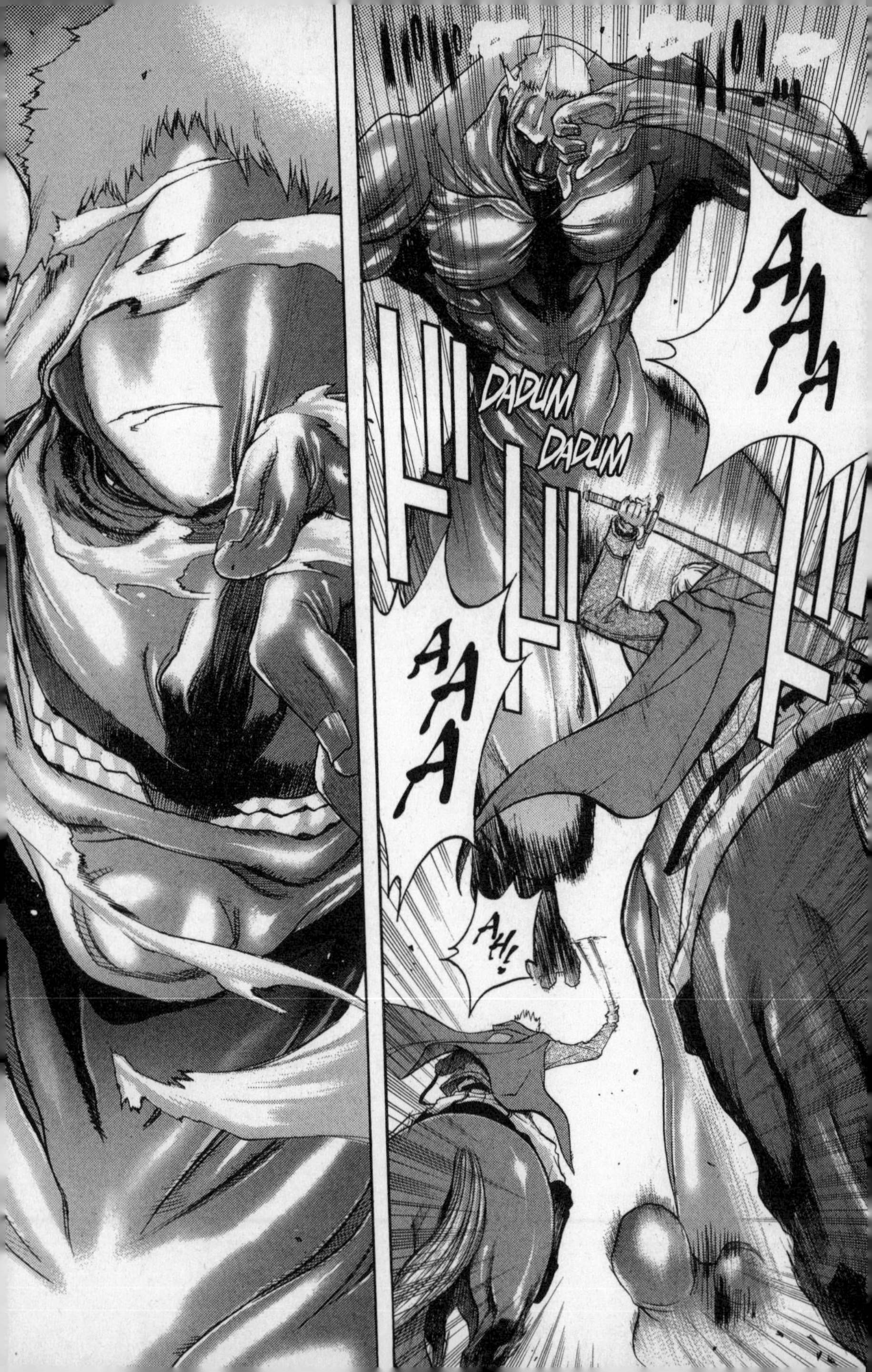
DADUM
DADUM
AH!!

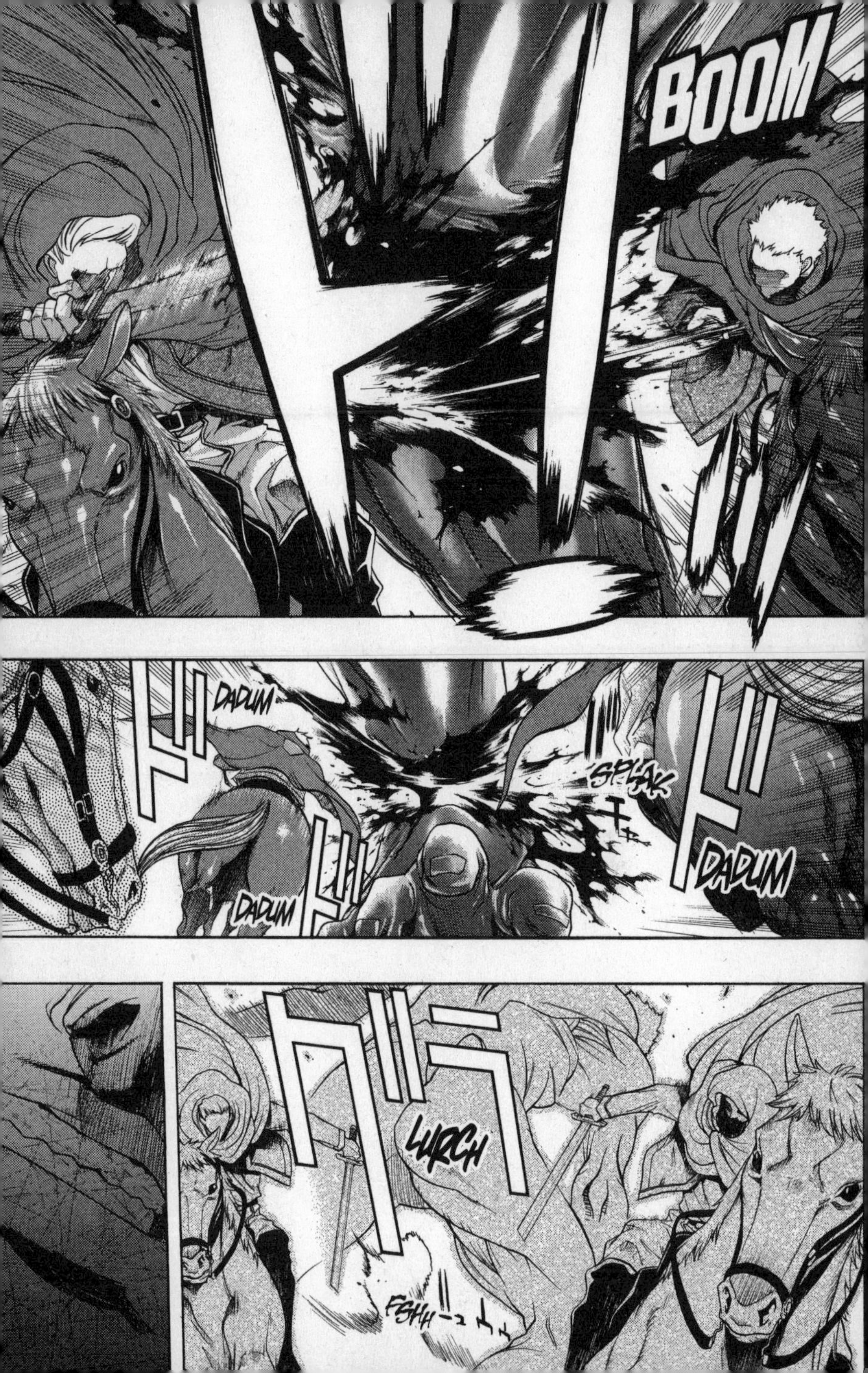
BOOM
DADUM
SPLAK
DADUM
DADUM
DADUM
LURCH
FSHH

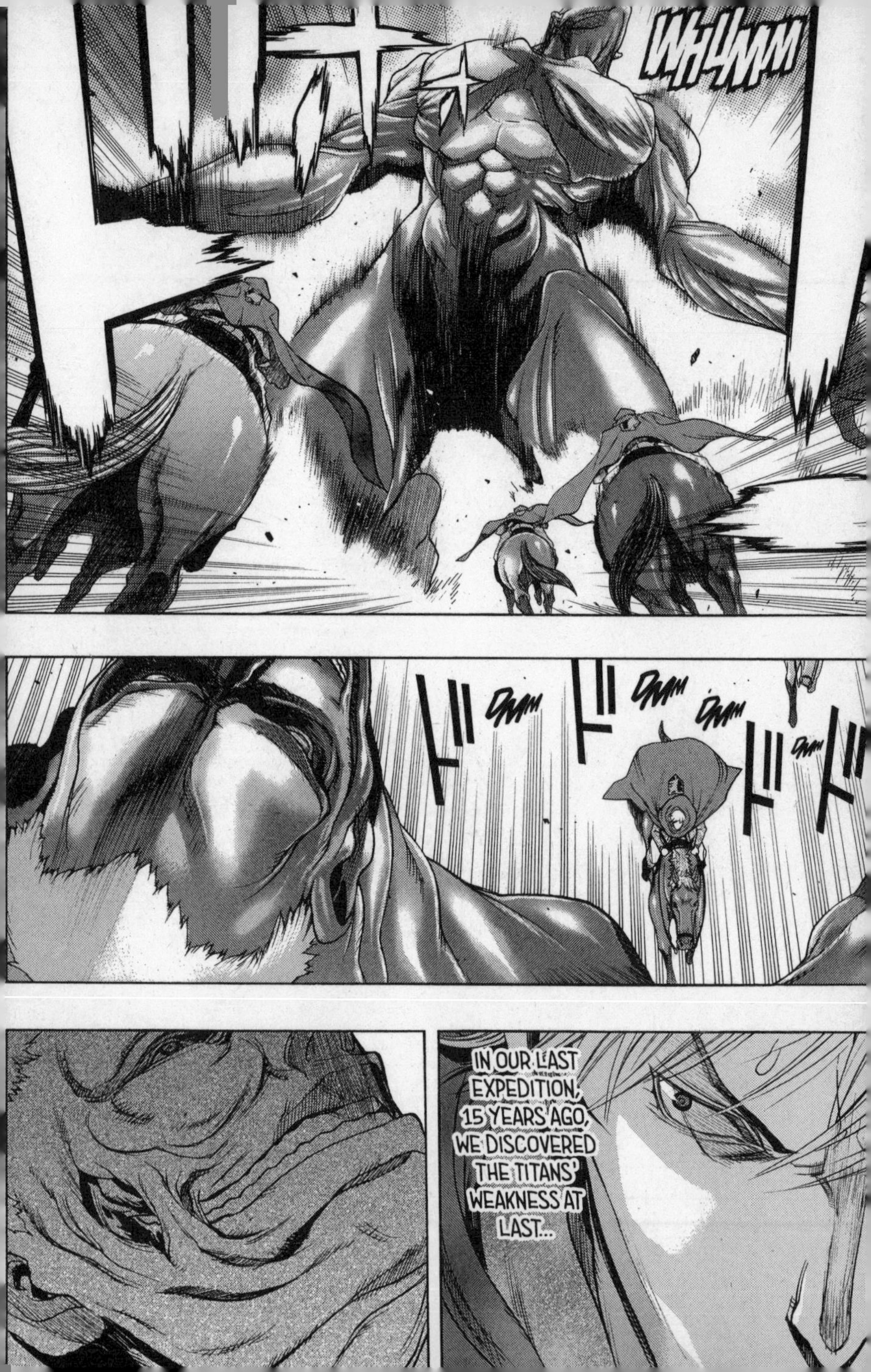
WHUMM
DMM
DMM
DMM
DMM
IN OUR LAST EXPEDITION, 15 YEARS AGO, WE DISCOVERED THE TITANS' WEAKNESS AT LAST...

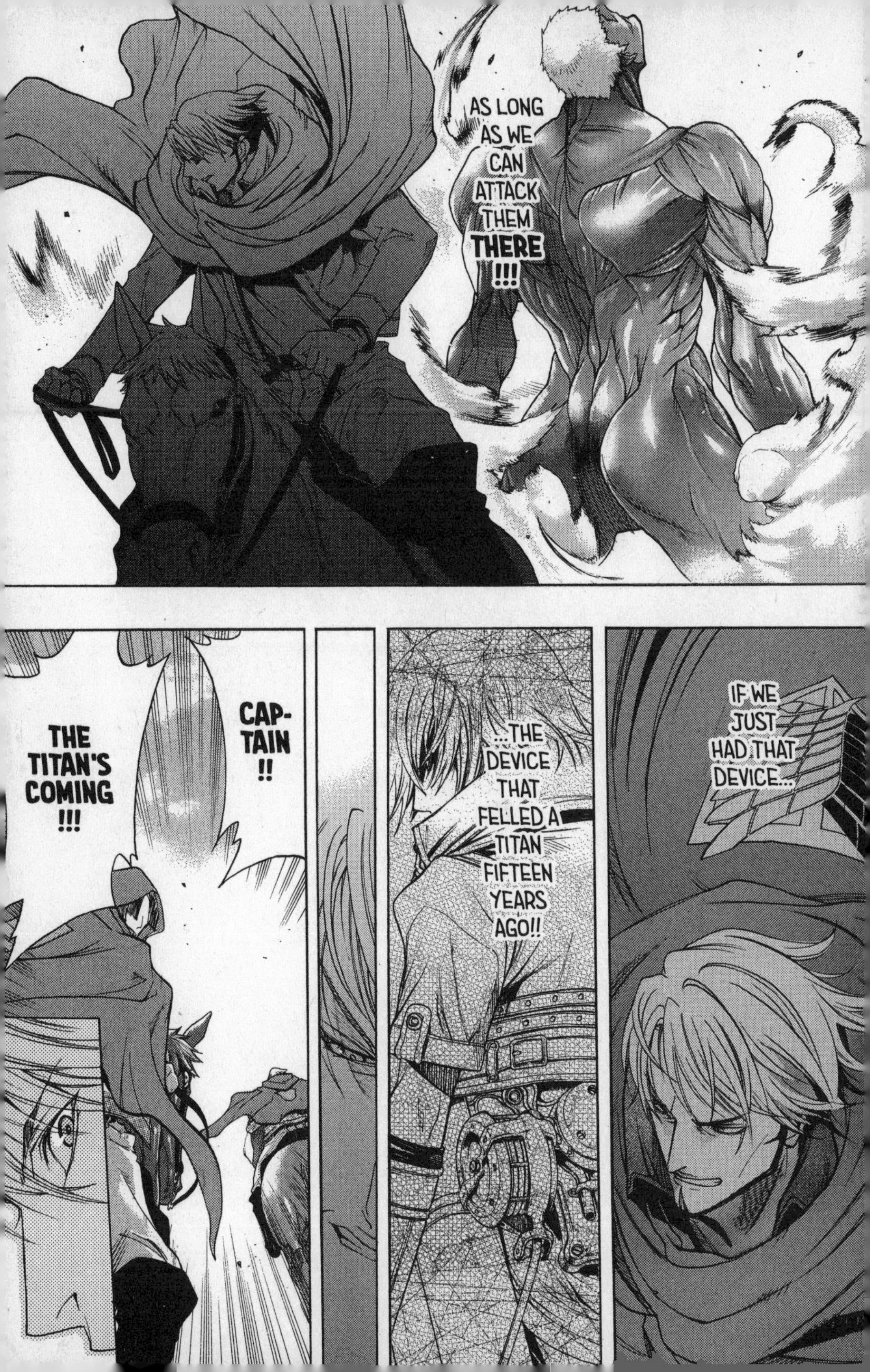
AS LONG AS WE CAN ATTACK THEM THERE!!!
IF WE JUST HAD THAT DEVICE...
...THE DEVICE THAT FELLED A TITAN FIFTEEN YEARS AGO!!
CAP-TAIN!!
THE TITAN'S COMING!!!

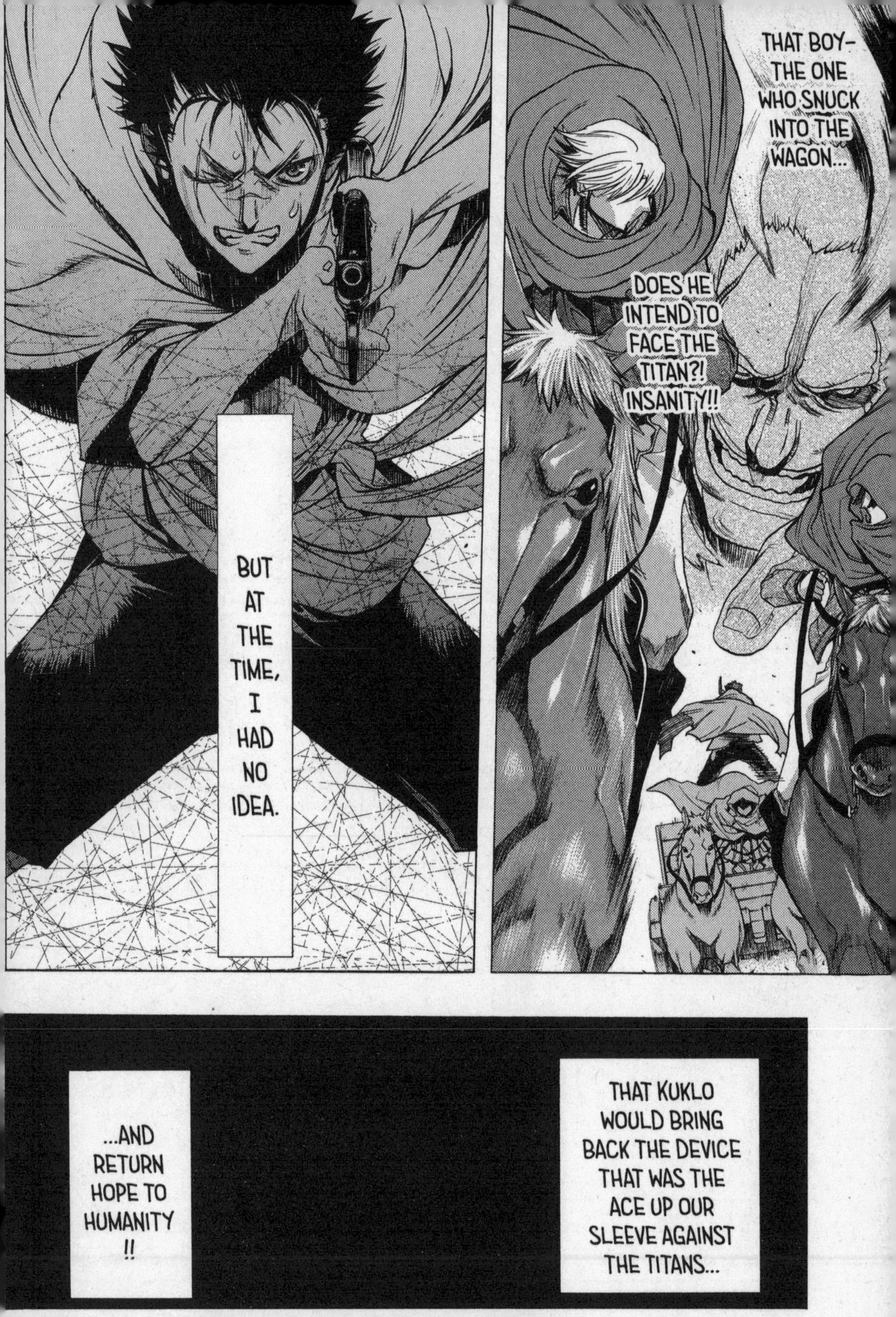
THAT BOY-THE ONE WHO SNUCK INTO THE WAGON...
DOES HE INTEND TO FACE THE TITAN?! INSANITY!!
BUT AT THE TIME, I HAD NO IDEA.
THAT KUKLO WOULD BRING BACK THE DEVICE THAT WAS THE ACE UP OUR SLEEVE AGAINST THE TITANS...
...AND RETURN HOPE TO HUMANITY!!

Carlo Pikale's Expedition Report · End

ATTACK on TITAN
BEFORE THE FALL

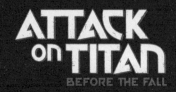

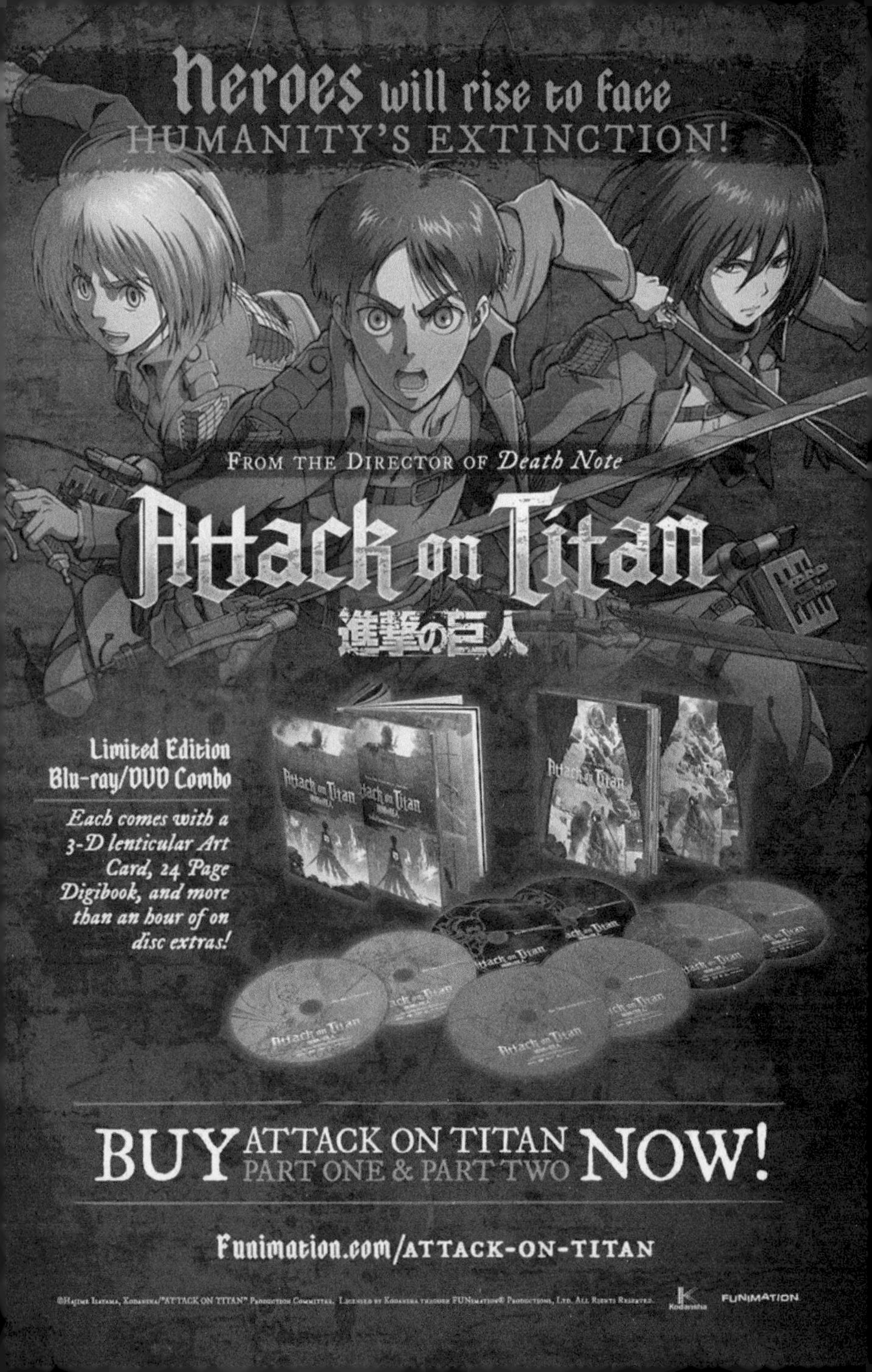
Heroes will rise to face
HUMANITY'S EXTINCTION!
FROM THE DIRECTOR OF Death Note
Attack on Titan
進撃の巨人
Limited Edition
Blu-ray/DVD Combo
Each comes with a 3-D lenticular Art Card, 24 Page Digibook, and more than an hour of on disc extras!
BUY ATTACK ON TITAN PART ONE & PART TWO NOW!
Funimation.com/ATTACK-ON-TITAN
©Hajime Isayama, Kodansha/"ATTACK ON TITAN" Production Committee. Licensed by Kodansha through FUNimation® Productions, Ltd. All Rights Reserved.
Kodansha
FUNIMATION

SANKAREA
undying love

"I ONLY LIKE ZOMBIE GIRLS."

Chihiro has an unusual connection to zombie movies. He doesn't feel bad for the survivors – he wants to comfort the undead girls they slaughter! When his pet passes away, he brews a resurrection potion. He's discovered by local heiress Sanka Rea, and she serves as his first test subject!

KC KODANSHA COMICS

SHERLOCK BONES

KC KODANSHA COMICS

DEDUCTIVE DOG DETECTIVE

When Takeru adopts a new pet, he's in for a surprise—the dog is none other than the reincarnation of Sherlock Holmes. With no one else able to communicate with Holmes, Takeru is roped into becoming Sherdog's assistant, John Watson. Using his sleuthing skills, Holmes uncovers clues to solve the trickiest crimes.

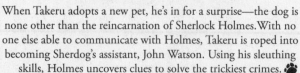

Say I Love You.

KC
KODANSHA
COMICS

Mei Tachibana has no friends — and says she doesn't need them!
But everything changes when she accidentally roundhouse kicks the most popular boy in school! However, Yamato Kurosawa isn't angry in the slightest—in fact, he thinks his ordinary life could use an unusual girl like Mei. But winning Mei's trust will be a tough task. How long will she refuse to say, "I love you"?

PRAISE FOR THE ANIME!

"This series never fails to put a smile on my face."
-Dramatic Reviews

"A very funny look at what happens when two strange and strangely well-suited people try to navigate the thorny path to true love together."
-Anime News Network

My Little Monster

OPPOSITES ATTRACT...MAYBE?

Haru Yoshida is feared as an unstable and violent "monster." Mizutani Shizuku is a grade-obsessed student with no friends. Fate brings these two together to form the most unlikely pair. Haru firmly believes he's in love with Mizutani and she firmly believes he's insane.

KC
KODANSHA
COMICS

NO.6

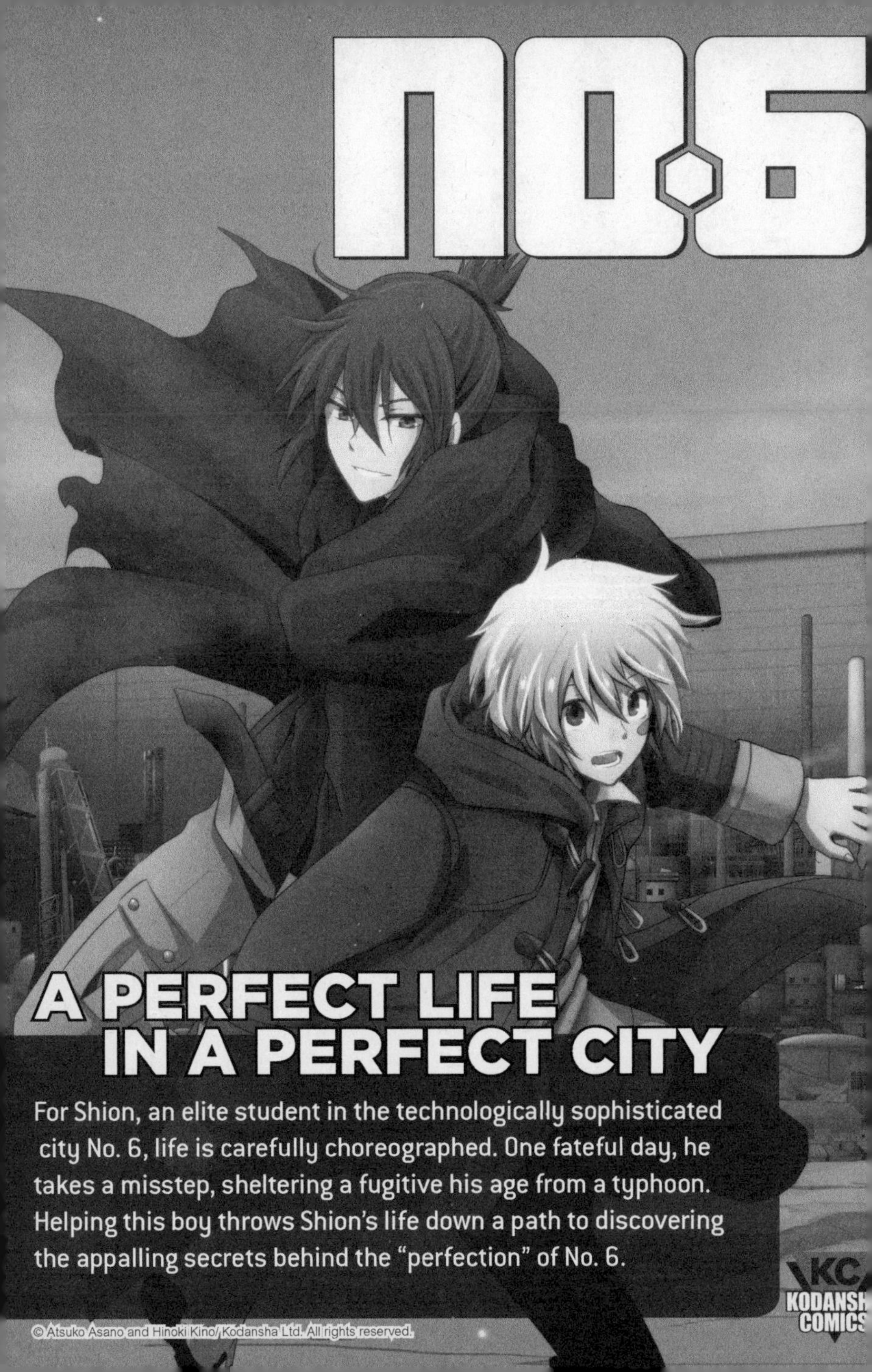

A PERFECT LIFE IN A PERFECT CITY

For Shion, an elite student in the technologically sophisticated city No. 6, life is carefully choreographed. One fateful day, he takes a misstep, sheltering a fugitive his age from a typhoon. Helping this boy throws Shion's life down a path to discovering the appalling secrets behind the "perfection" of No. 6.

KC KODANSHA COMICS

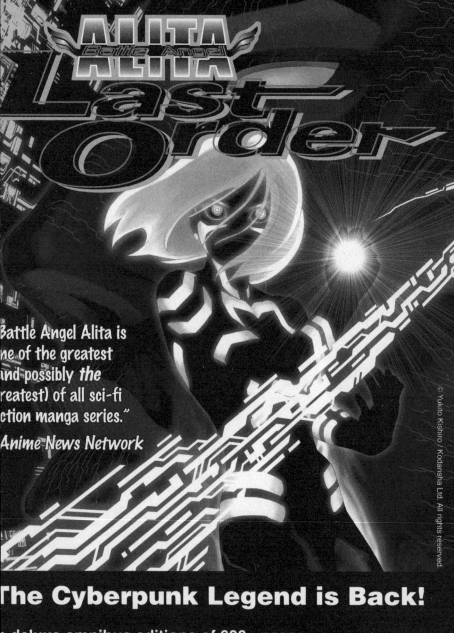

ALITA
Battle Angel
Last Order

"Battle Angel Alita is one of the greatest and possibly *the greatest*) of all sci-fi action manga series."

—Anime News Network

The Cyberpunk Legend is Back!

In deluxe omnibus editions of 600+ pages, including ALL-NEW original stories by Alita creator Yukito Kishiro!

KC
KODANSHA COMICS